Literary Trails of the North Carolina Piedmont

NORTH CAROLINA LITERARY TRAILS

is a project of the North Carolina Arts Council,

an agency of the Department of Cultural Resources

Linda A. Carlisle, Secretary, Department of Cultural Resources

Mary B. Regan, Executive Director, N.C. Arts Council

literary trails

of the North Carolina Piedmont

A GUIDEBOOK

Georgann Eubanks

Photographs by **DONNA CAMPBELL**

The University of North Carolina Press *Chapel Hill*

**PUBLICATION OF THIS BOOK WAS SUPPORTED
IN PART BY A GENEROUS GIFT FROM THE
WACHOVIA WELLS FARGO FOUNDATION.**

Designed by Richard Hendel
Set in The Serif and Scala Sans types
by Tseng Information Systems, Inc.
Manufactured in Canada

The paper in this book meets the guidelines for permanence and
durability of the Committee on Production Guidelines for Book
Longevity of the Council on Library Resources.

The University of North Carolina Press has been a member of the
Green Press Initiative since 2003.

Library of Congress Cataloging-in-Publication Data
Eubanks, Georgann.
Literary trails of the North Carolina Piedmont : a guidebook /
Georgann Eubanks ; photographs by Donna Campbell.
p. cm. — (North Carolina literary trails)
Includes index.
ISBN 978-0-8078-3333-9 (cloth : alk. paper) —
ISBN 978-0-8078-5979-7 (pbk. : alk. paper)
1. Literary landmarks—North Carolina—Guidebooks. 2. Authors, American—
Homes and haunts—North Carolina—Guidebooks. 3. North Carolina—
In literature—Guidebooks. 4. North Carolina—Intellectual life—Guidebooks.
I. Campbell, Donna, 1951– II. Title.
PS144.N63E94 2010
810.9'7565—dc22
                                                      2010015807

cloth   14 13 12 11 10   5 4 3 2 1
paper   14 13 12 11 10   5 4 3 2 1

CONTENTS

This literary guide is a book about books, a way to read your way across North Carolina as you travel. The eighteen tours included here will steer you to the spots that inspired our state's writers and the literary visitors who also found their muse here. As such, this narrative goes beyond North Carolina literature itself. It requires a deeper imagining—to see what these authors have seen, to breathe the air in the places where they have lived and worked and written, to consider their aspirations, fears, and struggles.

Writers have always been celebrities of a sort, characters in their own right who often spark a reader's curiosity about how they did their work and where, with what kind of pencil or typewriter or computer, and how they managed to harness their considerable gifts. This guide offers some of that backstory.

The featured poems, novel and story excerpts, and bits of personal memoir from these authors are intended to enhance your appreciation of what you're seeing, or in some cases, what you're *not* seeing because of the march of progress. Many of the Piedmont sites on these tours are not as they were when a particular writer lived or worked there.

The earliest stories of North Carolina's Piedmont are tales of fertile farmland and plentiful game that drew native peoples to establish settlements and protect their sacred places.

Later, the promise of such bounty drew the Quakers south from Pennsylvania—among them, Daniel Boone's father and mother, Squire and Sarah, a story told by North Carolina poet and novelist-turned-biographer Robert Morgan.

The Quaker influence is still profound in these parts. In this book we'll visit Centre, a tiny community south of Greensboro where the Quaker forebears of short story writer O. Henry (William Sydney Porter), young adult novelist Kathryn Worth (*They Loved to Laugh*), and legendary journalist Edward R. Murrow all lived in proximity to one another alongside the unremarkable rivulet known as Polecat Creek.

The Piedmont's agricultural assets eventually led into the industrial age as local and transplanted entrepreneurs took farm products—cotton, tobacco, and timber—and turned them into manufactured goods the nation needed (textiles, furniture) or wanted (cigarettes).

For decades in the late nineteenth and twentieth centuries, Piedmont (and mountain) people left the fields to labor in mills—performing backbreaking, monotonous, and deafening work. They could not help but distract themselves from their labors with the simultaneous manufacture of stories, gossip, music, and mysteries to ponder. As mill culture began to diminish, these stories became more precious—especially to the children and grandchildren of these people, who later came to marvel at the industry and diligence of their elders.

Many poems, plays, novels, oral histories, and memoirs about mill life in the Piedmont have been collected and published in the last several decades. But not all the writing is so recent. Remarkably, the worker uprising that took place at Gastonia's Loray Mill in 1929 was so dramatic that no fewer than six novels were written in the 1930s that aimed to portray, through fiction, developments in the organized labor movement. We'll consider these textile narratives, and we'll also have a look inside a cigarette factory through the eyes of Durham writer Mary E. Mebane, who worked for American Tobacco as a teenager.

Of course, the presence of African Americans in large numbers in the Piedmont has contributed significantly to the literature of the region. Alex Haley's monumental book, *Roots*, takes place, in part, in Caswell and Alamance counties. We'll visit the graves of Haley's ancestors and of the family of slaveholders who owned them. In Chatham County we meet George Moses Horton, an enslaved man who wrote the first collection of poems published by a black American in more than half a century and the first book of poems by an African American in the South.

We'll also learn how Harlem Renaissance poet Langston Hughes broke the color barrier in 1931 by dining in a whites-only establishment in Chapel Hill with the editors of a student literary magazine, much to the shock of many townspeople, black and white. We'll examine how North Carolina figured in the career of writer Zora Neale Hurston, who taught at North Carolina Central University for a semester and joined a writing group at the University of North Carolina at Chapel Hill led by playwright Paul Green. Shortly after Hurston left, Richard Wright came to Chapel Hill to work with Green on a stage adaptation of his novel, *Native Son*. And we'll commemorate the amazing life of poet and memoirist Pauli Murray, who was raised in Durham by a family with deep roots in the region.

We'll take both a walking and a driving tour of North Carolina's largest city, visiting the Charlotte mansion where Pulitzer Prize–winning writer John Hersey was married, the high school that both Charles Kuralt and Jan Karon attended, the neighborhood where short-story writer Charles Chesnutt got his first job away from home, and the house where Georgia novelist Carson McCullers wrote the first chapters of her classic novel, *The Heart Is a Lonely Hunter*.

Because of the outstanding universities in the Piedmont, this region has launched many writing careers. Trail 2 lifts up the tradition of generosity among teachers of creative writing that makes our state's writing community so strong. Partly because of this expansive literary community, the Piedmont has drawn a number of distinguished writers back home to North Carolina—novelists Michael Malone, Allan Gurganus, Jill McCorkle, and David Payne and poet and novelist Heather Ross Miller, for example. Other well-known writers who grew up elsewhere have made the Piedmont home for part, if not all, of the year. This group includes Annie Dillard, Maya Angelou, Louis D. Rubin, Lee Smith, Hal Crowther, Elizabeth Spencer, and the late Betty Smith, who wrote both *A Tree Grows in Brooklyn* and *Joy in the Morning* in Chapel Hill.

Finally, we'll answer some questions you probably haven't thought to ask. For example, where did humor writer David Sedaris get his first job washing dishes? What links Mark Twain to Mount Airy and Jack London to Stokes County? And what is it about the city of Charlotte that has prompted more than its expected quota of mystery and crime novels?

In the hope of fostering literacy and expanding our understanding of North Carolina and its literature, we invite you to take some time with these tours of twenty-eight counties in central North Carolina. The excerpts from Piedmont writers are intended to be read aloud as you tour. Many sites beg for a walk, a picnic, a reading or two, and a contemplative hour to witness the passing scene.

Some authors included along these trails are well known; others may have works that have fallen out of print; and some may be only locally or little known. The excerpted works appear here for their connection to a specific place, or for their historical significance in the state's literature, or for the bit of local culture or color they reveal. Traditionally, the Piedmont region has its eastern boundary at the Fall Line and includes Fayetteville, Raleigh, and the Sandhills. But the eastern guidebook that follows this one begins with Raleigh as the gateway to eastern North Carolina and will encompass the Sandhills as well.

Of course you'll find in these pages a great many distinguished writers who have significant bodies of work that reach far beyond the confines of the Piedmont and North Carolina. However, to give a full accounting of these writers' contributions is well beyond our reach. The chief purpose of this book, and of the Literary Trails series as a whole, is to encourage you to delve deeper when an excerpt creates curiosity. Ultimately, any effort to capture all of the state's writers in these pages is impossible. New works are coming out every day, and the North Carolina Arts Council's companion website for this project will continue to update the trails. Visit <http://www.ncliterarytrails.org> to learn about new and notable books and literary events.

We hope the introduction offered here will entice you to visit a library or bookstore and pick up some of the novels, poetry collections, memoirs, and creative narrative histories that have a North Carolina connection. We have taken care to include works from established publishers that should be readily available in each trail's region, if not statewide. Some out-of-print works can still be found in libraries and at used booksellers and through online vendors that specialize in finding obscure titles.

In a section at the end of each tour called "Literary Landscape," you'll find quick information on long-running creative writing workshops, university programs, seasonal festivals related to literature, and regular readings hosted by writers' groups, public libraries, and schools.

Try your hand at writing about the places you visit. There's always room for more North Carolina writers!

Georgann Eubanks

trail one

The
Western
Piedmont:
Mystery
and
History

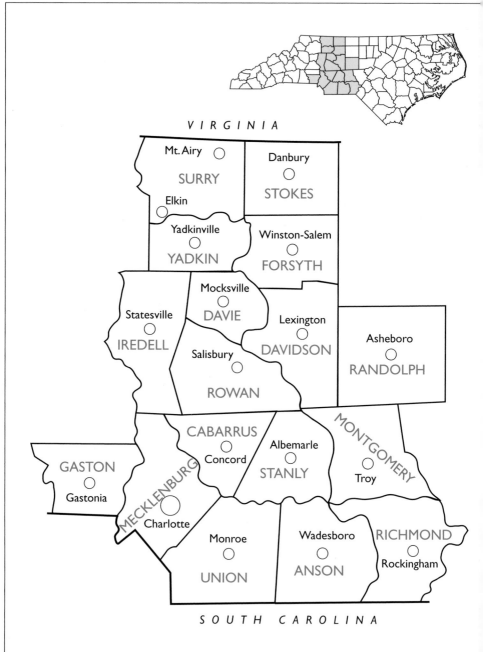

COUNTIES AND PRINCIPAL TOWNS OF
TRAIL ONE

All you had to do was turn the knob
until the light clicked on and soon you'd find
rising out of static was your life.
Everytime you heard "The Weave Room Blues"
or "Cotton Mill Colic No. 3" you felt
like a deer that risked a meadow, its eyes
lifted to see the barrel too late.
Someone had caught you in his sights,
hit you solid in the guts
with all the things that you had thought
you didn't want to think too long about.
But days later you'd catch yourself
humming those lines as you worked your shift.
Maybe it was the banjo and guitar,
the way they prettied up the words,
that made those songs lighten up your heart
like a deep water Baptist hymn.
Or maybe in the end it was the words,
the bare-assed truth making a stand
in a voice that could have been your own.

—From *Eureka Mill*, by Ron Rash
    (Corvallis, Ore.: Bench Press, 1998), 51.

Stretching from the ancient Saura Mountains in Stokes County on the Virginia border to the skyscrapers of Charlotte glittering like so many stacks of silver coins at the southernmost tip of North Carolina, this literary trail, perhaps more than any other, offers a window on North Carolina's transition from Old South to New. This corridor was the birthplace of North Carolina's once-dominant textile industry, celebrated in Ron Rash's poem and now disappearing into thin air like a radio signal.

The stories, novels, and poems of this region are full of mill whistles dividing the day into three shifts of eight hours each. In them, mill workers amble to and from their stick-built houses on the sides of red clay hills. Steamy summer nights and bitter winter darkness alike are marked by the clockwork of thundering trains barreling through backyards and the middles of towns, carrying products to faraway places.

Textile workers around the turn of the twentieth century reckoned with

3

diphtheria, Spanish flu, and TB and the quarantines that often accompanied them. They lived in small houses built by their employers, shopped at "the company store," and often endured squalid sanitation practices while also trying to bring a bit of the farms they left behind with them in the form of chickens, goats, and milk cows.

In the later literature about this slice of North Carolina history, many Piedmont writers express nostalgia for those earlier times when summers were slower and the absence of air-conditioning kept people outside on their porches, talking and watching their neighbors come and go.

As the Piedmont has moved from muscle to mind work and free trade has moved the textile industry to other countries, most of the mills have closed. Some durable old plants are being converted to shopping malls and condominiums or displaced by "clean rooms" where research and new product development in pharmaceuticals and food science have taken over. Banking and biotechnology are the new industries here, while the oldest of the mills hunker down along the banks of rivers, their bricks settling, their insides empty. With broken windows and "For Sale" signs, their brick towers and smokestacks still rise above neighborhoods where some shotgun houses are yet occupied and others are empty as seashells, hinting at so many past lives lived. This trail tours some of these old haunts and attempts to bring to life some of the stories and poems that help us understand the transition that's still under way.

Winston-Salem

Everyone in America knows this brand-name town, but the writers who have been shaped here tell a deeper story. Experience Moravian culture in Old Salem. Learn more about the literary deacons of Wake Forest University and explore African traditions of storytelling at Winston-Salem State University.

Writers with a connection to this area: A. R. Ammons, Maya Angelou, Brad Barkley, John Henry Boner, Will D. Campbell, Martin Clark, Jonathan Daniels, Paxton Davis, Charles Edward Eaton, John Ehle, Anna Catharina Ernst, Nathan Ross Freeman, Adelaide Fries, Larry Leon Hamlin, Frank Borden Hanes, Harold Hayes, Hunter James, Norman Katkov, Helen Losse, Milt Machlin, Penelope Niven, Jacqueline Ogburn, Patrick Reynolds, Bynum Shaw, Elizabeth Spencer, Douglas C. Waller, Edwin Graves Wilson, Emily Herring Wilson, Isabel Zuber

We begin in the town made famous worldwide by the tobacco products manufactured here. Writing in the 1940s, Raleigh journalist Jonathan Daniels offered an introduction to Winston-Salem during its heyday as a tobacco town:

> Maybe God built Winston-Salem. It is not a blasphemous idea. In His name Moravian brothers walked down the wood from Pennsylvania to begin their skilled and God-fearing community in the wilderness. And their past is kept in Salem in the old brick and stone houses with the hooded doors and the windows made with little panes. The old trees grow green in quietness. If Winston, swollen with the wealth of cigarettes and underwear and stockings, is only across a street, sometimes it seems also across a world. It is not. There is something more than a hyphen between the two towns. There is a Moravian blood in the factories and the banks. Some of the Scotch-Irish money has helped keep the old town sweet. There is a triumph

tour 1

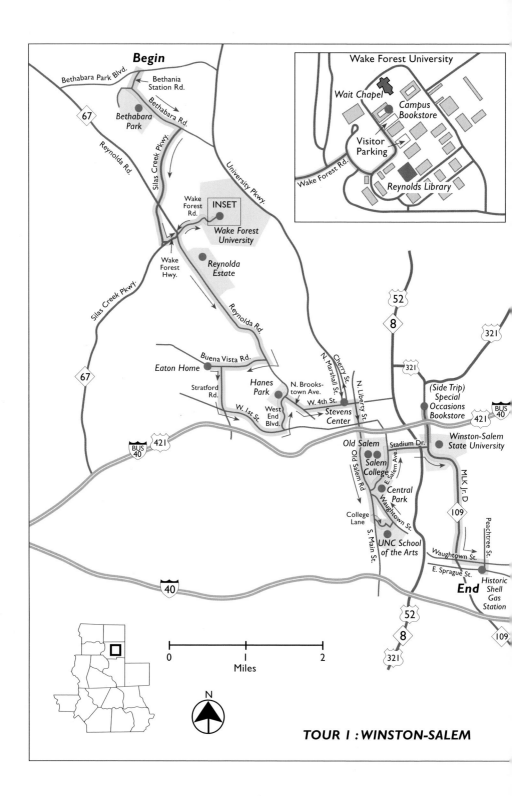

Begin

Bethabara Park Blvd.
Bethania Station Rd.
Bethabara Rd.
67
Bethabara Park
Reynolda Rd.
Silas Creek Pkwy.
University Pkwy.
Wake Forest Rd.
INSET
Wake Forest University
Wake Forest Hwy.
Reynolda Estate
Silas Creek Pkwy.
52
8
321
67
Reynolda Rd.
Buena Vista Rd.
Eaton Home
Stratford Rd.
Hanes Park
N. Brookstown Ave.
N. Marshall St.
Cherry St.
N. Liberty St.
321
(Side Trip) Special Occasions Bookstore
421
BUS 40
W. 4th St.
W. 1st St.
West End Blvd.
Stevens Center
BUS 40
421
Old Salem
Salem College
Stadium Dr.
Winston-Salem State University
Old Salem Rd.
E. Salem Ave.
Central Park
MLK Jr. D
109
College Lane
Waughtown St.
S. Main St.
UNC School of the Arts
Waughtown St.
Peachtree St.
E. Sprague St.
End
Historic Shell Gas Station
40
52
8
321
109

0   1   2
Miles

N

Wake Forest University

Wait Chapel
Campus Bookstore
Visitor Parking
Wake Forest Rd.
Reynolds Library

TOUR 1 : WINSTON-SALEM

in their attachment. After living together a long time the towns were formally united in 1913, the same year the first Camel cigarette was manufactured and if it was a wedding of new-rich and old gentleness, it had been a marriage of success as well as convenience all the same. — From *Tar Heels*, by Jonathan Daniels (New York: Dodd, Meade, 1941), 156.

Few towns in North Carolina have preserved as much of their heritage as has Winston-Salem. This tour begins at Bethabara, site of the earliest settlement of Moravians, now a small park in the sprawling suburbs on the northwest side of town.

■ BETHABARA PARK

2147 Bethabara Road

336-924-8191

Unlike the bustle of Colonial Williamsburg, Bethabara is a contemplative spot shaded by enormous black walnut trees. A number of restored and reconstructed buildings are set along a narrow lane through the park, requiring drivers to assume the speed of a horse and buggy. This 183-acre wildlife preserve also offers a museum and visitors' center where guided tours of the village and gardens are provided for a small fee.

Winston-Salem native Hunter James has documented the enormous changes to the landscape in this vicinity. James, a journalist who spent thirty-five years first at the *Baltimore Sun* and later at the *Atlanta Constitution*, returned here in 1989 to write and to restore the family home place on Becks Church Road less than a mile north of Bethabara. In *The Last Days of Big Grassy Fork*, James rails against the less-than-fragrant landfill and the flanks of industrial warehouses that now surround his property. He also weaves personal memoir with an irreverent, no-punches-pulled version of local history beginning with the arrival of the German Moravians:

The settlers chose the name Bethabara because their first settlement was never meant to be anything more than what its name suggested, [Hebrew meaning "House of Passage"], a temporary way station that awaited the building of Salem, the central congregation town and administrative center. All of that would come much later. Meantime, Bethabara itself grew rapidly to become a commercial center of more than passing importance, rivaling Salisbury, another German settlement of note, as one of the two largest towns west of the fall line. —From *The Last Days of Big Grassy Fork*, by Hunter James (Lexington: University Press of Kentucky, 2002), 18, 21.

Moravians are now a relatively small Christian sect represented around the globe, yet their Christmas love feasts are widely known and each year draw many participants to Bethabara and Old Salem. Paxton Davis, another Winston-Salem–born journalist-turned-memoirist, describes his boyhood encounter with the tradition:

The doors opened and women wearing plain white dresses entered the sanctuary carrying baskets of Moravian buns which they passed down each row of pews. By then our mothers had whipped out the inevitable linen napkins and ordered us, with glares threatening the cessation of Christmas, to put them on our laps. The buns were followed by trays of hot Moravian coffee, another delicacy, sweet and milky, that proved impossible to duplicate at home. That was the simple meal by which the Moravians commemorated brotherhood and God's love of man, and there was nothing like it in the experience of any of us, for it was not a sacrament like Communion and it was wholly free of supernatural overtones or hocus-pocus; it was simply an act of fellowship, as it seemed. —From *Being a Boy*, by Paxton Davis (Winston-Salem: John F. Blair, 1988), 173–74.

At Old Salem, down the road a ways, we'll revisit the Moravians, but for now the tour continues at a literary powerhouse and one of the most significant institutions of higher education in North Carolina, founded by another denomination, the vigorous Baptists.

■ WAKE FOREST UNIVERSITY

Continue down the narrow lane (Bethabara Road) that runs through the park. The road will soon widen and meet up with Silas Creek Parkway. Turn right on Silas Creek and follow it all the way to the major intersection with Wake Forest Road. Turn left onto Wake Forest Road, following the signs to the campus entrance just across Reynolda Road.

Once a Baptist college for men, founded in 1834 in the town of Wake Forest, sixteen miles north of Raleigh, today's Wake Forest University reopened on this site in 1956. Over the years, Wake Forest has accumulated a heady list of writers among its alumni. Among the university's literary faculty, probably none is more widely known than Reynolds Professor of American Studies Maya Angelou, a dynamic woman who began her career in entertainment before turning to writing. Angelou has led several lives around the globe—as singer, dancer, actress, political organizer, and poet. She made her literary debut with *I Know Why the Caged Bird Sings*, the 1969 autobiographical account of her checkered childhood in Stamps, Arkansas. The book is now a classic and is required reading in many classrooms worldwide.

Five more volumes of Angelou's autobiography followed, along with a number of poetry collections. Her best-known poem was written for the first inauguration of President Bill Clinton: "Here, on the pulse of this new day, / You may have the grace to look up and out / And into your sister's eyes, and into / Your brother's face, your country / And say simply / Very simply / With hope— Good morning."

Angelou came to North Carolina with the encouragement of her longtime friend, Wake Forest faculty member Dolly A. McPherson, a scholar of African American literature whose 1990 book, *Order Out of Chaos*, provides a definitive interpretation and context for Angelou's work.

Angelou also befriended Emily Herring Wilson, a poet, historian, and literary advocate who studied with Randall Jarrell at Woman's College (now University of North Carolina at Greensboro) and then married beloved English professor and longtime Wake Forest provost Edwin Graves Wilson. In this poem, Wilson, a white woman raised in segregated Columbus, Georgia, captures a visceral sense of the extraordinary physical presence and power of Angelou from their first meeting.

FROM A FAR PLACE
For Maya Angelou
So many mornings ago
I was the little girl
on the Avenue, sweeping
the sidewalk

You balanced a basket
on your head
like an Egyptian woman
in my school book.
Your thin dark skirt
rode between your legs.

The sweat you wiped away
clean with a white handkerchief
rolled in your sleeve.
We looked
back and forth.
I think
we never spoke.

Now you have come
from a far place
to visit home:
your dress dazzles,
your rings like diamonds,
are diamonds.
We drink white wine
as in a movie.
You speak
a beautiful and strange
way.

I watch
your body leave,
taller than anyone's,
your turban in the sun.

I in my child's body
run after you,
balance in your shadow
like a shadow.
—From *Balancing on Stones*, by Emily Herring Wilson
    (Winston-Salem: Jackpine Press, 1979), 30–31.

In 1992, just a few years after Angelou joined the faculty at Wake Forest, Emily Wilson organized a landmark conference for North Carolina women writers in Winston-Salem, featuring Angelou as keynote speaker. Wilson also commissioned local artist Anne Kesler Shields to create *Women of Letters: A Group Portrait of North Carolina Writers*, which now hangs over the circulation desk in the Z. Smith Reynolds Library, our main stop on the Wake Forest campus.

These thirty-two portraits of North Carolina women writers by Anne Kesler Shields
hang above the circulation desk in the Reynolds Library at Wake Forest University.
The paintings are mounted on a framework lined with pages from Lee Smith's novel
Fair and Tender Ladies.

DIRECTIONS

From the Gatehouse at the campus entrance, proceed past the Welcome Center and over two speed bumps. At the bottom of the hill, take a right (still Wake Forest Road). At the stop sign at the top of the hill, take a left. The Reynolds Library is the second building on the right with a large circular driveway in front. To park, pass the library. The next two lots on the right accommodate visitors.

Reynolds Library is home to the Maya Angelou Film and Theater Collection, preserving scripts and documents relating to Angelou's theater and television career, which included a major role in the television miniseries *Roots*, based on the book by Alex Haley.

It was here, too, that for many years Boone native Isabel Zuber, a poet, novelist, and short-story writer, made her living while developing her vivid Appalachian novel *Salt*, discussed in volume 1 of *Literary Trails*. Zuber was one of the founders of Winston-Salem's Jackpine Press (together with Emily Wilson and poet A. R. Ammons).

In addition to the handsome portraits of women writers at the circulation desk, the Gerald Johnson Graduate Lounge serves as a gallery for the portraits of a number of university writers who attended Wake Forest College when it was still located in the Wake County town of the same name. (Ask a librarian for permission to enter.) Gerald Johnson, a Scotland County native who worked alongside H. L. Mencken at the *Baltimore Sun* for many years, was far more liberal in his views than the contrarian Mencken. In his long career, Johnson wrote biographies, children's history books, two mysteries, and two novels, in addition to his prolific political commentaries. His novel about Thomasville is considered in Tour 11.

Wake Forest alumni and Shelby natives W. J. Cash, author of *The Mind of the South*, and his political antithesis, Thomas Dixon, are also commemorated in this room, alongside North Carolina's first poet laureate, John Charles McNeill, of Wagram.

A likeness of Laurence Stallings, who with Maxwell Anderson wrote the Broadway hit *What Price Glory*, is also here. Stallings's 1924 novel *Plumes*, a best seller in its time, was adapted for the film *The Big Parade*. Box office proceeds from the movie reached an all-time high in MGM history, at least until *Gone with the Wind* came along in 1939. Stallings was married to Helen Purefoy Poteat, daughter of William Louis Poteat, a science professor who served as president of Wake Forest College in the 1920s. In his day, Poteat somehow managed to convince the North Carolina legislature not to ban the teaching of evolution in public schools, as other states in the South had done following the Scopes trial. The campaign put Poteat at grievous odds with the Southern Baptist Convention and nearly cost him his job.

A. R. Ammons's portrait also hangs in the Johnson Room. Ammons, a native of Whiteville, studied biology at Wake Forest and became a dedicated scribe of nature through his poetic voice. As one of North Carolina's most honored writers, Ammons won the National Book Award twice and often came to Winston to visit his alma mater, teach, and eat at his favorite restaurant, the K&W Cafeteria, a chain that, like Krispy Kreme Doughnuts, originated in Winston-Salem. Ammons's work is featured in volume 3 of *Literary Trails*.

The Reynolds Library has among its holdings the papers and letters of Harold Hayes, the Elkin-born editor of *Esquire* magazine who helped to create the genre known as creative nonfiction. (Hayes is considered in the next tour.) Another Wake Forest writer, Bynum Shaw, graduated in 1948 alongside Hayes and pursued a career in journalism but would soon return to join the Wake Forest faculty, nurturing generations of would-be writers here. In addition to producing the fourth volume of Wake Forest's history, Shaw wrote four novels (*The Sound of Small Hammers*, *The Nazi Hunter*, *Days of Power*, *Nights of Fear*, and *Oh, Promised Land*), all available in Reynolds Library. His students included

Douglas C. Waller, a *Time* magazine correspondent and the author of several books on military history, and Michael Riley, who was named editor of the *Congressional Quarterly* in 2007.

Baptist preacher and civil rights activist Will Campbell is another Wake Forest alumnus whose 1977 autobiographical work, *Brother to a Dragonfly*, was followed by several novels and many other nonfiction books. Campbell, a Mississippian, was the inspiration for Doug Marlette's character Will B. Done in the comic strip "Kudzu." (See Tour 14.)

Before leaving the Wake Forest campus, poetry enthusiasts may also want to step over to the department of English on the second floor of Tribble Hall, where A. R. Ammons's typewriter is on display in the department's lounge, along with a number of first editions of his work. Former English professor and Wake Forest provost emeritus Edwin Graves Wilson inspired generations of literature students in this building. Following his retirement, Wilson edited a fine children's book, *Poetry for Young People: Maya Angelou*. The collection, illustrated by Jerome Lagarrigue, was published in 2007 to commemorate the fiftieth anniversary of the United Nations. Wilson provided both introductions and annotations to his Wake Forest colleague's poems. Angelou was the first living poet featured in this popular children's series, which has included Shakespeare, Robert Frost, Robert Browning, Langston Hughes, and Emily Dickinson.

Our tour of Wake Forest concludes with a fitting tribute by Winston-Salem poet Helen Losse, who speaks to another aspect of this university's engagement in the cultural life of the state.

THE TEAMS THAT ALWAYS WEAR BLACK
Nothing but basketball comes in March.
Everyone dreams of cutting down nets.
Who will reach deep to find strength
in muscles that ache but must not quit?

Look how chosen teams play
keep-away with beautiful slippers—
no longer afraid of the Spirit,
no longer afraid to think, *holy*.

Strong teams wear white, bend weary limbs
like forsythia branches, yellow and hardy.
Other teams wear black—
always black, under the bright lights.

There are no godmothers.

No pumpkins or coaches. Not even mice.

Everyone knows the clock will strike midnight.

And they don't really *dance* at this ball.

—From *Writer's Harbor* (May 2006), used by permission of Helen Losse.

■ REYNOLDA HOUSE

Adjacent to the university on Reynolda Road (retrace your route back to the Wake Forest campus entrance and turn left) is the former estate of the Reynolds family, whose tobacco products once dominated Winston-Salem, the town from which two cigarette brands derived their names.

On Reynolda Road, headed uphill from the Wake Forest campus, turn left at the first traffic light into Reynolda Village, a collection of some thirty buildings once used by staff and family members of the Reynolds clan. This elegant estate, originally comprising more than 1,000 acres, was created by Richard Joshua Reynolds and Katherine Smith Reynolds, who began construction of the main house, Reynolda, in 1917. It later became the principal residence of R. J. Reynolds's son-in-law Charles and daughter Mary Reynolds Babcock, a shy woman with a strong interest in gardening and philanthropy. Today the seventy-room "country house" is known as the Reynolda House Museum of American Art, where significant paintings by artists from three centuries are exhibited, along with Tiffany art glass, American pottery, and many of the original furnishings from the Reynolds family.

Writers often come to Reynolda to read and conduct workshops, surrounded by paintings by Grant Wood, Mary Cassatt, Jacob Lawrence, Thomas Hart Benton, and Andrew Wyeth, among others.

After having a look around the Village, stroll uphill through the gardens to tour the house, which is bordered by mature boxwoods, sturdy old magnolias, and festive topiary. (Call 336-758-5150 for hours and current exhibitions and events.)

Patrick Reynolds, the grandson of R. J. Reynolds, established the Foundation for a Smokefree America in 1989. In his family memoir published the same year, he describes the evolution of the grand residence:

When Mary [Reynolds Babcock] came into her quarter of the fortune [$30 million in 1936], she began to remodel the bungalow, making a new main entrance at the east wing . . . something that would afford the family some privacy since the public was now allowed onto the grounds to drive to the gardens. In the basement the Babcocks installed a bowling alley, pool table, and shooting gallery, as well as a mirrored bar, and beyond the east wing they added an eight bedroom guest house and an indoor swimming pool. By the late 1930s, Reynolda finally became what Katherine had hoped it would be twenty years earlier—a complete family estate.—From *The Gilded Leaf: Triumph, Tragedy, and Tobacco: Three Generations of the R J Reynolds Family and Fortune*, by Patrick Reynolds and Tom Shachtman (Lincoln, Neb.: iUniverse, 2006), 186.

This memoir, reportedly unpopular with a number of Reynolds family members, was nevertheless available in the Village Bookshop in Reynolda Village on the day we visited, along with a number of first editions of other North Carolina books, some long out of print. Patrick Reynolds, moved by his father's death from emphysema as a result of smoking, began his crusade against tobacco by selling his RJR stock and delving into the family history to write the memoir. But Reynolds was not the first to be struck by curiosity sufficient to base a book on the family's fortune and misfortunes.

At least two accounts—*Millionaire's Row*, a 1996 novel by Norman Katkov (scriptwriter for the *Ben Casey* television series), and *Libby*, a 1985 "true crime" book by Milt Machlin (author of *The French Connection*)—explore the death of Zachary Smith Reynolds, the youngest son of R. J. Reynolds. Not yet twenty-one, Zach was found on the sleeping porch at Reynolda with a gunshot wound to the head in July 1932. Reynolds was an avid flier and notorious reveler. He had married his second wife, Libby Holman, only a few months earlier. She was a Broadway torch singer who, as it turned out, was pregnant at the time of the alleged murder.

Zach Reynolds's first marriage at the age of eighteen to towel heiress Anne Cannon, of Concord, with whom he had also fathered a child, complicated matters in the settlement of his estate, even after the State of North Carolina, for lack of conclusive evidence, was forced to drop its murder indictment against the second wife, Libby Holman, and Albert Walker, Zach's best friend and personal assistant.

■ BUENA VISTA

Continue up Reynolda Road and "Millionaire's Row," as novelist Norman Katkov called it—"the long avenue of splendid houses" largely built from the enormous proceeds of Winston-Salem's tobacco and textile interests. Cross Coliseum Drive and continue to Buena Vista Road. Turn right onto Buena Vista.

Writer Paxton Davis describes this neighborhood where he was raised in the 1920s and 1930s:

> Buena Vista (in Winston-Salem pronounced "Bewna" and with Vista as in "is") was the latest and most ambitious of the neighborhoods developed around downtown as its periphery spread in every direction in the decade following World War I. . . . Buena Vista was new and comfortable with the tidiest thoroughfares and handsomest houses Winston-Salem could boast in its energetic assault upon the future. —From *Being a Boy*, 6, 8.

Buena Vista was also the childhood haunt of Charles Edward Eaton, one of the state's distinguished twentieth-century poets. Eaton was the youngest of eight children. His mother, originally from South Carolina, went to Salem College. His father, who came from a crossroads near Mocksville to the city of Winston to seek his fortune, was a great lover of poetry. Oscar Benjamin Eaton served as mayor of Winston for ten consecutive terms and was a principal architect of the merger of the towns of Winston and Salem, in 1913.

As the youngest in the household, Charles was doted on by his parents. His literary gifts were burnished through impromptu quizzes and recitations at the family dinner table. As he told poet Paul Jones in a 1992 interview: "When my mother was on her deathbed—she died when I was sixteen—my father called me in and said, 'Charles, we've decided that you are going to be a poet. And we hope and believe you will.'" It was a mantle he accepted with gratitude.

Eaton was very much a poet's poet. He studied for a year at Duke and then transferred to the University of North Carolina at Chapel Hill to focus on creative writing. As a graduate student at Harvard he met Robert Frost, who became a lifelong mentor and friend. Frost recommended Eaton for a fellowship at Bread Loaf (a long-running summer writing program in Vermont), where Eaton met poets William Carlos Williams and Archibald MacLeish, who also became lifelong friends. Of Frost, Eaton said, "He impressed me as a man, you see, and how much character and strength and long-lastingness comes into the career of a poet." It was this personal discipline and dedication that led Eaton to become one of North Carolina's most prolific formalist poets. He died in Chapel Hill at the age of eighty-nine. His boyhood home is at 2222 Buena Vista Road, fronted by a white picket fence.

THE APPRAISAL
Heretofore, hereafter, and herewith
I think of my father and his guns:

A sanguine, emotional man, part bronze,
Divided and yet blent, by tool and myth.

He was brought up to shoot more rabbits
Than any boy in Davie County;
Carolina is both rich and poor of bounty—
Papa kept a gun trained on his sensual habits.

When he became the Mayor of his town,
He hunted better, and, so I thought, demeaned
Me, holding furry corpses while he cleaned—
I still have dreams of bloody rabbits hanging down.

Harsh smell of dung in their little bodies,
A sound of shot against the pan—
I never liked the work but still can
Eat jugged hare with friends who euphemize.

Devotions in those days were absolute—
Papa saw me as both myth and tool:
Someone, steady as a god, must blood the Golden Rule
And show how strong men differ from the brute.
—From *The Man from Buena Vista: Selected Nonfiction,*
1944–2000, by Charles Edward Eaton (Cranbury, N.J.:
Associated University Presses, 2001), 22.

Paxton Davis, who was nine years younger than Eaton, lived around the corner at 608 Arbor Road and later at 707 Oaklawn, also nearby. Davis would go on to write for the *Winston-Salem Journal* and teach journalism at Washington and Lee University for twenty-three years. In his memoir he recollects the Winston of his boyhood—the foods, sports, holiday celebrations, popular culture, and religious practices—and his own coming-of-age as the privileged son of a lifelong Reynolds division manager. Davis even claims to remember the day in October 1927 when Charles Lindbergh flew over the city in the *Spirit of St. Louis.* Davis would have been two at the time, but his memory is accurate. Lindbergh had completed his record-breaking transatlantic flight to Paris that spring, a journey that began at a Long Island airfield owned by R. J. Reynolds Jr. Davis writes:

The Reynolds legend pervaded Winston life, the legend of a swashbuckling post-bellum redneck who'd whipped Buck Duke at his own game, and the Reynolds presence was visible everywhere: in the twenty-two story Reynolds Building, in 1931 North Carolina's tallest, standing at the center of town; in the long maroon trucks hauling hogsheads of leaf from warehouse to factory; above all in the acre upon acre of factories themselves, a long wave of red brick undulating across East Winston cheek-by-jowl with the numberless shanties where the black Reynolds laborers lived. Winston smelled pleasantly of tobacco most of the time and some said it smelled of money, too; and the Reynolds legend extended to the Wachovia Bank and Trust Company, which stood symbolically, symbiotically across Courthouse Square from the Reynolds skyscraper, to which it unarguably owed its prosperity. — From *Being a Boy*, 29.

By the 1950s, Winston-Salem was home to the largest tobacco manufacturing plant in the world, and it was in this era of extraordinary local prosperity that Mississippi writer Elizabeth Spencer chose to set her best-known work, *The Light in the Piazza*, a 1960 novella about Margaret and Clara Johnson, the wife and daughter of a Winston-Salem tobacco executive, who go to Italy on holiday. Spencer, who ultimately settled in Chapel Hill in the 1980s, witnessed her popular novella also take the form of a 1962 film starring Olivia de Havilland and Yvette Mimieux and, later, a 2005 Broadway musical. Spencer told interviewer D. G. Martin that she gave her American characters the hometown of Winston-Salem to avoid having her kinsfolk and neighbors in Mississippi and Alabama try to guess if the characters were based on actual people in those states.

■ DOWNTOWN WINSTON-SALEM

To visit the center of the city, return from Buena Vista to Stratford Road and turn right, following under Stratford's canopy of oaks to a busy, five-points intersection. Take a left onto First Street, which meanders toward the center of the city alongside the freeway on your right. After crossing Hawthorne Road, take the second left onto West End Boulevard. Winston-Salem–born novelist Martin Clark gives us a fictional picture of this neighborhood as he remembers it:

In 1969, when Evers Wheeling was a boy in Winston-Salem, North Carolina, men in filling-station uniforms still checked your car's oil, pumped high test gas out of heavy silver nozzles and cleaned your windshield with a spray bottle and a blue, quilted wipe. There was a man named Herman Stovall who worked at the West End Shell, where Evers and his family would stop for fuel and air and little Cokes with peanuts poured into the bottle. Herman was a bent, thin, wispy man, a skeletal bumpkin with a crew cut and big red ears. He could hold an inch-long ash on his cigarette, and he didn't think that astronauts had touched down on the moon and he didn't believe in gorillas, even though they'd been on exhibit in various zoos for over half a century. Herman would give Sundrop caps out of the drink machine and tin Prince Albert cans to Evers and the other kids who visited the station, and he would lean over the greasy cash register counter to show them cat's cradle tricks with a loop of grimy brown twine. Evers would take the soda caps home in a paper sack and scratch off the cork on their undersides, trying to win a free pop or a five-dollar bill.—From *The Many Aspects of Mobile Home Living*, by Martin Clark (New York: Knopf, 2000), 3.

West End's Hanes Park—named for the first family of Winston-Salem textiles and still a popular spot with kids—will soon come up on the left side of the boulevard. The Hanes family's stockings and underwear designs once defined the industry, but the family also has a literary legacy. Frank Borden Hanes, whose mountain novel-in-verse is considered in volume 1 of *Literary Trails*, has been a generous benefactor to the collections in the libraries at the University of North Carolina at Chapel Hill. Hanes has made possible a number of extraordinary purchases, including the papers of Irish poet William Butler Yeats. Hanes's philanthropy also helped to complete the acquisition of the papers of Louisiana novelist Walker Percy and Civil War historian Shelby Foote, both of whom, like Frank Hanes, attended UNC–Chapel Hill in the 1930s.

From West End Boulevard, with Hanes Park still on your left, turn right on Brookstown Avenue, and in five blocks turn left on West Fourth Street, which climbs a hill into downtown. Note the Stevens Center on the corner of Fourth and Marshall. Once a silent movie house, this theater is now the primary performance space for the UNC School of the Arts and the site of a number of world premieres over the years, including Neil Simon's *Lost in Yonkers*. Just down the block at 226 North Marshall is the Sawtooth Center for the Visual Arts, also a venue for literary gatherings.

Continue east on Fourth. Here the section of the street beginning at Cherry has been designated Larry Leon Hamlin Way, so named for the late founder of the National Black Theatre Festival, a gathering held every other year in

Winston-Salem since 1989, drawing to town such luminaries as playwright August Wilson and actors Sidney Poitier, Ruby Dee, Oprah Winfrey, and Denzel Washington.

Cross Cherry Street. Straight ahead is the section where most of the city's manufacturing once took place. Turn right on North Liberty Street, which will become Old Salem Road in a few blocks. A bit farther up Liberty Street, though no landmark on Glenn Avenue remains to commemorate it, was the shop where William E. "Jack" Ogburn Sr. repaired the jukeboxes he installed in diners, fish camps, and truck stops across North Carolina. Durham children's writer Jacqueline Ogburn commemorates her grandfather's career in *The Jukebox Man* (Dial Books for Young Readers, 1989), illustrated by North Carolina artist James Ransome.

■ OLD SALEM MUSEUMS AND GARDENS

From Old Salem Road, turn left on West Academy Street to enter the village of Old Salem just south of downtown. This well-preserved Moravian settlement is home to the Museum of Early Southern Decorative Arts and an extraordinary library and research facility housed in the Frank L. Horton Museum Center, at 924 South Main Street. The library's holdings are a treasure trove of resources on the arts, trades, genealogy, architecture, and cultures (including Native American and African American) of the preindustrial South.

African Americans had a significant presence among the Moravian faithful. Some were slaves; others were hired as free workers. Many spoke German and English. They worshipped and were buried in Moravian cemeteries, known as God's Acre, alongside their white counterparts. Interpretive exhibits about the role of Black Moravians in Old Salem can be found in the Salem Tavern and elsewhere. Today, some three-quarters of the Moravian faithful worldwide are people of color, largely due to evangelical efforts beginning in the eighteenth century in Africa, South America, and the West Indies.

The diaries and journals of all of these early settlers, which reveal much about the region's heritage, are a significant part of the Horton Center collection. Writer and scholar Adelaide Fries, born in Salem in 1871, dedicated her life to assembling and preserving the Moravian archives here. Her best-known work, *The Road to Salem* (1944), is a translation of an autobiography by Anna Catharina Ernst, who arrived at Bethabara in 1759, lived an arduous life of service, and survived four husbands. She is buried in plot number 186 in God's Acre, the Salem cemetery above the old town.

Another Salem writer, John Henry Boner, was born here in 1845 and lived

In Old Salem, costumed interpreters are available to answer questions about the historic Moravian settlement that lies south of the skyscrapers in downtown Winston-Salem.

for a time in the Salem Tavern where George Washington once spent the night. Like so many Winston-Salem writers to follow, Boner pursued a career in journalism. He served as literary editor of *New York World* and near the end of his life, in poor health, was a proofreader at the Government Printing Office in Washington. His poems in the collection *Whispering Pines* (1883) survive today in part because of their reissue by the late John F. Blair, the Winston-Salem publisher who selected the book to be the first produced by his press in 1954. Boner's poetry is of its time—lyrical and formal. This elegiac poem, which is appropriate to a tour of Old Salem, also gives a glimpse of Boner's wit, suggesting what might have been his attitude toward the visitors who now throng his hometown streets.

HOUSES IN AN OLD STREET
How eloquent are these of time long past!—
    An architectural text still plain to read,
Though sadly ravaged and decaying fast,
    Of a great epic—these the epicede
Of their departed era. Note the walls,
    The steps, the windows, and the carven doors.
Degenerate now are those once stately halls,
    With alien footsteps on their pillaged floors.
Forlorn, forlorn! There is no sadder thing
    In all the world than a forsaken home
About which vestiges of grandeur cling.
    But so it is, and even noble Rome
Is Rome no more; her meager remnant totters—
Cast-iron, paint, asphaltum, and globe-trotters.
—From *Poems*, by John Henry Boner (New York: Neale, 1903), 22.

Old Salem sits adjacent to Salem Academy and College, the oldest continuously operating educational institution for girls and women in the country. The college added a creative writing major in 2006, and its Center for Women Writers regularly brings authors from across the country to read and conduct workshops for students and the community. The center sponsors three national literary awards in fiction, poetry, and creative nonfiction. Carl Sandburg biographer Penelope Niven is the center's writer-in-residence. Another Niven biography details the life of Thornton Wilder, the author of *Our Town*.

■ UNIVERSITY OF NORTH CAROLINA SCHOOL OF THE ARTS

From Old Salem, return to Old Salem Road and continue south to the roundabout at the bottom of the hill and take the second road around the circle, which is South Main Street. The driveway into UNCSA is well marked and on the left beyond a cluster of storefronts.

As an unusual institution within the University of North Carolina system, UNCSA serves high school, college, and graduate-level students through its conservatory programs in dance, drama, music, filmmaking, and theatrical design and production. Students also take academic classes in the liberal arts as they prepare for professional careers in their disciplines. Founded in 1963 under the leadership of Governor Terry Sanford and his arts policy adviser, Asheville-born writer John Ehle (see volume 1), the school has nurtured playwrights, composers, and screenwriters alongside its talented performing artists. Literary travelers with children may especially enjoy a stroll through the outdoor movie set in the middle of campus, which re-creates a street scene, complete with a movie marquee, a Krispy Kreme Doughnut shop, and other familiar Winston-Salem storefronts.

Every year, through the Kenan Institute for the Arts, also housed on campus, the Kenan Writers' Encounters provide a series of public lectures, classes, and workshops by nationally recognized writers and artists for the purpose of bridging the worlds of art and letters. For more information, see <http://www.kenanarts.org>.

Exit the campus on the side opposite from where you entered and turn left on Waughtown Street. Take Waughtown back toward town. As you proceed through the roundabout, take the first right onto East Salem Avenue, which ascends toward downtown through Winston-Salem's Central Park. At the intersection with Stadium Drive, the entrance to Salem Academy and College is on the left. Turn right on Stadium Drive, which leads directly to the main entrance to Winston-Salem State University, across Martin Luther King Jr. Drive.

■ WINSTON-SALEM STATE UNIVERSITY

The pristine campus of this historically black university founded in 1892 is set high on a hill in east Winston. The campus will be particularly appealing to visitors with an interest in visual art and representations of stories from the African Diaspora. The Diggs Gallery (336-750-2458) presents rotating exhibitions from Africa and by African American artists and serves as a gathering spot for a range of campus programs related to history, storytelling, and literature. The university has hosted Nikki Giovanni, Alice Walker, and Gwendolyn Brooks among its many visiting writers.

In addition to the Diggs Gallery, which is located on the lower level of the O'Kelly Library very near the campus entrance, visitors should not miss the bold narrative murals by Gastonia native John Biggers in the atrium of the library. Other works by African American artists, including Romare Bearden, Selma Burke, and Stephanie Pogue, are also housed in the library.

Return to Martin Luther King Jr. Drive and turn left, heading south toward our last stop on this tour, a nostalgic landmark that is often pictured in books of twentieth-century Americana and described in a novel by Greensboro writer Brad Barkley.

A detail from Origins *—one of two murals created by Gastonia-born artist John Biggers for the atrium of the O'Kelly Library at Winston-Salem State University. Biggers's nephew, James Biggers Jr., an artist and teacher in Gaston County Schools, assisted with the installation.*

This place, it turned out, was an old Shell filling station, with two glass-topped gas pumps, regular and high-test, looming tall and rusty, and an old oil pit filled in with weedy dirt. The station itself was made of poured concrete, shaped to look like a giant scallop shell.

"Back in the forties, all of them were made like this. You know, Shell and shell, an advertising gimmick. This is the last one in the country. It's on the National Register of Historic Places."

He popped the door of the Lincoln and stepped out, and I followed him. We peered in through the dusty window of the door cut in the middle of the shell, the inside cramped by a small desk, a chair with a broken seat, a metal rack meant to hold motor oil or snack foods. On the desk was the ghost tracing of an old cash register outlined in heavy dust.

"Pretty cool place," I said. "Why are you showing it to me?"

"Because I bought it."

—From *Money, Love*, by Brad Barkley (New York: W. W. Norton, 2001), 327.

Barkley set his contemporary novel in and around Winston-Salem with side trips to the North Carolina mountains. Locals will recognize a number of familiar landmarks in this comic coming-of-age story about a young man caught between his father's insatiable appetite for fly-by-night moneymaking schemes and his mother's desperation to become a published poet. (Barkley has also written, with Heather Helper, two young adult novels set elsewhere.)

To see the outstanding retro-landmark, continue south on Martin Luther King Jr. Drive to its end at Waughtown Street and turn left. The next major crossroad is Peachtree Street. Turn right and the enormous shell is in the next block, on the left at East Sprague Street.

■ LITERARY LANDSCAPE

Forsyth County Public Library

660 West Fifth Street, Winston-Salem

336-703-2665

<http://www.co.forsyth.nc.us/LIBRARY/>

This downtown library loans nearly 2 million books per year. Winston-Salem residents from all walks of life come here to read, study, and relax. For the literary visitor, the North Carolina collection is a valuable cache of rare volumes of poetry and prose.

Authoring Action

8 West Third Street, Winston-Salem

336-831-1905

<http://www.authoringaction.org/>

Drawing on the talented recent graduates of the UNC School of the Arts, Authoring Action helps young people "publish, stage, and film their life experiences so that they can transform their lives, become leaders, and effect change in the world." The artistic director is poet and filmmaker Nathan Ross Freeman.

Delta Fine Arts Center

2611 New Walkertown Road, Winston-Salem

336-722-2625

<http://www.deltafinearts.org>

Creative writing workshops are occasionally offered by this community institution—the first nonprofit organized by African American women in

Winston-Salem. A lecture series and rotating exhibitions are the primary programs of the center, open Tuesdays through Fridays and most Saturdays.

BookMarks Book Festival

336-460-4722

<http://www.bookmarksbookfestival.org/>

info@bookmarksbookfestival.org

This free, one-day festival of books and writers takes place every September at Historic Bethabara Park.

Barnes & Noble

1925 Hampton Inn Court, Winston-Salem

336-774-0800

Across I-40 from Hanes Mall on the southwest side of town, this very large bookstore is accessible via Hanes Mall Boulevard.

Borders

252 South Stratford Road, Winston-Salem

336-727-8834

This bookstore features a café and a good selection of regional books, just south of the downtown freeway.

Special Occasions

112 North Martin Luther King Jr. Drive, Winston-Salem

336-724-0334

Probably no other bookstore in the United States has a better selection of Maya Angelou's many works (and she is a frequent customer). This large, freestanding shop just north of the freeway (I-40 Business) is on the east side of town. It stocks books by many other African American writers and celebratory gifts.

Shakespeare and Company Bookshop

Le Select Cafe

210 North Main Street, Kernersville

336-993-1050

<http://www.shakespeareinkernersville.blogspot.com>

Housed in the basement of an old furniture factory building in the heart of downtown Kernersville (a few miles east of Winston-Salem), this bookstore offers regular readings by local authors, exotic pastries, an in-store book club, and a large inventory of classic literature and books by regional writers.

Germanton : Danbury : Pilot Mountain : Mount Airy : Dobson : Rockford : Elkin

Climb Pilot Mountain. Explore the Yadkin River, sample North Carolina wines, and get a taste of the valley's colorful history through writers past and present.

Writers with a connection to this area: Frances Casstevens, Martin Clark, Bill Griffin, Harold Hayes, Maria Ingram-Braucht, Jack London, Helen Losse, Stephen Knauth, Joseph Mills, Michael Renegar, Mark Slouka, Trudy J. Smith, Hardin E. Taliaferro, Mark Twain, Amy Wallace, Irving Wallace, Lynn York

This tour features a somewhat odd assortment of storied sites that have led to a number of works of popular fiction and prize-winning nonfiction. Writers in these parts have been inspired by colorful characters from the countryside and by a wealth of ghost tales and freakish incidents of murder. The tales range from a surreptitious visit to the area by the likes of notorious bank robber John Dillinger to the curious story of "the original Siamese twins," Chang and Eng in Mount Airy.

We begin in the Stokes County town of Germanton, some seventeen miles north of Winston-Salem. This quiet village, with its fine art gallery, winery, and many historic homes, also has the distinction of having been home to Burea Jefferson Savage, business partner to adventure novelist Jack London (*Call of the Wild*) during the Klondike Gold Rush in Alaska. Savage, born near Pinnacle in Stokes County in 1862, set off for Alaska in the last decade of the nineteenth century and staked a number of claims. He returned to Stokes County to marry a local woman in 1902. His wife once recalled to relatives that she knew all the characters upon whom London had based his Alaska books. Savage and his wife and family finally settled back in Stokes County in 1906, where he worked as a banker,

tour 2

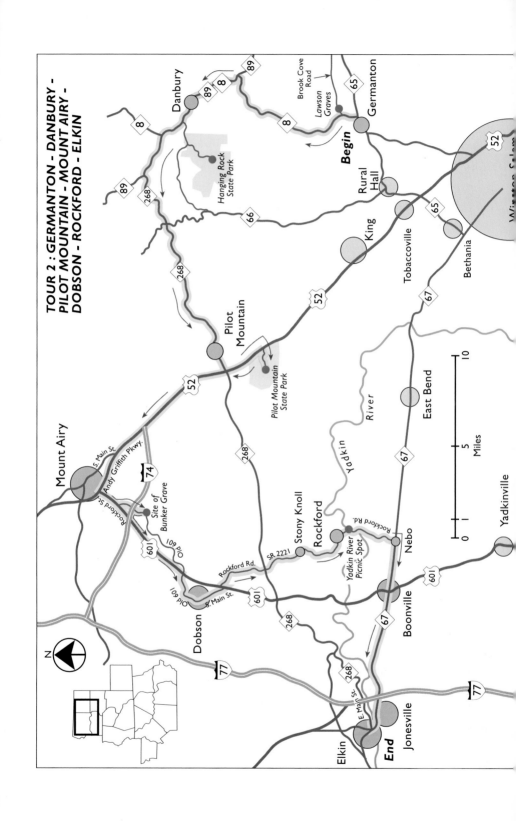

TOUR 2 : GERMANTON - DANBURY -
PILOT MOUNTAIN - MOUNT AIRY -
DOBSON - ROCKFORD - ELKIN

farmer, and one-time mayor of Germanton until he was gored by a bull and died on the family farm.

Following NC 65 through Germanton, turn left on NC 8 north toward Danbury. Watch for Brook Cove Road on the right, in less than a mile. Turn right and then take an immediate left on a narrow gravel private drive and follow it to the end.

Before you is Browder Cemetery, a small graveyard that holds the remains resulting from one of the saddest stories of domestic violence ever committed in North Carolina—the Christmas Day massacre of the Lawson family in 1929.

Tobacco farmer Charlie Lawson killed his wife, his six youngest children, and then himself. It was an event that continues to reverberate throughout Stokes County. The incident scandalized the state and led to three books, a documentary film, and at least five classic ballads, one of which reached the top of the charts in 1930.

White Christmas—Bloody Christmas: Finally the True Story of the Lawson Family Murders of Christmas Day, by the father-and-daughter writing team of M. Bruce Jones and Trudy J. Smith, was the first complete account of this story, which sold 13,000 copies before becoming a rare commodity.

As grim as the story is, perhaps equally dark are the ways in which the human urge toward voyeurism played out after the tragedy. Some 5,000 people reportedly attended the funeral of the victims.

As late as the 1970s, the Lawson house and farm further down Brook Cove Road was still being visited by curious tourists. At one point, a family member sold refreshments and souvenir pictures and charged admission to the crime scene. Charlie Lawson's brain went to Johns Hopkins for study. The crib of the youngest child, bloody sheets and all, went on tour as a side show at local carnivals.

For a time, rumors circulated that the family had been murdered by the notorious John Dillinger, though he could not have committed the crime from his jail cell in Indiana, where he was at the time. By 1933, however, he was out of prison, robbing banks again. That winter, Dillinger came through North Carolina with his gang to visit the site of the Lawson murder. The members of the Dillinger group each paid their 25 cents admission and took the tour, and then Dillinger left a note in the front door of the Lawson house taunting the local law officer, who did not recognize him as he passed through.

The Lawson family is buried near the middle of the cemetery. A large headstone bears the names of the parents and all but one child, James Arthur Lawson, who was not home at the time of his father's rampage. Arthur lived only to the age of thirty-two. His grave is nearby, separate from the others.

■ DANBURY

Backtrack to NC 8 and turn right, heading north toward Danbury. In ten miles, where 8 joins NC 89, bear left. Soon you'll be in the village of Danbury. Here the county library and courthouse (both on the right side of the highway) rest on grounds that once hosted a settlement of Native Americans whose many legends about the curative waters of nearby springs at Vade Mecum and the sacred Saura Mountains are part of the lore of the county. Once a resort town with a large, antebellum tourist hotel called Piedmont Springs, Main Street Danbury today offers a museum, a bakery and café called Artist's Way Creations, and the Dan River Company, which organizes trips by canoe and kayak on the river (336-593-2628).

Beyond Danbury, watch for signs to Hanging Rock State Park, only 1.4 miles to the left off the main highway. The park's fifteen-acre lake, foot and bridle trails, and roads were built in 1938 and provide a welcome spot to hike and view the Piedmont from an unusual elevation.

Continue north on NC 89 to the intersection with NC 268 and turn left. This road meanders through the Stokes County countryside and into Surry County to our next stop in Pilot Mountain. In this fertile, rolling landscape, tobacco is still a cash crop, though its profitability was in question as early as the Depression, according to this poem by Winston-Salem writer Maria Ingram-Braucht:

ONE STORY BENEATH THE PIN OAK
Sunday afternoon we're sitting
in the backyard spitting seeds out
of bought watermelons and my
father says it's the worst
summer since 1930 when they had to
replant tobacco four times,
on into July, before it took hold.
Six and a half acres brought
a hundred and forty dollars
at six cents a pound.
But there were some, he said,
only bought a half, a quarter
cent a pound.
One old man from Stokes County
crated up a bunch of chickens
to bring with him.

The Dan River flows through Moratock Park in the Stokes County seat of Danbury.

The auctioneer's fee was more
than his tobacco brought,
so he took his chicken money
to get back out into sunlight.
They sat around the camp,
laughing to keep from not laughing
at the fine mess they were in:
young'uns needed saddle oxfords
and notebook paper.
Daddy asked the man from Stokes
was he going to raise tobacco next year.
Oh yeah, he said, that's the only
thing they's any money in.
—From "One Story beneath the Pin Oak," by Maria Ingram,
    in *Thirtieth Year to Heaven: New American Poets*
    (Winston-Salem: Jackpine Press, 1980), 84.

Follow 268 until it meets US 52 and turn right. Then take an immediate left onto Bullington Lane, which quickly ends at East Main Street in Pilot Mountain. Turn right and follow East Main into town.

A winter view of Pilot Mountain and its distinctive knob as seen from an old tobacco farm, a few miles south of the summit.

■ PILOT MOUNTAIN

This village, which sits adjacent to the Piedmont's most unusual outcropping of stone, is also the setting for Lynn York's first novel, *The Piano Teacher: A Novel of Swan's Knob*. The book is part love story and part murder mystery, solved by York's unlikely heroine, the piano teacher, Miss Wilma Mabry, a character based on York's own piano teacher in town. Readers of the novel will not be surprised to learn that Pilot Mountain is full of sites that inspired York. The author says she was guided less by the literal map of streets and houses than the landscape of her memory.

"That meant that I felt free to borrow bits and pieces of Pilot Mountain and then imagine the rest," she says. The Coach House Restaurant, for example, where town patriarch Roy Swan and Miss Wilma go on their first date, was a real restaurant on West Main Street and was York's favorite place to eat growing up. The space is now occupied by a tanning salon.

York also frequented the soda fountain at "Surry Drug," now Mount Pilot Drug, at 119 West Main Street. She writes about a sandwich shop that the locals in the book refer to as "the Squeeze Box," because of extremely limited seating. It is indeed a tiny shop on the left side of Main, seemingly swallowed up by the parking lot that surrounds it.

From here, the tour heads to the top of the mountain from which the town takes its name. On Main Street, you'll once more meet up with NC 268 (now called Key Street). Turn left and follow 268 to US 52 and head south. Watch for signs to Pilot Mountain State Park at the very next exit on 52 South. The access road ascends the mountain and ends at a parking area just below the pinnacles.

■ PILOT MOUNTAIN STATE PARK

This evocative peak is visible for miles in every direction. From the parking area you can hike to the top of Little Pinnacle, where on a clear day you can see Hanging Rock State Park to the east and Winston-Salem to the southeast. The level, mile-long Jomeokee Trail—so named for the Native American word meaning pilot or guide—circles the knob.

There is another opportunity to hike at the bottom of the mountain near the entrance where the river section of the park provides a five-mile southward meander through the woods to the Yadkin River Trail. Watch for wildlife and consider this wistful reflection by Winston-Salem poet Helen Losse:

THE EAGLE AT SUNSET
   (Just North of Winston-Salem)
This trek begins near Pinnacle.

Yes, I've been here before:
A shadowed cow wades in a farmer's pond.

The sun becomes
a thin and setting line. A lone tobacco plant

moves thorny underbrush
aside, poking through. The *smell of money*

no longer dances in the wind.
Coiled cedar roots cling to the earth

like young octopi. I drink water
in long, refreshing gulps,

enjoy the evening, flanked by evergreens:
watching an eagle—diving

from Pilot's forbidden ledge, soaring in
concentric circles, charging the down-currents

of the gusty wind.
Then, a darkening silhouette: And he's lost

in the reddening sky.
—From *Domicile* (August 2001), used by permission of Helen Losse.

■ MOUNT AIRY

Our next stop, the largest town in Surry County, is due north on US 52. Forgo the I-74 bypass to the west. Head straight into town on US 52 (Andy Griffith Parkway) and turn right on Rockford Street (US 601). Mount Airy, the childhood home of Andy Griffith, was the inspiration for television's Mayberry, but it is also known today for its wealth of homegrown music and theater and an annual storytelling festival called Blue Ridge and Beyond, held each spring.

The Andy Griffith Playhouse, just ahead on the left at 218 Rockford Street, was built in 1920. This building originally housed the elementary school where North Carolina's most famous comedic actor learned to read and write. It later became the playhouse where he first practiced his craft. Today the building serves as headquarters for the Surry Arts Council (336-786-7998) and its enormously popular Mayberry Days festival, held annually during the last week in September. The Andy Griffith Collection, an assortment of memorabilia from the Mayberry television series and Griffith's acting career, is also on permanent display here, open seven days a week. The public library is across the street.

Municipal parking is available behind the buildings on Mount Airy's Main Street, so you can explore the town on foot. At 125 North Main Street, Mayberry aficionados can tackle an enormous pork chop and slaw sandwich from the 1923-vintage Snappy Lunch (336-786-4931) and then visit Floyd's Barbershop next door. Saturday mornings there's live local music across the way at the Downtown Cinema Theater at 142 North Main, where radio station WPAQ hosts its Merry-Go-Round broadcast from 11:00 to 1:30.

The literary visitor may also be gratified to learn that Mount Airy was the

Outside the Andy Griffith Playhouse in Mount Airy (aka Mayberry), an iconic tribute to the town's favorite son, alongside his television "son" Opie, the child-actor-turned-filmmaker Ron Howard. An identical sculpture is located in Raleigh's Pullen Park. Both were created by Studio EIS in New York.

birthplace of country singer Donna Fargo ("Happiest Girl in the Whole USA"), who has turned to writing poetry and greeting card copy in recent years. Fargo is celebrated, along with one-time Mount Airy residents Chang and Eng Bunker, through exhibitions at the historic Robert Smith House, 615 North Main Street (336-789-4636).

Chang and Eng Bunker, twins who were born conjoined at the breastbone in 1811, were often called "the original Siamese twins," because they actually came from Siam. Though P. T. Barnum first made them famous, many writers have since been intrigued by their remarkable story. Even Mark Twain, in a sketch published in 1869, uses Chang and Eng for an absurdist riff on the challenge of two personalities physically joined but with opposing temperaments, particularly in matters of religion and the consumption of alcohol:

> The Twins always go to bed at the same time; but Chang usually gets up about an hour before his brother. By an understanding between themselves, Chang does all the in-door work and Eng runs all the errands. This is because Eng likes to go out; Chang's habits are sedentary. However, Chang always goes along. Eng is a Baptist, but Chang is a Roman Catholic; still, to please his brother, Chang consented to be baptized at the same time that

Eng was, on condition that it should not "count."—From "Personal Habits of the Siamese Twins," by Mark Twain, *Packard's Monthly*, 1869, <http:// etext.virginia.edu/railton/wilson/siamese.html>.

Twain would return to the theme of twins as a metaphor for the divided self in his work as he wrestled to describe the harsh realities in the United States of slavery, racism, and a culture that tacitly encouraged people of mixed parentage to "pass" as white if their skin color was light enough. *The Prince and the Pauper* (1881) and *Pudd'nhead Wilson* (1894) lift up the fickle challenges of race and class as they are applied differently to "twin" characters. The usual interpretation of Clemens's choice of the pen name Mark Twain is as a reference to the riverboat term for the depth of water needed for safe passage, but Twain scholar Stephen Railton of the University of Virginia suggests that the name may also reflect the writer's lifetime literary preoccupation with twins. "Twain" literally means two items of the same kind.

In 1978, the father/daughter team of Irving and Amy Wallace published *The Two*, a biography of Chang and Eng. More than two decades later, two novels published about a year apart each take on the point of view of one of the twins. Darin Strauss's 2001 novel *Chang and Eng* is narrated in the voice of Eng and begins with the story of the Bunkers' arrival in nearby Wilkesboro. Mark Slouka's 2002 novel *God's Fool* is told in Chang's voice and uses the periods just before and during the Civil War as bookends to the tale of the brothers' origins on the Mekong River in Thailand. At the age of seventeen, Chang and Eng sailed for Europe, consigned by their mother to an opium trader for the sum of 300 pounds. In England, a medical researcher undertook an investigation of their anatomy and presented a paper about them to London's Royal College of Surgeons. Their fame quickly spread, and soon the brothers found themselves in the company of royalty and members of high society, who regarded them as fascinating curiosities of nature.

The brothers eventually signed a contract with P. T. Barnum and crossed the Atlantic to tour the United States with Tom Thumb and other "freaks" in Barnum's show. During this period, Eng converted to Christianity at the urging of Barnum's wife, but Chang was not so inclined.

The twins were twenty-three when they gave up the circus and settled in Wilkes County, North Carolina. There they married sisters—daughters of a local judge. Chang fathered ten and Eng eleven children, and eventually they moved to Surry County, where the two families spent two weeks at Chang's house and then traveled by wagon to spend two weeks at Eng's. As Slouka has Chang explain:

The gravesite of the original Siamese twins, Chang and Eng Bunker, who are buried with their wives, the Yates sisters, on a hill outside Mount Airy. The brothers helped finance the building of the church and cemetery here.

I think back on that time fondly. We all still lived in the house at Mount Airy then, Addy and Sallie making out as best they could, the children always underfoot.... What sweet days those were. I've never had tomatoes like the ones that grew there, trellising themselves on the children's crosses, bearing them down with the weight of their fruit.—From *God's Fool*, by Mark Slouka (New York: Knopf, 2002), 8.

Before leaving Mount Airy, you may want to visit the Bunker gravesite behind the White Plains Baptist Church at 614 Old Highway 601. From the Andy Griffith Playhouse, follow US 601 south. Cross US 52 and continue away from downtown. Watch for Walmart on the left and then turn left at the next available turn lane onto Old 601. In two miles you will pass over I-74. The White Plains Baptist Church is just beyond the overpass. The cemetery is on a dramatic hill in back of the older church building, and the Bunker gravesite is immediately adjacent to the church.

Chang and Eng financed the building of the church and the establishment of the cemetery. Every June their many descendants come here for a Bunker family reunion, which is open to the public. Backtrack to US 601 and turn left toward Dobson to continue the tour.

■ YADKIN RIVER VALLEY

Heading southwest on 601, this tour takes in long views of the fertile Yadkin Valley, where thermal belts moderate the influence of frost and farmers have made a dramatic turn in the last two decades from tobacco toward viticulture and the art of wine making. The climate here is friendly to grapes, and North Carolina's nascent wine industry is growing with each successive harvest. For her second book, *The Sweet Life*, novelist Lynn York follows piano teacher Wilma Mabry into marriage and the winemaking business. Wilma's new husband, Roy Swan, is the central character, who adores his grapes:

> On days like this, with a sweet breeze coming down from the Knob into the valley of his land, with the sun beaming down on his little crop of grapes, on his tomato vines and his face, Roy Swan imagined that he had been such a man for centuries, overseeing his land on a hillside, that he was reincarnated somehow—though that was in no way a Protestant teaching—that he had stood in such a field on a hillside in Umbria in 1730 maybe, holding warm grapes in his hand, more pleased with life than anyone on earth.—From *The Sweet Life*, by Lynn York (New York: Plume, 2007), 28.

Watch for signs along 601 directing visitors to various wineries. You can pick up maps and a calendar of events (including music and other special festivities) from most any vintner and chart your own tour of the vineyards dotted across the region. Grab a picnic, sample some wines, seek your own muse, and enjoy this poem by Joseph Mills, a member of the faculty at the University of North Carolina School of the Arts in Winston-Salem.

THE THIEF
When winemakers use the thief,
the long pipette to withdraw liquid
from the cask or carboy,
it looks like a violation,
as if they're performing
exploratory surgery

trying to determine
the state of what's inside.
Perhaps that's why
it has such a name,
an acknowledgement
of transgression
but also a suggestion
the wine no longer
belongs to its makers.

I think of the lost expressions
on painters' faces
after they sell canvases
they have worked on for months
or parents at airports in August
saying goodbye to children
who have chosen colleges
hundreds of miles away.
The winemaker's tool serves
as a constant reminder:
what we make is not ours,
someday our rooms will be empty,
love makes thieves of us all.
—From *Angels, Thieves, and Winemakers*, by Joseph Mills
   (Winston-Salem: Press 53, 2008), 16.

■ DOBSON

US 601 takes you to Dobson, the county seat of Surry County. Old 601, which veers off to the right as you approach, is the most direct route into town. The courthouse, at the intersection of Main and Atkins streets, is a key site in Lynn York's first novel and is the setting that novelist Martin Clark likely had in mind as he wrote *The Many Aspects of Mobile Home Living*. Clark's novel mostly takes place in the fictional town of Norton—like Dobson, about twenty-five minutes from Winston-Salem—where his main character, Evers Wheeling, serves as one of the youngest judges in North Carolina. Martin Clark delivers both a thriller and a meditation on class privilege in his first novel.

Our route continues through wine country to Rockford, a once-thriving antebellum settlement on the shores of the Yadkin River. Beyond the Dobson courthouse, continue on South Main Street (601 Business) out of town and take Rockford Road (sr 2221) on the left. Rockford Road crosses over the 601 bypass and continues through the countryside.

The land drops sharply on either side of the road just before you reach the beautifully maintained Rockford Methodist Church, built in 1914. A little farther down the hill on the right is the Rockford General Store with its broad, tin-roofed front porch and red benches set out for travelers to rest. The store's proprietors have built an amphitheater out back, which is the site of a Halloween celebration in October that includes the energetic telling of local ghost stories.

Roadside Revenants and Other North Carolina Ghosts and Legends (2006) is Michael Renegar's contribution to the growing collection of popular ghost tales from this area. According to the Rockford storekeeper, Renegar, who lives nearby in East Bend, often trades tales with local historian Frances Casstevens, a writer who also makes her home nearby in the pristine village of Huntsville. Casstevens is the author of *Death in North Carolina's Piedmont: Tales of Murder, Suicide and Causes Unknown* (2006) and *The Civil War and Yadkin County, North Carolina* (2005). As of 2010, Casstevens had published seven volumes about the Civil War, its notable figures from Yadkin, and its impact on the region, including a book about the staunch abolitionist Edward Wild, who trained African soldiers for the Union Army. Most of Casstevens's books have been published by McFarland Books of Ashe County.

Former North Carolina legislator Daniel W. Barefoot of Lincolnton provides a tale about Rockford's famous dog-ghost in his collection, *Haints of the Hills: North Carolina's Haunted Hundred, Volume 3* (2002).

Half a dozen structures in Rockford are on the National Register of Historic Places and date back to the eighteenth century. This village was once the county seat of Surry County and, as such, was visited by Andrew Jackson, Aaron Burr, and James K. Polk. The Grant Burris Hotel, established in 1794, hosted all three. It burned in 1974, but its four chimneys still stand directly across the road from the general store.

Hardin E. Taliaferro (pronounced "Tolliver") was a local humorist and preacher in the era when Rockford was the site of so much activity. His *Fisher's River Scenes and Characters* is an illustrated volume from 1859 that provides a window into the hardship of living here and the language of the white settlers who farmed the Yadkin Valley back then. One of Taliaferro's memorable char-

A common scene in the Yadkin Valley: spring brings new growth to grapes at Westbend Vineyards, one among the dozens of wineries in the region.

acters is Dick Snow, described as "a little above ordinary. He was a little stoop-shouldered, and moved quickly and with great ease. His face was quite paradoxical, wearing both a vinegar and pleasant appearance. His eyes were black, small, and restless, indicating quick perception, particularly of the ridiculous."

In this anecdote, Dick's speech is best read aloud for the full effect of Taliaferro's phonetic translations of the Yadkin vernacular:

> People in that country, at the time of which I speak, got nearly all their information by inquiry. They did not take the papers; the sound of the stage bugle never echoed through their hills and mountains. If a man went twenty miles from home, he might expect on his return to be quizzed not a little. Dick once went to Rockford, the seat of justice for Surry County, to court, when a certain "'Squire Byrd" was to be tried for murder. Expectation was on tiptoe. Dick returned, and was asked the news. He replied:
>
> "Thar warn't no trial; 'twas put off, an' 'Squire Byrd has gi'n siscurity for his exspearunce at the next court, so they 'least him."
>
> Dick had a pertinacious way of abbreviating nearly all his words, even when he knew better. He was a man of fine sense and good judgment, but

he wished to take "short cuts," and "talk jest like he'd bin larnt," and was too energetic to take time to pronounce whole words. Once he returned from court, and was giving his neighbors the news in the presence of his wife, who was a woman of good learning for that section, and said "sich an' sich" men were "'turned to court."

His wife was amused at him, and said, "Dick, why don't you call that word right?"

"Well, ree-turned, then, ef you will have it the long way," replied Dick. "Some folks are allers gwine the long way, but that ain't me. I gits right inter it, like a homminny-bird (humming-bird) inter a tech-me-not flower." —From *Fisher's River Scenes and Characters*, by Hardin E. Talliafero (1859), <http://docsouth.unc.edu/nc/taliaferro/taliaferro.html>.

Continue through Rockford on Rockford Road, which joins Old Rockford Road. At the bottom of the hill, the road turns sharply to the right and runs alongside a broad and shallow stretch of the Yadkin. A bridge soon crosses the river. On the left, a grassy picnic area provides the perfect place for a stop and a reading of this river poem by Charlotte writer Stephen Knauth:

RETURNING TO A COVE OF THE YADKIN
Hidden among frazzled catkins,
among rank whiskers of the Almighty,
life's golden purpose snores.
Mother and Father swimming in the river near dusk,
each particle of creation available for viewing
in the gold band of light between the river's surface
and the first tier of green fir. Approaching eighty
with a solid backstroke, her eyes closed, as though calmly pulling
the river downstream. He treads water, head bobbing
like an apple in a tub, Mao in the Yangtze. Do their
eyes still meet across the water as they once did?
No thought now of the chair's cold weight,
the letterbox laden with bills, the hidden vials.
Swimming past dark, through midnight's liqueur.
Swimming through trees and moon-burnt clouds, as if.
—From *Iron Horse Literary Review* (Fall 2001): 113.

■ JONESVILLE/ELKIN

Our final destination on this tour includes the historic towns of Jonesville and Elkin, also on the Yadkin River. From the picnic area south of Rockford, continue southeast on Rockford Road, which soon turns sharply to the right (straight ahead is Richmond Hill Church Road). Stay on Rockford Road for two miles to the little crossroads of Nebo and turn right on NC 67, which runs through historic Boonville and becomes Main Street in the town of Jonesville.

As you come into Jonesville, the landscape begins to lose elevation and a relatively new bridge spans the Yadkin and arches over Elkin's Main Street below it. Elkin, the larger of these two towns that straddle the banks of the Yadkin, sits high on the far side in Surry County. On the south side, Jonesville is in Yadkin County.

A good place to start your visit is the Yadkin Valley Visitors' Center at 116 East Market Street in Elkin (which is also NC 268). From literary history, Elkin's claim to fame is journalist Harold Thomas Pace Hayes, who spent his early years here. He was the son of a fundamentalist Baptist preacher and a mother with cultural interests. Hayes went on to Wake Forest College, eventually serving as editor of *Esquire* magazine for nearly a decade, beginning in 1964. A daring editor who followed his gut, Hayes is largely credited with launching what came to be known as "new journalism." He helped to spawn this radical surge in creative nonfiction when he began hiring writers at *Esquire* who used the tools of fiction to cover contemporary figures and events, treating their subjects as characters and dramatizing scenes with dialogue and action, sometimes only loosely based on fact. The reporters sometimes even took the liberty of first-person narration, thus becoming characters in their own articles—then considered a violation of journalistic standards in reporting news.

Norman Mailer, Tom Wolfe, William Styron, Gay Talese, Peter Bogdanovich, Dorothy Parker, James Baldwin, Nora Ephron, and John Berendt (many years later the author of *Midnight in the Garden of Good and Evil*) were among Hayes's stable of go-to writers. After beating out his rival from Duke University, Clay Felker, for the top editorial spot at the magazine, Hayes also took enormous design risks, including controversial (for the 1960s) depictions of boxer Sonny Liston as Santa for a Christmas issue, a photo in profile of Richard Nixon with makeup being applied to his face, and a portrait of heavyweight champion Muhammad Ali as Saint Sebastian with faux arrows piercing his torso above his signature silk boxing trunks. The formula worked. Circulation skyrocketed to nearly a million readers, and the magazine enjoyed nearly a decade of record revenues.

Hayes also wrote a seminal article on primatologist Dian Fossey on which the film *Gorillas in the Mist* was partially based. Late in life he wrote two books on ecology and had nearly completed a biography of Fossey when he was afflicted by a brain tumor that led to his death in 1989 at the age of sixty-two.

To get a bird's-eye-view of Harold Hayes's hometown of Elkin, leave your car and walk a bit farther down Market Street from the Visitors' Center to the old two-lane bridge, which now is open only to pedestrian traffic.

Though much about Elkin has not changed since Hayes's era, contemporary local writer and rural family physician Bill Griffin offers this poem as a meditation on the recent development you'll soon see sprawling across the foothills in the region:

DARK ADAPTED
Crouch atop the midnight ridge,
look back across the piedmont expecting
trees, streams, tobacco fields
all fused into one flat blackness,

but not so—the nightscape has been pierced
and bleeds pinpricks of mercury blue-white,
brawny thumbprints of halogen vapor
in strip mall clusters, at crossroads' sprawl,

or broadcast singly in farmers' sleepy yards—
each bright point the anchor of one soul's fear.
Black bear and red wolf once possessed the night;
now this sterile galaxy of assurances

is drilled and hammered into place and even defeats
the stars—they can't compete
at ground level with the glare.
But from this elevated vantage I look up

to vaster points of blue and brass
that still outnumber human aspirations:
suspended in the sphere of all and nothing,
in darkness not flat but enfolding, deep,

the flood tide of cosmos seeps through
to drench this speck of presence, to lap

at woods, fields, farms and rise
to fill these dark adapted eyes.
—Used by permission of Bill Griffin.

Griffin, who organizes the region's annual Foothills Favorite Poem Project, recommends a stroll through the Elkin business district. Proceed from the bridge to the concrete stairway down to Main Street. In several blocks, you'll find Diana's Bookstore, at 127 West Main Street (336-835-3142). This local institution is shoulder to shoulder with the headquarters for the Brushy Mountain Winery and the Reeves Theater, built in 1940. Elkin native Cicely McCulloch (who owns the bookstore) and her childhood friend Robin Turner are leading a three-county effort to restore the 700-seat facility for local arts events.

The Elkin Public Library (336-835-5586) is at the end of the block, at 111 Front Street. It's majestically perched on the bank of a swift creek with its very own wide waterfall visible from the western-facing windows.

■ LITERARY LANDSCAPE

Blue Ridge and Beyond Festival
Surry Arts Council
218 Rockford Street, Mount Airy
336-786-7998
<http://www.surryarts.org>
An international cadre of storytellers and music makers gathers in Mount Airy for this festival, hosted by the Surry Arts Council each spring.

Mount Airy Public Library
145 Rockford Street, Mount Airy
336-789-5108
<http://www.nwrl.org/mta.asp>
This facility, lit by daylight and passively cooled and heated, won an American Institute of Architects Design Award. It is outfitted with wireless Internet access and has extensive genealogical materials.

Mocksville : Cooleemee : Salisbury : Gold Hill

Follow the Yadkin River—a powerful inspiration to writers from Davie and Rowan counties, recent and long past.

Writers with a connection to this area: Kurt Corriher, Janice Moore Fuller, John Hart, Nathaniel Hawthorne, Hinton Rowan Helper, Langston Hughes, Harriet Jacobs, James Weldon Johnson, Hugh T. Lefler, Audre Lorde, Robert Morgan, Jim Rumley, Joanna Catherine Scott, Frances Fisher Tiernan (Christian Reid), Margaret Walker, Richard Walser, Henry Wiencek

This tour begins in territory once pioneered by Daniel Boone's parents and by Boone himself—a story skillfully told by North Carolina poet and novelist Robert Morgan. It also skirts by the estate, now a park on the Yadkin River, that once belonged to members of the Reynolds tobacco clan, who bought and expanded the manor house they named Tanglewood after Nathaniel Hawthorne's popular children's book *Tanglewood Tales* (1853).

But we begin at Cooleemee Plantation, a tract of 1,800 acres with four miles of frontage on the Yadkin River south of Tanglewood, an estate that has been placed into a conservation trust. Though visitors are discouraged, the plantation has two significant literary connections.

DIRECTIONS

From I-40 west of Winston-Salem, take exit 180 and head south on NC 801, proceeding through Advance, pronounced with the accent on the first syllable. At US 64, turn left. In a little more than two miles you will cross a wide bridge over the Yadkin River. Pull over and look southwest to see the edge of the Cooleemee Plantation, once commemorated by a state historic marker along this stretch of highway but now unmarked. Writer Henry Wiencek describes his first visit to the estate:

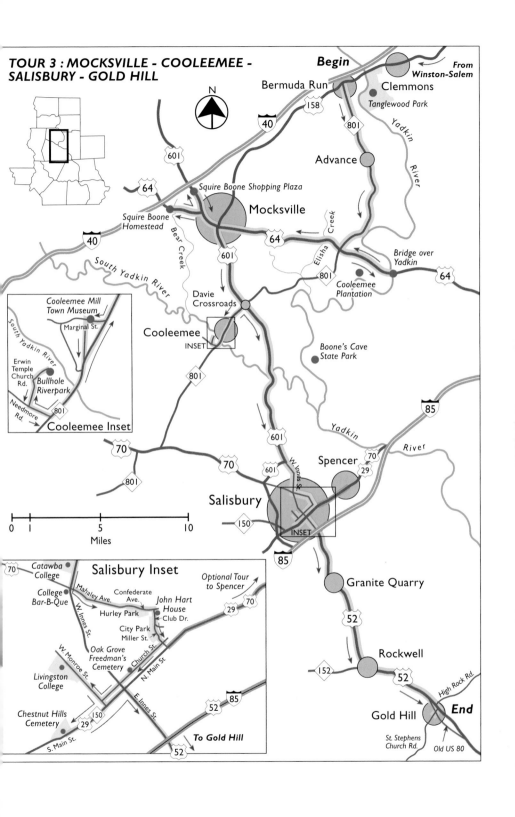

TOUR 3 : MOCKSVILLE - COOLEEMEE - SALISBURY - GOLD HILL

N

Begin

From Winston-Salem

Clemmons

Bermuda Run

158

Tanglewood Park

40

601

801

Yadkin River

Advance

64

Squire Boone Shopping Plaza

Mocksville

Squire Boone Homestead

Bear Creek

601

64

Elisha Creek

Bridge over Yadkin

64

40

801

Cooleemee Plantation

South Yadkin River

Davie Crossroads

Cooleemee Inset

Cooleemee Mill Town Museum

Marginal St.

South Yadkin River

Erwin Temple Church Rd.

Bullhole Riverpark

Needmore Rd.

801

Cooleemee

INSET

Boone's Cave State Park

801

85

Yadkin River

70

70

601

601

Spencer

70

29

801

Salisbury

150

INSET

W. Innes St.

85

0   1   5   10

Miles

Granite Quarry

Salisbury Inset

Catawba College

70

College Bar-B-Que

Mahaley Ave.

Confederate Ave.

John Hart House

Optional Tour to Spencer

29   70

Hurley Park

Club Dr.

W. Innes St.

City Park

Miller St.

Oak Grove Freedman's Cemetery

Church St.

N. Main St.

Livingston College

W. Monroe St.

52

Chestnut Hills Cemetery

150

29

E. Innes St.

52

85

S. Main St.

52

To Gold Hill

152

Rockwell

52

High Rock Rd.

Gold Hill

End

St. Stephens Church Rd.

Old US 80

The mansion at Cooleemee was a commanding presence. Lordly and gleaming, it stood atop a knoll not far from the Yadkin River in North Carolina, at the end of a gravel road that snaked through a pine forest. I emerged from the woods to see the house set on a pedestal of terraced gardens, painted a brilliant white, and guarded by a pair of magnificent trees, a flamboyant maple and a stately Southern magnolia. I approached it from below, like a supplicant.

Tall and heavyset, with a great wave of white hair breaking across his head, Judge Peter Wilson Hairston made an imposing figure as he stood in the doorway of Cooleemee Plantation—the very image of the Old South aristocrat. He wore a bathrobe and slippers—he had been, he explained, polishing the silver—but that did not in the least diminish the gravity of his presence. From the doorway boomed a powerful, resonant voice—truly the voice of a judge. The voice was a great gift, an instrument worthy of an actor, the perfect instrument, as I would find, for telling the old stories of the plantation across a candlelit dining table, with tumblers of bourbon within easy reach. . . .

"First things first. My name is spelled *Hair*ston, but it is pronounced *Hars*ton. If you can manage that"—now the smile emerged—"we'll get along just fine."

—From *The Hairstons: An American Family in Black and White*,
by Henry Wiencek (New York: St. Martin's, 1999), 3.

Henry Wiencek's prize-winning biography of the Hairstons took him eight years to write. The Hairston clan, he wrote, is likely the largest family in the United States because the white Hairstons, at the peak of their land holdings, owned forty plantations and some 10,000 enslaved people, who also bore the family surname. Cooleemee is reportedly the last of these large tracts, with a gorgeous Greek Revival mansion that's still intact. Confederate major Peter Hairston bought it in 1817 with his wife, Columbia Stuart Hairston, sister of Civil War general J. E. B. Stuart.

Long ago, the Davie County Hairstons gave up the practice of sharecropping that followed emancipation. In 1948, Judge Peter Wilson Hairston (described in the passage above) and his wife abandoned successful careers in Washington to come home and save the historic property from ruin. Hairston opened a small law practice in Mocksville and was later appointed to the bench by Governor Jim Hunt.

In 1978, despite threats from the Ku Klux Klan, Judge Hairston hosted a huge

The grand house at Cooleemee Plantation figures in Henry Wiencek's prize-winning biography, The Hairstons: An American Family in Black and White, *and in John Hart's second novel,* Down River. *Used by permission of The Land Trust for Central North Carolina.*

reunion at Cooleemee for some 3,000 white and black Hairstons and their guests. The purpose was to celebrate Cooleemee's designation as a National Historic Landmark. Squire Hairston, an African American elder whose grandfather had been a slave on the plantation, gave the keynote address. Unfortunately, racial tensions in North Carolina at the time made a National Guard detachment necessary for security at such an openly biracial event. (A year later, five demonstrators were gunned down at an anti-Klan rally in Greensboro.)

In his biography, Wiencek follows the family saga up to the moment when, a number of years after the Cooleemee reunion, at another family gathering in Greensboro, black members of the Hairston clan confronted the judge with the grief and anger they harbored about the heritage of slavery. The words spoken stung all parties, but the conversations and efforts at reconciliation have continued as all the Hairstons—some connected by blood, others by purchase, and some by both—wrestled with the ongoing fallout. Judge Hairston eventually placed Cooleemee Plantation in the Land Trust for Central North Carolina, making it one of the largest agricultural properties protected for posterity in the state. He died in 2007 at the age of ninety-three. His son still manages the property.

Salisbury novelist John Hart visited Cooleemee Plantation while Judge Hairston was still living, in order, as Hart put it, "to get a feel for a piece of land that large along the banks of the Yadkin." Hart's second novel, *Down River*, is partly inspired by his wistful longing for the nearly five hundred acres his own family once possessed on nearby High Rock Lake—land, Hart says, that had remained pristine from the time General Cornwallis camped there. When his parents divorced they sold the land, and it became a trailer park and dump site. Unable to return to that property, Hart visited the Cooleemee Plantation and began to imagine setting his novel there.

The river is my earliest memory. The front porch of my father's house looks down on it from a low knoll, and I have pictures, faded yellow, of my first days on that porch. I slept in my mother's arms as she rocked there, played in the dust while my father fished, and I know the feel of that river even now: the slow churn of red clay, the black eddies under cut banks, the se-crets it whispered to the hard, pink granite of Rowan County. Everything that shaped me happened near that river. I lost my mother in sight of it, fell in love on its banks. I could smell it on the day my father drove me out. It was part of my soul, and I thought I'd lost it forever.

But things can change, that's what I told myself. Mistakes can be un-done, wrongs righted. That's what brought me home.

—From *Down River*, by John Hart (New York: Thomas Dunne Books, 2007), 1.

Hart's depiction of the landscape is powerful. His thriller begins with the re-turn of a prodigal son, Adam Chase, to Rowan County. But because of his check-ered past Chase soon finds himself a potential suspect in a murder.

Hart says that trips to local vineyards also helped inspire his novel. From this scenic view of the Yadkin, backtrack on 64 and head west toward Mocksville.

Just a few miles after the crossroads with NC 801, you are in the vicinity of Elisha Creek—land that long ago belonged to Daniel Boone's father. Accord-ing to writer Robert Morgan, Daniel Boone was sixteen when his father, Squire Boone, became increasingly disenchanted with the Quaker community in Pennsylvania where the family lived. Squire stopped attending church meet-ings because he resented the opprobrium of the Friends when his older son, Israel, married a non-Quaker. Perhaps just as important, Squire had heard tales of beautiful lands to the south in Virginia and North Carolina that could be had cheap. Robert Morgan picks up the tale with his characteristic lyricism:

The Boones arrived on the Yadkin in the fall of 1751. The Yadkin and its feeder creeks moved fast enough to turn gristmills and saw mills. The bottomlands and meadows offered unsurpassed soil for farming, and the higher ground was ideal for grazing....

The soil along the river and tributary creeks of the Yadkin Valley was a rainbow of colors and textures. Near the streams, the ground, once cleared of roots and exposed to the sun, was a black alluvial powder, a mixture of silt and sand and rotted vegetation perfect for growing watermelons and corn, crops favored by loose, damp soil. In a rainy season streams sometimes overflowed and left standing pools in the hot sun that scalded the roots of species such as beans.

Farther from the river, on gently rising land that rarely flooded, the topsoil was rich brown, the color of dark roast coffee. Stiffer than the loam along the river, the dirt was still loose when plowed, with glittering bits of quartz and mica among its crumbs and sugary lumps. Among the brown cortex of soil were patches of silver clay drawn up by the plow, and yellow splotches of oxide-rich subsoil were exposed by cultivation or erosion, as well as beds and bands of red clay.

—From *Boone: A Biography*, by Robert Morgan (Chapel Hill: Algonquin
Books of Chapel Hill, 2007), 32, 33.

As legend has it, the Boones lived in a cave for a time on the opposite side of the Yadkin not far from Cooleemee Plantation. Today those grounds are the site of Boone's Cave State Park, more easily accessible from the town of Lexington in Davidson County than from this side of the river. Historical records also suggest that Squire and Sarah Boone and their children spent time on Elisha Creek and then obtained 640 acres on the west side of Mocksville, near Bear Creek.

Not long after coming to North Carolina, young Daniel Boone met a neighbor, Rebecca Bryan, and married her in 1756 in a ceremony conducted by his father, who had by then become a local magistrate. The newlyweds likely lived in a cabin on Squire's property for a time but then moved some miles north, building their own home place east of the present town of Farmington on the north side of I-40. Daniel and Rebecca lived there off and on for a decade.

Along US 64 west, closer to the town of Mocksville, once called "Old Mock's Field," it's hard to imagine the hardship of clearing land and setting up homesteads in this area. Robert Morgan conveys the toil and also the dangers posed to the settlers by native Sapona Indians, who did not always appreciate the white interlopers.

For his part, Daniel Boone respected the native peoples of the region and tried to avoid conflict with them. Morgan says the Cherokee named him "wide-mouth" because Boone "was prone to laughter and storytelling" (71).

It has been said that Boone had the temperament of an artist, that he was a poet of the woods, the hunt, the exploration of mysteries beyond the next ridge. Boone was described by the early biographer Timothy Flint as essentially a poet. He was an acute observer, studying the signs and weather and the Natives, and he felt an ancient kinship with the forest. He loved contemplation and solitude, yet was a good companion on the trail, popular with neighbors, fellow hunters, and scouts. The Indians seemed to be in awe of him (79).

A poet's sensibility Daniel Boone may have had, but he was not a good speller, as will be evident shortly at his father's gravesite.

■ MOCKSVILLE

Mocksville, the county seat of Davie County, is a pleasant village whose commerce includes a pet bakery and boutique, a soda shop, and plenty of antique dealers. At Main Street, turn right and go two blocks to reach the town square. Take a stroll and enjoy the historic architecture.

When you're ready, return to US 64, now joined with US 601. Turn left and stay on 64 when 601 veers north. In 1.4 miles, you'll come to the birthplace of Davie County's most notorious writer, Hinton Rowan Helper, commemorated by a state historical marker on the right.

Helper was born here in 1829, in what is now a renovated private residence that is on the National Register of Historic Places. The Evans Place, as it is known, was actually built on the site of Squire Boone's last residence. (The Boone land holdings in this area are also noted by a state historical marker 0.1 mile farther west on 64, just before the highway crosses over Bear Creek.)

Hinton Helper was an antebellum farmer who believed that slavery was a disaster for poor white growers like himself. He expounded on this thesis in *The Impending Crisis of the South: How to Meet It* (1857). North Carolina literary historian Richard Walser claims that the book was "second only to *Uncle Tom's Cabin* in its inflammatory effect upon the nation" at the time:

Helper was no sentimentalist, no fire-eating emancipator. He had no love for the blacks.... He simply wanted to rid the South of all slaves, to transport them to countries outside the United States.... He wrote that the system generated unproductive men and made "slaves" of the owners. He also argued that a vigorous literature could not be maintained under such a system.—From *Literary North Carolina: A Brief Historical Survey*, by Richard Walser (Raleigh: North Carolina Department of Archives and History, 1970), 20.

Helper's book was soon outlawed in North Carolina for its antislavery sentiments but embraced by abolitionists despite its ardent racism. One abolitionist, a Quaker book vendor in Guilford, was arrested and jailed for selling multiple copies. Meanwhile, the Republican Party reportedly distributed some 100,000 copies nationwide.

According to Richard Walser, Helper became the most despised citizen in the region because of his condemnation of slavery and was forced to leave Salisbury, where he was living at the time of the book's publication. He never returned to North Carolina but went on to serve in the U.S. State Department in South America and to write several more books, each more exaggerated in their declarations of white supremacy and advocacy for the deportation of persons of color from the United States.

Before leaving Mocksville, backtrack on US 64 and turn left on US 601 north for a short jaunt to visit the graves of Daniel Boone's parents. Watch for the Squire Boone Shopping Plaza on the right after Yadkinville Road merges into 601 from the right. This strip development unceremoniously flanks the old cemetery where Squire and Sarah Boone are buried. Their graves are toward the back, beyond an iron fence in an area surrounded by a low stacked-rock wall. The gravestones are so old that they have been framed in brick for protection.

Biographer Robert Morgan explains that Daniel Boone likely inscribed his father's stone, misspelling the death date of January the second as "Geniary tha 2." "The imaginative spelling," Morgan writes, "resembles that in many of the documents in Daniel's handwriting" (81).

■ COOLEEMEE

From this point, return south on US 601 for approximately six miles and turn right at Davie Crossroads on NC 801 south. In about a mile you'll come to the historic mill village of Cooleemee, set on the banks of the South Yadkin River, which flows southeast from here to join the Yadkin's main stream.

In recent years, Cooleemee citizens have worked hard as a community to document and preserve their textile heritage and share it with visitors. When you come into town, take a right on Marginal Street. Ahead on the left, at the corner of Church Street and surrounded by a chain-link fence, is the Cooleemee Mill Town Museum (336-284-6040), open Wednesdays to Saturdays from 10 to 4. This homegrown institution occupies the expansive Zachary-Holt House and presents a fascinating collection of everyday artifacts, photographs, quotations from oral histories, and other publications related to the mill in Cooleemee, which was established here at the very beginning of the twentieth century.

Today's grassroots preservation effort by former mill workers, amateur and professional historians, and volunteers in town has spread to embrace the region and has resulted in the publication of a magazine, *Bobbin and Shuttle*, full of photographs and stories from mill workers alongside interpretive articles by scholars.

Jim Rumley, a former textile worker, has compiled an extensive coffee-table volume, published in 2001 by the Cooleemee Historical Association. Among the many photographs and local tales, Rumley provides an account of the origin of "The Bullhole," a popular site on the South Yadkin River.

A Mr. McDaniel was an eye-witness and told it to a young Dorie Pierce who was known to soak up all river lore.

As the mill, the dam, and the houses were being built, the whole area was one giant construction site. Sometime around 1900, timbers were being cut and hauled from the Rowan side of the river to Cooleemee. An old Black man, whose name has vanished in time, had a beloved bull ox and was hard at work at the Shoals. His ox slipped on the rocks and went down into a swirling pool of water. The witness said that the old man loved that bull ox so much that he nearly went down with it and was spared a similar fate only because onlookers pulled him away. The bull was never seen again.

Ever since that day, this spot has been known to Cooleemee people as "The Bullhole." When water is up in the South Yadkin River you can still see that whirlpool.

—From *Cooleemee: The Life and Times of a Mill Town*, by Jim Rumley (Cooleemee, N.C.: Cooleemee Historical Association, 2001), 406.

To see the Bullhole at Cooleemee Falls up close, make your way from the museum back to NC 801 and turn right to cross the South Yadkin River. Take the first right on Needmore Road and the next right on Erwin Temple Church Road, which winds back toward the river. Signs direct you to the Bullhole Riverpark, which is down a well-maintained gravel road. There are bathrooms, a covered picnic pavilion, canoe access, and walking trails alongside this airy stretch of the river.

Return on 801 north to Cooleemee. At the junction with Watts Street, notice the historical marker that celebrates Cooleemee's best-known writer. Historian Hugh T. Lefler was born in 1901 on a farm near here and went to high school in Cooleemee before attending Duke University (then Trinity College). Lefler became a popular member of the faculty at the University of North Carolina at Chapel Hill. He coauthored several volumes on state history, which were widely used during his lifetime as texts for elementary, high school, and college students. One of Lefler's earliest books was a historical profile of the controversial Hinton Rowan Helper.

Continue north on 801 back to the intersection with 601 and turn right (south). Follow 601 for 9.5 miles toward Salisbury. Watch for signs to Catawba College.

■ SALISBURY

Salisbury is one of the Piedmont's older population centers. Squire Boone, in his role as a local official, helped lay out the streets in town, according to biographer Robert Morgan. The town is also chockablock with historic churches, graveyards, and homes that figured in the Civil War.

Salisbury is the birthplace of Cheerwine, the cherry-flavored, regional soft drink invented in 1917. It's a particularly effective digestive agent when consumed with any of the many local versions of Piedmont barbecue.

As for literary history, Salisbury is the birthplace of Frances Fisher Tiernan, who coined the term "The Land of the Sky" to refer to the North Carolina mountains in her travel writing, as discussed in volume 1 of *Literary Trails*. Publishing under the pen name of Christian Reid, she wrote more than forty light romances in the 1880s and a play celebrating the Confederacy entitled *Under the Southern Cross*. Proceeds from the play were used to underwrite a monument to Jefferson Davis. (Fort Fisher in Wilmington was named for her father, Confederate colonel Charles F. Fisher.) Today the author is commemorated by a historical marker on South Main Street, an engraved granite book set in the front yard of the Rowan Public Library, and in an exhibit of memorabilia from her life in the Rowan Historical Museum. Her gravesite is ahead on this tour.

US 601 turns sharply right as you get to the Salisbury town limits. Proceed straight ahead, however, following the signs to Catawba College on one of the town's main arteries, Innes Street. Catawba is a private liberal arts institution that was originally established in the town of Newton in Catawba County in 1851 but moved here in 1925. Catawba's resident poet and playwright, Janice Moore Fuller, proudly notes that the college's theater complex—including Keppel Auditorium, Hedrick Theatre, and Florence Busby Corriher Theatre—has premiered a number of new plays by professional and student playwrights in recent years. (Catawba's theater arts and music departments are among the school's largest.) Keppel Auditorium is also the site of the Brady Authors' Symposium each March, which has presented writers such as Pat Conroy, Lee Smith, Reynolds Price, Frances Mayes, Jodi Picoult, and Rick Bragg.

Catawba's recently renovated Corriher-Linn-Black Library (on the left side of Innes heading into town) houses the papers and books of the Poetry Council of North Carolina. The library's Thomas Wolfe Collection—more than 600 volumes, including first editions, various papers, and other ephemera—was a gift of lifelong collector Billy R. Wilkinson of Newton.

Just beyond the Catawba campus, at the intersection of Innes and Mahaley Avenue, look to the far right for College Bar-B-Que Drive-In (704-633-9953)—a location popular with locals. It is also the unnamed site of a scene in Salisbury novelist John Hart's first book, *The King of Lies*. Hart recommends the place for breakfast or barbecue.

From this intersection, turn left on Mahaley to reach the next destination, which figures in Hart's work and that of another Salisbury novelist, Kurt Corriher, who is director of the Center for Ethics and Faith at Catawba College.

The country club district of Salisbury more or less begins where Mahaley becomes Confederate Avenue. Though Corriher's fictional town is named Lake Elm, this neighborhood is most likely what the author had in mind in his thriller *Someone to Kill*:

The timing was fortuitous. The economic expansion of the fifties and sixties made Gustaf Pavlak a rich man, along with several dozen Lake Elm families who bought into the initial stock issue for Pavlak Equipment. By the time Gustaf's older son John graduated high school, the company employed six hundred people and earned annual revenues of over four hundred million dollars. Gustaf Pavlak built an eight-thousand-square-foot house on a hilltop near the Lake Elm country club. It was made of white brick, custom manufactured using a rare clay found only in the Appalachian mountains. —From *Someone to Kill*, by Kurt Corriher (New York: Macmillan, 2002), 68.

Corriher, who is a local playwright and actor in addition to his administrative and teaching role at Catawba College, was born in nearby China Grove. Likewise, his protagonist, John Pavlak, just happens to serve on the staff of a local college. As the novel opens, Pavlak's soon-to-be-ex-wife, a journalist, and her young daughter are mysteriously killed by a car bomb. While much of the novel's action takes place in Berlin, Germany, where Pavlak goes to search for clues to the murder and is pursued by the FBI and CIA as a suspect himself, the story eventually returns to North Carolina. Pavlak's father, mentioned in the passage above, holds the key to the mysterious deaths.

Another literary landmark in this neighborhood is found at the corner of Club Drive and Confederate. The white house on Club Drive set on the hill overlooking City Park is where John Hart says he imagined the main character of his first novel, Jackson Workman Pickens, living unhappily with his wife. It also happens to be the house where Hart grew up.

Truth be told, I disliked the house; it was too big, too visible. I rattled in it like a quarter in a tin can. But I always liked to sit there at the end of the day. It was warm in the sun. I could see the park, the oak trees made music of the wind. I would try not to think about choices or the past. It was a place for emptiness, for absolution, and rarely was it mine alone. —From *The King of Lies*, by John Hart (New York: Thomas Dunne Books, 2006), 17.

Hart was born in Durham, the grandson of the late Deryl Hart, a Duke surgeon and later president of the university from 1960 to 1963. Hart's father also went into medicine, along with three other siblings. John, who spent much of his youth in Salisbury, followed the family norm by beginning at Davidson College as a premed student but changed his major to French literature after studying abroad in France. (His mother had been a French teacher.) Hart then took graduate degrees in law and accounting and worked for a time as a banker, a stockbroker, and an attorney before quitting to write full time. He wrote most of *The King of Lies* in the Rowan Public Library.

Turn right from Confederate onto Club Drive, following alongside City Park. As Club curves left, go straight ahead on West Miller Street. At the stop sign for

The childhood home of Salisbury novelist John Hart was the inspiration for the fictional residence of his protagonist, Jackson Workman Pickens, in Hart's first novel, The King of Lies.

North Jackson Street, proceed ahead with a short jog to the right on Miller. Then take the next right on North Church Street and follow it seven blocks. Note the restored Grimes Mill on your right just before you cross the railroad tracks.

■ OAK GROVE FREEDMAN'S CEMETERY

This landmark, at the corner of West Liberty Street and North Church, began as a burial ground for African Americans in 1770. The area was later separated by a fence and then a sturdy granite wall so as not to connect with an adjacent graveyard for white people. During the first half of the twentieth century, vandals violated this African American cemetery—bodies were disinterred and the historic grave markers disappeared.

This epigram from poet Langston Hughes is one of several literary quotations chiseled into the pink granite wall that flanks the Oak Grove Freedman's Cemetery in Salisbury. Artist Maggie Smith and landscape architect Sam Reynolds designed the public art installation.

In 2006, with support from the National Endowment for the Arts, Salisbury's Waterworks Visual Arts Center began a public art project to create a powerful tribute to the 150 persons, enslaved and free, who were buried here. Artist Maggie Smith and landscape architect Sam Reynolds installed pink granite walls inscribed with lines of poetry from African American writers, including Langston Hughes, James Weldon Johnson, Audre Lorde, and eastern North Carolina's Harriet Jacobs, whose birthplace is in Edenton. Jacobs's words follow a stair-stepped wall along the Church Street side of the graveyard. The wall drops lower and lower with each powerful phrase:

> I kneeled by the graves of my parents.
> A black stump at the head of my mother's grave was
> all that remained of a tree my father had planted. . . .
> I seemed to hear my father's voice come from it,
> bidding me not to tarry till I reached freedom.
> —From *The Deep Wrong; or, Incidents in the Life of a Slave Girl*,
>   by Harriet Jacobs (Oxford: Oxford University Press, 1862), 138.

■ LIVINGSTONE COLLEGE

The next stop illuminates another chapter in the story of Salisbury's African American population. Continue down Church Street six blocks to West Monroe Street and turn right. Livingstone College, at 701 West Monroe Street, is surrounded by a historic neighborhood that remains relatively unchanged since the school's move here from Concord in 1882 under the leadership of the AME Zion Church. The college's founder, Joseph Price, is buried in the Poets and Dreamers Garden, which is on the left side of the administration building at the center of campus. The garden is a pleasant spot, with bronze busts of writers Lorraine Hansberry, Langston Hughes, and William Shakespeare set among formal, boxwood-lined walkways.

Pioneering writer Margaret Walker taught at Livingstone from 1941 to 1942 and again from 1945 to 1946. Her 1942 volume of poetry, *For My People*, is a collection of ballads, sonnets, and free verse that draw recognizable portraits of people from many walks of life. When it earned the Yale Younger Poets Award, it was the first time such a prestigious national award had gone to an African American female.

FOR MY PEOPLE (EXCERPT)
For my people lending their strength to the years, to the gone years and
   the now years and the maybe years, washing ironing cooking scrubbing
   sewing mending hoeing plowing digging planting pruning patching
   dragging along never gaining never reaping never knowing never
   understanding....

For the cramped bewildered years we went to school to learn to know the
   reasons why and the answers to and the people who and the places
   where and the days when, in memory of the bitter hours when we
   discovered we were black and poor and small and different and nobody
   cared and nobody wondered and nobody understood; ...
—From *The Oxford Anthology of African-American Poetry*, ed. Arnold
   Rampersad and Hilary Herbold (New York: Oxford University Press,
   2006), 93.

This long, lyrical poem—probably Walker's best known—bears a full reading. Her groundbreaking 1965 novel *Jubilee* is the tale of an enslaved family during and after the Civil War. It won the Houghton Mifflin Fellowship Prize, though North Carolina writer Wilma Dykeman, writing in the *New York Times Book Review*, called it "uneven."

Poet Margaret Walker began her teaching career in 1941 at Livingstone College in Salisbury and published her first collection, For My People, *the following year. Photo by Carl Van Vechten, courtesy of the Van Vechten Trust.*

Based on her grandmother's stories and extensive research, the novel took Walker more than thirty years to write, during which time she raised four children, took care of her disabled husband, taught at several universities, and worked as a journalist, magazine editor, and social worker. *Jubilee* generated significant literary consideration and debate, so much so that Walker wrote a book in 1972 explaining how she devised the novel and dismissing claims that the book only confirmed the romanticized South of *Gone with the Wind,* even if told from an African American perspective.

Among Walker's later works are two collections of essays, a volume of transcribed conversations with poet Nikki Giovanni, a passionate volume of poetry on the civil rights movement of the 1960s, and a book on the work and life of Richard Wright, whom Walker first befriended, along with Gwendolyn Brooks, during their employment with the Works Progress Administration in Chicago in the 1930s. Walker later helped Wright in his research for *Native Son.*

In 1988, Walker sued author Alex Haley, alleging that his book *Roots* infringed upon her copyright to *Jubilee,* but the case was dismissed. She died in

1998 in Chicago but is remembered every year on July 12, designated as Margaret Walker Day in Jackson, Mississippi, where she taught for many years at Jackson State University.

■ CHESTNUT HILLS CEMETERY

From the Livingstone campus, it's a short drive to the gravesite of Frances Fisher Tiernan, aka Christian Reid. Return on West Monroe Street toward downtown. In six blocks, turn right on South Main Street (US 70). In another six blocks, the cemetery will be on the right. Enter the gates and follow the paved drive straight ahead and up a knoll. Tiernan's grave is surrounded by a low wall fashioned of large, white, rough-hewn bricks. A Salisbury pink granite bench, a commemorative stone, and a large Celtic cross sit inside the wall.

Local poet Janice Moore Fuller says that many notable Salisbury residents are buried here in Chestnut Hills, including Civil War commanders, U.S. congressmen, and actor Sydney Blackmer, who played the devil in the film *Rosemary's Baby*. Fuller's own relatives—including Royal Loflin, who built a number of houses in Salisbury's West Square Historic District—are also buried here. Fuller offers this remembrance from her youth:

WHAT THE DEAD SEE
Chestnut Hills Cemetery
He had a pimpled countenance,
angel wings spread—guarding what?
The yew tree? The maroon DeSoto,
cloudy plastic stretched across its windows,
parked too close to my mother's plot?

The crow did what crows do: perched
on a headstone, cawed now and again,
let the sun extract the purple hidden in its wing.
It hopped to another grave, watched me watching it,
then cocked its head away. I could see only one eye,

exact as a rifle sight. What did the dead see?
The roots of the yew tree inching toward them?
The still earth filled with failed crocuses
never opening a passage to the sky?
When I was little, my cousin and I would lie

on our sides facing each other, each headed
the opposite way. Downside up, we'd talk for hours,
making all the weird faces we could.
The familiar made strange, my cousin an alien,
mouth in her forehead, blank spread of skin

where she ought to be kissed. Could I still loop
my arm inside her arm and walk along the beach?
Maybe the dead see us like this: upside down,
combing what we should be shoeing, smirking when we
should be crying, laughing at all the wrong parts.
—From *Séance*, by Janice Moore Fuller (Oak Ridge, Tenn.:
    Iris Press, 2007), 15.

The downtown district is the final stop in Salisbury. From the cemetery entrance, turn left on South Main Street and drive nearly up to the intersection with Innes Street and look for on-street parking. Take a stroll. You might try a Cheerwine and hamburger or hot dog from Hap's Grill, just across Innes at 116 North Main (recommended by John Hart). Up and down both of these streets are many worthwhile stops—a general store called Okey Dokey & Co., an old grocery, Barnhardt's Hardware, a wine shop, galleries, and more. Stop by the Visitors' Center at 204 East Innis for detailed maps and information on historic neighborhoods. If you're so inclined, you can also continue north on Main Street all the way to the adjacent village of Spencer, where children generally find the emphasis on trains very entertaining. (The North Carolina Transportation Museum is here. Call 704-636-2889 for details.)

And, finally, if you spend the night in Salisbury or allow some extra time for touring, consider driving down to Gold Hill, just fourteen miles south on US 52 (East Innes Street). Watch for signs to Historic Gold Hill and turn right across the railroad tracks. Historic Gold Hill Park is at 735 Saint Stephens Church Road.

■ GOLD HILL

Tom clicked his tongue and off they went in the dim light along the narrow dusty lane, out onto the dusty road leading north to Salisbury. Past the mining office and the blacksmith, past the crouched row of miners smoking and talking sideways to each other on the porch outside the general store, past the post office and the saddler and the grog shop, the attorney's office, the Presbyterian church, its manse and graveyard, past Miz

*The village of Gold Hill—a combination of original and replica structures that recollect
the setting of Joanna Catherine Scott's historical novel,* The Road to Chapel Hill.

Hedra drinking early morning coffee on her porch, sagging in her heavy-
bottomed chair, her speculative, almost vicious eyes, unwaving hand, on
up the clattering road beside the train line, fine dust trailing in a low red
cloud.

   As the din of Gold Hill fell away behind them, the ruined hills gave way
to woods and then to farms, and woods again, and farms. The mule trotted smartly, as mules never do, and the air was clear and silent, only Tom's
voice, deep and gentle and assuring, calling out encouragement from time
to time. The day turned warm, the sky bright blue. Eugenia pulled the
blanket off her knees and tossed it behind her in the cart. She felt light, as
though she would float off with happiness, Tom's voice circling and circling round her head like some large kindly bird.

—From *The Road from Chapel Hill*, by Joanna Catherine Scott (New York:
   Berkley Books, 2006), 71–72.

Chapel Hill novelist Joanna Catherine Scott begins her Civil War novel in
Gold Hill. Eugenia Mae Spottswood has been forced to leave her comfortable,
aristocratic life in Wilmington when her father makes a bad business deal and

ends up as a miner in Gold Hill. Enduring the foreign hardships of cooking and keeping house in this rough mining encampment, Eugenia finds herself attracted to Tom, her father's slave. For his part, Tom is determined to find freedom and ends up enlisting in the Union Army. Scott provides a vivid portrait of the hardships of secession in Piedmont North Carolina and of the terrors of the escalating war.

Today, historic Gold Hill may at first seem a little hokey with its plank sidewalks, old streetlamps, rustic benches, and storefronts, which might have been built for the set of a Hollywood western, but the mining village also has an authentic old post office, a rock jailhouse, and a handsome green space for outdoor performances. In this seriously isolated bit of countryside where gold was once the speculative attraction, you'll likely find at least one eatery that's open and several charming antique and gift shops.

■ LITERARY LANDSCAPE

Davie County Public Library
371 North Main Street, Mocksville
336-753-6030
The Martin-Wall History Room at this library has not only extensive county genealogy records and resources but also several handsome volumes about Davie County history for sale. The Davie County Library also supports a branch in Cooleemee.

Cool Beanz Café and Books
65 Court Square, Mocksville
336-753-0453
A good selection of coffees and teas and used paperbacks makes this a warm stop on a cold day.

The Literary Bookpost
110 South Main Street, Salisbury
704-630-9788
This friendly bookshop, home to three cats on the day we visited, is a great supporter of regional writers. When John Hart's second novel came out, the store reportedly ordered 1,600 copies, the largest order the publisher ever remembered receiving from one bookstore. The shop hosts frequent readings and signings.

Escape the Daily Grind

316 South Salisbury Avenue, Spencer

704-636-0160

According to poet Janice Moore Fuller, this spacious coffee and pastry shop in Spencer, just a short distance from Salisbury, sponsors open-mike readings by local authors.

Rowan Public Library

201 West Fisher Street, Salisbury

704-216-8228

<http://www.lib.co.rowan.nc.us>

As befitting a town with such a long history, this library has an unusually large collection of local materials related to history and genealogy, in the Edith M. Clark Room upstairs. A fabulous digital archive of local postcards is part of the online collection.

Statesville : Mooresville : Davidson : Huntersville : Concord

Learn more about the literary legacy of Davidson College and consider the origins and influence of NASCAR on writers along this route.

Writers with a connection to this area: Anthony Abbott, Joseph Bathanti, Jeffrey Beam, Doris Betts, Sally Buckner, Martin Clark, Patricia Cornwell, James Gay, William Harmon, John Hart, Scott Huler, Ralph Johnson, Catherine Landis, D. G. Martin, Sharyn McCrumb, Richard McKenzie, Rosie Molinary, Randy Nelson, Alan Michael Parker, Sheri Reynolds, Steven Sherrill, Judith Minthorn Stacy, William Styron, Theodore Taylor, Charles Wright

■ STATESVILLE

To be a child in the tall house where I grew up in Statesville, North Carolina, was to live marooned on an island. Along the front limit of the large yard ran a busy highway which—for several centuries—I could not grow old enough to cross. In back, the lot became a garden and fruit orchard before it stopped at the end of railroad tracks where I was not allowed to play. Twice a day the last surviving steam engine in that part of the state puffed slowly by toward Taylorsville, and twice a day I stood at the limits of a honeysuckle bank to wave to the engineer. Sometimes he put out a hand the size of my head, and waggled the fingers inside his striped denim glove.

On both sides of our old-fashioned house lived old-fashioned couples who trained roses over white arbors, and were forever setting seedbeds between us like barriers. I had no brothers and no sisters. Most of the girls I knew at school lived close together in a cluster of brick cottages, miles away from an old house in a bypassed part of town.

tour 4

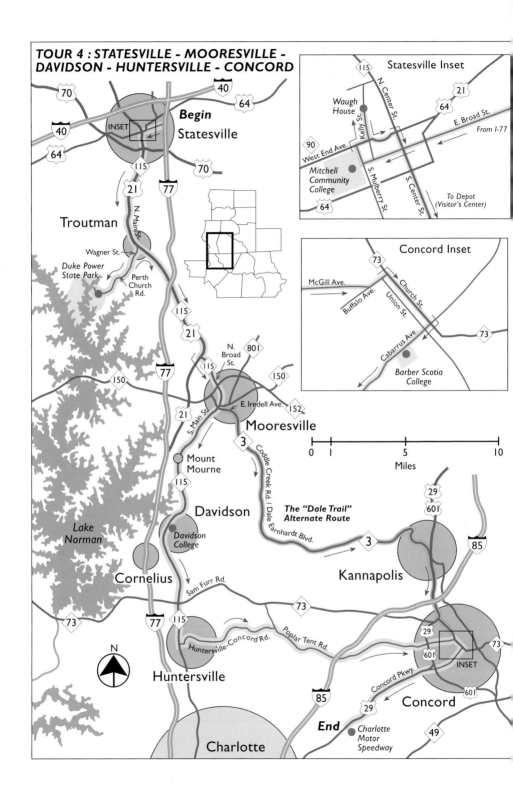

TOUR 4 : STATESVILLE - MOORESVILLE - DAVIDSON - HUNTERSVILLE - CONCORD

Begin
Statesville

Troutman

Wagner St.

Duke Power
State Park

Perth
Church
Rd.

N. Main St.

Lake
Norman

N. Broad St.

Mooresville

Mount
Mourne

Davidson

Davidson
College

Cornelius

Sam Furr Rd.

E. Iredell Ave.

Coddle Creek Rd. / Dale Earnhardt Blvd.

The "Dale Trail"
Alternate Route

Kannapolis

Huntersville-Concord Rd.

Poplar Tent Rd.

Huntersville

Concord Pkwy.

Concord

N

Charlotte

End
Charlotte
Motor
Speedway

0   1   5   10
Miles

Statesville Inset

Waugh
House

N. Center St.

Kelly St.

West End Ave.

E. Broad St.

From I-77

Mitchell
Community
College

S. Mulberry St.

S. Center St.

To Depot
(Visitor's Center)

Concord Inset

McGill Ave.

Buffalo Ave.

Union St.

Church St.

Cabarrus Ave.

Barber Scotia
College

INSET

I did the things marooned children have always done. I made society ladies from kitchen matches—impaled grapes for their heads, inverted morning-glory blooms for ball-gown skirts. An apple tree became a team of horses, its crooked limbs saddled with old newspapers and bridled with lengths of clothesline.

—From "Spies in the Herb House," in *The Astronomer and Other Stories*, by Doris Betts (New York: Harper & Row, 1965), 1–2.

Like the narrator of "Spies in the Herb House," novelist and short story master Doris Betts was an only child, the daughter of William Elmore and Mary Ellen Freeze Waugh. Doris's father worked in one of Statesville's many cotton mills (now gone), and in Doris's early years the family lived on the edge of the mill village in a small house (also gone) where both Doris and her mother were born. "Nobody my age was born in a hospital," Betts once said.

Doris learned to read by the age of four, and in her isolation as an only child she took to books. As she once explained in an interview with the local newspaper, "I didn't even understand fully where books came from. But somewhere in there you get your first library card and you check out a book, open it up and smell the pages, and you can't wait for the summer to lie underneath the apple tree and read. From love of reading I thought that would be the best thing in the world to do—to make books."

Betts's early fascination with reading took her to the local public library—familiar territory that would later be reflected in the creation of at least two notable characters who are librarians—Nancy Finch, the protagonist in the 1981 novel *Heading West*, and the less sympathetic Agnes Parker in the short story "Miss Parker Possessed," collected in *The Astronomer and Other Stories* (1965).

When Doris was fourteen, the Waugh family bought a house at 233 Kelly Street on the west side of Statesville, not far from the Associate Reformed Presbyterian Church on Broad Street, where Doris's deeply rooted Christian faith and her immersion in the elegant language of the King James Bible began.

Making good use of her early gift for the essay, Doris Waugh began publishing a column in the *Statesville Daily Record* in high school. Upon graduation, she enrolled at Woman's College, now the University of North Carolina at Greensboro, and married law student Lowry Betts in her sophomore year. Betts helped to support their partnership by returning to journalism, leaving college midstream so that Lowry could finish school in his native South Carolina. In 1953 she won the *Mademoiselle* College Fiction Contest for a short story, which then led to the publication of *The Gentle Insurrection and Other Stories*. Published

Doris Waugh Betts in her early years of teaching at the University of North Carolina. Courtesy of North Carolina Collection, University of North Carolina Library at Chapel Hill.

when Betts was only twenty-two, the book won the UNC Putnam Prize, judged that year by Pearl S. Buck, Marjorie Kinnan Rawlings, and James Street. (The collection was reissued by LSU Press in 1997.)

Lowry and Doris Betts soon began their family and relocated to Chapel Hill, where Lowry went to law school, and then to Sanford, where he began his law practice. Betts wrote her first novel, *Tall Houses in Winter* (1957), followed by *The Scarlet Thread* (1964), set in the late nineteenth and early twentieth centuries and depicting the dramatic changes brought to a small town in North Carolina by the textile industry. In 1966, Betts was invited to teach part-time at the University of North Carolina at Chapel Hill, without a baccalaureate degree—a remarkable story, to be picked up later in this volume when we reach Chapel Hill and consider Betts's eminent career as a professor of creative writing and head of the UNC–Chapel Hill faculty for several years.

Betts's early story collections and novels are excellent introductions to North Carolina's Piedmont region. To visit the landmarks of Doris Betts's youth, take the Broad Street exit off I-77 (two exits south of I-40). Follow Broad Street west toward downtown Statesville. This handsome route is lined on both sides by mature pin oaks, which form a shady canopy in summer. Soon Broad widens to a boulevard. The new Iredell County Public Library—but not the one Betts frequented—was completed in 2005. It's to the right off Broad on Tradd Street just as you come into the central business district. The Associate Reformed Presby-

The house where Statesville writer Doris Waugh Betts penned her first prize-winning essay, "Meet American Citizen Mr. Brown."

terian Church, which Betts attended, is in the very next block of Broad on the right before the intersection with Center Street. (Statesville has preserved a great many Queen Anne and Neoclassical homes in the four historic districts surrounding the business district, which are worth exploring.)

To see the house where Betts lived as a teenager (still a private residence), continue on Broad to the entrance to the Mitchell Community College campus. Set on a wooded knoll, this school was named for the daughters of Elisha Mitchell, for whom North Carolina's tallest mountain was named. Men were not admitted to study here until 1932.

Turn right on Mulberry Street, the birthplace of writer Theodore Taylor, a longtime California resident who has written more than two dozen popular young adult books and another dozen novels in a long career that has included many years in Hollywood. Taylor still proudly claims his North Carolina roots.

From Mulberry, it's a quick right turn onto West End Avenue and then an immediate left onto Kelly Street. The house is the fifth on the left, flanked by a large hemlock on the right and a mature dogwood on the left. From here, Statesville High School, where Betts was graduated in 1950, is only a few blocks away on North Center Street. Everything the family needed was in walking distance, since, as Doris tells it, the Waughs "didn't own a car until after I was married."

Return to West End Avenue and turn left, back toward the business district, noting the Romanesque Revival building facing Kelly Street on the corner, home to Congregation Emanuel, one of the oldest Jewish assemblies in North Carolina.

Beyond the Emanuel synagogue on the left is the Old Fourth Creek Burying Ground at 202 West End Avenue. This historic cemetery served as the town's only burying site until 1880.

James Gay was Iredell County's anointed, if not officially appointed, poet laureate in the years following the Revolutionary War. Veterans often commissioned Gay to write and publicly recite his verses for town celebrations such as those held in this cemetery. Gay is also reportedly the author of the first poetry book written in North Carolina.

Contemporary poet and novelist Joseph Bathanti has written a number of poems about the sites, landscapes, and people in Iredell County, including this cemetery. His work was conceived in the eleven years he served on the faculty of Mitchell Community College. One of Bathanti's Iredell poems is installed in the old Train Depot.

To visit, follow West End Avenue back to Center Street (NC 115/US 21) and turn right, past City Hall on the left and the new Statesville Civic Center on the right. Continue downhill and go through a railroad underpass; the road then climbs sharply. Depot Hill, as it is known, was the site of Tom Dula's hanging in 1868—a story made famous by the Kingston Trio and told and retold by many North Carolina writers, including Manley Wade Wellman, discussed in volume 1, and, more recently, novelist Sharyn McCrumb, who mentions the hanging in her novel *Ghost Riders* (2004).

The Statesville depot is on your left. Built in 1911 and restored, it is now the Statesville Visitors' Center (704-878-3436), offering brochures and maps to a variety of area attractions. Bathanti's poem "The Stonecarver" is inside.

Ahead, we venture into the countryside, where the steady pursuit of dairy and livestock farming has remained viable. In fact, Iredell County has the largest population of dairy cattle in North Carolina.

Large tracts of open space have served farmers here for centuries. Among the fine old plantings and volunteers on the rural byways are cedars that still delineate property lines and flank livestock fences, though more and more housing developments associated with regional growth spawned by Charlotte and nearby Lake Norman are transforming the rural scenery.

Statesville-born poet and teacher Sally Buckner has often written about the

Iredell landscape and about Stanly County to the south where her family later moved. "We lived in a little brick house on a dirt road right off what is now Highway 21—virtually 'out in the country' then," she says.

Buckner, a contemporary of Doris Betts, has taught creative writing at every level from kindergarten through graduate school. She retired in 1998 after twenty-eight years on the faculty of Peace College in Raleigh. A political activist who has also provided thoughtful leadership in North Carolina's literary community, Buckner served as editor of two important anthologies, *Word and Witness: 100 Years of North Carolina Poetry* (1995) and *Our Words, Our Ways: Reading and Writing in North Carolina* (1999).

In this poem, written in the voice of her mother, Buckner describes the hardships of the Depression era and how her father, George, contributed to the family's Christmas celebrations.

CEDAR

Always cedar.
Fir trees didn't grow in Iredell County,
and George never considered pine or hemlock,
which suited me fine: I loved the scent of cedar
spicing the entire house from the very minute
those feathery branches ruffled through the door
until right after Christmas, when we flung
its carcass, picked as clean as chicken bones
outside where it could dry till fit for firewood.

In early years, he'd combine his search
for a tree with a hunting trip, return grinning,
tree on one shoulder, rabbits on the other.
Later, when whatever disease the doctors
couldn't find a name for drew the muscles
in his legs so tight he could barely walk—
lurched like a drunken sailor—he would drive
far out in the country, scanning the winter roadside
till he found a likely candidate, straight and full,
which he could manage to clamber to, cane
clasped in one hand, ax in the other.

Never paid or asked permission. Lord, why would he?
We were all tree-poor those days, wouldn't miss a cedar
more than a dandelion. Nobody'd thought

of using tillable land for Christmas trees.
When Hoover was still making promises,
who would have laid down a cherished dollar
for something to toss away after just a week?

When George got home, he'd nail two boards in an X
for the tree's support. I'd swath them with a blanket.
The girls would help him string the lights, then wind
cellophane garlands through the greenery.
Meanwhile I'd whip Lux Flakes to a frothy lather;
dried on the branches, if you'd squint your eyes,
you'd swear that it was snow. Altogether,
it was some kind of pretty.

Eighteen years now, he's been gone. At first,
my boy still at home, I'd buy a tree—
resenting every dollar—fix it up
the best I could all by myself. Then later,
hoisting trees got to be beyond me.

I purchased one advertised as "everlasting,"
needles, branches, trunk—all aluminum.
Don't use lights, just big red satin balls.
The children, when they come, never complain.
The grandchildren exclaim, "Red and silver!
Look at it shine!" And it lasts year after year—
not half the trouble of a woodland tree.

But I still miss the scent of cedar.
—From *Potato Eyes*, vol. 17/18 (1998), used by permission of Sally Buckner.

■ TROUTMAN

From Statesville, continue south on NC 115 across Third Creek to Troutman, where the Barium Springs Home for Children has been in operation since 1891. This Presbyterian institution was featured in the 2006 PBS documentary *Homecoming*, produced by a former resident, Richard McKenzie, who first shared his own story in *The Home: A Memoir of Growing Up in an Orphanage* (1996).

As you come into Troutman proper, divided by what used to be a railroad track and now returned to green space and a sidewalk that runs the length of town, look for signs to Duke Power State Park, to the right. A fine place to picnic, read a book, or cool your feet, this park makes a nice side excursion. Turn right on Wagner Street, which soon becomes Perth Church Road. Follow the signs, and in less than 1.5 miles bear right on State Park Road.

When in the 1960s Duke Power Company created North Carolina's largest lake by damming the Catawba River, the sprawling growth of suburban Charlotte that has pushed north along its edges was not completely foreseen. Most of Lake Norman's 500 miles of shoreline are now devoted to private development, but here, along one of the lake's northernmost fingers, Duke Power State Park is still rustic.

This area is also the setting for Iredell County native Steven Sherrill's second novel, *Visits from the Drowned Girl* (2004). Sherrill attended Mitchell Community College, where, he is proud to claim, he earned a diploma in welding and also studied creative writing with Joseph Bathanti. He went on to earn an MFA in poetry at the University of Iowa's Writers Workshop. His first novel, *The Minotaur Takes a Cigarette Break*, is a fantastical account of Greek mythology's Minotaur, who does a stint as a line cook in a North Carolina barbecue restaurant.

Sherrill's second novel paints a sometimes grim if realistic picture of the ongoing economic transition in the region and its profound impact on working-class people. The novel's central character, Benny Poteat, services cell phone, water, and radio towers in and around Buffalo Shoals on Lake Norman, painting and repainting them and changing lightbulbs. Buffalo Shoals is located at the northernmost tip of Lake Norman where Iredell County meets Catawba County. As Benny Poteat surveys the world from a dizzying height, he witnesses a shocking event:

> That day, as with countless days before it, from two hundred feet up, the Carolina Piedmont spread out 360 degrees around him, county bleeding into county: dogwood, pitch pine, and red-dirt hills for mile after mile. It was spring, wet and fecund. Benny Poteat had been climbing towers, legally, since he was fifteen years old, and fifteen years later he still loved the struggle between the late-March winds and the rigid metal framework he buckled himself to Monday through Thursday, weather permitting, well into winter. So, while it's true that Benny Poteat had seen a lot of things from up there, mostly he just did his job and bore witness to hour upon mundane hour in sometimes vertiginous solitude. He was rarely prepared for the extraordinary. In fact, he'd be hard pressed to come up with anything that could have prepared him, truly prepared him, for what he saw that day.—From *Visits from the Drowned Girl*, by Steven Sherrill (New York: Random House, 2004), 4.

Benny sees a young woman shuck her clothes and backpack on the shore and disappear into the Catawba River. Benny can't help himself. He climbs down from his perch and rummages through what is left behind in the girl's backpack—a series of homemade videotapes. From this point forward, life gets much more complicated for Benny as he seeks out the family of the drowned girl but cannot bring himself to tell them what he saw from the tower.

■ MOORESVILLE

From Duke Power State Park, return to NC 115 and head south to Mooresville, once a booming cotton mill town now known as "Race City." Today the National Association for Stock Car Auto Racing (NASCAR) is celebrated in a number of attractions that have given new life to the area. More than sixty racing teams are headquartered in the vicinity. The best known is Dale Earnhardt, Inc., the company and philanthropic foundation established by the late NASCAR driver, also known as "The Intimidator," who died in a 2001 crash in Daytona, Florida. Earnhardt's son, Dale Junior, known as "Little E," still lives near Mooresville on a large tract where he has built a faux western town for his friends' amusement and a helicopter pad for his comings and goings.

It may come as a surprise that auto racing has been pursued in fiction and nonfiction by at least two prominent female novelists from North Carolina. The first to assay the topic was Sylvia Wilkinson, who was born in Durham and studied with poet Randall Jarrell at the University of North Carolina at Greensboro, where Jarrell declared her the most gifted prose writer he'd ever taught. Wilkinson's pace to publication was swift from the start. She won both national and North Carolina honors for her five semiautobiographical novels published from 1966 to 1982. All are set in North Carolina.

Wilkinson ventured into the world of nonfiction in 1973, driven by her fascination with auto racing. *The Stainless Steel Carrot: An Auto Racing Odyssey* was her first foray. A decade later, Algonquin Books of Chapel Hill published Wilkinson's *Dirt Tracks to Glory: The Early Days of Stock Car Racing as Told by the Participants*. Wilkinson's sixth novel, *On the Seventh Day God Created Chevrolet* (1993), is set in North Carolina in the 1960s and depicts a young man's journey to break into stock car racing.

Sharyn McCrumb, who loves her native state's popular legends and lore, likewise found herself revved up by the racing industry here. "Midnight in Mooresville" is the title of the first chapter in McCrumb's *St. Dale*, a novel that follows a group of devoted NASCAR fans on a pilgrimage to all the racetracks where the late Dale Earnhardt drove his stock car.

Like the larger-than-life apparition of the racing giant who appears to a loyal fan in Sharyn McCrumb's novel St. Dale, this 900-pound, nine-foot-tall statue of NASCAR legend Dale Earnhardt created by artist Sam Bass stands in the heart of his hometown of Kannapolis.

The novel begins with one female fan's mysterious midnight encounter with the late Earnhardt. He arrives in his white racing suit as an apparition on the side of the road in Mooresville ready to change her flat tire—a scene McCrumb writes as an event of biblical (or Elvisean) proportions. Using *Canterbury Tales* as her inspiration, McCrumb's novel is a meditation on the humanity of our modern-day heroes. McCrumb was so inspired by her NASCAR immersion that she wrote a second novel, *Once around the Track* (2007), detailing the development of a Winston Cup racing team, all women except the driver, who is selected because he is "pretty."

If you're a racing fan, you might consider a side trip to visit the Earnhardt team's headquarters, known as the "Garage Mahal," at 1675 Coddle Creek Road, where you'll find an exhibition of pictures, cars, and trophies amassed by the team. Watch for NC 3 signs south of the junction of NC 115 (North Broad Street) and Highway 152 as you are coming into the heart of downtown Mooresville. NC 3, also called the "Dale Trail," goes off to the left across the railroad tracks and runs all the way through Earnhardt's hometown of Kannapolis and into Concord.

There's more to Mooresville than auto racing, however. Davidson College

English professor Randy Nelson grew up here. His 2006 short-story collection, *The Imaginary Lives of Mechanical Men*, has a comic tale of two misfits who work in a florist shop and deliver funeral arrangements to churches up and down NC 115.

Mooresville is also the landscape for the novels of Judith Minthorn Stacy. Born in Michigan and married right out of high school, Stacy is the working mother of four children. Various jobs have contributed to her capacity as a fiction writer and humor columnist. When she left Michigan and settled with her family here, Stacy found fodder for the novels *Styles by Maggie Sweet*, *Maggie Sweet*, and *Betty Sweet Tells All*. Her fictional town of Poplar Grove bears a sure resemblance to Mooresville. The Dixie Burger in the novels might well be the spectacularly retro What-a-Burger Drive-In, which you will see across the railroad tracks on your way out of Mooresville. Stacy's characters are constantly driving along the same route as this tour:

> She pulls out of the parking lot, then onto East Main and Townsend Avenue. She passes the city limits sign, the That'lldu Bar and Grill, the Farmer's Market, then under a bridge spray painted with the warning JESUS OR HELL. Within seconds there are rolling hills, dotted with clover. Cattle graze on the hillside. She rolls down her window. The air is sweet and thick. She can feel it on her skin. —From *Betty Sweet Tells All*, by Judith Minthorn Stacy (New York: HarperCollins, 2002), 69.

"Race City" has also been swept up in the rapid development around Lake Norman, but Mooresville's small-town character has so far been preserved downtown. While you are passing through, don't miss the makers of Deluxe Ice Cream, Mooresville Ice Cream Company (704-664-5456). The plant, at 172 North Broad Street, is on the right side of the railroad tracks as you are headed south. According to writer Ann Wicker, a Mooresville native who now lives and writes in Charlotte, Deluxe is a rich, old-fashioned concoction that has been manufactured here since 1924 and is only sold locally in restaurants and grocery stores. You can also buy it retail at the plant on weekdays from 7 to 5.

■ DAVIDSON

Continuing south on NC 115 out of Mooresville, the countryside soon takes on the rural character that Judith Minthorn Stacy describes. Over the next ten miles, you'll pass through Mount Mourne, a pre–Revolutionary War settlement originally famous for its church *and* its tavern. Then you'll cross the county line from Iredell County into Mecklenburg County and find yourself in the charming village of Davidson and the campus of its liberal arts college of the same name.

Among the many books that have been written in this college town over the years, one local volume deserves first mention. Ralph W. Johnson and his father, Walter, were among the most successful businessmen in Davidson throughout the twentieth century. *David Played a Harp: A Free Man's Battle for Independence* is Ralph Johnson's memoir, published in 2000 shortly before his death. In it he describes life in the African American community here when Jim Crow laws were in full force.

Ralph Johnson opened his first barbershop when he was sixteen and continued in the business for fifty years, employing as many as seven African American barbers at any given time. In his memoir, Johnson delivers a stunning picture of the era, his remarkable entrepreneurship in light of the times, and his controversial dance with white power during segregation. He recounts how he was surprised and hurt when he became the subject of protests by Davidson students in the late 1960s, because his barber shop had always exclusively served white customers during regular business hours. White Davidson students demanded that Johnson serve black customers on an equal basis. The ensuing tensions caused Johnson to close his shop for good in 1971. He waited nearly thirty years to publish his side of the story.

At his death, Johnson's estate funded a scholarship for African American students at Davidson. He also deeded his real estate holdings to the college, asking that they be used as affordable housing for lower income families to counter rising real estate values in town.

Among many other literary lights that have come through these parts was novelist and Virginia native William Styron, who began his college education here in 1942. Styron wrote for the school newspaper and literary magazine, but his college career was interrupted when he decided to enlist in the Marine Corps and left campus before his eighteenth birthday. Following a summer of officer training in 1943, Styron transferred to Duke University to study with the legendary William Blackburn (discussed later in this volume). Styron would go on to write such controversial classics as *The Confessions of Nat Turner* and *Sophie's Choice.*

Tennessee native Charles Wright graduated from Davidson in 1957 with a degree in history, but he claims that his poetic muse did not arrive until after his departure for military service in Italy. Davidson College is nevertheless proud to claim him. Wright's 1997 collection *Black Zodiac* is one of the most honored books of American poetry in the twentieth century.

A strong creative writing curriculum and faculty have continued to produce a raft of books by Davidson grads in more recent decades. Poet and novelist Alan Michael Parker directs the program in creative writing and is also a core faculty member in the Queens University low-residency MFA program in Charlotte.

Anthony Abbott, much-beloved faculty member and longtime head of the Davidson English department, is retired but continues to teach a few writing courses each year. Three poetry collections preceded Abbott's two novels. In his 2005 poetry collection *The Man Who . . .* Abbott offers this vision of his present life as a retiree living on Lake Norman:

THE MAN WHO LOVED MONDAYS
scratched a living in the briarpatch
for forty years or more. "Oh, it's Monday,"
his colleagues moaned with long mouths.

"Don't throw me in the briarpatch,"
he'd say to himself, curving his hands
like Brer Rabbit's paws. Monday morning

he sat at his desk, sheer joy crinkling
in his eyes, lectures to write, books
to read, students to talk to long

into the lazy afternoons of fall,
the crisp mornings of winter,
when his boots would crunch

the first footprints into the new snow,
into the soft mornings of spring
when the yellow forsythia came

and then the burst of the azaleas
pink and white below his high
window. These days forever coming

Monday after glorious Monday
where the blessed thorns make the blood
run and the quick brain and the turtle

One more Davidson alumnus of importance to the state's literary life is syndicated newspaper columnist D. G. Martin. Since 1999, Martin has been interviewing writers from across the state on the half-hour public television program *Bookwatch*. Martin's father, David Grier Martin, was president of Davidson from 1958 to 1968, overseeing the tumultuous period of integration that Ralph Johnson wrote about.

To learn more about Davidson's literary history, visit the E. H. Little Library, located directly behind the domed Chambers Hall at the very center of the Davidson campus. The library's Davidsoniana Room contains books by and about Davidson faculty and alumni.

Before you leave, Davidson graduate and local writer Rosie Molinary, author of *Hijas Americanas: Beauty, Body Image, and Growing Up Latina*, also suggests a stop in the Lingle Chapel of Davidson College Presbyterian Church. "The brick entrance faces Main Street," she says. "Walk inside (it is usually unlocked during the day) and you'll find a small chapel with gentle light and walls like a blank slate. I discovered it while an undergraduate at Davidson and, years later, it still offers me the same peace and serenity."

■ HUNTERSVILLE

From Davidson, continue south on Main Street, which seamlessly becomes North Main Street in the charming village of Cornelius and continues on into the adjacent town of Huntersville, once the home of journalist LeGette Blythe, whose important biographies are discussed in volume 1 and later in this book. Huntersville was also the site of a prison (now closed) that served as inspiration for scenes in two novels: Charlotte writer Judy Goldman's *Early Leaving* and Joseph Bathanti's *Coventry*, both to be discussed later in this volume.

If your visit here happens to fall on a Saturday between June and September, watch for the farmers' market signs and turn left onto Huntersville Concord Road. After you pass Town Hall and the Police Station, the shelter where farmers set up their wares will be on your left. There are other open-air farmers' markets in Statesville, Mooresville, and Davidson. The scene described here by Davidson poet Alan Michael Parker could happen at any one of them:

THE OFFERING
Summer air like hot bread
at the farmers' market on a Saturday—

when a pregnant woman in a purple sari
went down in the crowd

and was lifted up and laid upon a table,
the basil and banana peppers shoved aside.

Her three-year-old son climbed up too;
her husband fanned her

with a bouquet of tiny yellow flowers,
all he had. Her three-year-old son

tried to slide inside her clothes.
Security arrived, two retirees on a golf cart,

swaggering in matching baseball hats,
fans of the Atlanta Braves, and a doctor

hurried over, set aside his cantaloupes.
Her husband waved his flowers;

how so much living can make a man
afraid of wanting more. Upon the table

her body surrendered,
one heartbeat, and another, faster.

The doctor gave her water, sat her up,
held her wrist and counted silently,

his expression formed into a question.
On the table next to her, someone had

left a mottled tomato, then someone else
dug a cuke from a bag,

a teenager pushed forward with a melon,
and then others came with offerings

to the smiling husband clutching
the mangled yellow flowers:

cherry tomatoes, zucchini, okra;
fear, helplessness, joy.
—From *Elephants & Butterflies*, by Alan Michael Parker
    (Rochester, N.Y.: BOA Editions, 2008), 59–60.

■ CONCORD

This tour concludes with a bucolic drive east through the Piedmont country-side to the town of Concord, pronounced by locals with equal emphasis on the "con" and the "cord," unlike the New England villages of the same name where the "n" and "r" are inaudible.

To reach Concord, continue east from the farmers' market on Huntersville Concord Road. Turn right when this road dead-ends into Poplar Tent Road, so named for the pole tent that served for a long time as one of the first churches established by Scots-Irish immigrants between the Catawba and Yadkin rivers. George Washington even spent a night in 1791 along this road at the Phifer Home, long gone but commemorated by a state historical marker. Poplar Tent runs all the way to US 29/601, where it becomes McGill Avenue, which in turn becomes Buffalo Avenue and ends at Church Street in downtown Concord. Turn right.

Though the mills are no longer operating, for the most part, the economic boom that created Concord and nearby Kannapolis is still evident in the number of elegant houses in the area. Concord is the birthplace of poet William Harmon, a University of North Carolina professor known for his own poetry and for the poetry anthologies he has assembled containing the most popular 100 poems in English and the finest 500 poems from Chaucer to Plath, as selected by some 550 critics, poets, and editors. Harmon has also served as the editor of *A Handbook to Literature*, through many editions.

Poet Jeffrey Beam, now a botanical librarian at UNC–Chapel Hill and poetry editor of *Oyster Boy Review*, also grew up nearby, on the outskirts of Kannapolis. Beam wrote this tribute to his grandmother, who went to work in the cotton mill at age thirteen, retired from Cannon Mills at sixty-five, and lived to the age of ninety-three.

THE LOOM
Willie Mae Gill, 1903–1995
She lived for cotton,
the growth of sons,
one daughter lame, a mother
ornery, mean.
She walked with coleus,
gloxinia, begonia stems,
rooting in a well-dug humus from

the woods. Sung hymns,
washed pots, forgave.
Left nothing undone.
Molted in summer's tomato-scent air,
in winter took wings
warped by textile's shuttle.
No searing hardship, no
humidity, feared.
Not any fabric
weaves on any loom.

—From *What We Have Lost: New & Selected Poems,*
1977–2001, by Jeffrey Beam (Hillsborough, N.C.: Green
Finch Press, 2002), enhanced spoken word CD.

Continuing south through Concord, watch for Cabarrus Avenue West and turn right. In the first block on the left is historic Barber Scotia College, where leading African American educator and presidential adviser Mary McLeod Bethune studied. Bethune's essay arguing against segregation was among those in *What the Negro Wants,* a controversial collection published by the University of North Carolina Press in 1944.

Cabarrus Avenue soon becomes Concord Parkway (US 29) and passes through a pastoral area of horse farms before we reach the very edge of Cabarrus County, where the Charlotte Motor Speedway has become a major industry for the area.

Some 200,000 people regularly flock to the speedway, packing the seats above the track. During the week of qualifying races, fans come in campers and set up housekeeping. The facility itself is gargantuan, dwarfing any professional football or baseball stadium anywhere.

Sharyn McCrumb's NASCAR pilgrims arrive in Concord in chapter 15 of the novel *St. Dale.* Their guide is a has-been driver named Harley Claymore, who endures the tour with hopes of getting back into the sport.

McCrumb, Sylvia Wilkinson, and others have recently given the NASCAR phenomenon a literary liaison, but no one explains the magic of racing better than Raleigh writer Scott Huler. In *A Little Bit Sideways,* Huler first documents NASCAR as a brand-new reporter for the *Raleigh News & Observer.* He sets out to follow from sunrise to sunrise what happens on a given week in autumn at the Charlotte Motor Speedway.

Huler comes to the conclusion that a significant part of the appeal of NASCAR is in the simplicity of old-fashioned machines competing in the era

Influential educator and presidential adviser Mary McLeod Bethune studied at Concord's Barber Scotia College as a young woman and was among a group of African American writers whose antisegregation essays were published in What the Negro Wants *by UNC Press in 1944. Photo courtesy of Documenting the American South, UNC–Chapel Hill.*

of the mysterious black box known as the computer. Taking his thesis partly from Humpy Wheeler, who built the speedway, Huler argues that the languid sport of baseball, played without a time clock in broad, slow-growing fields, once helped the country manage the transition from agricultural life to the industrial revolution. Today, he goes on to suggest, NASCAR is helping us cope with the transition from mechanical to digital. NASCAR, by this reckoning, is just another turn in the social upheaval and economic transition from low tech to high tech that Piedmont literature helps to explain. But Huler's prose also does more. It gives the reader an unforgettably visceral account of a NASCAR race, excerpted here, but powerful just the same:

The start.
    That's why you're here. It's all been leading up to this. For this you came. From the moment you drove up to the speedway and heard the whine

of a single car testing on the track, from the first moment a race car reached out to you with that noise, you were mad to get inside. . . . The rest of the week was a rush of images and sensations—the heat of the sun, radiating back from those four banked asphalt turns. The endless hours of practice, the cars droning around the track singly or in bunches. The sickly sweet exhaust smell of the garage. The qualifying and requalifying. The sound of rebel yells reverberating all night long. The pain of stinging sunburn. The grogginess of dehydration mixed with the beer and fatty food constantly on offer from friendly infielders. . . . And then the noise. . . .

You thought you understood. But now, when the green flag drops and, half a mile away, in Turn 4, those drivers get in the throttle, you hear a noise that starts a fear, an awe, a surrender in your chest.

And then echoing back on itself from the high-banked asphalt turns, *it gets louder*. It rises so loud that it leaves sound behind and becomes a new kind of perception, a sort of air-pressure plasma; your ears give up. The screaming roar breaks up into staticky fragments, a noise so buffeting and profound that it surpasses the very concept of hearing. . . .

So you stop listening, and you do by instinct what the others do by tradition: you scream. You scream, you howl, you tilt your head back and let 35 years of civilization out in a long, roaring bellow. So do the others, and as you catch your breath, as you wipe tears from your cheeks and try to regain some sense of where you are, you see the most unusual thing. . . .

Goose bumps. Goose bumps from your wrist, up along your arm to your elbow, and from there all the way up your neck to the base of your hair. Goose bumps. . . .

You try to explain, in long terms about sound, culture, unity, and participation, about sports, marketing, television, and the great American need to just do something, but it's hard. Then you come to the short version. You saw God.

And that's it. *You saw God*. You know where he *lives*. You've been to his *house*. It's between Turns 1 and 2 in the Charlotte Motor Speedway *and all are welcome*!

—From *A Little Bit Sideways: One Week Inside a NASCAR Winston Cup Race Team*, by Scott Huler (Osceola, Wis.: MBI Publishing, 1999), 230, 232–33.

Bookland

1619 East Broad Street, Statesville

704-873-5545

Statesville's only general-interest bookstore has an eclectic regional selection and is located inside the Signal Hill Mall on Broad Street.

Iredell Public Library

201 North Tradd Street, Statesville

704-878-3090

<http://www.iredell.lib.nc.us>

This astonishingly airy and attractive new facility has a spiral staircase leading up to the Local History Room, which features information on Doris Betts, among other Iredell luminaries.

Mooresville Public Library

304 South Main Street, Mooresville

704-664-2927

<http://www.ci.mooresville.nc.us/library>

In the heart of town, this library boasts a new addition with ample computers and a lively gang of patrons.

Main Street Books

126 South Main Street, Davidson

704-892-6841

This stalwart independent shop has a strong North Carolina section and hosts writers for readings and book signings in close collaboration with the college's creative writing program. You may find some poetry collections here that are otherwise hard to locate.

Davidson College Bookstore

704-894-2349

<http://www.davidsoncollegebookstore.com>

Though the obvious emphasis is on textbooks, this bookstore also carries books by faculty. Located next to the Richardson Stadium in the Knobloch Campus Center, it is closed on weekends.

Davidson Public Library

119 South Main Street, Davidson

704-416-4000

<http://www.plcmc.org/locations/branches.asp?id=8>

In the heart of downtown on the campus Green, this branch of the Public Library of Charlotte–Mecklenburg County caters to children and also has a popular book rental program for the latest best sellers.

Books-a-Million

8301 Concord Mills Boulevard (on I-85), Concord

704-979-8300

This shop is part of what Cabarrus County folks like to tout as the number one attraction in North Carolina—the Concord Mills Mall.

Concord Main Library

27 Union Street North, Concord

704-920-2050

<http://www.cabarruscounty.us/library>

Located in Concord's historic business district, this library serves as the main facility for the Cabarrus County library system and hosts a wide array of book clubs focusing on different genres.

Uptown Charlotte (Walking Tour)

Stroll through North Carolina's most cosmopolitan city while discovering its durable literary traditions. Visit the celebrated ImaginOn, the Queen City's amazing children's library, and learn about the lost neighborhood of Brooklyn, where Charlotte's African American community first put down roots.

Writers with a connection to this tour: Asa Paschal Asanti, Dorothy Barresi, LeGette Blythe, Erskine Caldwell, W. J. Cash, Charles W. Chesnutt, Burke Davis, Harriet Doar, Tony Earley, Judy Goldman, Lucinda Grey, John Hart, Robin Hemley, Langston Hughes, Dot Jackson, Jody Jaffe, Kenji Jasper, Mary Kratt, Rose Leary Love, Susan Ludvigson, Joe Martin, Edgar Lee Masters, Carson McCullers, Rolfe Neill, Aimee Parkison, Dannye Romine Powell, Barbara Presnell, T. J. Reddy, Charles Shepard, Marian Sims, R. T. Smith, William Styron, Charleen Swansea, Dede Wilson

The town was in the middle of the deep South. The summers were long and the months of winter cold were very few. Nearly always the sky was a glassy, brilliant azure and the sun burned down riotously bright. Then the light, chill rains of November would come, and perhaps later there would be frost and some short months of cold. The winters were changeable, but the summers always were burning hot. The town was a fairly large one. On the main street there were several blocks of two- and three-story shops and business offices. But the largest buildings in the town were the factories, which employed a large percentage of the population. These cotton mills were big and flourishing and most of the workers in the town were very poor. Often in the faces along the streets there was the desperate look of hunger and of loneliness.—From *The Heart Is a Lonely Hunter*, by Carson McCullers (Boston: Houghton Mifflin, 1940), 5.

tour 5

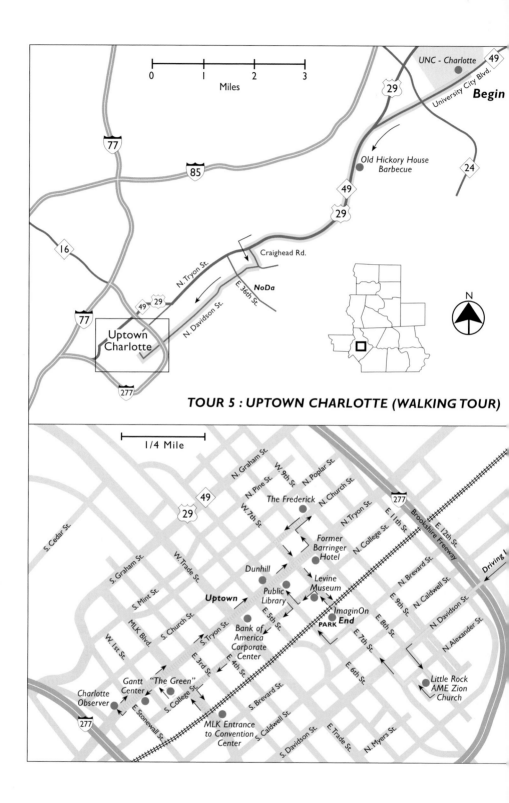

TOUR 5 : UPTOWN CHARLOTTE (WALKING TOUR)

This description of a fledgling southern city is Charlotte in the 1930s. In September 1937, Georgia-born Carson McCullers moved here as a newlywed with her husband, Reeves, who had landed a job in Charlotte's financial sector. Carson, only twenty years old, spent that fall and winter in a local boarding-house drafting the novel she initially titled "The Mute." The book, her first, turned out to be a classic.

Like Asheville, Charlotte has been a magnet to more than a few literary giants, including Erskine Caldwell, W. J. Cash, William Styron (briefly), and even Edgar Lee Masters. The city has also spawned an enormous crop of its own writers—many, curiously enough, in the genre of the murder mystery, which we'll consider more fully in Tour 6.

Charlotte's Novello Festival of Reading is a nationally recognized literary gathering that takes place every fall, and the Novello Festival Press holds the distinction of being the nation's only public library–sponsored literary pub-lisher. (See <http://www.plcmc.org/novello_press/>.) But even before Novello came on the scene, Charlotte's public library had published a number of vol-umes important to the city's literary history.

Notable among these books is *The Imaginative Spirit: Literary Heritage of Charlotte and Mecklenburg County, North Carolina*. Poet and historian Mary Kratt put together this 1988 compendium of more than ninety writers' profiles. According to Kratt, Charlotte's literary narrative goes back to the 1700s, when a local blacksmith, Adam Brevard, wrote a satirical poem to express his outrage at the behavior of town leaders. By his tone and choice of medium, Brevard ap-parently started a trend: poetry has always been a popular genre in Charlotte, and a satirical approach to local controversy is still a perennial pastime among city writers.

Indeed, North Carolina's largest city is known by turns as the "Queen City" (after Queen Charlotte, wife of England's King George III) and the "Hornets' Nest" (so called by the occupying British Army in 1780 because of the relent-less stinging opposition to the Brits mustered by the fierce Scots-Irish settlers). These two monikers have also seemed to shape some long-standing Charlotte traits. Dramatic divisions along class lines dating from the textile era and the penchant for rancorous public debate have provided ample fodder for genera-tions of local authors writing fiction and nonfiction.

Today, Charlotte is also North Carolina's Queen of Arts. Corporate leaders have made enormous investments in the city's cultural infrastructure, and both classical and edgy manifestations of creativity are everywhere.

At times, this creative exuberance has come up against another, more tradi-tional force: Charlotte is and has always been a city of many churches. It is the birthplace of the world's most famous evangelist, Billy Graham (a favorite son), and was the headquarters of the now-defunct PTL Club, run by Jim and Tammy Faye Bakker (generally a sore subject). As early as the 1930s, Charlotte novelist Marian Sims (a friend of Carson McCullers) was quick to point out the curious contradictions created by Charlotte's big-city ambitions and its thick religious roots:

> A church on every corner and more murders than Chicago; prohibition and more speakeasies, I imagine, than New York ever had. The best roads and the worst slums in America. Ministers carting voters to the polls in bootleggers' cars to uphold the dry law. . . . Sunday golf at the country clubs and no golf for the poor devil who has to play on a public course in the city limits.—From *Call It Freedom*, by Marian Sims (Philadelphia: J. B. Lippincott, 1937), 39.

Fast forward to 1994, when novelist Tony Earley gives us another look at Charlotte's contradictions in the midst of its breakneck growth. Earley writes about members of his own generation, whose parents worked in the textile mills but who, upon coming of age, were forced to seek new means of livelihood in the postindustrial South. In the short story "Charlotte," Earley's dispirited narrator describes his life in the city where big-time sports have replaced the staged dramas of brute conquest and defeat on the southern wrestling circuit of his parents' era:

> Now Charlotte has the NBA, and we tell ourselves we are a big deal. We dress in teal and purple and sit in traffic jams on the Billy Graham Parkway so that we can yell in the new coliseum. . . . In the old days in Charlotte we did not take ourselves so seriously. Our heroes had platinum-blond hair and twenty-seven-inch biceps, but you knew who was good and who was evil, who was changing over to the other side and who was changing back. You knew that sooner or later the referee would look away just long enough for Bob Noxious to hit Lord Poetry with a folding chair. . . . In the old days our heroes were as superficial as we were—but we knew that— and their struggles were exaggerated versions of our own. . . . Now when we march disappointed out of the new coliseum to sit unmoving on the parkway, in cars we can't afford, we have to think about the things that are true: everyone in Charlotte is from somewhere else. Everyone in Charlotte tries to be someone they are not.—From *Here We Are in Paradise*, by Tony Earley (Boston: Little, Brown, 1994), 34–35.

As Tony Earley's nostalgic story "Charlotte" describes, the city's enthusiasm for wrestling in the 1960s marked a different era. Pictured here is the city's first coliseum. When it was built in 1955 it was the largest unsupported steel dome in the world. Photo courtesy of the Charlotte Observer.

Kenji Jasper, a one-time contributor to the *Charlotte Observer* and on-air personality for Black Entertainment Television, writes about what many have characterized as Charlotte's formulaic aspirations to instant big-city status:

Charlotte was the furthest I had ever been outside of DC. The city seemed artificial, like it had been grown in a lab. It didn't have a voice or a tradition. But at least it was quiet.

From the highway all I could see was suburban turf. There were stretches of houses and trees and shopping areas and grocery stores. But then it looked like they had just dropped six or seven blocks of large buildings and tall skyscrapers in the middle of it so that they could call it a city.
—From *Dark*, by Kenji Jasper (New York: Broadway Books, 2001), 21.

As this tour points out, Charlotte's historic buildings continue to fall to the wrecking ball while new and interesting skyscrapers rise. With these shining towers coming into view, we begin on the northeast side of the city.

■ UNIVERSITY OF NORTH CAROLINA AT CHARLOTTE

Since its founding in 1965, this relatively young university has been a launching pad for the careers of a number of fine writers, including poets Asa Paschal Asanti, Susan Ludvigson, T. J. Reddy, and R. T. Smith, among others. Over the years, the faculty has included novelist and nonfiction writer Robin Hemley (who wrote his seminal textbook, *Turning Life into Fiction*, here) and American Book Award winner Dorothy Barresi, a poet. Today, poets Barbara Presnell and Lucinda Grey are among the creative writing faculty. Presnell's work lifts up life in the state's historic textile mills. Grey was associated with the *Southern Poetry Review*, a journal that was headquartered in Charlotte for many years and that still sponsors an annual poetry prize named for North Carolina poet Guy Owen. UNC-Charlotte offers a master's degree with a concentration in children's literature, the only such degree offered in the state and one of a handful offered in the United States.

Beyond UNC-Charlotte, 29 and 49 merge to become North Tryon Street. The Old Hickory House BBQ comes up on the left near the corner of Gloryland Avenue. Charlotte poet and novelist Judy Goldman strongly recommends a meal here, and she also set a scene in this restaurant in her novel *Early Leaving*. The book chronicles a picture-perfect Charlotte family that falls apart when their teenage son, Early (only a toddler in this excerpt), commits murder. Early's overprotective mother struggles to come to grips with her role in this family tragedy. Here she remembers happier times:

We didn't eat out very often, but when we did, it was at one of the inexpensive places in town. Olde Hickory House Barbecue Restaurant, in North Charlotte, was our favorite. It was what we could afford in those days, and the food was good. The address seemed to be a symbol for the way things were taking shape for us: Gloryland Avenue. As simple as our life was then, there was an ease to it. A good-natured hopefulness.

One night, Peter and I sat across from each other in one of the red vinyl booths lining the knotty-pine walls, the lamp between us a little covered wagon. Early sat in one of the restaurant's old wooden highchairs at the end of the table.

The waitress brought our sweet iced tea, her fingernails clicking as she set the wet glasses in front of us. "And how old are you, you cute little thing?" she asked Early in a drowsy voice. Her accent was a mixture of southern and something else, maybe Appalachian.

He laughed, drawing his whole body up. I answered for him, the way mothers do, like a ventriloquist, "I'm eighteen months old."

—From *Early Leaving*, by Judy Goldman (New York: HarperPerennial, 2005), 13–14.

■ NODA

Before we reach Uptown for the walking tour, consider a stop in Charlotte's historic arts district, NoDa (short for North Davidson). Proceed on North Tryon across Sugar Creek Road. The next intersection is Craighead Road. Turn left, and in a half mile, after crossing the railroad tracks (Southern Railway's main line), turn right on North Davidson Street.

This area was once a bustling industrial corridor where several mills and their accompanying residential villages were constructed early in the twentieth century. On your right are the old Mecklenburg and Johnston mills; the latter shut down in 1975, the very last of Charlotte's many textile operations to close. Below NoDa's central crossroads at 36th Street is Highland Mill #3, the first in Charlotte to be powered by electricity. Plans call for all three historic mill buildings to be transformed into apartment and/or retail space.

Short-story writer and UNC-Charlotte faculty member Aimee Parkison offers this narrative guide to NoDa's unusual artistic assets:

Just on the edges of the Uptown skyscrapers and Downtown townhouses are the tastefully renovated homes of North Charlotte's historic mill village and the eclectic restaurants, shops, and galleries of NoDa. On North Davidson Street, galleries display contemporary works of local artists. Whether serious or ironic, kitschy or keen, the work is vibrant, surprising, and inspired. In fact, the artists are usually within an arm's reach to discuss their process during the twice-monthly gallery crawls.

Those hungry for more than inspiration can delve into the cozy charm of the Smelly Cat Coffee House, where visual artists, filmmakers, musicians, writers, and students hobnob in the afternoons and into the evenings.

After nightfall, in the background, live music rushes through the open doors of bars camouflaged behind crowds of music-lovers, window-gazers, gallery-crawlers, and theater-goers. Somewhere lurking behind the scent of spilled beer are the emerging voices of local creative writers performing poetry slams or flash-fiction readings in the occasional breaks between songs.

■ BROOKLYN

To appreciate what Uptown once looked like, before urban renewal, we make one more quick stop on our way into the city's center. From NoDa, continue on North Davidson toward Uptown Charlotte, passing over I-277 and through a traffic circle at Ninth Street. Turn left at the next block on East Eighth Street. Cross North Alexander Street and take the next right on North Myers Street. This spur dead-ends into the parking lot of the former Little Rock AME Zion Church, which also served as home to Charlotte's Afro-American Cultural Center for many years. Follow the driveway around the church to the right to see the 1890 shotgun houses that once sat on Bland Street, a few blocks away from the heart of Charlotte's historic African American neighborhood of Brooklyn.

At the beginning of the twentieth century, Brooklyn lay mostly to the south of the Uptown crossroads of Trade and Tryon streets. The neighborhood was home to many African American businesses and churches and to the first independent public library for blacks in North Carolina, established in 1903. Today Brooklyn has all but vanished, but a 1965 memoir preserves many memories of the neighborhood. Beloved teacher, poet, and musician Rose Leary Love wrote the account of Brooklyn's heyday.

As Love explains, shotgun houses like the ones in Brooklyn were common in Charlotte and were the fuel for a devastating fire in 1917 that she witnessed as a teenager:

The fire had started in a small shotgun house (which was a common name for a very inferior type of wooden structure) on a side street and had quickly spread to the tinderbox houses on each side of us. The fire then raced down Caldwell Street helped by flying sparks which set houses on fire on both sides. —From *Plum Thickets and Field Daisies: A Memoir*, by Rose Leary Love (Charlotte: Public Library of Charlotte and Mecklenburg County, 1996; reissued by Novello Festival Press, 2005), 179–80.

The flames jumped from roof to roof; in all, more than forty homes were destroyed that day. Love goes on to suggest that this disaster was the beginning of Brooklyn's end. Land speculators began constructing cheap rental housing to replace the single family cottages that burned. Brooklyn—once featuring side-yard gardens planted with collards in fall and okra, corn, and potatoes in summer—became a slum, she says. The neighborhood's congenial mixture of African American professionals, poor people, and those in between had moved

The atrium of ImaginOn: The Joe and Joan Martin Center, which serves as home to the children's library and a professional theater.

elsewhere by 1965 when she finished her memoir, and almost all of Brooklyn's original buildings had been razed as part of an urban renewal plan. Love wrote to save her memories, if not her neighborhood.

■ UPTOWN WALKING TOUR

Exit the church parking lot and turn right onto Seventh Street. After crossing Caldwell, turn left at the next block on Brevard and then take a quick right onto Sixth Street. Ahead on the right is the ramp to a parking garage that overlooks Charlotte's light rail transit line where it crosses Sixth Street. The first ninety minutes in this parking lot are free for visitors to ImaginOn, which is the first stop on our walking tour of Uptown. (Please note that from this point forward this tour is not easily navigated by car because of one-way streets. However, a quick hop onto the trolley or Lynx Blue Line can minimize some of the walking up and down College Street if needed.)

Take the elevator from the parking deck to the ImaginOn lobby, where you can have your ticket validated. If this lot is full, other fee parking lots are located around the block on Seventh Street between College and Brevard streets.

■ IMAGINON: THE JOE AND JOAN MARTIN CENTER

300 East Seventh Street, Charlotte
704-416-4600
<http://www.imaginon.org/>

ImaginOn is a collaborative venture of the Public Library of Charlotte and Mecklenburg County and the Children's Theatre of Charlotte. The result? A literacy playground with a mission of bringing stories to life. As home to both a library for children and teens and a professional children's theater, ImaginOn is an extraordinary multimedia center that encourages the exploration of stories in all forms—written, spoken, and electronic. Programs and exhibitions help young people express themselves using a variety of tools.

ImaginOn's full name honors two of Charlotte's civic leaders: the late Joe Martin, a former Bank of America executive, and his wife, Joan. After his retirement from the bank, Joe published two books. *On Any Given Day* (2000) is a memoir written with Ross Yockey chronicling Martin's heroic fight against Lou Gehrig's disease. His 2001 novel, *Fire in the Rock*, is a coming-of-age story of two boys whose friendship in the Jim Crow South crosses racial lines. Martin wrote the latter with special software that allowed him, despite near total paralysis, to type out his narrative by moving his eyes.

ImaginOn is worth a visit with or without children. The building is Mecklenburg County's first county-owned LEED-certified facility, and it is both light-filled and lighthearted. (LEED stands for Leadership in Energy and Environmental Design.) As you tour the building, look for small posted signs that identify some of the recycled or rapidly renewable materials used in its construction and finishes.

Begin your tour on the first floor. Here you'll find Spangler Children's Library, the StoryLab exhibition and program space, the Round storytelling room, and entrances to ImaginOn's two theaters—the 570-seat McColl Family Theatre and the Wachovia Playhouse. The Children's Theatre of Charlotte presents a full sea-

Larry Kirkland's public art installation outside ImaginOn commemorates the writing career of journalist and Charlotte Observer *publisher Rolfe Neill.*

son of productions in both venues, and the library uses them for author appearances, film series, and other events.

As you meander up the ramp that spirals through the building, notice the upper levels of the StoryJar towering above the StoryLab. Each marble in the jar represents a story that a visitor has left behind at ImaginOn, and the characters and props hanging above the jar are a few of the ideas that might inspire such stories.

On ImaginOn's upper level you'll find a technology lab, studios used for acting classes for students between the ages of three to eighteen, a multimedia production studio where young people can produce movies and music, and the Teen Loft, which is reserved for twelve- to eighteen-year-olds. On your way back down the ramp, look up to see the giant skylights that provide much of ImaginOn's indoor lighting.

Leaving the building by the main entrance, be sure to stop by Larry Kirkland's public art piece, *The Writer's Desk*. Built on a superhuman scale, the installation features old-fashioned writing tools—pen, ink, pencil, and typewriter keys. This landmark tribute was commissioned by friends of Mount Airy native Rolfe Neill, who served as publisher of the *Charlotte Observer* from 1975 to 1998.

Neill was also one of the founders of the library's Novello Festival of Reading, held annually since 1991. The sculpture incorporates a number of quotations—barbed, funny, and inspiring—from Neill's long-running Sunday columns in the city's newspaper.

Continue uphill on Seventh Street and across the Lynx tracks.

■ LEVINE MUSEUM OF THE NEW SOUTH

200 East Seventh Street, Charlotte
704-333-1887
<http://www.museumofthenewsouth.org>

A bit farther up the block, the Levine Museum of the New South offers a permanent exhibition, *Cotton Fields to Skyscrapers: Charlotte and the Carolina Piedmont in the New South*, which documents the evolution of the region since 1865 and lends a bit more context to the literature excerpted in this trail. North Carolina writers regularly come here to lecture and read as part of the Levine's monthly programming. The museum gift shop carries a number of titles—mostly historical nonfiction. Call or check the Internet for hours and a monthly program schedule.

■ PUBLIC LIBRARY OF CHARLOTTE AND MECKLENBURG COUNTY

310 North Tryon Street, Charlotte
704-416-0100
<http://www.plcmc.org>

From the Levine, continue up Seventh Street and take a left on College. You'll pass the back side of Spirit Square on your right, the home of regular poetry slams, plays, and documentary exhibits offered by The Light Factory. At the next corner, turn right on Sixth. The building on your right is Charlotte's Main Library, where quotations from dozens of writers adorn all sides of the columns under the portico. Take your time and enjoy the good words. Note that the main entrance to the library is on Sixth (not Tryon, as the address suggests).

The Public Library of Charlotte and Mecklenburg County was begun as a subscription service housed above a bookstore on South Tryon Street in 1891. In 1903, on its present site, the Carnegie Library opened, which served as Charlotte's main library until the old building was razed and the present facility was constructed and opened to the public, in 1956. Charlotte writer Dede Wilson's poem describes her husband's early memories of the original building:

THE CARNEGIE LIBRARY
That post-war summer,
the boy lived in the Churchill Apartments,
sat on the sidewalk
in early evening heat,
chair propped against the wall,
walked with his parents
south on Church to Trade,
to the Selwyn Hotel or the S&W
for cafeteria suppers.
Mornings he walked up Sixth
alongside the Dunhill Hotel,
crossed Tryon, the trolley rails
pressing under his brogans,
and turned left. Glancing up
at the dome, columns and pediment
of the Carnegie Library,
he skipped up the steps,
pushed at the wooden door.
He was there to help Miss Ring
pry open a shipment of books,
paste the due-date sleeves inside,
and—after she'd inked the numbers
in white—shellac the spines.

The old library—oak, doors, steps, stone—
like ink on an old book's spine, is gone.
—Used by permission of Dede Wilson.

Today the library has more than twenty branches across the county. It was named National Library of the Year in 1995 and Library of the Future in 1996, and it was the winner of the 2006 National Award for Museum and Library Service.

The literary visitor must be sure to visit the Robinson-Spangler Carolina Room on the third floor. This sturdy collection of North Carolina literature includes many first editions and some rare surprises. It was among these volumes in the old Carnegie building that Burke Davis, a sportswriter in the mid-1940s for the *Charlotte News* (the city's one-time afternoon newspaper), began his research into what would become a series of historical novels and biographies that were hugely popular in Charlotte and beyond.

Also, don't miss the gallery space outside the Carolina Room designed to present rotating exhibitions on city history. One favorite display offers views of Charlotte in the days of novelists Carson McCullers and Marian Sims. Local historian and poet Mary Kratt grieves the loss of the rural countryside, the character of the landscape, and the Charlotte she knew as a girl:

WHERE THE WOODS WERE
Barechested carpenters saw and nail.
The few remaining birds compete
with workmen's radio rock and roll.
The residential air replete with hammering
tolls loveliness lost.
                    I watch the crane,
hear the men cheer as the roof beam falls
in place there along the measured line.
They piss in the corner where wrens
once sang in the muscadine.
—From *Spirit Going Barefoot*, by Mary Kratt
    (Davidson, N.C.: Briarpatch Press, 1982), 28.

In the front lobby as you depart the library, copies of the anthologies and prize-winning volumes of fiction and nonfiction published by the library's Novello Festival Press are available for purchase. Proceeds from these books—sold nationwide—are used to support library programs here.

■ **CHARLOTTE CONVENTION CENTER**

501 South College Street, Charlotte
704-339-6000
<http://www.charlotteconventionctr.com>
From the library's main entrance turn left and head back to College Street. Turn right at the corner and follow College across Fifth and Trade and continue three more blocks to Martin Luther King Jr. Boulevard. Turn left on MLK Boulevard and cross the rail line. On the far side of the tracks on the right is the MLK Boulevard entrance to the Charlotte Convention Center. Inside, a series of murals along the concourse document parts of Charlotte's history relevant to this tour.

The mural Remembrances of Charlotte's Second Ward: Brooklyn and Blue Heaven, *by poet and visual artist T. J. Reddy, celebrates the value placed on education in Charlotte's historic African American neighborhoods.*

The mural of longtime Charlotte poet and visual artist T. J. Reddy, *Remembrances of Charlotte's Second Ward: Brooklyn and Blue Heaven*, relates to the city's historic African American community of Brooklyn, which included the land where the Convention Center stands today. Blue Heaven was an adjacent neighborhood on the far side of today's I-277.

The title of Juan Logan's mural, *I've Known Rivers*, comes from a Langston Hughes poem, "The Negro Speaks of Rivers": "I've known rivers: / I've known rivers ancient as the world / and older than the flow of human blood in human veins. / My soul has grown deep like the rivers" (*Crisis*, June 1921).

Hughes, a major poet of the Harlem Renaissance, reportedly visited relatives in Charlotte in the 1950s. Logan's painting also commemorates the Brooklyn neighborhood and its most famous religious institution, Sweet Daddy Grace and the House of Prayer, which is now headquartered near Johnson C. Smith University. Note also the stylized shotgun houses in the work.

Ruth Ava Lyon's mural, *The Goodliest Land*, refers to the first words written in English about North Carolina, often quoted fondly by journalist Charles Kuralt, whose literary roots in Charlotte are discussed in the next tour. (If you are

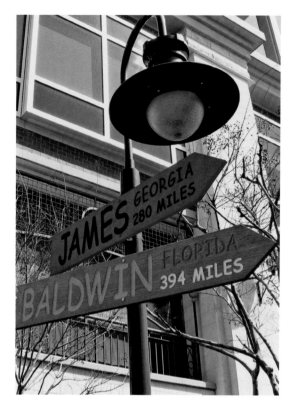

At The Green, several whimsical geographic markers not only locate Charlotte's distance from other towns and cities but also create an opportunity for literature lovers to search for the names of famous writers.

interested in seeing more of Charlotte's extensive public art collection, the city's light rail service—the Lynx Blue Line—comes directly into the Convention Center right here. Public art installations are at every station along the line in either direction.)

■ THE GREEN

between South Tryon and College streets

704-358-9898 (for entertainment schedule)

Exit the Convention Center the way you came in, cross the tracks, and return to the corner of MLK Boulevard and College Street. To your left, in the middle of the next block on the opposite side of College from the Convention Center, look for an open space called The Green. The entrance is flanked by two bronze columns of books. This three-tiered park is full of funky artwork celebrating literature. Children can make a scavenger hunt of finding the bronze pages that have "flown" from the books and are strewn throughout the park. They feature quotations from well-known writers and poems from local Piedmont Middle School students.

Without looking too hard, you'll find other literary references and riddles in the park's public art. Concrete chess tables invite a game or two, as does a hop-scotch grid built into the ground. An interactive fountain, piped-in sounds, and the proximity of several eateries make this a busy spot. The Green hosts musical entertainment on some days at lunchtime and sponsors movies, music, and games of bocce some evenings. Head uphill through the park to South Tryon Street and turn left, passing under the old neon Ratcliff Florist sign to reach the intersection of Tryon and Stonewall.

■ HARVEY B. GANTT CENTER FOR AFRICAN AMERICAN ARTS AND CULTURE

551 South Tryon Street, Charlotte
704-547-3700
<http://www.ganttcenter.org>
The new home of African American culture in Charlotte, now known as the Gantt Center, fronts East Stonewall Street. It houses the Hewitt Collection of African American Art, which is outstanding for its paintings by some twenty artists, including Charlotte natives Romare Bearden and Charles Alston. The center also regularly hosts rotating exhibits, concerts, plays, dance performances, literary readings, and lectures. Check the website for current events.

The Gantt Center, built to fit a lot only 45 feet wide and 400 feet long, has an unusual design and is decorated with panels reminiscent of an African quilt pattern. At the top of the building is an open-air terrace. The distinctive four-story interior stairway at the center of the building, visible from the street, is symbolic of the biblical Jacob's ladder, an important icon in the African American community, as explained by Rose Leary Love, teacher and writer from Charlotte's Brooklyn community, who explored the hardships of segregation and the balm of religious faith in her memoir:

Many onlookers from time to time have wondered how it has been possible for various members of the race to overcome innumerable obstacles, weather avalanches of prejudice and adversity, and yet climb Jacob's ladder singing the staunch, inspiring lines of comforting old songs. . . . Over and over they have beseeched their maker "to make a way out of no way," and countless times, the answers have come. —From *Plum Thickets and Field*

Daisies: A Memoir, by Rose Leary Love (Charlotte: Public Library of Charlotte and Mecklenburg County, 1996; reissued by Novello Festival Press, 2005), 154.

Jacob's Ladder was also how people referred to the Brooklyn neighborhood's Myers Street School, where young Rose Leary was a student. Opened in 1882 as Charlotte's first black public school, the frame schoolhouse was enlarged many times as the student population grew and the demand for classrooms increased. With these additions came the need for multiple fire escapes, which crisscrossed the exterior and gave the building its nickname.

A couple of blocks northwest of the Gantt Center, on South Mint Street (near today's Bank of America Stadium), the first major African American fiction writer in the United States, Charles Waddell Chesnutt, worked as assistant to the principal of the Peabody School from 1873 to 1877. (The school no longer stands.) Chesnutt's father's grocery in Fayetteville had failed and his mother had passed away, so young Charles, only fourteen but already working as a pupil-teacher in the Freedman's School in Fayetteville, was sent to Charlotte to assume a more challenging position and to earn money for the family. He began keeping a journal during his Charlotte years, and in 1880, at the age of twenty-two, he revealed his deepest wish, to become a writer:

> I think I must write a book. I am almost afraid to undertake a book so early and with so little experience in composition. But it has been a cherished dream, and I feel an influence that I cannot resist calling me to the task.... The object of my writing would not be so much the elevation of the colored people as the elevation of the whites—for I consider the unjust spirit of caste which is so insidious as to pervade a whole nation, and so powerful as to subject a whole race and all connected with it to scorn and social ostracism—I consider this a barrier to the moral progress of the American people: and I would be one of the first to head a determined, organized crusade against it.—From the journal of Charles W. Chesnutt, <http://www.online-literature.com/charles-chesnutt/>.

■ **THE *CHARLOTTE OBSERVER***

600 South Tryon Street, Charlotte
704-358-5000
<http://www.charlotte.com>

Across from the Gantt Center on the corner of West Stonewall and South Tryon is the headquarters of the *Charlotte Observer*. In addition to publisher Rolfe Neill and the long list of Charlotte's mystery and crime novelists to be considered in the next tour, many other journalists have come through this stalwart institution, honing their craft in preparation for tackling a longer form of writing—mostly novels. Among their ranks is 1970s feature writer and investigative reporter Dot Jackson. Even as she made her living as a journalist, Jackson had squirreled away a completed novel, first under a mattress and then in an unplugged refrigerator until the family secrets she'd revealed in her manuscript had lost their potency. That novel, *Refuge*, was published in 2006 by Novello Festival Press, the year Jackson turned seventy-four.

Reporter Charles E. Shepard delivered his suspenseful exposé, *Forgiven: The Rise and Fall of Jim Bakker and the PTL Ministry*, in 1989. (His earlier *Charlotte Observer* coverage of the scandal surrounding the Charlotte-based evangelist earned him a Pulitzer Prize.) Elizabeth Leland, a reporter who won the Ernie Pyle Award for her journalism, published *A Place for Joe: A True Story of a White Southern Family, a Black Man, Their Lifetime Together and Their Love for One Another*, in 1997.

Harriet Doar, longtime *Observer* book editor and columnist and cofounder of North Carolina Press Women, was "a nurturer and promoter of North Carolina writers," says Red Clay Books publisher Charleen Swansea, who lived in Charlotte for many years and launched the city's poetry-in-the-schools program. Doar's poems were collected in 1983 in *The Restless Water*. Her successor at the newspaper, Dannye Romine Powell, a prolific poet whose work is featured in Tour 10, has provided many probing interviews of southern writers over the years.

■ TRADE AND TRYON

Head back on Tryon toward The Green and continue five more blocks to the epicenter of Charlotte, where Trade Street crosses Tryon. Here four magnificent bronze sculptures by Raymond Kaskey—titled *Transportation, Future, Commerce*, and *Industry*—occupy the four corners of Charlotte's central square. In *Industry*, a child peeking out from under the skirt of a woman wearing a headscarf commemorates the role of the women and children who worked in the textile mills.

In his first novel, Burke Davis described this crossroads as it appeared in the early twentieth century, but he gave Charlotte the fictional name Elizabeth:

A wind from the west, out of the foothills, harried the leafless elm branches in the square and molded the skirts of the women passing along the streets. It dried the rutted mud in the street leading up the hill. In its breathing it piped a thin tune on the finger of the Presbyterian steeple, like the thin voice of God. Gusts shivered the great glass panes of Trade Hotel facing the square and flapped the new yellow sign on the corner:
Watch Elizabeth Grow! 100,000 by 1920!
—From *Whisper My Name*, by Burke Davis (New York: Rinehart, 1949), 4.

Like Thomas Wolfe, Davis had local readers guessing which citizens he had in mind when he created his fictional characters. As Mary Kratt explains, "People wore out the books reading about the Scotch-Irish town of Elizabeth where Cornwallis camped and independence was declared early, where Jeff Davis heard the news of Lincoln's death on a street corner, and where Jews and Catholics were so rejected that the Jewish protagonist became a Gentile and Methodist to set up a dry goods store in town" (*The Imaginative Spirit*, by Mary Kratt, 37).

According to Davis's 2006 obituary, the novel was loosely based on the experiences of an executive at Ivey's Department Store, a historic building that stands a block away from Trade and Tryon, at West Fifth and Church. Charlotte journalist Harry Golden had given Davis the germ of the story and encouraged him to write the novel.

Other important writers have passed through this crossroads. In 1914, when he was twelve, Erskine Caldwell, the future author of some thirty novels, including *Tobacco Road* and *God's Little Acre*, spent a summer in Charlotte learning about religious tolerance from a Jewish shopkeeper on Trade Street. It was a lesson Caldwell never forgot and which he recounts in his 1968 memoir, *Deep South: Memory and Observation*.

In the summer of 1944, Edgar Lee Masters, author of *Spoon River Anthology*, moved to Charlotte and joined the North Carolina Poetry Society, organized here in 1932.

The elderly Masters lived in the Selwyn Hotel, which stood only one block west of the square on the northeast corner of Trade and Church streets. The year before moving to Charlotte, Masters had collapsed in his apartment at the Chelsea Hotel in New York City, where he was living with his second wife, a woman thirty-three years his junior. After she nursed her husband back to health, Ellen Coyne Masters needed a job. She found employment in Charlotte as a teacher and went on to create the first full-fledged English department at the private Charlotte Country Day School. Mrs. Masters was teaching her pri-

The 1929 Dunhill Hotel (right) has a cameo role in John Hart's novel The King of Lies *and has hosted a number of literary luminaries during their visits to Charlotte.*

vate school pupils up the road from the public school where in 1945 Charles Kuralt enrolled in the sixth grade. Meanwhile, Edgar Lee Masters spent his days looking out the window of the Selwyn, writing every morning and occasionally going out to meet with other Charlotte poets.

While you're at this intersection you may want to step into the grand lobby of the Bank of America Corporate Center, at 101 North Tryon. North Carolina artist Ben Long, whose first ambition was to become a writer, has created three fresco panels that fill the atrium with images of industrious Charlotteans. The central panel in particular celebrates chaos and creativity.

Continue walking north on Tryon.

■ THE DUNHILL

237 North Tryon, Charlotte

If Charlotte has a hotel even faintly resembling New York's famous Algonquin, it is this refurbished sixty-room gem. The Dunhill has been a popular spot for writers ever since it opened as the Mayflower Manor in the unfortunate year of 1929. Salisbury novelist John Hart has his main character come to the hotel for a clandestine meeting with a private investigator in his novel *The King of Lies*: "The Dunhill Hotel was on Tryon Street in downtown Charlotte. It had a great bar, full of deep and shadowed booths, and would be almost empty on a Sunday night" ([New York: Thomas Dunne Books, 2006], 84).

■ THE BARRINGER HOTEL

426 North Tryon, Charlotte

Continue down Tryon two more blocks. On the opposite side of the street from the Dunhill is the former Barringer Hotel, now Hall House, which has served as a residence for seniors for many years. This twelve-story, red-brick structure, now threatened with destruction, was built in 1940 and billed then as Charlotte's most up-to-date hotel. It once accommodated movie stars Judy Garland, Tyrone Power, Joan Crawford, and Gloria Swanson.

The elegant hotel also played host to seventeen-year-old William Styron, who came here with a classmate from Davidson College in 1942 to ply himself with beer before visiting a less-glamorous hotel of sorts nearby. The rite of passage that followed the drinking became fodder for fiction in Styron's 1979 novel *Sophie's Choice*. His character Stingo narrates: "The comedy [was] played out with a tired old whore from the tobacco fields in a two-dollar-a-night flea-bag hotel in Charlotte, North Carolina" ([New York: Random House, 1992], 32).

As Styron explained to the *Charlotte Observer*'s Dannye Romine Powell in a 1994 interview: "I was so filled with beer I don't remember a great deal about it. I remember getting on the bus back to Davidson very fulfilled." Styron wrote about the incident and its aftermath once more in a comedic essay, "A Case of the Great Pox," collected in the posthumous volume *Havanas in Camelot* (2008). Not long after his visit to the Barringer, Styron was called to Parris Island, South Carolina, for Marine Corps officer training. When he became ill, he spent several weeks in the base infirmary convinced that he had contracted syphilis from the Charlotte encounter.

■ THE FREDERICK

515 North Church, Charlotte

Past the Barringer is Eighth Street. Turn left and walk one block up Eighth to North Church Street. Diagonally across Church in the next block up, beyond two frame houses, is The Frederick. This brick apartment building, originally outfit-

The Frederick on Church Street in Charlotte was where writer W. J. Cash kept an apartment and wrote his landmark work, The Mind of the South.

ted in 1927 with "bachelor apartments" for men and "housekeeping units" for single women and families, is where W. J. Cash lived alone, playing his Wagner recordings much too loud to suit his neighbors and writing *The Mind of the South*, still considered a classic treatise on the character of white southerners of his era.

Cash first put his ideas on paper in a 1929 article by the same title for the *American Mercury*. The magazine's publishers, Alfred and Blanche Knopf, were so taken with the piece that they encouraged Cash to expand it into a book. The release date for the book kept being postponed through the mid-1930s as Cash struggled with several drafts while he also fulfilled his duties as a reporter for the *Charlotte News*. (The newspaper was headquartered a few blocks away at South Church and West Fourth.) In the original *Mercury* article, Cash, who was clearly immersed in, if not impressed by, the bustle and ambition of a growing Charlotte, pulled no punches:

One hears much in these days of the New South. The land of the storied rebel becomes industrialized; it casts up a new aristocracy of money-bags which in turn spawns a new noblesse; scoriac ferments spout and thunder toward an upheaval and overturn of all the old social, political, and intellectual values and an outgushing of divine fire in the arts—these are the things one hears about. There is a new South, to be sure. It is a chicken-pox of factories on the Watch-Us-Grow maps; it is a kaleidoscopic chromo of stacks and chimneys on the club-car window as the train rolls southward from Washington to New Orleans.

But I question that it is much more. For the mind of that heroic region, I opine, is still basically and essentially the mind of the Old South. It is a mind, that is to say, of the soil rather than of the mills—a mind, indeed, which, as yet, is almost wholly unadjusted to the new industry.
—From "The Mind of the South," by W. J. Cash, *American Mercury*, October 1929; available at <http://www.wjcash.org/WJCash1/WJCash/WJCash/THE.MIND.OFTHE.SOUTH.html>

Here the walking tour of Uptown ends. To return to ImaginOn, head down Church Street from Eighth to Seventh Street and turn left. Cross Tryon and College streets and catch the elevator inside ImaginOn to return to the parking deck.

■ LITERARY LANDSCAPE

J. Murrey Atkins Library
University of North Carolina at Charlotte
1201 University City Boulevard, Charlotte
704-687-2030
<http://library.uncc.edu/>
UNC-Charlotte's Special Collections houses more than a million manuscripts. Of special literary note are the papers of novelist Marian Sims and 300,000 items from Harry Golden. The New South Voices Project is an ongoing library initiative that has its roots in the interviews of prominent North Carolinians conducted by LeGette Blythe, who served as writer-in-residence at UNC-Charlotte beginning in 1967 and was the author of a history of Charlotte.

Real Eyes Bookstore
3306 North Davidson Street, Charlotte
704-377-8989
<http://www.realeyesbookstore.com>
Real Eyes is the center of NoDa literary activity, with regular Sunday storytelling sessions for children, a women-only book club, and many other special

events. The store is the primary organizer of the annual fall Charlotte Literary Festival.

Blumenthal Performing Arts Center and Spirit Square
130 North Tryon Street, Charlotte
704-333-1598
<http://www.blumenthalcenter.org>
This center serves as residence for Charlotte's leading dance, opera, theater, and musical companies. Spirit Square, also administered by the Blumenthal, is a former church down the block, with an entrance at 345 North College Street. It hosts a monthly poetry event with nationally recognized masters of the spoken word.

Great Aunt Stella Center
926 Elizabeth Avenue, Charlotte
704-944-6014
<http://www.greatauntstellacenter.org>
This former church hosts concerts, literary events, conferences, and weddings.

Charlotte Neighborhoods (Driving Tour)

Who-done-it is a big deal in Charlotte, the city that may have more crime writers than criminals. Examine the evidence: visit the haunts and hangouts that inspired their fiction. This tour also encompasses more of Charlotte's broader literary history and its contributions to the state's reputation for fostering fine wordsmiths.

Writers with a connection to this area: Cathy Smith Bowers, Marion Cannon, Fred Chappell, Patricia Cornwell, Mark Etheridge, Frye Gaillard, Harry Golden, Judy Goldman, Anne Underwood Grant, John Hersey, Terry Hoover, Henry Houston, Jody Jaffe, Paul Jones, Mary Kratt, Charles Kuralt, Elizabeth Lawrence, Fred Leebron, Amon Liner, Carson McCullers, Tamar Myers, Cathy Pickens, Diana Pinckney, Kathy Reichs, Kathryn Rhett, Carl Sandburg, Marian Sims, Faye Sultan, Charleen Swansea, Katharine White, Robert Whitlow, Ann Wicker, Emily Wilson

Though Charlotte is most often pictured as a collection of impressive skyscrapers, it is also a city of distinctive neighborhoods, which have been described over the years by many of the city's writers. In fact, Charlotte writers love to set scenes around town and use real place-names in their fiction and poetry. These neighborhoods form the basis for this driving tour.

■ SOUTH END

Leave Uptown via South Tryon Street to visit a neighborhood of bungalows and small storefronts dating from the 1920s and 1930s known as the South End. From the end of the last tour, exit the ImaginOn parking deck on Sixth Street, turn right and cross College to reach Tryon Street. Turn left. Follow South Tryon (NC 49) over I-277 and through two major intersections—first Morehead, then Carson. It's only 0.6 miles to the

tour 6

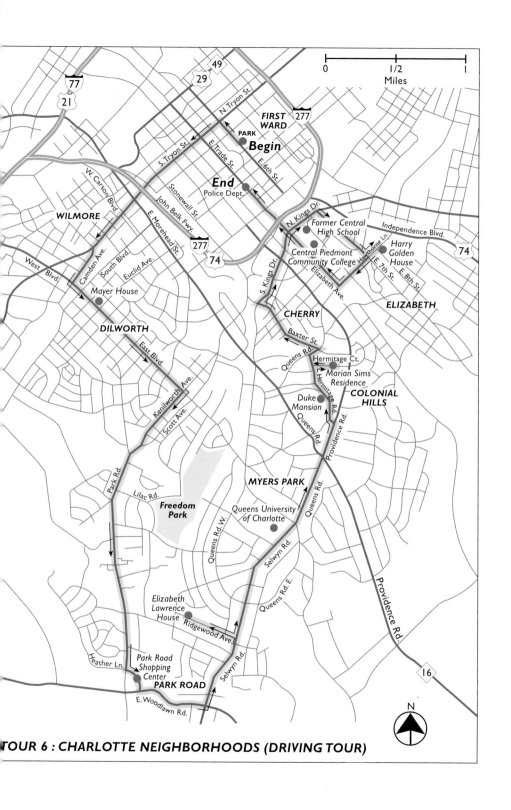

TOUR 6 : CHARLOTTE NEIGHBORHOODS (DRIVING TOUR)

traffic light where Summit Street is on your right and Camden Road forks to the left. Follow Camden as it runs alongside the Lynx Blue Line.

Immediately on the left is the Charlotte Art League, which occasionally hosts literary events, in addition to its exhibitions and weekend gallery crawls. Then, at 1531 Camden, you'll see the offices of the *Charlotte Post*, the city's longest-running African American weekly newspaper. Henry Houston established the publication in 1878, and in the early years he ran the paper out of his Brooklyn home on East Second Street—now Uptown's Martin Luther King Boulevard.

On the right at 1614 Camden is one of Charlotte's most authentic southern eateries, Price's Chicken Coop. Recommended enthusiastically by Charlotte novelist Judy Goldman, a visit to this cash-only restaurant usually involves standing in one of several lines to order and then taking out generous portions of old-fashioned fried chicken, potato rounds, and hushpuppies by the sackful.

Continue on Camden across Park Avenue to the intersection where West Boulevard (on the right) becomes East Boulevard. Turn left on East. The next intersection is South Boulevard. Though the tour goes straight ahead on East, the literary visitor may want to take a short jaunt down South Boulevard. The historic Atherton Mill, still in operation when novelist Carson McCullers lived in the area, is now one of many popular destinations along this street where Charlotteans shop for home furnishings.

In the first block on your right, at 1820 South Boulevard, is the Pewter Rose, a restaurant that appears in Jody Jaffe's first equestrian mystery, *Horse of a Different Killer*. Jaffe's fictional fashion writer, Natalie Gold, declares this high-end establishment with its multinational menu to be "the best lunch place in town." It's still a favorite among the Charlotte literati for lunch and dinner, according to longtime *Creative Loafing* writer and editor Ann Wicker. (Wicker recently compiled and edited *Making Notes: Music of the Carolinas* for Novello Festival Press—a collection of essays on songwriters and musicians from the region.) Another local favorite, a bit farther down at 1910 South Boulevard, is La Paz Restaurante, a Mexican café where crime writer Kathy Reichs and others have set scenes in their Charlotte-based novels.

■ **DILWORTH**

The tour continues on East Boulevard into the Dilworth neighborhood, which has drawn writers and artists for decades. Anne Underwood Grant, who ran her own advertising agency in Charlotte, finally quit her day job to write her first murder mystery, *Multiple Listing*. Grant's droll protagonist, Sydney Teague, lives and works as a communications consultant in Dilworth. She describes the neighborhood:

> For me Dilworth is the only part of Charlotte that doesn't seem to have been created during the eighties. . . . The neighborhood was first laid out in the second half of the nineteenth century and bustling by the 1890s. . . . The houses are substantial, not necessarily in size but in construction and quality. Styles are hodgepodge from Tudor to Queen Anne to early Crafts-man. . . . Every yard has at least one hundred-year-old tree, usually an oak. . . . All the roofs are steep pitched, multi-angled, no matter what the style. The rest of Charlotte is uniformly Georgian. . . . If I were a bird and looking for an interesting place to roost in Charlotte, North Carolina, I'd make a beeline straight for the roofs of Dilworth. — From *Multiple Listing*, by Anne Underwood Grant (New York: Dell, 1998), 49–50.

In 1937, writer Carson McCullers and her new husband came straight from their wedding in Columbus, Georgia, to Dilworth. They made their first home together at 311 East Boulevard. Their two-room furnished apartment was inside the Mayer House (now the Copper Restaurant). Here McCullers began *The Heart Is a Lonely Hunter*, her first and most celebrated novel.

According to McCullers's biographer, Virginia Spencer Carr, the apartment's kitchen was so tiny that the refrigerator had to be kept in the bedroom, along with three huge dressers, an iron bed, two bookcases, and a table that served as both Carson's writing desk and the dining table.

McCullers's husband, Reeves, who also had aspirations to write, worked to support the couple during their early marriage as an investigator for the Retail Credit Corporation. Both suffered from respiratory problems, and, fearing a cold winter in the Mayer House, they soon moved across town to 806 Central Avenue, where they had a much bigger kitchen and a room apiece for writing. That apartment house (now demolished) was also cold, and Carson eventually began working at the Charlotte Public Library, where, her biographer writes, "she frequently warmed up her insides by surreptitiously sipping sherry from her ever-present thermos" (*The Lonely Hunter: A Biography of Carson McCullers*, by Virginia Spencer Carr [Athens: University of Georgia Press, 2003], 78).

McCullers submitted her first six chapters and an outline for the rest of the novel in the spring of 1938. It won the Houghton Mifflin Fiction Prize. In August 1940, Richard Wright reviewed the book in the *New Republic*, the same year his own novel, *Native Son*, came out. "To me," he wrote, "the most impressive as-

*Now used as a restaurant, this large apartment house on East Boulevard in
Charlotte served as home to Carson McCullers as she began her first novel,*
The Heart Is a Lonely Hunter, *in 1937.*

pect of *The Heart Is a Lonely Hunter* is the astonishing humanity that enables a
white writer, for the first time in Southern fiction, to handle Negro characters
with as much ease and justice as those of her own race" (195).

McCullers's novel is full of misfits, mill hands, and the African Americans she
saw daily on her forays into Charlotte. As it turned out, the first eight months
of the McCullerses' marriage—all in Charlotte—would be their happiest. The
couple divorced in 1941 and later remarried, but their troubles were ongoing.
Despondent, Reeves McCullers killed himself in 1953.

Today it is possible to go inside the Mayer House for a meal. Copper, a nou-
veau Indian restaurant, comes highly recommended by Charlotte poet Diana

Pinckney. While you're in the neighborhood, you might sprint across the street to Paper Skyscraper—a gift and card shop with an eclectic selection of books on Charlotte history and architecture along with local literature. It's at the corner of East Boulevard and Euclid Avenue.

Continue ahead on East and turn right on Kenilworth Avenue, which soon joins Park Road.

■ PARK ROAD SHOPPING CENTER

Over the next two miles this tour heads deeper into the southern suburbs of Charlotte, where much of the land was once given over to forest or farming, with fields of cotton and corn, dairy barns, and unpredictable creeks, says local historian and poet Mary Kratt. Freedom Park, Charlotte's largest park, is only a few blocks away, accessible by Lilac Road on your left. Our destination, however, is Park Road Shopping Center, a landmark with several distinctions at the corner of Park and Woodlawn Road. Turn left into the shopping center before you get to the light at Woodlawn and try to imagine the dairy cattle that once grazed here. In the early twentieth century, this land belonged to William Franklin Graham Sr., whose son Billy, the future evangelist and prolific writer, was born here in 1917. Billy Graham, a lanky fellow who never particularly excelled in school, adored baseball and hot rods. He spent his childhood tending his prized goats and devouring Edgar Rice Burroughs's *Tarzan* series, his favorite reading material.

Before his fall from grace, Charlotte televangelist Jim Bakker had bought the Grahams' two-story home that was on this site and moved it brick by brick to his now-defunct Christian theme park, Heritage Village, across the state line in South Carolina. Eventually the Graham family acquired the house once again and moved it to another location in Charlotte, the Billy Graham Library, which opened in 2007 near Charlotte Douglas International Airport. Visitors may tour the fully furnished house, which sits in front of a barnlike library and visitors' center designed to recall the Graham farm.

Chapel Hill poet Paul Jones also grew up in this neighborhood. Jones is one of the founders of the North Carolina Writers' Network and the architect of ibiblio.org, "The Public's Library," hosted online by the University of North Carolina at Chapel Hill. He introduces his poem about the shopping center:

The Park Road Shopping Center, the remembered location of this poem, was the first modern mall—although we would now call it a strip mall—

in Charlotte in 1956. *Brown vs. Board of Education* was decided on May 17, 1954. To my young, and now older mind, the opening of the shopping center and the Supreme Court decision were concurrent.

DIVIDING WATERS

Signs divided the waters
when all the creeks were rerouted
around the evangelist's
father's field and crops withered
as the shopping center sprouted
and red hills of clay mounted
in red dust and oily mists.

Even their hair was crimson:
men at break—the setting sun—
their hard work clinging to them
made them all seem one red race
but too soon they were replaced
—as if by some magic whim—
by clean careful concrete men.

What was to come next was grand:
a new J.C. Penney's store
with tiles that set departments
apart like pools of rain
that captured only one tint:
the boy's section was lime green,
the toys brown, sports blue and more.

My grandmother took me in
—I think I was about four—
and the grand old man himself
held the door as in we poured
to gawk at the full shelves,
wonderfully uniform bins,
and the tall tight-lipped women.

Thirsty in all this outpour,
I looked for water fountains
and found two flanking a door

one shiny metal marked "White"
and a white one called "Colored"
new but with a dripping drain
still the colored one seemed right.

I stepped up for a cool sip;
one hand bravely on the knob
thinking I had made the slip.
With a rough yank, I was robbed
of my try for those colors
and shoved over to the other
by my silent grandmother.

But there the water ran red.
My lips looked like they had bled
a blood common to all kids;
the drips draining on the tiles
ran into the Young New Styles
section like Biblical curses.
I drank deep and almost burst.
—"Dividing Waters" by Paul Jones, from "Sunday Reader"
    (Raleigh: *News and Observer*, August 17, 2003).

Though the anchor stores of Jones's memories are no longer here, Park Road Books, established in 1977, is the city's longest-surviving independent bookstore, with excellent customer service (704-525-9239 or <http://www.parkroad books.com>).

■ ELIZABETH LAWRENCE HOME

Follow one of the main arteries in the Park Road parking lot to its terminus on East Woodlawn Road and turn left. In a half mile, turn left on Selwyn Road and watch for Ridgewood Avenue upcoming in 0.4 miles. Turn left on Ridgewood to see number 348, where North Carolina's most acclaimed garden writer, Elizabeth Lawrence, lived for many years.

When I was a little girl, my mother took great pains to interest me in learning to know the birds and wildflowers and in planting a garden. I thought that roots and bulbs and seeds were as wonderful as flowers, and the

Distinguished horticulture writer Elizabeth Lawrence lived and gardened at this site on the edge of Charlotte's Myers Park neighborhood for thirty-five years.

Latin names on seed packages as full of enchantment as the counting-out rhymes that children chant in the spring. I remember the first time I planted seeds. My mother asked me if I knew the Parable of the Sower. I said I did not, and she took me into the house and read it to me. Once the relation between poetry and the soil is established in the mind, all growing things are endowed with more than material beauty.—From *A Garden of One's Own: Writings of Elizabeth Lawrence*, ed. Barbara Scott and Bobby J. Ward (Chapel Hill: University of North Carolina Press, 1997), 3.

Georgia-born Elizabeth Lawrence lived in several places across the South before her family moved to Raleigh so that she and her sister might attend prep school at St. Mary's. After completing her undergraduate degree at Barnard, where she immersed herself in literature, Lawrence came back to the capital city to become the first woman to enroll in the landscape architecture program at North Carolina State University.

Lawrence had already recognized that she could not earn a living as a poet, but her love of literature and her ability to turn a phrase lifted her writing about gardens and gardening to a sensuous level. In the 1930s, she began to publish articles about plants and trees in magazines such as *House & Garden*. As her writing gained popularity, Lawrence found her mailbox filled with warm correspondence from her devoted readers, many of whom became fast friends.

Among them were Mississippi novelist Eudora Welty and Katharine S. White, one of the principal editors and a garden columnist for the *New Yorker* magazine from its founding in 1925. (The literary visitor may remember that Katharine White's son from her first marriage is the *New Yorker's* longtime fiction editor Roger Angell, and her second husband was the extraordinary E. B. White, perhaps best known for his children's book, *Charlotte's Web*, and his essential grammar guide, *The Elements of Style*, coauthored with William Strunk Jr.)

Winston-Salem poet and women's historian Emily Herring Wilson edited the letters of Katharine White and Elizabeth Lawrence, published in 2002 as *Two Gardeners: A Friendship in Letters*. Much like a biography, the collection offers a satisfying portrait of two eloquent and sensitive women, their times, and their mutual love for both word and spade work. Other collections of Lawrence's writing—including her long-running columns in the *Charlotte Observer* and her very first book, *A Southern Garden*—continue to be mainstays in the libraries of gardeners in the South and beyond.

Lawrence's home, where she lived from 1948 until her death, in 1985, is still a flowering sanctuary. Plans call for the property to be transferred from private ownership to the stewardship of a nonprofit organization. In the meantime, tours of the grounds may be arranged by contacting the Elizabeth Lawrence Foundation at tours@elizabethlawrence.org.

Wing Haven Gardens and Bird Sanctuary, up the block at 248 Ridgewood Avenue, hosts thousands of visitors annually and is open several days a week. Wing Haven is a three-acre refuge created by Elizabeth and Edwin Clarkson, in 1927. The Clarksons were fast friends and neighbors of Miss Lawrence. The prolific Mary Kratt wrote an account of the Clarksons' development of Wing Haven. She tells how the newlyweds arrived in Charlotte by train in 1927 after their honeymoon. It would be the first time Elizabeth Clarkson saw what was to be her new home:

> Elizabeth gasped. The house stood stark and solitary in a field of hard, red mud with nothing green except a few waist-high pine seedlings. Eddie led her around back to the single tree, a spindly willow oak. Since Eddie did not have the door key to the house, they climbed in a window. He led her into

the living room where his wedding present waited, a mahogany Steinway baby grand piano.

The next day Elizabeth started her garden.

—From *A Bird in the House—The Story of Wing Haven Garden,* by Mary Kratt (Charlotte: Wing Haven Foundation, 1991), 8.

Backtrack to Selwyn Avenue and turn left.

■ MYERS PARK

What Charlotte lacked in architectural glory it made up for in the splendor of its trees. Tall, graceful, arching halfway to heaven; they're considered the jewels in the Queen City's crown and the pride of its residents.... The biggest and most majestic trees live on the many Queens Roads, a labyrinth of streets all with the same name that runs through Myers Park, one of Charlotte's oldest and toniest neighborhoods. No one has ever explained why five or six streets bear the same name. The only thing I can figure is that Queens Road is the high-dollar, old-money address in town, so the developers just kept naming more and more streets Queens Road to cash in.

—From *Horse of a Different Killer,* by Jody Jaffe (New York: Fawcett Columbine, 1995), 19–20.

Perhaps Jody Jaffe exaggerates a bit for the sake of humor, but Queens Road East, Queens Road West, and the original Queens Road, designed in 1911, are three different thoroughfares that meet each other at odd and confusing angles throughout Myers Park. Follow Selwyn north and you will soon see Queens East (right) and Queens West (left) and, at 1900 Selwyn, Queens University of Charlotte.

■ QUEENS UNIVERSITY OF CHARLOTTE

Dating back to 1857, this institution has a lively literary history, first as a woman's college and now as a coeducational university. Among its graduate programs is a low-residency master of fine arts in creative writing. Students from across the country come twice a year for the on-campus component of the degree and between sessions work from home via correspondence with their instructors. Among the poetry faculty is Cathy Smith Bowers, who was named North Carolina's poet laureate in January 2010. A past poet-in-residence at Queens, she's much beloved by her students. Novelist Fred Leebron heads the program and has brought in as teachers up-and-coming and veteran writers, including his wife, a gifted memoirist, Kathryn Rhett.

Leebron's second novel, *Six Figures*, tells the story of an ambitious young couple who move to Charlotte from the West Coast to advance their careers in nonprofit work but soon find that they still have a ways to go to afford the finer things in town. Leebron's characters perpetually pass through Myers Park to reach their more modest neighborhood. The reminder of the limits of their salaries grates on them:

> Now they were passing the stores and shop fronts of Myers Park—Mars Park they'd first thought it was called by the lush accents, Mars Park—gourmet coffee, gourmet Italian take-out, gourmet ice cream, gourmet bagels. The car rocked so gently it was like a boat, and they sailed along the border of Elizabeth, one of those up-and-coming neighborhoods that had been almost accessible to them.—From *Six Figures*, by Fred Leebron (New York: Alfred A. Knopf, 2000), 104.

Ultimately Leebron's couple is unlucky, and what begins as a novel of manners becomes a story of random violence, mistrust, and big-city, white-collar deceit.

In addition to the MFA program, Queens has long offered writing workshops to the local community through what is now called the Center for Lifelong Learning. Notable among the faculty in this program is Cathy Anderson, a professor of business and former provost at Queens, who writes under the pen name Cathy Pickens. Her mysteries include *Southern Fried* and *Done Gone Wrong*.

In the early 1960s, Charleen Swansea taught a creative writing class at Queens that was open to the community and included Charlotte poet, philanthropist, and civil rights activist Marion Cannon, the widow of textile magnate Martin L. Cannon Jr. Though Swansea says that she and Cannon initially disagreed vehemently about the relative merits of rhyme in poetry, they nevertheless became friends.

After an unhappy dispute with the Queens administration over whether a visiting student from Africa enrolled at Johnson C. Smith College could join their workshop, the writing group abandoned Queens and began meeting at Swansea's house on nearby Westminster Place, where they soon created literary history, not only for Charlotte but for the entire region.

With Cannon's financial backing and Swansea's chutzpah, the group launched *Red Clay Reader*, a literary journal that was published annually from 1964 to 1971.

There's an atmosphere of creative tension in the South these days and more hot-hearted writing than ever before. So the RED CLAY READER got its start in southern pride. We wanted a place to show off the quantity and quality of this new writing and it also seemed high time to give an argument to William Faulkner's myth that the South is forever stunted by an unredeemable guilt. — From *Red Clay Reader* (the first collection), Charlotte, N.C., 1964, 2.

And with this opening volley, entitled "Why We Did It," Charleen Swansea (then Whisnant) introduced the first issue of the *Reader*, which included work by Leon Rooke, Fred Chappell, Doris Betts, Reynolds Price, Lawrence Ferlinghetti, Stanley Kunitz, Romulus Linney, and literally dozens of others who would soon become mainstays of North Carolina literature. Harriet Doar's interview with William Styron in the inaugural issue discusses the novel he was midway through writing at the time, *The Confessions of Nat Turner*. Rumi scholar Coleman Barks's first published poem also appears.

"But who will buy such a publication?" Marion Cannon had asked early on.

"Libraries!" said Swansea. "We'll print it in hardcover and tell them it's a book!"

From the era of the Freedom Riders of the civil rights movement and on into the fledgling years of the women's movement, *Red Clay Reader* published some of the nation's most revolutionary artists and writers, including Lillian Smith, Jack Kerouac, Alice Walker, and Kate Millett. Charlotte poet Amon Liner served as poetry editor. All *Red Clay* writers were paid for their work, which was unusual for most literary journals. The group edited and pasted up the *Reader* on Swansea's back porch, where the tops of a washer and a dryer and a sawhorse table served as production desks.

Determined to make every issue more stupendous than the last, Swansea dogged famous writers, urging them to submit something for publication. After four years of such hounding, Norman Mailer gleefully submitted a piece to Swansea that she says was "too pornographic to print." The *Reader* became, in its time, the most widely circulated literary magazine in America, with 5,000 paid subscriptions. Swansea says the name became the inspiration for North Carolina's Broadway-bound musical group of the 1980s, the Red Clay Ramblers.

Ultimately, the number and range of submissions became overwhelming to its small staff, and the *Reader* suspended publication. But Swansea and Cannon soon turned their talents to Red Clay Books, another enterprise that published dozens of new and established writers, primarily women. Charleen Swansea would go on to establish Charlotte's poetry-in-the-schools program, bringing some of the best-known poets of the era and many former *Red Clay Reader* contributors to read and teach in the Mecklenburg County schools. Meanwhile, Marion Cannon stopped rhyming and grew stronger as a poet. According to Swansea, Cannon's *Collected Poems* was reprinted five times and made more money than any other title published by Red Clay Books.

CREATION
One needs so little to create
If bridges, planes and towers
Are not the goal:
A scrap of linen, strands of wool, a needle;
A pot of dirt, a seed, a bulb,
Or just a pencil and a piece of paper.
— From *Another Light*, by Marion Cannon
   (Charlotte: Red Clay Books, 1974), 19.

■ DUKE MANSION AND COLONIAL HEIGHTS

Continue up Selwyn, which becomes Queens Road beyond Queens University. At the intersection with Providence Road, where Queens turns to the left, continue straight ahead on Providence. The next street on your left is Hermitage. Turn left and then bear to the right on Hermitage Road. Cross Ardsley and look for 400 Hermitage, on your left.

This grand white house, which James B. Duke bought in 1919 and then tripled in size, became the southern headquarters for Duke and his daughter, Doris, during the early 1920s as he developed his hydroelectric plants in the region. In its heyday, the mansion featured a fountain with a fifty-foot plume, created by water piped some twelve miles from the Catawba River to the lawn. Now on the National Register of Historic Places, it was also the site of the creation in 1924 of the Duke Endowment.

The Duke Mansion also has a couple of rather surprising literary connections. Besides playing host to any number of plays, art events, and festivals over the years, the mansion figures in Ross McElwee's autobiographical film *Bright Leaves*, which was based on the filmmaker's obsession with the 1949 novel *Bright Leaf*, written by University of North Carolina dance and drama professor Foster Fitzsimmons. Through a series of investigative interviews in the film, McElwee tries to figure out if the Fitzsimmons novel and subsequent Hollywood movie, starring Gary Cooper and Patricia Neal, were based on the story of his great-grandfather. John Harvey McElwee purportedly invented a logo picturing a bull for his own tobacco product, only to have it appropriated by the Dukes for their signature Bull Durham tobacco. Lawsuits over the logo ultimately ruined McElwee's great-grandfather.

In the course of the movie's investigation, Ross McElwee's longtime pal and high school writing teacher, Charleen Swansea, accompanies him to the mansion, where they marvel at the wealth behind it, wealth that McElwee's family never acquired.

Though it is not mentioned in the film, the Duke family only kept the house for ten years and then sold it in 1929 to Martin L. Cannon, father-in-law of poet Marion Cannon, Swansea's friend and the financial backer of *Red Clay Reader*. When Frances Ann Cannon (Marion's sister-in-law) staged her grand wedding at the estate in April 1940, one of the guests was her old flame, John F. Kennedy, whose *Profiles in Courage* would win the Pulitzer Prize in 1957.

The groom was also a literary star in the making—*Time* magazine journalist John Hersey, who had begun his writing career as personal secretary to Sinclair Lewis, the first American to win the Nobel Prize for Literature. Hersey's first novel, *A Bell for Adano*, would win the Pulitzer Prize in 1945. His best-known work, *Hiroshima*, was first published in its entirety in a 1946 issue of the *New Yorker*. It was the only material in the issue—no cartoons, no other stories or commentary. It sold out within hours. (Hersey also wrote the introduction to *Let Us Now Praise Famous Men*, by novelist James Agee and photographer Walker Evans, arguably one of the most important documentary collaborations of the twentieth century.)

Continue on Hermitage Road for 0.2 miles and turn right on Hermitage Court. Look for number 519 on the right. This address, among the centenary oaks and elegant camellias, is one of the houses where Marian Sims wrote her blistering novels of social critique, excoriating Charlotte's stratified class system of the 1930s and 1940s. She also published more than forty short stories in magazines such as *Saturday Evening Post*, *McCall's*, and *Collier's*. Sims wrote what she knew—the Charlotte country club scene. She was the wife of a local judge who was also the first chair of the North Carolina ABC (Alcoholic Beverage Control) Board. Marian Sims was a well-known member of Charlotte's golfing, bridge-playing, book club, and gardening set, yet she was quick to allow her fictional characters to lift up the hypocrisy they (and she) saw everywhere.

As Mary Kratt explains in *The Imaginative Spirit*, Atlanta novelist Margaret Mitchell was so smitten with Sims's second novel, *World with a Fence*, that she wrote an effusive letter in 1936, congratulating Sims on writing successfully about "normal" southern people. (Of course, Mitchell meant normal *white* people; Sims in her time was not particularly enlightened in matters of racial equality, but she was sympathetic to the plight of poor people of all colors.)

Sims's 1940 novel, *City on a Hill*, exposed corruption in the fictional city of Medbury, where bankers, politicians, and clergymen worked piously to maintain an ordinance banning Sunday commerce while ignoring more serious issues of poverty and violence in the city.

Return to Hermitage Road and turn right. At Queens Road, turn right, then take the next left onto Baxter Street, which leads into the historic Cherry neighborhood.

■ CHERRY

In her many turns around town, crime novelist Kathy Reichs brings her characters in the novel *Bare Bones* into this historic African American neighborhood in Charlotte, which was built on the site of original slave cabins and named for a hillside grove of cherry trees, now long gone. John and Mary Myers, whose open land had once been a cotton farm, developed this self-contained village in 1891, well in advance of Myers Park, which bears their name. Charlotte developers have set their sights on much of the area, while longtime homeowners have also begun restoring some of the historic bungalows here.

Continue on Baxter across Cherry Street to the traffic light at South Kings Drive. Turn right to visit the Elizabeth neighborhood.

■ ELIZABETH

Two important literary landmarks occupy the Elizabeth section. The first is Central High School. Cross Charlottetown Avenue, Third Street, and Fourth Street, and on the right, at the intersection with Elizabeth Avenue, you'll see the campus of Central Piedmont Community College, where Central High's main building is still in use by the college.

It was to this spot that writer James Baldwin came south in 1957, for the first time in his career, to report on the progress of school desegregation in Charlotte for *Harper's* magazine. Only a few years before Baldwin's visit, Central High had among its students future CBS correspondent Charles Kuralt, novelist Jan Karon, University of North Carolina system president Dick Spangler, literary doyenne Charleen Swansea, and poet and local historian Mary Kratt.

By the time he entered Central High, Charles Kuralt was already committed to journalism and dreamed of becoming editor of the *New York Times*. Born in Wilmington, Kuralt had lived in Onslow County and several other southern

Writers Charles Kuralt, Jan Karon, Charleen Swansea, and Mary Kratt were among the graduates of Charlotte's Central High School, now part of the campus of Central Piedmont Community College, which also has a strong literary tradition.

cities before moving to Charlotte in 1945, when his father was appointed welfare superintendent for Mecklenburg County. In junior high, Kuralt had been generously encouraged by his eighth-grade teacher, Anne Batten, who supervised the student newspaper. By age thirteen, Kuralt had landed his own radio program on the local ABC affiliate and was being paid 10 cents per column-inch for his writing in the *Charlotte News*. His voice matured early, and Kuralt continued his radio work throughout high school, honing his writing skills for the spoken word and gaining national notice for his gifts. In tenth grade he wrote an essay that was singled out from among 250,000 entries in a contest sponsored by the National Association of Broadcasters. Part of Kuralt's prize was a trip to the White House to meet President Harry Truman.

In the eleventh grade, fifteen-year-old Kuralt published a piece in *North Carolina English Teacher* demonstrating the agile lyricism and concrete details of people and places for which he would become best known:

'Tis the night before Christmas. 'Tis evening of a gloomy Sunday that is cold and wet. In the parks, the trees stand firm, their bare boughs creaking in the wind. The sky is overcast; the damp wind sniffs at every lamp post and deserted alleyway.

In the big churchyard on Trade Street, the rocks are wet. The gravel paths, clean from many rains, are neat against the dead brown of faded grass. Mist falls upon the asphalt.

In the windows of all the stores, the "Merry Christmas" signs hang, their silvered lettering staring out on the street. The neon gets mixed up in the mist. In one shop window, dressers in felt slippers are already at work, taking away the displays, getting ready for the big post-Christmas sales. They take down the fake holly wreaths, cotton, silver dust, and speak choppily to each other, their mouths full of pins.

—From *Remembering Charles Kuralt*, by Ralph Grizzle (Asheville: Kenilworth Media, 2000), 71–72.

Kuralt would go on to the University of North Carolina at Chapel Hill, where he succeeded Rolfe Neill as editor of the *Daily Tar Heel*. Early on, Kuralt was labeled a Communist for his editorials favoring the *Brown v. Board of Education* decision of 1954. He returned from college in the summers to work for WBT radio in Charlotte, a CBS affiliate. Then, before completing his degree, Kuralt took a job in his senior year with the *Charlotte News*. He soon distinguished himself with a column called "People," for which he won the Ernie Pyle Award. By 1957, he was on his way to New York. CBS had summoned Kuralt to a job in broadcasting that would last thirty-seven years.

In 1984, Kuralt paid tribute to his native state on the occasion of North Carolina's 400th birthday. *North Carolina Is My Home* is a love letter (in the form of a coffee-table book, a recording, and a video) that combines Kuralt's prose with the music of the late Charlotte composer-pianist Loonis McGlohon, a collaboration that resulted in a new state song and very few dry eyes among devoted Tar Heels at its debut on public television.

■ HARRY GOLDEN HOME

To reach the second literary landmark in the Elizabeth neighborhood, continue on North Kings Drive to East Seventh Street and turn right. On your right, beyond the intersection with Charlottetown Avenue, is Independence Park. The next major cross street is Hawthorne Lane. Turn left on Hawthorne and then right on Eighth. Pull over immediately to see the historic house on the corner, at 1701 East Eighth Street.

From 1973 to his death, Charlotte's most famous newspaper publisher lived

The witty and irreverent journalist Harry Golden wrote biting editorials in his national newspaper, the Carolina Israelite. *This residence on Eighth Street in Charlotte was his last.*

in this bungalow after retiring from his monthly duties as sole writer and editor of the *Carolina Israelite*.

Born in Ukraine, Harry Golden grew up on New York's Lower East Side, where he opened a stock brokerage firm after a couple of years of college. In 1929, he declared bankruptcy and was convicted of mail fraud and sentenced to five years in Atlanta's Federal Penitentiary. After his release, he worked for newspapers in New York and Norfolk, Virginia, before settling in Charlotte, in 1941. He launched the *Carolina Israelite* the next year, with a press run of 800 copies. At the peak of its influence, the paper's nationwide circulation reached 14,000 readers—many of whom were clergy of all faiths. Among the more than two dozen books he wrote, Golden was probably proudest of his biography of Carl Sandburg and the relationship he established with the poet, who lived in Flat Rock, North Carolina, during the last twenty-two years of his life.

Frye Gaillard—author of a definitive book on the desegregation of Charlotte's public schools and the cofounder, with Amy Rogers, of Novello Festival Press—describes Golden's influence on public discourse during his time:

Mixed in with the displays of ego and the flashes of seriousness, there was also a comic quality about Golden's style. It was there even in his ap-

Harry Golden (right) wrote a biography of poet Carl Sandburg. The two compare notes on the porch of Sandburg's Flat Rock home known as Connemara. Photo courtesy of Special Collections, J. Murrey Atkins Library, UNC-Charlotte.

pearance: the suspenders, the oversized cigars, the twinkle in his eye be-hind the dark-rimmed glasses. Perhaps that is why he could get away with something far more threatening, far more subversive in the South of his day, than ringing proclamations about his own Jewish heritage. Between the 1940s and the late 1960s, Golden emerged as one of the nation's lead-ing opponents of white supremacy, and he did it with satire. He mocked the hallowed institution of racial segregation.... It is difficult to say what impact Golden had on Charlotte. He was not especially popular or honored in the city. But he did push his case with cleverness and tenacity, making the leap with ease from his concern over the oppression of Jews in Europe to the oppression of blacks in America. And his very outrageousness may have added legitimacy to more moderate voices.

—From *The Dream Long Deferred: The Landmark Struggle for Desegregation in Charlotte, North Carolina*, by Frye Gaillard (Columbia: University of South Carolina Press, 2006), 18–19.

Golden began his newspaper in 1942 in a house on Elizabeth Avenue. Carl Sandburg did his best to explain his friend's unusual editorial process in the foreword to Golden's best-selling collection of columns, *Only in America*, which was also adapted for Broadway:

Whatever is human interests Harry Golden. Honest men, crooks, knuckle-heads, particularly anybody out of the ordinary even if a half-wit, any of them is in his line. He writes about them. He drops the sheets of writing in a barrel. Comes the time of the month to get out his paper, *The Carolina Israelite*, he digs into the barrel and finds copy.—From *Only in America*, by Harry Golden (Cleveland: World Publishing, 1958), 13.

Golden also appeared on Edward R. Murrow's popular television interview program, *Person to Person*, in his trademark suspenders with the wooden barrel of columns by his side. Golden corresponded with governors and presidents, writers and opinion leaders. He covered the Adolf Eichmann trial for *Life* magazine, in 1962, and wrote speeches for Robert Kennedy. He was briefly engaged to poet Marion Cannon in their later years and was known to enjoy wild games of poker with other writers at Cannon's townhouse off Providence Road.

Golden ceased publication of his newspaper in 1968 because of illness. Richard Nixon gave him a pardon for his federal conviction in 1974. A decade later, he died in this house on Eighth Street. For years, Golden's dear friend Anita Brown kept the house as it had been when the writer was alive. The current owners of the house still have copies of his newspapers that were left behind.

Return to Hawthorne Lane and turn left. Follow Hawthorne to Elizabeth Avenue and turn right on Elizabeth, which becomes Trade Street soon after you cross I-277.

■ CHARLOTTE-MECKLENBURG POLICE DEPARTMENT

The final stop on this tour is the Charlotte-Mecklenburg Police Department, at 601 East Trade Street, a spot worthy of reflection due to the uncanny number of crime novels, legal thrillers, and detective mysteries that have issued from the Queen City in the past several decades. However, it doesn't take a detective to recognize a more mundane reason. Arguably, Charlotte is no more prone to crime or corruption than any other urban center is, but perhaps the example of Patricia Cornwell with her multiple book contracts helped speed the local rush toward crime and suspense novels.

Now a whole host of successors has followed, setting novels in familiar sites all around town, including this building, where a striking Ben Long fresco in the lobby illustrates the many facets of police work. Park in the metered lot between the police headquarters and the large parking deck that fills the block and have a look.

Of Charlotteans who have turned to crime writing, the largest source are reporters from the *Charlotte Observer*. This tour has already introduced Jody Jaffe. Mark Etheridge, an *Observer* editor and third-generation journalist, also put his experience to work in the 2006 murder mystery *Grievances*. Terry Hoover, another newspaper veteran, has been praised for her Steve Harlan mystery, *Double Dead*. Working in the 1960s, Hoover's protagonist solves crime without the benefit of high-tech electronics.

Then there's the Charlotte attorney-turned-novelist Robert Whitlow, whose books give a new meaning to the term "the Christian mysteries." From a faith-based perspective, he writes legal thrillers set in the South.

Charlotte can also lay claim to a practicing forensic-psychologist-turned-novelist in Faye Sultan, who launched her Portia McTeague series of novels about—guess what?—a forensic psychologist working in Charlotte. The books, written with contributor Teresa Kennedy, are *Help Line* and *Over the Line*.

After living in various spots around the world, Tamar Myers settled in Charlotte and as of 2010 has more than thirty books to her credit, including the Den of Antiquity mystery series, which revolves around an antique dealer who sells her wares across the Carolinas.

Then there are the academics with a second life of crime writing. In addition to Queens professor Cathy Pickens, who has a shelf of novels to her credit, Kathy Reichs probably tops the list of those who have put Charlotte in the national who-done-it limelight. Reichs is on the anthropology faculty at the University of North Carolina at Charlotte and is an internationally recognized forensic expert who works regularly with North Carolina's and Quebec's chief medical examiners. Reichs was called in to assist in the identification of human remains in Rwanda, at the World Trade Center, and at the exhumation of bones in France believed to be those of St. Thomas Aquinas. Besides her world travel, Reichs divides her time between Charlotte and Montreal, as does her smart and smart-alecky protagonist, Temperance Brennan.

And, finally, there was O. Weldon Terrell, a mysterious novelist who turned out to be the late Queens University president Billy O. Wireman, along with professors Robert W. Whalen and Richard T. Goode, who combined their middle names to create a nom de plume for two thrillers and a book of nonfiction. Case closed.

■ **LITERARY LANDSCAPE**

Main Street Rag Publishing Company
704-573-2516
<http://mainstreetrag.com>

M. Scott Douglass is managing editor and publisher of the poetry, first novels, and short fiction collections, along with an annual anthology and a quarterly magazine of poetry, prose, interviews, reviews, and art, called *Main Street Rag*. Because *MSR* owns its own bindery equipment, the company also helps writers who wish to self-publish, under its Pure Heart Press imprint.

Charlotte Writers' Club

<http://www.charlottewritersclub.org>

For more than eighty years, the Charlotte Writers' Club has hosted monthly meetings, workshops, readings, contests, and other special events. For the past several years, the club has also published an anthology of contest winners' and members' writing. The group meets most third Tuesdays of each month, September through May, at 7:00 P.M., at Joseph-Beth Booksellers.

Joseph-Beth Booksellers

South Park Mall

4345 Barclay Downs Drive, Charlotte

704-602-9800

<http://www.josephbeth.com>

This enormous store features a comprehensive selection of regional literature upstairs and a full service restaurant and coffee shop downstairs. Local writers regularly present their work and/or sign books.

Barnes & Noble Sharon Corners

4020 Sharon Road, Charlotte

704-364-0626

This bookstore features weekend story times for children, regular author events, a coffee shop, and a strong selection of regional literature.

Mecklenburg County Courthouse

832 East Fourth Street, Charlotte

One block east of the intersection of Elizabeth Avenue and McDowell Street is the county courthouse, where artist Robin Brailsford and North Carolina poet laureate emeritus Fred Chappell used a clever array of texts to adorn the exterior pedestrian corridors of this multistoried facility. Entitled *We Hold These Truths*, the public art installation considers the path to liberty through the words of writers throughout history.

Mount Holly : Belmont : Gastonia

Discover the literature that's been spun from the city that once had the largest number of looms and spindles in the South and the region that had more cotton mills in the 1920s than any other place on earth.

Writers with a connection to this area: Sherwood Anderson, Stewart Atkins, LeGette Blythe, Max Childers, Olive Tilford Dargan (Fielding Burke), Thomas A. Dixon, Pamela Duncan, June Guralnick, Grace Lumpkin, Don Mager, Dorothy Myra Page, William Rollins, Flora Ann Scearce, Chuck Sullivan, Mary Heaton Vorse, Ella Mae Wiggins

RAP

    For Scott Douglass
Out of the ordinary, alongside,
a car pulls up in this ant-line. I look
across. Like neighbors, light to light, for blocks,
we creep. Their boom concusses air inside
my closed windows. Four boys (weave, cap turned,
dreads, white rolled up doo rag) rock their torsos
like jerky metronomes, and their wide mouths
chant the virility of unbroken
uncompromised joy. Clasping the moment
as if the throbbing bass were the heartbeat
of the cosmos and they rode its center,
they rap along one voice joined together.
I switch off the news on my radio
because theirs is plenty enough for now.
—From *Drive Time*, by Don Mager (Charlotte: Main Street
    Rag Publishing Company, 2008), 33.

Johnson C. Smith University English professor Don Mager provides an unusually joyful image of the daily commute along one of the many corridors leading into and out of down-

tour 7

TOUR 7 : MOUNT HOLLY - BELMONT - GASTONIA

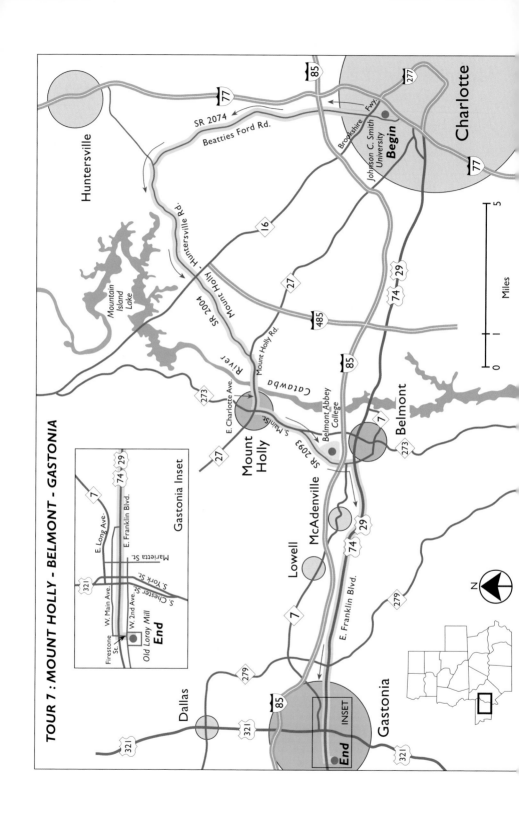

town Charlotte. This tour begins at Johnson C. Smith University, on Beatties Ford Road.

■ JOHNSON C. SMITH UNIVERSITY

Johnson C. Smith University, at 100 Beatties Ford Road, a private, liberal arts university, was established in 1867. The neighborhood surrounding this historically black college (now university) came to be a focal point for the relocation of many of the displaced residents of the Brooklyn section of Charlotte, as described in the last two tours.

The annual Lyceum Program offers a number of public lectures, readings, and spoken-word events. A student-run writing group, the Black Ink Monks, hosts monthly poetry slams on campus, and the organization's members often perform at other venues in the city. Check the university website for current events. <http://www.jcsu.edu>

■ MOUNT HOLLY

Proceed on Beatties Ford Road for 7.7 miles and turn left on Mt. Holly Huntersville Road. In 6.7 miles, the road merges with NC 27 and continues across the Catawba River to enter the town of Mount Holly and, at the same time, Gaston County, so named in 1846 for Judge William J. Gaston of New Bern. Gaston served on the state Supreme Court, was a member and financial backer of North Carolina's fledgling Catholic Church at the time, and was an outspoken abolitionist and advocate for free black suffrage. Also an occasional poet, Gaston wrote "The Old North State," which eventually was put to music, in 1927, and became North Carolina's official song: "Then let all those who love us, love the land that we live in, / As happy a region as on this side of heaven."

NC 27 is called East Charlotte Avenue within Mount Holly, and the railroad track running parallel to it was the first to be laid in the county, in 1860. Mount Holly got its name in 1875, when the Mount Holly Cotton Mill (honoring the New Jersey textile town of the same name) opened on North Main Street. It is now the oldest surviving mill building in the county.

From scores of farms in the region, heavy loads of ginned cotton came riding the rails into towns like Mount Holly, Belmont, and Gastonia. Thousands of people from the mountains and foothills, who came here also by rail seeking work, fashioned the cotton into yarn and cloth. According to North Carolina historian Kathy Ackerman, in *The Heart of Revolution: The Radical Life and*

Machinery sits idle in a textile mill in Mount Holly.

Novels of Olive Tilford Dargan, Gastonia by 1927 "had more looms and spindles within a radius of a hundred miles than any other southern city and more textile plants than any other country in the world" (68). By 1939, Gaston County could lay claim to producing 80 percent of the finest combed cotton yarn in the United States.

Stories of twentieth-century mill workers are still told here, though the old plants where they worked three shifts a day are increasingly being put to other uses. In Mount Holly, the center of operations for the city itself is in a retrofitted mill beside the railroad tracks alongside NC 27.

From 27, turn left on South Main Street, park, and have a look around this recently renovated historic town center. Imagine Mount Holly in its textile heyday through this narrative poem by Gastonia newspaperman Stewart Atkins, who as a teenager was one of the founders of the North Carolina Poetry Society. Atkins's story of hardship, common among mill workers, takes its theme from many a sad song of despair and rebellion from the era.

LOVE IN A COTTON MILL
Whirring spindles spin swiftly under the blue electric
    night-time daylight,
And I stood and watched her.

She had lips that made you think of ripe cherries in the
 sun and her hair was spun red-gold.
She was the fastest girl in the mill at her machine. Her
 hands moved like lightning.
Her name was Naida. Maybe she read it in a book. She
 read a lot of books. (She went up through the
 seventh grade in school before her old man made
 her quit to go to work.)
Her sisters were named Ruth, Mary, Margaret—things
 like that.
Her parents named her Martha.
But she changed it when she got old enough to read.
Her eyes were yellow-green, and I loved her.
Probably I fell in love with her the first time I saw her standing by her
 machine.
But I realized it only gradually.
The boss gave us half an hour for a breathing spell at
 midnight.
Somehow, she and I got in the habit of sitting out on the concrete mill
 steps, eating our lunch together,
 smoking cigarettes, drinking Coca-Cola, looking
 at the stars, and talking.
She told me how she hated the mill, the people, the
 surroundings, how she wanted to get away to go to
 college and be somebody.
One night I missed her from her machine.
The next day I went to her home.
She was sick.
There was no money for a doctor.
The company doctor came, felt her pulse, took her
 temperature.
"Give her some aspirin," he said wearily. "She'll be
 all right."
The next week she died.
I've quit crying now. But I hate the mill—since she's
 gone.
The new girl at her machine is slow and gets things in
 a hell of a mess.

She's gone, and her old man has to do without his
　　Saturday-night quart now.
She's gone and at midnight my cigarettes don't taste
　　good anymore, and my Coca-Cola sticks in my
　　throat.
—From *The Halting Gods*, by Stewart Atkins (Emory University, Ga.:
　　Banner Press, 1952), 16–17. Courtesy of Emory University.

Cigarettes and Coca-Cola, Milky Way candy bars and the night drone of heavy machinery are details that enliven a 1932 novel about Gaston County by Sherwood Anderson, best known for his 1919 novel in stories, *Winesburg, Ohio*. His lyrical language conveys the repetitive motion and music of the mill:

In a cotton mill at night. You are working there. There is a roar of sound—a sustained roar—now low, now high—big sounds . . . little sounds. There is a singing—a shouting—a talking. There are whispers. There is laughter. Thread laughs. It whispers. It runs softly and swiftly. It leaps. Thread is like a young goat on the mountains of the moon. Thread is like a little hair snake running into a hole. It runs softly and swiftly. Steel can laugh. It can cry out. Looms in a cotton mill are like baby elephants playing with mother elephants in a forest. Who can understand inanimate life? A river coming down out of a hill, over rocks, through a quiet glade, can make you love it. Hills and fields can win your love as can also steel made into a machine. Machines dance. They dance on their iron legs. They sing, whisper, groan, laugh. You get woozy headed sometimes seeing and hearing all the things going on in a mill. It is worse at night. It is better, wilder, more exciting at night. It tires you more.—From *Beyond Desire*, by Sherwood Anderson (New York: Liveright Publishing, 1961), 282.

Continue south on South Main Street in Mount Holly, which soon runs into NC 273. Follow 273 a few more blocks to a fork and bear right on old 273, also known as Belmont–Mount Holly Road.

■ BELMONT ABBEY

Ahead on the left is the extraordinary campus of Belmont Abbey College. This private, liberal arts school and monastery dates from 1876 and is still tended by a group of Benedictine monks, for whom theology, literature, and gardening are intense pursuits. In the early 1960s, future North Carolina poet

Belmont Abbey College was founded in 1876 by Benedictine monks, who occupy
a monastery on the grounds. Popular North Carolina poet-in-the-schools
Chuck Sullivan was a basketball standout here.

Chuck Sullivan came here from New York City to play college basketball. He was
recruited by the voluble Al McGuire, who had been hired by Belmont Abbey for
his first head coaching job following his career as an NBA player.

An aggressive recruiter, McGuire often traveled to New York City, seeking
talent on the asphalt courts of Manhattan. He reportedly brandished photos of
the quad at Duke University, telling his young prospects that the Gothic campus was Belmont Abbey's. McGuire was also known for his creative use of language, referring to referees as "zebras" and college administrators as "memos
and pipes."

McGuire's acolyte, Chuck Sullivan, went on to become a popular poet in the
schools, touring North Carolina as "a circuit rider for the cause of verse," as he

puts it. Sullivan wrote the following poem for the former athletic moderator at Belmont Abbey. The poem is rendered in calligraphy on a banner that hangs in the monastery on campus.

THE CHIME OF LOVE AND HONOR (EXCERPT)
For Father Raphael Bridge O.S.B.
The hushed rowdy roundball congregation
Of The Fox and his Yankee Crusaders
Bent to worship on the cold floor
Before an early morning Abbey altar

Our Faith flickering shadows
Confessed by all the candles'
Working out of salvation
In the chilled crypt's light

And with the world just dying
For first light there we were
Wise guys on our knees
Needful and greedy for grace
In the Abbey's cellar of belief
Out of which the cathedral
daily spires toward
Belmont's rising hidden sun.
—From *Zen Matchbox*, by Chuck Sullivan (Charlotte: Main Street Rag Publishing Company, 2008), 29.

■ **BELMONT**

Continue south on Belmont–Mount Holly Road across I-85. The Gaston County Visitors' Center is immediately on the left, should you require a map or additional local information. Ahead is Belmont's Main Street leading into the thriving downtown where there are several possible spots for a meal, local antiques, and ice cream. Belmont is another mill town where a single textile family—the Stowes—is largely responsible for the town's assets, including an attractive park and amphitheater in the town center, used year-round for concerts, festivals, and other community events, and Daniel Stowe Botanical Garden, a 450-acre preserve and formal garden eight miles south of Belmont near Lake Wylie.

Huntersville journalist and historian LeGette Blythe wrote about the

Stowe family. Among his many volumes documenting the lives of prominent North Carolinians, such as the Penland School's Lucy Morgan and Crossnore's Dr. Mary Martin Sloop (discussed in volume 1 of *Literary Trails*), Blythe also produced *Robert Lee Stowe, Pioneer in Textiles* in 1965, a book that offers a glimpse of Gaston's history and a perspective on the industry that defined it for so long.

To visit the county seat of Gastonia, take US 74 west from Belmont.

■ GASTONIA

That week something unusual happened at the mill. People at work at their looms or frames suddenly found themselves being watched by strange men. If one of them went for a drink of water, the man stood looking at his watch, and put down something in a book when they came back. It was very distressing, for the watching kept up over several days....

In the third week hank clocks were installed on the machines, and people were paid by the time the hank clock registered....

Automatic spoolers were put in, and when this was done thirty-five people were used where one hundred and sixty had been used before. Weavers who had tended eight to twenty looms now had nearly one hundred each: but when it was found that people fainted too often the number was reduced a little. Most of the women had to give up weaving.
—From *To Make My Bread*, by Grace Lumpkin (Champaign: University of
  Illinois Press, 1995), 329.

In this 1932 novel, Georgia writer Grace Lumpkin describes "the stretch out" that occurred in Gastonia and in other mill towns in the 1920s, which led to an unprecedented period of violence and unrest in the region. In the 1920s, mill owners began demanding increased productivity while decreasing workers' pay. Layoffs followed the installation of machinery that promised greater efficiency in the production of thread and cloth. Mill workers, already living in poverty, were being forced to stretch out the workday and speed up their efforts or lose their jobs.

To see Gastonia's Loray Mill, the site of the most famous labor strike of the era, continue on US 74 (East Franklin Boulevard), which becomes West Franklin as it crosses Marietta Street in the center of downtown Gastonia. (Main Avenue, one block north, runs parallel to Franklin.) Continue on West Franklin across US 321 and soon you will see Loray towering five stories above West Gastonia. It is 0.7 miles from 321 to Firestone Street, named for the company that last occupied the old mill building. Turn left on Firestone and right on Second Avenue to

Gastonia's Loray Mill was the site of a dramatic strike in 1929 that resulted in the publication of at least six novels in the 1930s. Sherwood Anderson and Olive Tilford Dargan were among those who wrote about the bloody worker uprising here.

get a closer look at the site and the surrounding houses that yet survive in the neighborhood.

The worker uprising that took place at Gastonia's Loray Mill in 1929 was so dramatic that in the 1930s no fewer than six novels were written that aimed to portray, through fiction, developments in the organized labor movement, including the rising influence of the Communist Party. Among them was Sherwood Anderson's *Beyond Desire* and William Rollins's experimental *The Shadow Before*. Critics panned both of these novels, and they have gone out of print. Four novels by women writers of the era have been republished in recent years, as feminist scholars and university presses have discovered their value as part of the historical record.

In addition to the politically charged novel by Grace Lumpkin, who disavowed her Communist sympathies later in life, Dorothy Myra Page, a white southerner, published her novel, *Gathering Storm: A Story of the Black Belt*, in the Soviet Union and made no pretense about its strident political agenda. As Glenda Gilmore explains in *Defying Dixie: The Radical Roots of Civil Rights*, "Its theme was the triumph of class solidarity over traditional racial divisions" (91).

Page effectively depicts the sometimes strained efforts at solidarity among previously segregated black and white mill workers and the lynchings and other horrific consequences suffered by African Americans, who joined ranks with their white counterparts.

But perhaps the most evenhanded novel of the period came from Mary Heaton Vorse, a journalist who had been covering the labor movement in the United States since 1912 and managed to get to Gastonia ahead of most of the rest of the national press to report on events as they unfolded for *Harper's*. Vorse lived in a boardinghouse for six weeks with one of the northern organizers of the Gastonia strike.

The result — Vorse's 1930 novel *Strike!* — is well written and perhaps comes closest to the actual events of the day. She tells the story through the eyes of two different journalists — both male. When Roger Hewlett arrives in Gastonia, he drops his bag at the hotel and takes a jitney to the mill village:

> A huge and silent mill dominated the community. Around it was the mill village, running crazily up and down hill, every house like the other, bare wooden shacks standing in red mud on brick stilts. The little houses seemed like a flock of chicks beside a monstrous hen, as if the mill had hatched them from square wooden eggs. Well, in a way, it had, Roger reflected. — From *Strike!*, by Mary Heaton Vorse (Champaign: University of Illinois Press, 1991), 4.

It was here that the drama began developing, on April 1, 1929, when some 1,800 workers, led by a small band of Communist organizers, began their strike against the Loray Mill. Responding to reports of the presence of "Communist agitators from the North," the governor, Max Gardner, sent in the National Guard, though the troops were conspicuously absent on the night that a mob destroyed union headquarters. Police arrested a number of strikers, many of whom soon returned to work.

Undaunted, women from the mill villages continued to picket Loray. As April turned to May, some of these women were beaten and arrested. Eventually, some sixty-two striking families were evicted from company housing and began living in makeshift tents supplied by strike organizers.

In June, local police raided the tent village. The able-bodied male workers — mountain men who had always kept their rifles handy — could stand no more. They fought back. Four Gastonia police officers were wounded, and the chief of police was shot and died the next day, though it was never clear whether the culprits were some police officers under the influence of alcohol during the raid.

Whipped up by the local press, a mob of Gastonia professionals and other citizens sympathetic to the mill owners rushed in and destroyed the tent village. The Communist leaders of the strike and fourteen others were arrested and charged with conspiracy to murder.

Reporters from across the nation now poured into town to witness the bizarre events that followed, including a wax figure of the murdered police chief dressed in his bloody uniform and trotted into the trial as part of the prosecution's case. Mary Vorse gave fictional names to most of the characters in her novel who were based on real people, but she did not disguise Shelby-attorney-turned-novelist Thomas A. Dixon, author of *The Clansman* (which became the basis for the film *Birth of a Nation*). Dixon makes a cameo appearance in the courthouse as a lawyer deputized to stand guard during the trial, and Vorse hints that he was among the rush of hooded citizens who had descended on the tent village.

Ultimately the court declared a mistrial, and violence once again erupted, stretching into Charlotte and elsewhere. During this episode, the local labor movement's beloved singer and songwriter Ella Mae Wiggins—only twenty-nine years old and the mother of nine children—was shot in the chest as she rode in a truck on her way to a union rally. She was buried as the mourners sang her most famous song, "The Mill Mother's Lament":

We leave our homes in the morning,
We kiss our children good-bye,
While we slave for the bosses
Our children scream and cry.

And when we draw our money,
Our grocery bills to pay,
Not a cent to spend for clothing,
Not a cent to lay away.

A second trial took place in the fall of 1929 that involved another round of high drama in the courtroom and resulted in seven convictions. The Communist organizers jumped bail and fled to the Soviet Union.

Asheville poet, playwright, and short-story writer Olive Tilford Dargan had never attempted a novel before finding herself so moved by the events in Gastonia that she started *Call Home the Heart*. This fictional account is based loosely on the story of Ella Mae Wiggins. Dargan published it in 1932 under the pseudonym Fielding Burke.

The Storyteller—*a sculpture by artist Frank Creech*—
is on permanent display in the Gaston County Library.

Dargan's novel influenced contemporary North Carolina novelist Pamela Duncan to write *Plant Life* (2003), a novel that addresses the challenges of North Carolina's female mill workers in the present era of free trade and cheap foreign labor. Likewise, contemporary Raleigh playwright June Guralnick loosely based her play *Finding Clara* on the 1929 strike at the Loray Mill. Ella May Wiggins's grandson was in the audience for the production, mounted by the Southern Appalachian Regional Theater in 2002.

Another contemporary writer who deals with this watershed era in North Carolina history is Flora Ann Scearce of Carteret County. She wrote two novels, *Singer of an Empty Day* (1997) and *Cotton Mill Girl* (2006), after finding a journal kept by her mother, Sippy.

Return to downtown Gastonia on West Main Avenue. Since the late 1970s Gastonia has become a town divided by the Southern Railway line, which sits well below street level in a curious concrete ravine (on your left). On the north side of the track are most of the county and city government buildings; on the south side is what remains of historic downtown Gastonia. Local writer Timothy Craig Ellis has published several volumes of local history and lore and maintains a website, <http://www.vintagegastonia.com>, which offers travelers more information on the local architecture. Ellis is also the curator of the Loray Historical Collection at Loray Baptist Church.

Two other, more lighthearted Gastonia books deserve mention. Max Childers's 1993 comic novel, *Alpha Omega*, offers the story of a man released from prison in South Carolina who takes a bus back home to Gastonia to put his newfound rock-and-roll skills to work in his quest to become the next Elvis Presley. Jeff Diamant's *Heist! The $17 Million Loomis Fargo Theft* chronicles the absurd but true story of an employee of Loomis Fargo. He made off with a truckload of cash and fled to Mexico but left his loot in the care of married friends. When they moved from a trailer into a $635,000 mansion near Crowder's Mountain, in Gaston County, and paid in full for a Toyota minivan with twenty-dollar bills, the FBI caught on. (Diamant originally covered the story for the *Charlotte Observer*.)

■ LITERARY LANDSCAPE

Gaston County Public Library
1555 East Garrison Boulevard, Gastonia
704-868-2164
<http://www.glrl.lib.nc.us/>
The North Carolina Room has a wealth of materials pertaining to the textile era and its music. For many years, librarian Carol Reinhardt has made Gaston County a literary destination, organizing readings and workshops, often with a multi-arts slant.

Matthews : Monroe : Wingate : Marshville : Wadesboro : Rockingham : Hamlet

Go back in time from contemporary Charlotte to the era when cotton was king and agricultural life was dominant in the southernmost part of North Carolina. This rural landscape comes alive in the poetry and prose of a surprising crop of writers.

Writers with a connection to this area: Daniel Bailey, Joseph Bathanti, Jonathan Daniels, Virginia DeBerry, Donna Grant, Jaki Shelton Green, Langston Hughes, Mary Kratt, John Lawson, Sharyn McCrumb, Lawrence Naumoff, Louis D. Rubin Jr., Gene Stowe, Timothy Tyson, Alice Walker, Carole Boston Weatherford, Tom Wicker, Robert F. Williams

Whenever I push my shovel deep into my Carolina red-clay garden, I wonder what lies hidden. Usually I find only cutworms, roots, a stone; but just when I forget to be watchful, my hoe clinks against metal: a harness ring from a plow horse long ago, a pale green medicine bottle, a white shard of china with a faint wisp of blue design. Since we bought this knoll and field five years ago, I have grown accustomed to the knowledge of other women who have worked this earth and lived in a house on the foundation stones that still lie beneath the great oaks. Great-grandmother was born here. These pieces of their lives waited like fragments of a message from these and other southern women and men who knew and now rest from the freedom and tyranny of the land.

I live on the edge of a shiny New South city that is far more concerned with its modern image than with history. The question is, "How do we look? How fast are we suc-

tour 8

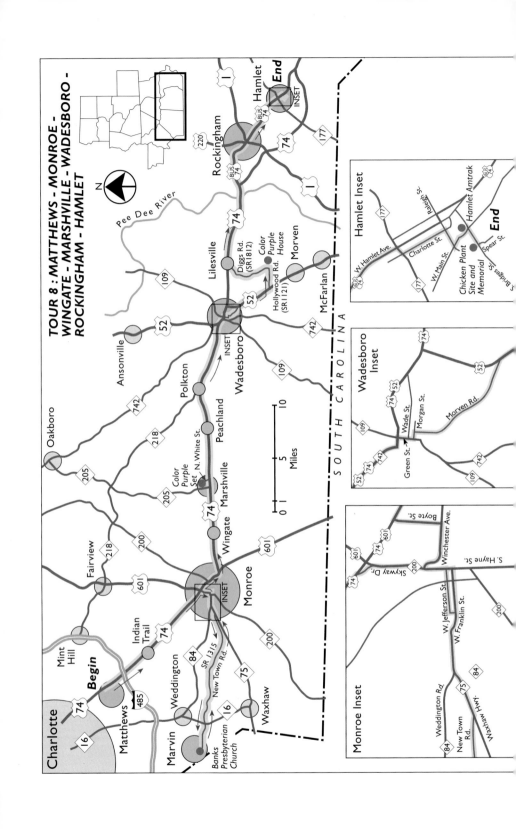

TOUR 8: MATTHEWS - MONROE - WINGATE - MARSHVILLE - WADESBORO - ROCKINGHAM - HAMLET

ceeding?" Rarely do I hear, "Who are we and where did we come from? How did we make this journey?"

—From "Finding the Pieces," in *The Only Thing I Fear Is a Cow and a Drunken Man*, by Mary Kratt (Durham: Carolina Wren Press, 1991), vii.

■ MATTHEWS

Charlotte's suburban sprawl follows us for a time on this tour as we head east. Along our route, new subdivisions seem to spring up like mushrooms after an autumn rain, but they will soon give way to signs of the past such as those that Mary Kratt wrote about from her home place on nearby Sardis Road. Begin by heading southeast on US 74, which in Charlotte is known as East Independence Boulevard. Before leaving Mecklenburg County, you'll pass through the burgeoning community of Matthews, originally called Stumptown for the remnants of trees that studded the landscape as farmers began clearing the land for cotton planting in the early 1800s. Matthews today is an affluent bedroom community with a quaint downtown (off 74 to the right on Sam Newell Road).

Matthews is also home to regional mystery writer Daniel Bailey, who worked for many years as chief deputy sheriff of Mecklenburg County before his appointment as sheriff, in 2008. Bailey oversees the largest sheriff's jurisdiction between Washington and Atlanta, which makes his second career as a mystery writer rather remarkable. His first two novels, set in South Carolina, are *Justice Betrayed* and *Execute the Office*.

Beyond Matthews, 74 crosses into Union County and passes through the town of Indian Trail. The Waxhaw Indians originally occupied this area. They built sturdy lodges and farmed an expanse of land that stretched from south of today's Charlotte as far west as Monroe. In the eighteenth century, British explorer John Lawson traversed this area on his survey of the Carolina interior and wrote enthusiastically in his journal about how well the Waxhaw people lived:

Upon our Arrival, we were led into a very large and lightsome Cabin, the like I have not met withal. They laid Furs and Deer-Skins upon Cane Benches for us to sit or lie upon, bringing (immediately) stewed Peaches and green Corn, that is preserv'd in their Cabins before it is ripe, and sodden and boil'd when they use it, which is a pretty sort of Food, and a great Increaser of the Blood.—From *A New Voyage to Carolina*, by John Lawson (1709), <http://docsouth.unc.edu/nc/lawson/lawson.html>, 33.

Unfortunately, it would take only two decades for the Waxhaw people to be nearly wiped out by contact with European settlers who brought smallpox and other diseases with them to the Carolinas.

This area also lays claim to two U.S. presidents: James K. Polk, born in Mecklenburg County near Pineville, and Andrew Jackson, whose birthplace is disputed. He was born either near Waxhaw in Union County or just across the state line, in South Carolina.

■ MONROE

In fifteen miles we come to Monroe, the county seat of Union County and the place where, in 1888, William Henry Belk, at the age of twenty-six, opened a department store he called the New York Racket. Belk sold bargain items from his 1,500-square-foot store downtown and was instantly successful. He soon convinced his brother, John Belk, a physician, to give up his practice and join him. Over the years, the Belk brothers built the largest privately owned department store chain in the nation. Their story was first documented in the biography *William Henry Belk: Merchant of the South*, written by Huntersville journalist LeGette Blythe.

To visit downtown Monroe, turn right on Skyway Drive (NC 200). You'll soon come into Monroe's historic district, which sits on a hill with the old courthouse at the highest point. The original Union County courthouse, dating back to 1886 and now restored, is one block east of Skyway Drive. The building houses a significant collection of archival materials about the county's heritage.

Monroe is probably best known as the hometown of the late Jesse Helms, one of North Carolina's longest-serving and most controversial senators, who was first elected in 1973 and retired from his seat in 2003. Helms's father, "Big Jessie," was Monroe's police chief for many years and was the focal point of a story often told by another Monroe native, who aspired to be a writer but instead became involved in politics and then exiled himself from the United States.

Robert F. Williams was eleven years old in 1936. One September day he happened to be downtown when police chief Helms began battering a black woman with his fists. The woman collapsed to the pavement, and Helms literally dragged her to the jail. White onlookers laughed; black men stood by watching in pained silence. As historian Timothy Tyson, born in Raleigh, North Carolina, writes, Williams never forgot the scene nor his shame and anger:

Robert Williams repeated this searing story to friends, readers, listeners, reporters, and historians. In the late 1950s, Williams used the story to help

The Union County Courthouse in Monroe dates from 1886 and houses historic memorabilia and genealogical archives.

inspire African American domestic workers and military veterans of Monroe to build the most militant chapter of the National Association for the Advancement of Colored People (NAACP) in the United States.... It contributed to the fervor of his widely published debate with Martin Luther King Jr. in 1960 and fueled his hesitant bids for leadership in the black freedom struggle. Its merciless truths must have tightened in his fingers on the night in 1961 when he fled Ku Klux Klan terrorists and a Federal Bureau of Investigation (FBI) dragnet with this wife and two small children, a machine gun slung over one shoulder. Williams revisited the bitter memory on platforms that he shared with Fidel Castro, Ho Chi Minh, and Mao Zedong. He told it over "Radio Free Dixie," his regular program on Radio Havana from 1962 to 1965.—From *Radio Free Dixie: Robert F. Williams and the Roots of Black Power,* by Timothy B. Tyson (Chapel Hill: University of North Carolina Press, 1999), 2.

Tyson's biography tells the story of Williams's lifelong political struggles and his perpetual effort to challenge the status quo within the civil rights movement. *Radio Free Dixie* could be heard at night on the AM airwaves, even in North Carolina.

From this modest town, both Robert Williams and Senator Jesse Helms became controversial figures. Of course, Williams's story is the lesser known. The reason he spent so many years outside the country, according to biographer Tyson, was that the FBI's preoccupation with his connections to leaders in the Communist Party (which he never joined) caused him to fear for his family's safety.

In the 1960s, Williams took a firm stand against Martin Luther King Jr.'s tenets of nonviolence. The world he had experienced in Monroe, he said, was far too dangerous for a man or woman not to carry the protection of firearms, as guaranteed by the second amendment to the Constitution. Years before the Black Panther movement, Williams encouraged his African American neighbors to bear arms and prepare "to meet violence with violence." He joined the National Rifle Association in 1950.

As a young man, Williams first left Monroe to work in auto manufacturing in Detroit while his wife, Mabel, stayed behind to open a day-care center. (Mabel's mother worked as a maid for the Belk family, and Mabel was named for one of the Belk daughters.) Williams enrolled for a time at Elizabeth City State, served briefly in the army at the end of World War II, and then continued his education at West Virginia State College, in 1949. He transferred to the North Carolina College for Negroes (now North Carolina Central University) in Durham and ultimately returned to Monroe to enroll at Johnson C. Smith, in Charlotte, where his grandfather had also studied following his emancipation from slavery. He also served for a year in the Marine Corps following his graduation from college.

Williams dreamed of a literary career and was already publishing poetry during his school years. His first notable prose piece came out in *Freedom*, a New York City newspaper published by Paul Robeson. As Tim Tyson reports, the "story appeared on the same page with an article by young Lorraine Hansberry, who would soon begin work on her classic play *A Raisin in the Sun*" (69).

While at Johnson C. Smith, Williams met Harlem Renaissance poet Langston Hughes, who apparently came to campus while visiting relatives in Charlotte. Hughes encouraged the young poet to pursue a career as a writer, but Williams would soon publish a poem expressing what would become his life's work—not literature but activism:

GO AWAKEN MY PEOPLE

Go awaken my people wherever they sleep
Tell them that we have a rendezvous to keep;

Go tell my people that the dawn is on the scene,
Tell them to behold a sight the world has never seen.
Go tell my people that the night is in the past;
Tell them that the dawn of heaven breaks upon the world at last.
Let them harken to the trumpet, the thunder of the drum;
Go awaken my people sound the great alarm!
Go tell my people that John Brown's spirit sweeps the universe;
Tell them the tide of freedom rises as the dams of oppression burst.
Go tell my people to enter their standard in fight,
Tell them to break their chains and throw their fears to the night.
Go awaken my people from Texas to Virginia,
Tell them of our glorious brothers in the colony of Kenya.
Go tell my people that the dawn has come,
Sound the trumpet beat the drum!
Let the tyrant shudder, let the oppressor tremble at the thunder,
For the tide of humanity rises to sweep the despot under.
Go awaken my people wherever they sleep,
Tell them that we have a rendezvous that we must keep.
—Used by permission of Mabel R. Williams and John C. Williams.

Stories of racial violence, Klan activity, and lynching are a dominant theme in the written and oral histories of Union County. One more recent book, however, offers a surprising story from the early twentieth century.

Former *Charlotte Observer* reporter Gene Stowe's *Inherit the Land: Jim Crow Meets Miss Maggie's Will* documents the history of three white women—Susan Ross and her daughters, Maggie and Sallie—who took a black child, Bob Ross, into their home and "raised him as an equal member of the family." Bob eventually married and he and his wife and later their daughter remained in the Ross household. Maggie and Sallie, who never married, wrote identical wills bequeathing their home place to the African American Rosses, but Maggie's will was ferociously challenged by relatives after her death in 1920.

Stowe explains that Maggie Ross was related to the governor of North Carolina at the time and was the richest woman in Union County when she died. She left the Bob Ross family not only her house but also hundreds of dollars, two gold watches, and 800 acres near Marvin, a little village due west of Monroe, nearly on the South Carolina state line. As Stowe tells it, the court case that challenged the will was dramatic. The prevailing beliefs that informed the testimony of the white relatives were harsh:

No jury in the south would give a black man and a black woman eight hundred acres in a white community, especially when 109 of Maggie's cousins were claiming the land. This was the white man's world. Maggie supped with black people; slept in the same bed as a little black girl; shared shoes, dresses, even underwear.... Southern women with sense didn't act that way. Such testimony proved that she wasn't simply sentimental or sometimes charitable with these people. She wasn't just doting; she was a dotard.—From *Inherit the Land: Jim Crow Meets Miss Maggie's Will*, by Gene Stowe (Jackson: University Press of Mississippi, 2006), 4.

Stowe, a Monroe native, began writing about the court case in the 1990s as a series for the *Charlotte Observer*. After meeting the descendants of Bob and Mittie Bell Ross, he was so taken with the tale that he then wrote several drafts of a novel on the subject. However, once he got his hands on the transcripts of the trial, Stowe realized he needed to write a nonfiction account. Or, as one of his friends quipped, the book is actually "a true story based on a novel."

As it turned out, the all-white jury in Monroe found in favor of Miss Maggie's wishes and allowed the land to remain in the hands of the Bob Ross family and, Stowe says, loosened forever the cultural proscriptions surrounding interracial land transactions in the county.

Readers of Stowe's book can visit the crossroads of Marvin by taking West Franklin Street (NC 75/84) out of Monroe. Follow 75 west as it forks to the left toward Waxhaw and then watch for New Town Road, which soon comes up on the right. Follow New Town Road, which will cross the railroad tracks and make its way some fifteen miles to Marvin, not far beyond the intersection with NC 16. Look for the old Marvin Methodist Church on the right. Just beyond is an open area where the Ross sisters' house once stood. (It has been moved by relatives to Mecklenburg County and restored.) Park at the Banks Presbyterian Church on the right and cross the road to visit the graves of Maggie (Margaret) and Sallie (Sarah) Ross. They are buried on the far left side of the church cemetery. The African American Rosses are buried in the old AME Zion Church cemetery nearby, though that congregation has also moved its church building a few miles away.

Backtrack to downtown Monroe, turning back north on Skyway Drive. Once across the railroad tracks, take the next right onto Winchester Avenue and travel eight blocks east. Turn left on Boyte Street. This was Robert Williams's neighborhood. Boyte continues ahead to US 74. Turn right on 74 to continue the tour.

■ WINGATE

A few miles east of Monroe is the village of Wingate, where the Jesse Helms Center houses the papers and memorabilia of the late senator and is open to the public. Wingate University's attractive campus, festooned with crepe myrtles and bisected by the railroad, is on the left side of US 74. This Baptist-affiliated, four-year private school emphasizes the liberal arts.

■ MARSHVILLE

Marshville, the birthplace of country singer/songwriter Randy Travis, is the next town along this route. Watch for Main Street coming in on the left and continue to the next traffic light at White Street. Turn left on White. This block was used as the setting for the in-town scenes in the film version of Alice Walker's epistolary novel *The Color Purple*. According to *The Film Junkie's Guide to North Carolina*, by Connie Nelson and Floyd Harris, the moviemakers hauled in dirt to cover the pavement and laid down planks over the sidewalks to re-create the novel's turn-of-the-century Georgia village, where the characters occasionally shopped for provisions. You can still see the word "Livery" painted on the brick facade of Marshville Auto Body, on the right. On the left is the storefront where the characters Celie (played by Whoopie Goldberg) and Sophia (Oprah Winfrey) shopped.

From Marshville, continue east and cross the county line into Anson County, also known as the Bluebird Kingdom of the World, as a sign on US 74 proclaims. In the 1940s, the ever-eloquent Jonathan Daniels of the *Raleigh News and Observer* wrote a poignant portrait of Anson County and one of its most prominent residents, Hugh Bennett, an environmentalist ahead of his time:

Anson County, where Hugh Bennett was born, is on the Pee Dee River, which Stephen Foster considered first when he searched the map for a two syllable Southern river about which to make a song of homesickness. He chose Suwannee at last, which has certainly fitted into the world's mouth, but the Pee Dee is home, too, of the old folk and the old land. Up above the big power plants and huge aluminum works it is the Yadkin River and runs, swift and tawny, from green mountains behind the estates of the Winston-Salem millionaires through the big lakes to make more power and drain more land than any other river in North Carolina. Earth has gone off with the rain. The river is not to blame. Riches grow now behind the blue windows of textile factories beside it, and far away, too, at the end of the long power lines which run back from it. But riches also went down it to South Carolina and the sea for decades before it was harnessed. Rich earth goes down it still, not to come back. —From "The Rivers Are Red," in *Tar Heels*, by Jonathan Daniels (New York: Dodd, Meade, 1941), 174–75.

Daniels goes on to tell about Hugh Bennett's campaign to introduce new agricultural practices to halt severe soil erosion in the area. Thanks to Bennett, Anson County claims the first official soil and water conservation district ever designated. As Daniels also points out, Bennett's preaching about conservation in the 1930s invoked the central thesis of Thomas Wolfe's last novel, *You Can't Go Home Again*: "There really is no such thing," Bennett said, "as returning to the places and people you remember from your youth. You realize that, on this old earth with its endless changing processes, we are all transient visitors; and you begin to count your score" (176).

Of course, the mills and factories Daniels writes about in *Tar Heels* are now industrial dinosaurs, and the Anson County landscape still remains distressed in places. In the poem "Drought," Appalachian State English professor Joseph Bathanti writes: "The corn chants / to be buried in August / It prays the land / lie fallow / under merciful heaven" (from *Anson County*, by Joseph Bathanti [Boone, N.C.: Parkway Publishers, 2005], 23).

Bathanti takes his readers to dozens of stops on the back roads of Anson County in this poetry collection and invokes the ghosts of those who have labored over the land for centuries. Anson also inspired the setting for Bathanti's haunting 2006 novel, *Coventry*, a mysterious and bleak story of prison life told from the points of view of both guards and their captives.

■ WADESBORO

At the city limits of Wadesboro on US 74, note the historical marker commemorating environmentalist Hugh Bennett's birthplace. Ahead is a wide boulevard leading into Wadesboro, the county seat of Anson County, another town, like Monroe, set on a hillside. To visit the uptown area, follow 74 to the intersection of NC 109 (Green Street) and turn right. On your right you'll see the Anson County courthouse, which has a bit part as the immigration office in the film version of *The Color Purple*.

Inviting benches, set around town, encourage visitors to tarry. An effort is also under way to restore the town's 1925 theater, the Ansonia (one block east of Green), where both Gene Autry and Roy Rogers made appearances in the 1950s.

Wadesboro has a number of galleries and museums. A neighborhood of striking houses, many dating back to the antebellum period and some open to the public, flanks the uptown area near the cemetery. *Far from the Tree*, a novel by the New York writing team of Virginia DeBerry and Donna Grant, is set on the outskirts of Wadesboro. Grant and DeBerry met in Manhattan as models and became close friends. Together they launched the fashion magazine *Maxima* before moving into their successful literary collaboration, which to date has resulted in five novels created over a decade. In *Far from the Tree*, sisters Celeste English and Ronnie Frazier are surprised when they inherit an old house in Prosper, North Carolina, at their father's death—an asset they didn't even know belonged to their large African American family. Before putting the house on the market, the sisters decide that they need to see the old home place. Ronnie flies from New York to Charlotte, where a real estate agent meets her at the airport. He describes the town as they make their way east on US 74:

"Prosper itself appears pretty typical. Small southern town full of personal history and mystery. A lot has probably changed since your family left and a lot is likely the same as forty years ago. Population hasn't fluctuated, one way or the other, more than a hundred people in over sixty years. Depending on who's counting, the racial mix is about even. There's a brand new Winn-Dixie, and a small radio station. The house was fairly large for its time, not many that big owned by us. And you've got a good-sized piece of land."—From *Far from the Tree*, by Virginia DeBerry and Donna Grant (New York: Macmillan, 2004), 146.

From here, we proceed to another location used in the filming of Alice Walker's *The Color Purple*, not far outside Wadesboro, but a full tank of fuel is a good idea because the area is sparsely populated and service stations are few.

DIRECTIONS

From the intersection of Green (NC 109) and Wade in the center of Wadesboro, proceed south one block and turn left on East Morgan and then take the first right on Morven Road, which will merge with US 52 south within a mile. Follow 52 past Country Club Road on your left and then watch for Hollywood Road, also on your left, where you will turn. (Hollywood Road used to be called Wastewater Treatment Center Road before the movie makers came to town!) Proceed on Hollywood until it dead-ends at Diggs Road.

The private, tree-lined driveway straight ahead that leads up to the house is off-limits, but turn left on Diggs, and you'll soon see a place to pull over on the side of the road to get a good view of the classic farmhouse with front porches

The elegant Anson County farmhouse that appears in the movie version of Alice Walker's novel The Color Purple *is now a private residence plainly visible from Diggs Road outside Wadesboro.*

on the first and second stories that comes early in the film as the residence of Mister.

According to a special feature in the 1995 Warner Brothers DVD edition of the film, Spielberg's crew constructed buildings and other temporary facades on this property during the summer they spent filming here. In ninety-five-degree heat they even managed to create a mock snowstorm across the Anson landscape using Epsom salts and a biodegradable flocking material.

Continue north on Diggs Road until it runs into 74 and turn right (east) to continue the tour.

■ ROCKINGHAM

The Richmond County towns of Rockingham and Hamlet have begun to blur boundaries, but on 74 going east Rockingham comes first after you cross the Pee Dee River. To see the heart of this town of tree-lined streets and handsome old houses, take 74 Business through Piney Grove and into town, rather than I-74 (also known as the G. R. Kendley Freeway/Andrew Jackson Highway), which bypasses both Rockingham and Hamlet to the east and south. As 74 Business narrows to two lanes at Five Points, it becomes Rockingham's West Broad Avenue.

Rockingham is a stop for the NASCAR pilgrims in Sharyn McCrumb's novel *St. Dale*. McCrumb's characters come to lay a wreath at the now-defunct North Carolina Motor Speedway, aka "The Rock," to honor their fallen hero, racer Dale Earnhardt. But before the ceremony, the group stops for lunch in a barbecue restaurant draped in checkered flags and festooned with Earnhardt photos and memorabilia:

> The Intimidator stared down at the restaurant's patrons, stern faced in his black and white Goodwrench firesuit, his eyes obscured by the usual dark sunglasses. A glass fronted curio cabinet from the Hickory Furniture Market displayed die cast replicas of the number 3 Monte Carlo and its predecessors, along with a collection of Earnhardt caps, coffee mugs, statuettes, framed 8 × 10 photos, and glass-framed posters of the car and its driver at different race tracks or posed in publicity stills.—From *St. Dale*, by Sharyn McCrumb (New York: Kensington, 2005), 240–41.

Continue on Broad Avenue (74), which will become West Hamlet Avenue in a few miles.

■ HAMLET

Our tour ends in the town named for every proverbial small town. Hamlet has long been known for its trains and *the* Trane, jazz saxophonist John Coltrane, who is celebrated along with a number of other African American jazz artists in several books by poet and children's author Carole Boston Weatherford, of High Point.

> TRANE TRAVELIN' (EXCERPT)
> *for John Coltrane*
> 1. The Old Ship of Zion.
> Morning, Mr. Day.
> Fifth house from the corner,
> the family ark buoyed
> young John in a sea
> of whiteness, swung low

as the choir steered him
straight and narrow
toward a band of angels
at the colored school.
He blew that horn
like Gabriel but still
got into devilment
with Cousin Mary once in a while.
They knew better than to play
on the tracks. Mother, may I
take a baby step? Take two
giant steps; I dare you.
Blue train-a-coming.
The Goldsboro Express!
Get on board, little children.
    Get on board.
—From *Stormy Blues*, by Carole Boston Weatherford
(New Orleans: Xavier Review Press, 2002), 63.

John Coltrane was born here in 1926, the same year as Hamlet's most celebrated writer, Tom Wicker. According to Lewis Porter's biography, *John Coltrane: His Life and Music*, at the time of their son's birth Coltrane's parents lived in a boardinghouse at the corner of Hamlet Avenue and Bridges Street, now commemorated by a state historic marker. Tom Wicker's parents also lived on Hamlet Avenue, but on the opposite side of the tracks in the more affluent (white) part of town.

Neither home place stands today, but Hamlet's much-photographed Queen Anne passenger train depot, which more or less marks the divide between the two neighborhoods of these celebrated citizens, has been restored to its former glory and houses the National Railroad Museum and Hall of Fame. To visit the station, follow Hamlet Avenue (74 Business) past the Sandhills Regional Medical Center on your left and turn right on NC 177. At the next corner, turn left on Charlotte Street.

Charlotte Street is where Coltrane's grandfather continued to live long after young John and his parents moved to High Point. Follow Charlotte Street several blocks to Raleigh Street and turn right. Cross the railroad tracks and take the first road to the left, Vance Street, which meets West Main Street in a block. Several historic storefronts are directly in front of you. Turn left on Main and the depot is just ahead on the left.

The Hamlet Depot has been restored to its early glory as remembered in the nonfiction of Louis D. Rubin Jr. and Tom Wicker.

There were those everywhere who knew Hamlet as an inevitable stop on the rail trip to Florida. From older generations a few still remembered that before the age of dining cars the old terminal restaurant in Hamlet had been a memorable eating place for weary travelers.—From *A Time to Die*, by Tom Wicker (New York: Quadrangle/New York Times Book, 1975), 12.

John Coltrane (whose family name was sometimes misspelled in genealogical records as "Coaltrain") and Tom Wicker both had relatives who worked for the railroad. Coltrane's grandfather was a dining steward; Wicker's father held a position high enough in the Seaboard Air Line to qualify the family for a free travel pass, which young Tom used often.

Curiously, these autobiographical details emerge in *A Time to Die*, Wicker's award-winning account of the 1971 inmate uprising at Attica State Correctional Institution, in New York. In the narrative, Wicker periodically reflects on his upbringing in the segregated South and at one point finds a shared appreciation for Coltrane's music with an African American reporter who is also covering Attica. (Wicker was among a select group that had been invited by the inmates to serve as observers of the ultimately futile negotiations that were intended to quell threatened violence.)

Wicker wrote the account of his Attica experience in the third person, referring to himself as a character. At one point he reminisces about the day in the 1930s when school was cancelled in Hamlet because President Roosevelt's special train from Warm Springs, Georgia, was coming through town:

> The Presidential train stopped for a few palpitating minutes with Secret Service men at every car entrance, but it was early in the morning and no one else made an appearance. Every window was shaded. Some said that just as the train pulled out, at the last moment, in the last window of the last car, the blind went up and a few lucky souls caught a glimpse of the famous smile and the uplifted chin. Although he was not one of those so fortunate, to Tom Wicker that day, it was as if the greatness of the world had embraced him and his town (135).

In the course of more than two dozen books, including nine novels, Wicker has time and again addressed his own privilege as a white man and his discomfort with the harsh disparities between black and white that he witnessed as a boy in Hamlet. Wicker graduated from the University of North Carolina at Chapel Hill and worked on newspapers in Aberdeen, Lumberton, and Winston-Salem before leaving his home state. He went on to work at the *Nashville Tennessean* and the *New York Times*. Wicker wrote what many consider one of the most accurate accounts of the assassination of President John F. Kennedy, which he witnessed from the press bus in the presidential motorcade. He also wrote an unsentimental and highly praised analysis of Kennedy's presidency for *Esquire* magazine editor Harold Hayes, an Elkin native.

Another eminent writer of Wicker's generation, Louis D. Rubin Jr., also has wistful memories of Hamlet and its depot. In an essay, Rubin recalls his encounters with the little gas-electric train, called the Boll Weevil, that originated in Savannah, ran through his hometown of Charleston, and on into Hamlet, where riders could then catch any number of larger passenger trains to far-flung destinations in every direction. Named after the pest that ravaged cotton crops up and down the same corridor, the Boll Weevil represented the opening of new routes to economic betterment for the once-isolated Georgia and South Carolina sea islanders—African Americans who were finally able to leave the coast by train in the 1930s. As Rubin writes: "Throughout the South there were many trains like the little Boll Weevil. In Eudora Welty's beautiful novel *Delta Wedding*, a little train named the Yellow Dog—in actuality the Yazoo and Delta—brings cousin Laura McRaven from the city of Jackson to the cotton lands of the Mississippi Delta."—"The Boll Weevil, the Iron Horse, and the End of the Line: Thoughts on the South," from *A Gallery of Southerners*, by Louis D. Rubin Jr. (Baton Rouge: Louisiana State University Press, 1982), 199.

Rubin, who founded Algonquin Books of Chapel Hill, goes on to relate his lifelong fascination with the little train that white folks seldom rode. To Rubin, the Boll Weevil stood for so many changes that were coming—by rail and otherwise—to the tattered culture of the Old South.

In a fit of nostalgia, Rubin attempted to ride the Boll Weevil in the 1950s, only to find that it had already been replaced by a much larger, air-conditioned, diesel-powered coach. Two decades later, on a trip by car, Rubin once more came to Hamlet and discovered that the Seaboard Line was no more and that its replacement, Amtrak, had downsized dramatically here. Nevertheless, Rubin made his way to the old wooden railroad hotel, which was still functioning. Its restaurant, full of patrons black and white, were sitting together and laughing. For Rubin, the sight was emblematic of the changes he had witnessed over his life and also a contradiction of the perennial worry in some literary quarters that the South and its distinctive southern literature would soon disappear:

The South has been with us for some time now, and there seems to be little reason not to assume that it will continue to be the South for many years to come. It has changed a great deal—it is always changing, and in recent decades the change has been especially dramatic. But there is little evidence that it is changing into something that is less markedly southern than in the past.... An identifiable and visible South remains, and its inhabitants continue to face the same underlying human problems as before, however much the particular issues may change.—From *A Gallery of Southerners*, by Louis D. Rubin Jr., 217–18.

In 2005, another North Carolina writer, Charlotte-born Lawrence Naumoff, published a novel about Hamlet that underscores Rubin's thesis about the simultaneous presence and absence of change. In 1991, Hamlet experienced the worst industrial disaster in North Carolina history. The Imperial Foods chicken processing plant, less than a block from the train depot, caught fire due to a faulty hydraulic line. The plant, which had somehow never been inspected in its eleven years of operation, had all but two exit doors locked from the outside as a deterrent to theft. Twenty-five workers died, and another fifty-four were badly injured.

Naumoff's novel, which has been called "docufiction," describes the actual events, though he invented the family that the story most closely follows. "That's what the demands of creating a drama and a narrative do, and it's that freedom and that range of creation that makes a novel what it is—not journalism," Naumoff writes in the preface.

All the oxygen in the vicinity, all the available air in the town of Hamlet, rushed toward the flames, drawn there in the same way that the people of the town now parked their vehicles and stood, shoulder to shoulder, hundreds and then thousands of them, the entire town, watching the spectacle, not laughing, not talking, just arms folded and touching each other in the mass, leaning against each other without knowing it, the crowd now as one, holding everyone within it up, and quiet, not a sound, not a word coming from all those people held back behind police and fire lines. — From *A Southern Tragedy in Crimson and Yellow*, by Lawrence Naumoff (Winston-Salem: Zuckerman Cannon, 2005), 202.

As painful to read as the events that inspired it, the novel is a rumination on poverty and workers' rights. It serves as a searing record of a disaster that led to criminal convictions of the plant managers and has since prompted legislative measures to avoid its repetition. Two memorials were erected to honor the workers by different factions in the tumult that followed the fire.

Piedmont poet laureate Jaki Shelton Green also wrote a powerful tribute to the Hamlet victims:

TRIBUTE TO THE MEN AND WOMEN WHO PERISHED IN THE IMPERIAL
CHICKEN PLANT FIRE IN HAMLET, NORTH CAROLINA (EXCERPT)
i feel this song my every question,
my what for, my how come,
my what did i do to be so black and blue
and it answers me by and by
in this new grave i choose
it answers like a moan.

no train came through those doors
no train whistle took us
out of there
—From *Breath of the Song: New and Selected Poems*, by
Jaki Shelton Green (Durham: Carolina Wren Press, 2005), 50.

To see the plant site and memorial, continue past the depot, cross the tracks, and take the first right on South Bridges Street. Just beyond a stand of trees on the right is an empty lot where the chicken plant, which had earlier been an ice cream manufacturing operation, once stood. A brick walkway leads into the memorial site on the right, immediately across from the entrance to Spear Street.

■ LITERARY LANDSCAPE

Union County Library
316 East Windsor Street, Monroe
704-283-8184
<http://www.union.lib.nc.us>
With a lively mix of book clubs that meet at all hours and the Hope Dawson Perry Multicultural Collection (endowed by a public schoolteacher), this library is a standout. A regular schedule of authors' visits, a Hispanic services program, and creative writing workshops for teens are among the many programs in this bustling facility.

Union County Writers' Club
P.O. Box 496
Monroe, NC 28111
<http://www.unioncountywritersclub.org>
This enthusiastic group meets monthly at the Union County Arts Council, on Main Street in Monroe, and sponsors workshops, contests, and an annual literary tea.

Hampton B. Allen Library
120 South Greene Street, Wadesboro
704-694-5177
<http://www.srls.info/anson/ansonIndex.html>
In the heart of uptown Wadesboro, the library is a good first stop for information about historic sites. The library has a special section for African Ameri-

can literature and a raft of public-access computers. The library also sponsors a bookmobile, the "Condensed Version."

Thomas H. Leath Memorial Library
412 East Franklin Street, Rockingham
910-895-6337
<http://204.211.56.212/richmond.html>
This large, attractive facility next to a terraced park is a couple of blocks north of Business 74 on US 1 in the residential heart of town. The library's friends group hosts one or two annual author events and a used-book sale.

Hamlet Public Library
302 Main Street, Hamlet
910-582-3477
A good place to survey Tom Wicker's books and to research local genealogy, this small, contemporary library is five blocks west of the depot.

Norwood : Aquadale : Albemarle : Badin

Meet the "Writing Rosses of Stanly County," probably the most prolific family in all of North Carolina literary history. Explore how one family could produce—in a single generation—a poet, a short story writer, and two novelists.

Writers with a connection to this tour: Jean Ross Justice, Susan Meyers, Heather Ross Miller, Ruth Moose, Fred Ross, James Ross, Eleanor Ross Taylor, Peter Taylor

This tour begins in Norwood, a town that sits on the western shore of Lake Tillery in Stanly County. Established as a trading center in the 1800s, Norwood's colorful history has been preserved in two novels written by brothers James and Fred Ross. The Ross sisters, Eleanor and Jean, have also written extensively about their native region, in poetry and prose, respectively. Fred's daughter, poet and novelist Heather Ross Miller, continues the family's distinguished literary legacy from her home near Morrow Mountain.

James Ross's 1940 novel, *They Don't Dance Much*, set during the Depression, celebrates the long tradition of Stanly County revelry made possible by prodigious local corn crops. His younger brother Fred's 1951 novel, *Jackson Mahaffey*, is also set along the banks of the Rocky River, but a bit earlier—during the Prohibition era under President Taft. Corn liquor flows freely through both books.

Approaching Norwood from the south, US 52 crosses the Rocky River. From the bridge, you can see the surrounding landscape. In pre–Revolutionary War times, North Carolina's first licensed tavern sat not far from this spot at the confluence of the Pee Dee and Rocky rivers. The tavern was built to serve travelers passing along the King's Highway, which ran from Charleston to Boston. Many early settlers made their way through this region, including Francis Asbury, the famous

tour 9

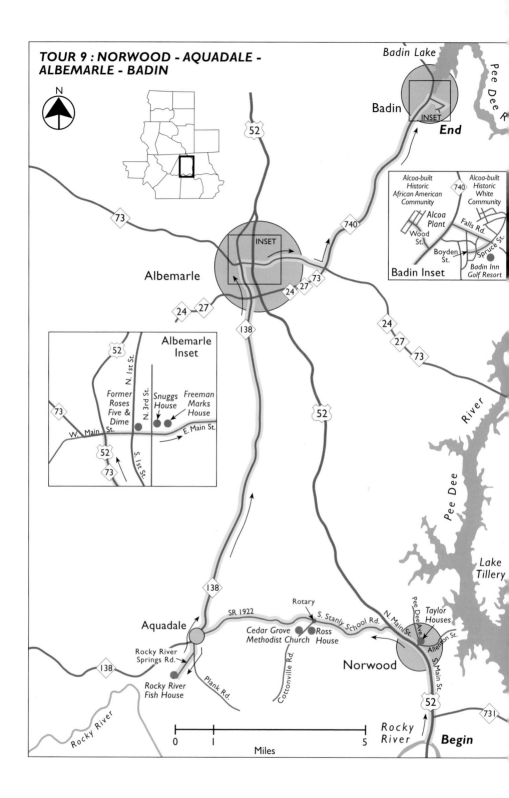

TOUR 9 : NORWOOD - AQUADALE - ALBEMARLE - BADIN

N

52

73

740

Albemarle

24 27

24 27 73

138

24

27

73

Badin Lake

Pee Dee R.

Badin

INSET

End

Alcoa-built Historic African American Community

740

Alcoa-built Historic White Community

Alcoa Plant

Falls Rd.

Wood St.

Boyden St.

Spruce St.

Badin Inset

Badin Inn Golf Resort

Albemarle Inset

52

N. 1st St.

N. 3rd St.

Former Roses Five & Dime St.

Snuggs House

Freeman Marks House

73

W. Main St.

E. Main St.

52

S. 1st St.

73

52

River

Pee Dee

Lake Tillery

138

Rotary

SR 1922

S. Stanly School Rd.

Taylor Houses

Pee Dee Ave.

N. Main St.

Cedar Grove Methodist Church

Ross House

Aquadale

Rocky River Springs Rd.

Rocky River Fish House

Plank Rd.

Cottonville Rd.

Norwood

Allenton St.

S. Main St.

52

731

Rocky River

Rocky River

Begin

0   1   5

Miles

The Writing Rosses of Stanly County: (left to right) James, Eleanor, Jean, and Fred.
Photo courtesy of Heather Ross Miller.

bishop who brought Methodism to North America and who preached in these parts in 1785, a legacy that Fred Ross underscores in his novel.

Indeed, Fred Ross barely disguised local geography and history in his narrative. The Rocky River is called the Wild River, Norwood is called Center (which was its actual name in the early 1900s), and Wadetown to the south is probably the author's fictional name for Ansonville or Wadesboro.

During the horse-and-buggy days of Prohibition, Stanly County was, as Fred Ross describes it, occupied by staunch Christians (mostly female) and liquor-making, hard-drinking, and gambling men with a special fondness for cock-fighting. Jackson Mahaffey was decidedly one of these renegade brethren, though he also had a strong entrepreneurial streak that led him to build a grist-mill on the river.

Following Bishop Asbury's celebrated visit, brush-arbor revivals became commonplace here. The swelling sound of hymns and hot preaching carried a great distance on summer nights. Early on in the novel, Mahaffey rigs up his old mule and buggy to investigate one such meeting and is instantly smitten by a pretty woman he sees there. Mahaffey tries his best to listen to the preacher:

I could tell right off the bat that he was a Methodist. He was tall, hungry looking, and poorly dressed. All faiths held brush arbor meetings, but the

Methodist preachers were easy to spot. They preached whether they got paid or not. See a raggedy, hound-lean preacher and nine times out of ten he would be a sprinkling Methodist. It seemed that their nature required that they try to grow good fruit on dry and thorny ground. Not that that made any impression on me. —From *Jackson Mahaffey*, by Fred E. Ross (New York: Bantam Books, 1951), 14.

Mahaffey soon wheels and deals to get a new buggy and suit of clothes to pursue the woman from the camp meeting. The novel proceeds from their rocky courtship to marriage to Mahaffey's brief conversion to Methodism and then to his attempt at abstinence from both home brew and cockfighting. Ultimately, Mahaffey cannot surrender his vices. He decides instead to run for a state senate seat to win back the waning respect of his wife, Molly. He enlists the help of a newspaper editor and a barber by telling them how to describe the key planks of his campaign:

"You tell the merchants that I'm for a higher retail price. Tell the buyers that I'm for a lower retail price. Tell them that hire that I'm for longer hours and lower wages. Tell the hired help that I'm for shorter hours and more pay. Remind the church members that I was converted last summer and just tell the others that I'm Jackson Mahaffey. I'm for whatever the voter wants. It might be best if you'd sort of feel out each person before you promise anything" (207).

And with this campaign strategy, Mahaffey defeats the stodgy incumbent, Pink Lilly, and is off to a life of public service in Raleigh at the book's conclusion.

Fred Ross was the only one of his siblings who stayed in Stanly County for most of his life. His first career had been as a pitcher in the semiprofessional baseball league sponsored by the textile mills in North and South Carolina. He also worked at the Alcoa plant in Badin from 1936 to the mid-1960s, where he served as payroll clerk and editor of Alcoa's employee magazine.

Fred Ross told reporter Bernadette Hoyle in an interview that he never intended to be a writer. "It was the rationing during World War II that made me turn to writing," he said, tongue in cheek. "I couldn't buy gun shells. I couldn't buy gasoline for my car or my outboard motor. My sister Eleanor, whom I more or less raised, still held to some affection for me, and she suggested I write."

Ross later edited newspapers in Mount Holly, Lillington, and Jonesville. His neighbors in Stanly, however, remember his talent for baseball. He once went up against Shoeless Joe Jackson, former standout center fielder for the Chicago

White Sox. The contest between Fred Ross on the mound and Jackson in the batter's box took place long after Shoeless Joe had been expelled for life from organized baseball. (He was a member of the team that came to be known as the "Black Sox," which in 1918 threw the World Series to Cincinnati.) Jackson had by this time returned home to South Carolina to play baseball illegally in the textile leagues.

According to Stanly County historian Les Young, Ross, already a couple of strikes ahead of the legendary batter, threw an inside pitch at Shoeless Joe's belly, thinking he would surely finish him off. Jackson sent the ball sailing over the right-field fence.

Fred Ross's elder brother, James, was also a baseball standout, attending both Elon and Louisburg colleges on baseball scholarships. James Ross served in World War II, studied at Columbia University, and then launched a career in journalism, which was largely spent at the *Greensboro Daily News*. His novel, *They Don't Dance Much*, was published in 1940, then reissued in 1975 as part of Southern Illinois University's Lost American Fiction Series, and issued again in 1986 by a publisher in London.

Much of the novel's action takes place at a Stanly County gas station that the owner decides to refashion into a roadhouse, where he and the novel's narrator (his employee) traffic in card games, slot machines, dancing, and local-made liquor. Smut Mulligan's roadhouse and a few tourist cabins that rent by the hour are set along the river road just outside the fictional town of Corinth (James Ross's version of Norwood), which would also put them very near US 52 and the Rocky River.

The name Corinth echoes the ancient Mediterranean towns of Troy and Carthage: their North Carolina counterparts are not far from here—Troy in Montgomery County and Carthage in Moore County. The narrator, a local farmer down on his luck, is Jackson T. McDonald, a name strikingly similar to Fred Ross's Jackson Mahaffey.

Crime novelist Raymond Chandler blurbed the first edition of *They Don't Dance Much*, calling it "a sleazy, corrupt but completely believable story of a North Carolina town." Others compared the unvarnished quality of James Ross's prose to early Hemingway. As this passage suggests, a more recent source of comparison might be Larry Brown's stark novel *Father and Son*.

Toward dark Old Man Joshua Lingerfelt came out to see what the new place was like. He walked around it, tapping the walls with his walking stick that was made out of hickory and puffing his stinking old corncob pipe. After awhile he came inside and sat down at the counter. He was an old man that went to the war in Cuba. He had a wooden leg and got a pension from the government. He was bald-headed and didn't have any teeth. Not even false teeth. But that didn't make much difference. He drank most of his meals anyway. He beckoned me over to where he was.

"Gimme a beer boy," he said, and spat on the floor. I got him the beer, and he grabbed it quick so as not to let any of the foam get away from him. He smacked his lips and sucked in his gums. "What in the devil you all mean putting up a place like this out here in these piney woods?" he said.

—From *They Don't Dance Much*, by James Ross (London: Harrap Limited, 1986), 76.

Standing on the banks of the Rocky River today, the literary visitor can only imagine the stories these woods could tell, but clearly they fired the imaginations (and perhaps the competitive spirits) of the Ross brothers. Next we meet the Ross sisters, Eleanor and Jean.

■ NORWOOD

From the Rocky River, continue north on US 52. Watch for the water tower near the center of Norwood and turn right at the traffic light onto Pee Dee Avenue. In the second block, park on the street and look left to locate the Norwood Public Library and the adjacent Norwood Museum, at 207 Pee Dee Avenue. Call for hours (704-474-3416).

On your right is the First United Methodist Church, and next door, at 129 Allenton, is the house that once belonged to poet Eleanor Ross Taylor, sister to Fred and James Ross. Eleanor's husband, the short-story master Peter Taylor, bought the house across the street at 128 Allenton—one of more than a dozen homes the couple bought and sold throughout their fifty-one-year marriage, which took them around the South and Midwest to fulfill Peter's many academic appointments and guest-teaching stints.

Upon their graduation from Norwood High School, Eleanor Ross and her sister, Jean, attended Woman's College, now the University of North Carolina at Greensboro. Eleanor studied with novelist and literary critic Caroline Gordon and her husband, poet Allen Tate. Peter Taylor's biographer, Hubert H. Alexander, reports that Allen Tate found Eleanor Ross to be a natural talent and compared her to Emily Brontë (who, of course, also had a sister—Charlotte—who wrote). Tate and Gordon helped Eleanor to win a fellowship to the graduate program in creative writing at Vanderbilt University. There she met Peter Taylor, a gregarious man who befriended almost every top American writer of his time.

Peter Taylor had studied with Alan Tate and with literary lions John Crowe Ransom and Robert Penn Warren. He was particularly close to poets Robert Lowell and Randall Jarrell. After his marriage to Eleanor Ross and a stint in the service during World War II, Taylor landed his first teaching job, in Greensboro, along with Randall Jarrell, who became a trusted reader of Eleanor's poetry. During Taylor's tenure at Greensboro, he and Eleanor spent several summers in Norwood, in this house and in another house that had belonged to Eleanor's mother out in the Stanly County countryside.

Though Eleanor Ross Taylor's writing life often took a back seat to her husband's, her gifts as a poet were always widely recognized in literary circles. Her poems have been heralded by feminist scholars for their clear-eyed reckoning of sexism. In reviewing her work for the *Virginia Quarterly Review* in the fall of 1972, Robert Mazzocco wrote: "Mrs. Taylor is a little like a Southern belle who has uncharacteristically read all the big books, thought all the gray thoughts, who is a bit fearful perhaps of expressing grief or depth of the cruel chemical wit of which she is capable, yet who, against 'cyclonic gust and chilly rain,' expresses them forthrightly anyway."

She composed this heartbreaking elegy upon losing her beloved brother, Fred:

THESE GIFTS
Fred Ross, 1913–1993
We take nothing out of this world
except yarns you invented at
    the feedsack that fed the planter
    as it worked the pear-tree field
    minding small sibling in straw hat,
except the willow at the springhead
    you dug out (home for the funeral I saw only
    workers pouring out of Textile-Cone).

the non-curricular you majored
    in   your rabbit boxes   bantam
    Easter egg that outpipped
    all your cousins',
your silly melon crop that   green-
    streaked hogs   wallowed branchside
    your gun where is it? and the squirrels
    you toppled out of trees and ate fried.

your diary's secrets (rouged schoolgirls
    trailed me down the playground:
    "Tell Fra-yd—I love him!"),
    the banjo that you swapped a jacket
    for then yo-lee-lay-hooed to
    on front steps at dusk,

the empties clinking in your desk
    among the last abandoned novel's
    pages (music that knows that winning loses),
except your grim voice miles away
    after my *You spend your day—?:*
    Waiting for dark!
even last year's tall skeletal
    smile that took me by the hand
    never a *Mayday mayday* from the stark
    porch's canes and
            calendars wherein
    our parents called down
    to the last one up *Be sure*
    to put the fire to bed;

you take your cache that flares and flashes
    out   a recent breath.
—From *Late Leisure*, by Eleanor Ross Taylor (Baton Rouge:
Louisiana State University Press, 1999), 38–39.

After Peter Taylor's death, in 1994, Eleanor Ross Taylor continued writing and publishing from her home in Charlottesville, Virginia. The Taylors' son, Ross, is also a writer.

A collection of photographs, memorabilia, and some twenty books written by members of the Ross family, including foreign language editions, are on permanent display in the Norwood Museum. When the "Writing Rosses Collection" was officially dedicated, poet and novelist Heather Ross Miller (Fred's daughter) was on hand. Miller, who retired to Stanly County after a career on the creative writing faculties of the University of Arkansas and Washington and Lee University, now teaches writing part-time at nearby Pfeiffer University. She is often asked how one family could, to a person, take such an interest in creative writing. "My grandparents loved to tell stories and to gossip," Miller explains, "especially on the front porch after supper in the summer, or in front of the dining room fire in winter. They both were especially good mimics and loved to act out the stories they told."

In addition to the Ross collection, the Norwood Museum features an eclectic array of local mementos and memorabilia that lift up Norwood's history as a mill town where baseball was the primary means of entertainment, as it was in so many Carolina textile towns.

Jean Ross Justice, the youngest of the original writing Rosses, lives in Iowa City, where she settled with her late husband, poet Donald Justice. (He won both the Pulitzer Prize and the Bollingen Prize and was invited to serve as U.S. poet laureate, though he declined for health reasons.) Jean Justice is a short-story writer whose work has appeared in many national magazines over the decades. She met her husband at the University of North Carolina at Chapel Hill when they were in graduate school. Her collection, *The End of a Good Party and Other Stories*, was issued by the University of Tampa Press in 2008.

To reach the Ross family home outside Norwood, we head toward Aquadale, a tiny crossroads where Jean and Eleanor taught for a time. Proceed north on US 52 (North Main Street in Norwood). Just beyond the city park on your right, proceed left at the fork, on South Stanly School Road, heading east toward Aquadale and Oakdale. To see the house where all four writing Rosses were raised, go three-quarters of the way around the upcoming traffic circle and take Cottonville Road to the south. The very first residence on the left, surrounded by mature trees, is the house and farm described in the earlier poem by Eleanor Ross Taylor. Jean Ross Justice also borrowed from a memory of her aging parents' last days together in this house to create the short story excerpted here:

In the late afternoon he and Rilla sat on the back porch and stared out at the backyard, toward the old garden plot, the corn crib and granary. A dusty haze hung against the woods in the distance. One of them would say again that it was still too dry; they'd say again that the days were getting shorter. Occasionally a car passed out front; he listened as it went on down the road, heading toward the long slope in front of the church, a weariness in the sound as it died away.

They would discuss supper. Eat what was left of what their daughter-in-law had brought last time? What she cooked was sometimes too rich for them, but they told her it was first-rate. Perhaps tonight they would open a can of stew.

What was left to talk about? *Remember*—that was the word they used most. Remember the black snake that lived out in the henhouse, cleaning up the rats, eating an egg every day or so, till it died from swallowing

The Ross homestead figures in the fiction of Jean Ross Justice and her niece, Heather Ross Miller, whose literary gifts were shaped early on in this household of storytellers.

a china nest egg? "Funny it couldn't tell," Rilla murmured. "Poor old snake! Oh Lord." He'd shown a neighbor the black snake, coiled on a rafter, and the neighbor said he couldn't have stood having it there. The snake didn't bother the hens, though, why should he kill it?

—From "Toward the End: Variations on a Theme," in *The End of a Good Party and Other Stories*, by Jean Ross Justice (Tampa: University of Tampa Press, 2008), 21–22.

Heather Ross Miller, who now owns the house but lives near Badin, remembers staying at the family home place with her grandparents. It was here that she listened avidly as a child to family gossip and stories from her hiding place under the dining room table or out on the porch. On Sundays, young Heather would be escorted by her grandfather down Cottonville Road to the Cedar Grove Methodist Church, now a much larger complex on the right about a tenth of a mile beyond the home place. Upon their arrival for Sunday school, as Heather tells it, her grandfather would pull out his handkerchief and dust off her patent leather shoes—a scene that is reprised in Miller's first novel:

I sat in my grandfather's Sunday School. Cedar Grove had only a one-room, white wooden Methodist Church and there were dark heavy curtains, like burlap, strung on rails to divide off the classes. The screech of those curtain rings skittering along the rail would always put my teeth on edge and make the skin of my neck prickle.—From *On the Edge of the Woods*, by Heather Ross Miller (New York: Atheneum, 1964), 7.

The power of place in fiction can hardly be overstated when three remarkable writers each take a turn with such a setting. In a memoir in progress, Jean Ross Justice re-creates a scene from the Ross household:

Sometimes a fragment of music comes to me, a theme from a Beethoven symphony, say, and it brings a fragment of feeling, then a fuller memory. My older brother James is sitting in the living room, his record player of 1940 or '41 turned up high, making the floor quiver. Beethoven, Mozart or Brahms. I hear the music from some distance away, perhaps the bedroom next door, or passing through on my way to the kitchen. There's pleasure in hearing it, as well as the satisfaction of an obligation, a need to know this music. (I have just finished high school, and am serious about 'culture'—haunted by lists of things to read and to listen to.) I don't join him; I understand he has some private use for the music. He sits listening, holding a large glass which once held peanut butter, his glass, big enough to carry a good supply of water upstairs, where he works and sleeps. He is nearly thirty, but is living at home in order to write full-time. He's published a novel already, and has left a job with the Internal Revenue Service in Greensboro to try this. Sometimes—perhaps this afternoon, judging from the volume of the music—there is whisky mixed with the water in the big glass. (We call it "liquor.")
Outside as the floor vibrates in the living room, my father is taking the

milk buckets to the barn to milk. My mother will be preparing to put out cold supper on the kitchen table, or making a fire in the wood stove to scramble eggs or cook rice, something hot to go with the cold vegetables left from midday dinner. They do not want to know about the liquor, if any, in the glass. The music goes on, beautiful and poignant.

—From a memoir in progress, used by permission of Jean Ross Justice.

To continue to Aquadale, return to the traffic circle and proceed east on South Stanly School Road. At Aquadale Road and the railroad tracks, turn left onto NC 138, which soon turns into Plank Road (a toll road built of wooden planks in the 1800s). Do not turn right with 138 toward Oakboro. Instead continue on Plank Road another 200 yards and turn right onto Rocky River Springs Road. In approximately a half mile, pull into the parking lot of the rough-hewn, barnlike Rocky River Springs Fish House on the right (704-474-3052 or <http://www.rrsfh.com>).

This historic restaurant opens at 3:30 P.M. on Thursdays through Sundays, but for the literary traveler, whether you grab a bite to eat or not, longtime creative writing instructor, poet, and short-story writer Ruth Moose gives us a little history: "My first short story, 'The Swing,' is set at Silver Spring Baptist Church, near Aquadale. And the place to eat in Stanly County when I was a child was always Rocky River Springs Fish Camp. They have the best tea in the world, sweet tea that comes from the natural springs there that gave Aquadale its name. For a time there was a hotel, and people came from all over to drink the healing waters. The hotel burned and the Fish House is near where it stood, which is also near the springs from which you can still drink the waters if you bring your own containers. Some do and swear it promotes longevity."

Originally called "the healing place" by the Indians, this tract of land was home to several different springs, each offering a different primary mineral—iron, arsenic, magnesium, sulfur, and copper. Throughout the 1800s, real-estate developers and tourism entrepreneurs created various accommodations and amusements for the summer residents and pilgrims who came to the town of Silver, as it was originally called. At one time or another, the area featured a bowling alley, pool rooms, a roller skating rink, a merry-go-round, and a dance pavilion. Evangelists came to preach here. Tourists flocked to the various hotels that were built and that then burned down over the years.

Unfortunately for Silver, however, the building of the railroad in 1914 brought in a new crop of developers. In the attempt to dig out a grand swimming pool and a deeper well to feed it with the healing waters, dynamite blasting actually destroyed the integrity of the various mineral springs and lowered the water level so drastically that the resort business literally dried up, as did the once-thriving town known today as Aquadale.

Having grown up in an area named and defined by water, it only makes sense that Ruth Moose would write this poem:

LAUNDRY
All our life
so much laundry;
each day's doing or not
comes clean,
flows off and away
to blend with other sins
of this world. Each day
begins in new skin,
blessed by the elements
charged to take us
out again to do or undo
what's been assigned.
From socks to shirts
the selves we shed
lift off the line
as if they own
a life apart
from the one we offer.
There is joy in clean laundry.
All is forgiven in water, sun
and air. We offer our day's deeds
to the blue-eyed sky, with soap and prayer,
our arms up, then lowered in supplication.
—From *Making the Bed*, by Ruth Moose (Charlotte:
    Main Street Rag Publishing Company, 2004), 49.

■ **ALBEMARLE**

From Aquadale, go north on NC 138 (Aquadale Road) for nearly ten miles all the way across NC 24/27. Continue to the next major intersection and turn right on West Main to reach Albemarle's central business district.

Notice the pawnshop in the brick building on the right at the corner of Main and First streets. The top of the facade is engraved with the name Fitzgerald

A corner in Albemarle that was once the site of Rose's Five and Dime, a setting used in two short stories by local writer Ruth Moose. The store's manager for many years was the father of Albemarle-born poet Susan Meyers.

and the date, 1927. This building was, for many years, the Rose's Dime Store in Albemarle.

> Ellis spends a lot of time at the dimestore in town. She goes maybe two or three times a week. She walks to town just to look. Most of the time she doesn't buy anything but a cherry Coke and some Nabs, sits in the drugstore booth and sucks ice. "They got the prettiest towels in Rose's," she tells Shelby. "They'd look so good when we get our house." —From *Dreaming in Color*, by Ruth Moose (Little Rock, Ark.: August House, 1989), 13.

Many North Carolinians know that the Rose's chain was founded in the town of Henderson, in Vance County. In 1915, the enterprise began as a "5, 10, and 15 Cent Store," and the hundred or so stores existing today from Delaware to Georgia serve towns with populations of fewer than 50,000. This Rose's in Albemarle clearly stoked the imagination of Ruth Moose, who set scenes here in her stories "Peanut Dreams" and "The Blue-Eyed Jesus," both from *Dreaming in Color*. Moose has taught creative writing for many years at the University of

North Carolina at Chapel Hill and still draws on this section of the state for inspiration.

Coincidentally, during the 1940s and early 1950s poet Susan Meyers's father managed the Albemarle Rose's, with its "clicking fans and oily floors," as she describes it. (A sample of her work appears in the next tour.)

Meyers recommends a visit to the Snuggs House at 112 North Third Street. It's the third-oldest house in Stanly County and began as a log cabin. Isaiah "Buck" Snuggs kept adding on until it took on a Victorian appearance. The Federal-style Freeman Marks House, around the corner at 245 East Main Street, is the oldest public building in the county. Both houses are open for tours. Call for hours (704-986-3777).

■ **BADIN**

Badin is a mill town unlike any other in North Carolina. Follow East Main Street through Albemarle to the intersection with NC 740 and turn left to reach this village, approximately six miles away.

A French engineer named Jean Jacquett came to Stanly County in 1910 and identified a narrow section of the Yadkin River that L'Aluminium Français and its president, Adrien Badin, had determined to be suitable to dam for power. Operating in the United States as Southern Aluminum, the company bought the land and planned to create a lake, powerhouse, plant, and town for the workers who would smelt aluminum here. French engineers designed a town that followed the contours of the land rather than the squared-off grid of a typical mill village. They designed quadraplex apartments for the mill workers and bungalows, cottages, and other amenities for the supervisors and mill owners. When World War I broke out, the president of the company, Badin, turned to the Mellon family of Pittsburgh, whose U.S. monopoly on bauxite (the mineral used to make aluminum) made the Badin project a desirable acquisition for Alcoa. The French went home to fight the Germans and Alcoa finished the dam. The pig aluminum ingots they began manufacturing were then shipped north to be made into finished aluminum.

As you come into town, Wood Street, on the left, leads uphill to the historically segregated African American mill village, which offers a good view of the aluminum plant below. Return on Wood Street and continue a short distance north on NC 740, to the third street on the right, Falls Road, which leads into the center of Badin's other mill village, the one built for the white workers and plant executives, as described in fiction by Heather Ross Miller, who grew up here:

The French architects and landscapers who designed the mill village of Badin also built these quadraplexes for the mill workers.

We all lived in apartments down below The Club. There was also a big white-columned Annex to The Club where people stayed in rooms dusted by maids and ate in the dining room cooled by ceiling fans with blades the size of palm trees.

Fluff caddied on the golf course for people like the Copps. Miss Jessie never played golf, but she could be seen going into the dining room in the Annex with various escorts, usually new engineers down from the Pittsburgh office, or new technicians training lazy Southerners to read gauges and adjust dials in the rotary stations.

But she lived in a row-house apartment the same as we did, Fluff down on Kirk Place, near the golf course. Miss Jessie right around the corner on Boyden from me on Spruce. And at the edge of town, in the farthest horizon, sat the smelter, poisonous as a toad, spewing and belching its noisy fire, those silvery ingots stacking up inside its wire fences.

—From "Miss Jessie Dukes and Kid Heavy," by Heather Ross Miller, in *Crossroads*, published by *North Carolina Humanities Council* 7, no. 3 (December 2003): 4.

The Badin Inn and Annex were originally built to house company officials, their guests, and the schoolteachers who were brought in to serve the children of Alcoa workers. In Champeen, *a novel by Heather Ross Miller, the inn is an ever-present symbol of company management.*

Time and again Heather Ross Miller has written poetry and fiction about her upbringing in Badin. Her 1999 novel, *Champeen,* is told in the voice of a precocious and incurably curious girl now grown, who once had free run of the village during its heyday as a company town. The novel gives a vivid portrait of an era when, Miller says, "no one ever locked a door and children could walk downtown to see Roy Rogers at the movies and walk back home in the dark."

Streetlights winked on in town, reflected along the rippling lake at the far end across from Carolina Aluminum. Carolina Aluminum kept booming and hissing and shrieking the way it had all my life in Badin, North Carolina, oblivious toward the people who tended it and lived beside it. —From *Champeen,* by Heather Ross Miller (Dallas, Tex.: Southern Methodist University Press, 1999), 200.

After Alcoa Aluminum ceased production, Badin incorporated as an independent entity. Details of town history are documented in the Badin Historic Museum, <http://badinmuseum.com>, at 60 Falls Road (704-422-6900).

Nearby, a townhouse apartment in one of the Alcoa quadraplexes is furnished with period pieces from the 1920s and is open to visitors when the museum is open on Sunday afternoons.

Today, the former clubhouse and annex are part of the Badin Inn (704-422-3683). Nearby Badin Lake provides recreational boating, swimming, and fishing. Each September, during the Best of Badin Festival, some 2,000 guests come to experience an art show, street dance, food, and fireworks.

■ LITERARY LANDSCAPE

B&D Book Store
951 North 1st Street, Albemarle
704-986-2102
<http://www.banddbookstore.net>
The friendly proprietors of this store, nine blocks north of Albemarle's West Main Street, offer new and used books. They will also help you locate first editions and hard-to-find volumes on the Internet.

Morrow Mountain : Troy : Star : Seagrove

North Carolina's ancient Uwharrie Mountains still hold secrets that several writers have tried to explain. Visit the region's remote and scenic rivers, venture out on the networks of hiking trails, and imagine, as these writers have, what life must have been like for the earliest explorers of this unspoiled and unsung preserve.

Writers with a connection to this area: James Applewhite, Michael Causey, Jim Lavene, Joyce Lavene, Margaret Maron, Susan Meyers, Heather Ross Miller, Fred T. Morgan, Eugene E. Pfaff Jr., Dannye Romine Powell

AT MORROW MOUNTAIN
On a slope of this mountain,
everything seems so simple.
Out my window, birch, oak, poplar,
the crazy mosaic of pine bark.
I eat when I'm hungry—bread,
cheese, peaches. Wind whorls somewhere
at the tops of trees. Are you miles away
or thousands of miles away? Last night,
a family of raccoons nudged
at my screen. Deer, necks angling
to the ground, stray close
to the porch, bolt at the rustle
of paper. I surprise myself
alone. I'm bolder than I thought.
Yesterday, I hiked miles through woods,
then swamps, followed the curve
of the Pee Dee River, climbed boulders
to see the waterfall. In a few hours
I'll pack up, head back. I'll miss
the silence here, the scatter
of light on leaves, appearing,

tour 01

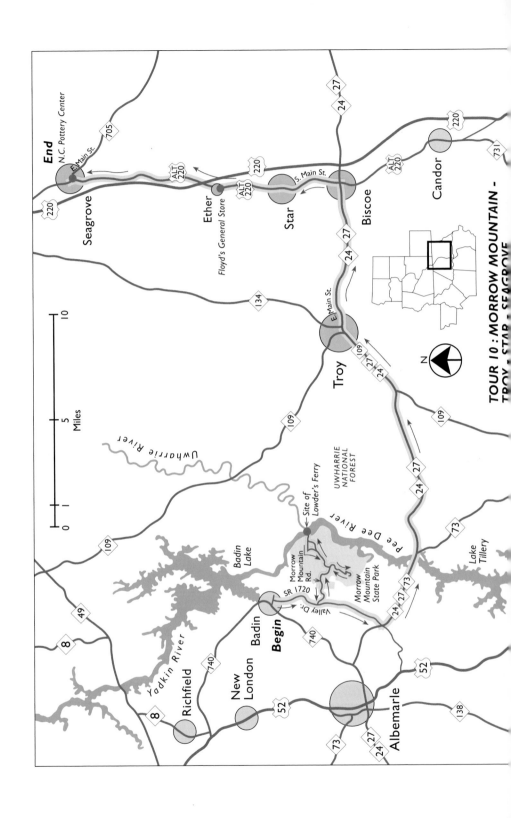

TOUR 10: MORROW MOUNTAIN –
TROY, STAR, SEAGROVE

*A simple wooden marker points the way for hikers heading
to the summit of Morrow Mountain.*

disappearing. A warning: When
I arrive, don't gauge my presence
by my distance. Reach for me.
—From *At Every Wedding Someone Stays Home: Poems*,
  by Dannye Romine Powell (Fayetteville: University of
  Arkansas Press, 1994), 21.

This tour begins in the quiet preserve of Morrow Mountain State Park, only
a few miles from Badin. Leave Badin on Valley Drive, heading south, and watch
for the state park entrance on the left. Stop by the stone-built information center to pick up a map. From here you can reach the top of Morrow Mountain by
car or by hiking a three-mile trail. If you are driving, head to the right where the
main road forks, a few hundred yards beyond the information center.

At the summit, there's a picnic shelter and an easy 0.8-mile trail that loops
around the peak. You can see several other nubby mountains in the ancient
Uwharries from here. Badin's Alcoa plant is to the north. Alcoa has preserved
most of the land between the summit and the aluminum plant for public use.
The park also fronts a significant stretch of the Yadkin River from just below

*Near the site of Lowder's Ferry, the Yadkin and Uwharrie rivers join
to become the Pee Dee River, which flows into Lake Tillery.*

Falls Dam to the beginning of Lake Tillery, which you can see to the south. In
between is the area at the confluence of the Uwharrie River where the Yadkin
changes its name to the Pee Dee.

To view the meeting of these three luminous rivers up close, descend the
mountain and proceed straight ahead, following park signs to the boat launch.
Heather Ross Miller's novel *Gone One Hundred Miles* recounts the life of
Dr. Francis Kron, the first physician in Stanly County, who made his home near
here. At the road's end, on the riverbank, is the former site of Lowder's Ferry,
which from 1883 to 1923 carried passengers—first on horseback or in buggies
and later in automobiles—across the water on a wide barge. These travelers
of old were usually making their way along the Salisbury-Fayetteville Market
Road, which ran through here. Dr. Kron once called the Market Road "perhaps
as bad a specimen of public road as can be started."

For hikers, Fall Mountain Trail (4.1 miles) and Three Rivers Trail (0.6 miles)
begin from this parking lot. A public swimming pool and a stone bathhouse
built by the Civilian Conservation Corps in the 1930s are nearby and open to
swimmers in season for a small fee.

From here, head back on the main road and follow the signs to the Kron House restoration. Dr. Kron, called "Tscharner" in Miller's novel, was a daringly experimental gardener and cook, and he raised his two daughters to join him in his horticultural pursuits.

> Doctor Tscharner sowed the land and made it prosper. He captured the swarming of its bees. He calculated the running of its shad in spring water.... The rarity and wealth of Doctor Tscharner's table took on the scope of his notoriety. Larkin natives came as much to see the curious gardens and perhaps glean a taste, as to have their ills treated.—From *Gone One Hundred Miles*, by Heather Ross Miller (New York: Harcourt, Brace and World, 1968), 44–45.

Miller's novel is narrated in a style appropriate to the period it imagines. Doctor Francis Kron was born in Prussia in 1793. After he married, he and his wife traveled to North Carolina to live with her relatives in Montgomery County. For a time Kron taught French at the University of North Carolina at Chapel Hill, living as a guest in the house of Elisha Mitchell, for whom Mount Mitchell was named. Kron then took a degree in medicine at the University of Pennsylvania before purchasing nearly 300 acres around Morrow Mountain. Kron's duties as sole physician to a sparse population of hardscrabble farmers and ne'er-do-wells in this rugged landscape were demanding. He offset his wearisome work by cultivating his fascination with plants, particularly vegetables and fruit trees.

For dramatic effect, Miller conflates her Doctor Tscharner's death by lightning with an actual occurrence from the period: a destructive tornado that in 1884 blew away the lumber collected to build what was to have been the home of ferry operator David Lowder. The local devastation from the storm led to Morrow Mountain's being called "Naked Mountain" for a time. Kron's actual death date is disputed among historians, but his "daybook" of writings about his horticultural exploits, many letters, and one of his diaries is preserved in the Southern Historical Collection at the University of North Carolina at Chapel Hill.

On a weekday in winter, Morrow Mountain is quiet, the forest undergrowth diminished, and the deer plentiful and curious. In summer, the park is undoubtedly busier, but if you are a writer looking for a quiet escape, this setting could prove to be productive. Six vacation cabins that can each accommodate up to six are available for rent—by the week in the summer and for shorter periods in spring and fall (704-982-4402).

In winter, the resident deer are not shy in Morrow Mountain State Park.

To continue this tour, return to the park entrance. Turn left on Valley Drive, going south to the intersection with NC 73/24/27. Turn left toward Troy. As you cross the bridge at the top of Lake Tillery, look north, upstream. The vast and relatively unsullied Uwharrie Mountains stretch from this point northeast in a series of peaks with simple names such as Horse Trough, Walker, Dennis, Lick, and Rabbit. Though NC 73 soon peels off to the south, stay on 24/27. You will shortly see parking for the Uwharrie National Recreation Trail, which leads deep into the forest for more than twenty miles.

■ TROY

He gazed off into the distance at the larger Uwharrie mounds. At one time, they had been the highest mountains in the eastern United States, so old that the Appalachians and even the Rockies were mere youngsters in comparison. But that had been in the Pleistocene Age; now, they were little more than large foothills that rose abruptly from the flat piedmont of North Carolina.

Gazing at the ethereal blue haze of the low mountains, he realized again the almost magnetic force they exerted; perhaps one reason most people who were born here stayed, except the most ambitious, was an inexpressible sense of bonding with the land. Even those that left, as he

had, for educational or career goals, seemed to gravitate back within a few years. Certainly it was a place of "roots," of the *old* underlying and subsuming everything that could be called *new*.
—From *Uwharrie*, by Eugene E. Pfaff Jr. and Michael Causey (Greensboro, N.C.: Tudor Publishers, 1993), 14.

Eugene Pfaff and Michael Causey (a pseudonym for M. L. Hester Jr.) have written a mystery told from multiple points of view that successfully captures the flavor of the region. Literary tourists will be pleased to know that the hero of *Uwharrie* is a librarian. The authors also hint at the possibility that some descendants of the Indians and British among the Lost Colony who disappeared on North Carolina's coast might have landed in these mountains.

Meanwhile, the indefatigable Fred T. Morgan, another local author, devoted his life to collecting oral histories and legends from the residents of the Uwharries. As he told us in the foreword to his first book and again in the more recent collection of character sketches and oral histories called *Uwharrie Bizarres* (John F. Blair, 2007), this region is surprisingly remote to be so close to the heart of the industrialized North Carolina Piedmont.

Unending green forests cloak the Uwharries, taming the river gorges and smoothing the stark precipices and gashy ravines. Little brown roads and a few hard-surfaced ones snake through the region, along with streams, logging trails, and overgrown wagon roads. Big lakes spread out into the valleys and crevices of the hills. Unless you know just where to look, you are likely to miss most of the signs of early human occupancy and enterprise that give this land its heritage: dams, grist mills, fords, ferries, covered bridges, foot bridges, rock quarries, sawmills, and courthouse sites, as well as many, many old homeplaces, gold mines and graveyards.—From *Ghost Tales of the Uwharries*, by Fred T. Morgan (Winston-Salem: John F. Blair, 1968), n.p.

As Morgan would have it, these hills are something like Alaska—a land so remote that people can drop out and disappear or at least lead uninterrupted lives characterized by strange habits and odd preoccupations. As Morgan suggests, "Catch a native oldster in the right mood, and he will talk with such color and fascination that you will wish you could stay for supper."

Troy, the seat of Montgomery County, is the central gateway to the 50,000-acre Uwharrie National Forest, purchased by the federal government in 1931 and designated a national forest by President John F. Kennedy in 1961. For detailed information, the district ranger's office is two miles east of Troy on NC 24/27. Call 910-576-6391 or stop by for maps.

For the literary traveler who'd rather sit on a rock and just read for vicarious adventure, local coauthors Jim and Joyce Lavene have created a series of murder mysteries set in the Uwharrie region. In *One Last Goodbye*, part of the mystery is the 1944 crash of a U.S. Navy airplane into the waters of Badin Lake—an actual incident that also figures in Heather Ross Miller's novel *Champeen*, discussed in the previous tour.

From the downtown square in Troy, continue east on 24/27 to the intersection with US 220 in Biscoe. (If it's early summer, note the profusion of peonies in many yards along this route.) Also take note of the peach trees (there's a North Carolina peach *named* Biscoe), and then head north on old US 220 Alternate, where flea markets abound. Eschew the new I-73/74 to enjoy a closer inspection of what is now known as North Carolina's Central Park, a region in the process of redefining itself following the decline of textile manufacturing. This poem by Duke University professor James Applewhite presents a familiar scene of economic hardship:

STATE ROAD 134
Down N.C. 134 past the township of Troy:
places not much in anyone's thoughts,
Wadesboro, Mt. Gilead, Calvary Church.
One yard spired
with the heartening thumb-bells of foxglove.
Road going past where the quick dog evaded
a truck in the monstrous heat: where
a hawk lay dead in a rumple of feathers,
a cow stood still under sweet gum scrub
and switched its tail.

I witnessed the chimney of a house long burnt
beside a ditchbank flooded with Cherokee rose.

And a field at my random turning
laid open and alone,
sky's rim back like an eyelid fringed
with the clay soil's fledgling pines.
Two board shacks with
windowpanes crushed by the heat,
paint bruised off by a weight of deprivation.

*The community of Star is at the geographic center of
North Carolina in Montgomery County.*

What balm of Gilead
descends for this mother, baby
on the hip of her luminous jeans?
In what hollow of mind
has even Christ held such features?

Face of a black boy vacant almost
as the country turning,
fields' loneliness sitting on his eyelids
too pure almost to be endured
in this forgetful distance.
—From *Selected Poems*, by James Applewhite
    (Durham: Duke University Press, 2005), 3.

■ STAR

This little village, approximately three miles north of Biscoe, is the state's
geographical center. Its public library (truly *the* central library in North Carolina) is housed in a small storefront.

Continuing north on US 220 Alternate, the next village is Ether. Here, at Hogan Farm Road, is Floyd's General Store, established in 1910. Just beyond the socket wrenches and hunting caps and beside the antique dentist's chair toward the back, you'll find a surprising collection of books for sale, including some titles by true-crime writer Jerry Bledsoe and novelist Tim McLaurin. Floyd's also has an unusually good supply of toys and candy.

In seven more miles, we come to Seagrove—the pottery pilgrim's mecca, but there's a literary connection, as well. Margaret Maron, one of the state's most accomplished mystery writers, used Seagrove as the setting for *Uncommon Clay*, another in her series of Deborah Knott novels. Knott is a judge and investigator who comes to the area to preside over an ugly divorce case, but she's not so busy as to miss the main attraction here. Early on, Knott slips away from the courthouse, grabs a bite of lunch, and goes in search of a few pieces of pottery. She begins at the North Carolina Pottery Center (one block east of the intersection of US 220 Alternate and NC 705; follow the signs). Knott explains the local drill:

The center displays representative pieces from most of the surrounding potteries, each keyed to a simple map of the area. . . . Since no one at the center can let you buy a sample outright, you're encouraged to go foraging on your own. Potteries are found on both sides of Highway 705 as well as along the branching roads. Most are right on the road, but others are up narrow dirt lanes, hidden from casual view by stands of cedar and pine, with only a small sign to tell you you've arrived. I found a half-dozen pieces whose style and color appealed to me, marked my map, and was on my way by one-fifteen.

At that, I barely had time to check out three or four places in the next hour, because you can't just go in and look at only platters. There's so much tactile variety, so many intriguing shapes, all demanding to be touched and held. The shops themselves were interesting, too. Some had regular museum pedestals with single pieces displayed like works of art, others stacked up rough planks and bricks and loaded the planks down like a discount warehouse. Some of the shops were separate showrooms, some were table and racks at one end with the potter and wheel at the other end, up to his elbows in wet clay as the wheel spun around and bowls magically emerged from the lump beneath his hands.

Although I didn't find my platters, I bought a grotesque face jug at one place and a large flower pot at another. At still another, I stood mesmer-

A face jug—one of many local styles of earthenware exhibited at the North Carolina Pottery Center in Seagrove.

ized as the potter turned out several cereal bowls in a row without a hair's worth of difference between them.

—From *Uncommon Clay*, by Margaret Maron (New York: Warner Books, 2001), 74–75.

Heed Deborah Knott's example and allow plenty of time for your pottery tour. Maron also quotes in her novel from a useful history of the artists in the region, Charles Zug's *Turners and Burners: The Folk Potters of North Carolina*, which is on sale with a number of other books about the region at the North Carolina Pottery Center.

This tour concludes with a poem by Susan Meyers, who grew up in Albemarle. "Area Pottery" is a common road sign in the vicinity of Seagrove.

AREA POTTERY SIGN MISREAD
AS *ARS POETICA*
    Seagrove, NC
1.
It's like confusing the tropes of *poetry*—
line by line, turn by turn—with *rotary*,

whose wheel also turns, but with more roar
(less iridescence) and patter.

It's like settling on a turnip for a treat,
taking the last radish on the tray,
mending a hem with tape.

It's like gossip unworthy of repeat,
the horse that won't trot,
the leaky bucket hanging from a frayed rope.

2.
The way hands curve as if cupping a pear,
clay in every pore,
what comes next so smooth it's rote.
The way a farmer knows his crop,
by head and heart, to sow and reap.

A gesture yields surprise, a stripe.
A flick becomes a scrape.
Hard to tell the potter
from the poet,
harder yet to tell the bowl from prayer.
—Used by permission of Susan Meyers.

■ LITERARY LANDSCAPE

Montgomery County Public Library
215 West Main Street, Troy
910-572-1311
<http://www.srls.info/montgomery/montIndex.html>
NC 24/27/109 join West Main Street in Troy. This library is one block west of
the junction and is part of the Sandhills Regional Library System. The spirited
librarians in this system regularly read and recommend books to patrons on
their website, with special attention to the works of local authors.

Asheboro : Randleman : Lexington : Thomasville

This tour is pure nostalgia: for the cotton mill culture that bonded workers and families in a common pursuit, for the amenities of small-town life in the Piedmont of the last century, and for a few of the indigenous treats of the region—barbecue, penny candy, and fried okra.

Writers with a connection to this area: Jerry Bledsoe, Cathy Smith Bowers, Braxton Craven, Sue Farlow, Charles Frazier, Holly George-Warren, Gerald White Johnson, Barbara Presnell, Margaret Rabb, Sandra Redding, Dale Volberg Reed, John Shelton Reed, Jack Riggs, Chris Costner Sizemore, Richard Walser

Leaving Seagrove on the last tour, you may still be wondering why so many potteries sprang up in this area. Poet Barbara Presnell explains that it was the early demand for jugs to harbor Randolph County's fine homemade liquor. Presnell also provides the following personal introduction to the place where she was raised:

I grew up in the late 1950s and 60s in Asheboro, the third child of a high school educator/counselor and the production superintendent at a small textile mill. Both sides of the family settled in the county over 200 years ago, on sprawling farms with many children. My grandfather operated a blacksmith shop and buggy repair business in town. On the other side of the family were farmers and Quakers—industrious, devout people.

I spent Saturdays traipsing around after my father at the mill or riding along the county roads looking for farms or fishing holes somebody at work had told him about. I knew the sewing ladies and the plant owners by name—

tour 11

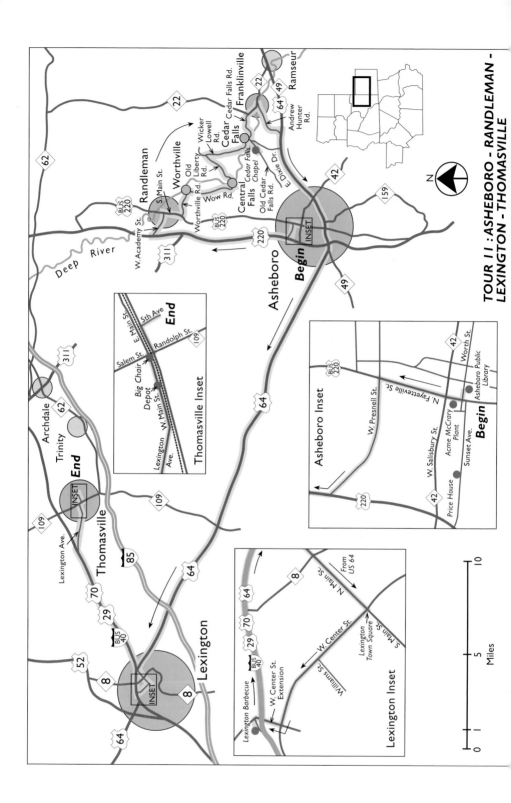

TOUR 11 : ASHEBORO - RANDLEMAN - LEXINGTON - THOMASVILLE

and they knew me. We'd visit my grandmother, a snuff-dipping mother of ten, who lived in a house on Main Street heated by a pot-bellied stove. Every month or so, we'd have to cut her a fresh toothbrush from a sweet gum branch. Sundays we'd head to the other end of the county where my mother's people lived, in Randleman, or Worthville, along the Deep River. Even though they were country raised, they were proper, bridge-playing people who kept a neat house on one of Randleman's downtown streets. I'm still meeting cousins I never knew existed. Most of the time we only have to trace back a generation or two before we find the link.

These are the people I write about, sometimes real and sometimes imagined. They cane chairs like my father did, and grow cucumbers and tomatoes in their side gardens, even though they have good jobs in town. They love their families and church. They struggle with a North Carolina that is changing too quickly, and sometimes they feel like they're being left behind. Sometimes they don't want to go.

■ ASHEBORO

Begin at the Randolph County Library, at the corner of Cox and Worth streets—a good place to park to explore Asheboro's downtown area on foot. Remarkably, this library has created an online index of all the titles published over the years by county residents. It includes such surprises as author Chris Costner Sizemore, better known as the subject of the film *The Three Faces of Eve*, portrayed by Joanne Woodward. Sizemore, who lived in the county but eventually settled in Florida, wrote three books about her experiences with multiple personality disorder.

Holly George-Warren, writer and contributor to nearly two dozen books on music and musicians and one-time editor of Rolling Stone Press, has a special connection to the Asheboro library. Her architect father designed the building, and her mother, Martha, was a librarian who engaged many North Carolina writers to speak here and at various book clubs in town.

In 1939, novelist Reynolds Price moved to Asheboro with his parents. His father, an appliance salesman for Carolina Power and Light, was transferred from Roxboro.

When I was six and ready for school, we moved into the only house my parents ever built. It was three miles outside Asheboro, among rocky hills that in Europe or the Mideast would be called mountains. The realtor's name for the neighborhood was Dogwood Acres, and it's now a crowded suburb, but we were pioneers. In 1939 there were few other houses, and on every side there were deep stretches of hardwood and pine and clear small streams. —From *Clear Pictures: First Loves, First Guides*, by Reynolds Price (New York: Atheneum, 1989), 94.

Five blocks west of the library, at 625 Sunset Avenue, is where Price's family later lived in town. In 1944, the family moved to Raleigh, when Price's father was offered a job with the Farmers Cooperative Exchange.

From the prosperous war years to the present, Asheboro has maintained its manufacturing base and is still home to one of the few successful textile plants operating in the region. Walk or drive west on Worth to its end at North Fayetteville Street and take a little jog across to Trade Street. Here is Acme McCrary, a plant that fills the whole block, up and down North Street.

This company has always provided many amenities for its workers, according to poet Barbara Presnell. She learned to swim in the company pool and has fond memories of the bowling alley that was here for employee use:

INDUSTRIAL LEAGUE BOWLING
Treva's husband throws a strike
every time he's up. She quit school
at fourteen, but Treva does the numbers
like a mathematician: ten plus ten plus
ten plus ten to three hundred at the last frame.
She works first shift sewing machine

at Stedman's. He sands for Dixie Furniture
but Dixie couldn't make a team, so he's on
with Stedman's by marriage, the ringer.
Their two kids come to Tuesday league night.
They'll know the ball like their own bones
long before they start at the mill.

When Treva's up, she wipes hands on her skirt,
tugs her blue-striped bowling shirt
—the company logo scripted on the back—
vees petite fingers in her six-pounder,
and throws. Seven down. Three more for a spare.
Tonight Klopman's eases ahead after the first game.

Stedman's a strong second. Bossong's best
was called in early for machine repair,

and they're a weak third without him.
Then it's Harrelson Rubber, Acme-McCrary,
Pinehurst, in that order. When your day
is the up-down-up-down arm of a needle

in cloth, a twenty-minute lunch,
when you're bad to slip stitches or tangle thread,
and your boss lives in the white house
so big your cousins drive to town just to see it,
you own the ball or you die. This
will save you: the necessary roar of the roll

down the alley, wild scatter of the hit,
a boy setting pins and sending balls
back to hands that can spin, slide, knuckle, toss,
that can make split pins fall, hands
with grease in their creases, grease under nails,
sewer's hands with thread burns scarred into palms.
—From *Piece Work*, by Barbara Presnell (Cleveland:
    Cleveland State University Poetry Center, 2007), 41–42.

To continue this tour's exploration of mill culture and literature, travel on Cox Street north from the library until it merges with Greensboro Street. At Presnell Street, turn left and take I-73/74 north, the fastest route to Randleman, another historic mill town. Just beyond the exit to High Point on US 311, take the Randleman exit and bear right onto West Academy Street.

■ **RANDLEMAN**

The first landmark here is Blue Mist Barbecue, one of a trio of local restaurants in business for more than fifty years and favored among writers (including Holly George-Warren) for the fried okra, among other delicacies.

One of Randleman's most famous legends takes place along the Deep River and was first published in the *Greensboro Patriot* in 1874. "The Story of Naomi Wise or the Wrongs of a Beautiful Girl" was written by "Charles Vernon," but older folks around here remember that the author was actually Braxton Craven, a one-time preacher and the teacher of "Mental and Moral Science" at Trinity College, where he also served as president some years before the school moved from Randolph County to Durham to eventually become Duke University.

The tale of Naomi Wise is still told in song by Wilkes County's Doc Watson, and, according to writer D. G. Martin, the story may have been the inspiration for a vignette in Charles Frazier's *Cold Mountain*, although Frazier's protagonist, Inman, halts the murder, saves the woman, and punishes the man who would have killed her. Randleman native Sandra Redding, a journalist and poet, offers this version from a more contemporary viewpoint:

NAOMI WISE

> *Randleman, NC—In the early 1800s Naomi Wise, pregnant and*
> *unmarried, was pushed off the banks of Deep River by the father*
> *of the unborn child. Many claim her footprint still remains,*
> *embedded in a rock, near the site of her unfortunate demise.*

Naomi
you weren't too wise
to get took in
by a mustached man
spinning those sticky lies
by the magnolias.
No, Naomi
that wasn't wise.
Born too soon
for pale pink pills
Diaphragms
or IUDs
now you drift
neath the deep Deep River
with craw-dads
and cold catfishes
while I criticize
Naomi
who wasn't wise.

—From *North Carolina's 400 Years: Signs along the Way—*
An Anthology of Poems by North Carolina Poets to Celebrate
America's 400th Anniversary, ed. Ronald H. Bayes, with
Marsha White Warren (Durham: Acorn Press, 1986), 7.

West Academy Street meets Naomi Street near the center of Randleman. Bear left at the fork, continuing on Academy. Ahead on the left is the Richard Petty Museum, honoring Randleman's best-known citizen. Next door is the old

Fading evidence of the dominance of tobacco in Randleman: the popular
Piedmont brand of cigarettes also included baseball cards in each pack.

Randleman School, and behind it, down the hill, you can see the ruins of a large mill on Deep River and its brick smokestack, the first of many on this tour.

Local poet Sue Farlow recommends a visit to the old St. Paul's Methodist Episcopal Church, now a museum on High Point Street, where town history is interpreted through artifacts and other material culture from the area. The church itself, built of handmade bricks and painted inside by artist Ruben Rinks in the nineteenth century, is adjacent to a very old cemetery where many early citizens are buried, including mill owner John Banner Randleman, for whom town was named, in 1876.

Head south on Main Street (US 220) a couple of miles to the intersection with Worthville Road (SR 2122) and turn left.

■ CENTRAL FALLS

In another two miles, turn right on Wow Road, which is a 2.7-mile roller coaster ride to the village of Central Falls. The main attraction here, according to Barbara Presnell, is the Old Rock Store, a curiosity built entirely of quartz stones, now called the Cornerstone Café and featuring "Maw-Maw's Cooking."

Once popular with mill workers, it has been in business since 1932. From this community of old mill houses, turn left on Old Liberty Road in front of the store. Follow Old Liberty until it meets Wicker Lowell Road and turn right.

■ CEDAR FALLS

Wicker Lowell Road leads into the bucolic mill village of Cedar Falls, where a footbridge on the right crosses the river to a picnic area with sheltered tables. The original Cedar Falls mill is on the left at the intersection of Whites Memorial Road and Loftin Pond Road.

Cedar Falls established the first cotton mill in Randolph County, built here in 1836, and, as the historic marker explains, this mill manufactured more cotton cloth than any other in the state for the Confederate Army. Turn right on Loftin Pond Road to see the mill owner's "big house" up the hill and the enormous yew tree in the front yard. Then continue just a few yards ahead to the fork with Old Cedar Falls Road (Bike Route 7) and bear right. Cedar Falls Chapel, dating from 1844, is on the right. The church's graveyard is a good spot to stop and read another poem by Barbara Presnell and consider all the lives that were dedicated to the manufacture of cloth here.

THE UNWEARING: A BENEDICTION
Then, at last, when machines shut down,
the crank and clatter of their work
quiet at this long shift's end,
when the bobbins are empty,

whistles have stopped blowing,
freight has been loaded on its beds
and is gone, when sore backs
and burly afternoons behind

concrete walls have gone,
when all the plants
have closed their doors,
there will be nothing left

but the spinning earth,
its tight weave of water and root,
soft fabric of morning,
each imperfection counted one

The first cotton mill in Randolph County was chartered in 1828 in Cedar Falls.
A picnic area for visitors sits alongside the Deep River, which powered the mill.

by one, nothing left but the world's
rhythm, the manufacture of its seasons,
nothing but the voices of our ancestors
talking above the roar,

and then we will take off the cloth
and there will be only thread
and then not even thread
or the need for thread

and we will bless each day's creation,
the sweat and rip that wove it,

Cedar Falls Church and cemetery recall the lives of the town's earliest textile workers, who made more shirts and drawers for the Civil War effort than any other mill in North Carolina.

the oily grace that gave it to us,
how it feels against our skin.
—From *Piece Work*, by Barbara Presnell (Cleveland:
    Cleveland State University Poetry Center, 2007), 3.

Our trip along the Deep River comes to an end in the town of Franklinville. Backtrack to the intersection with Wicker Lowell Road and Whites Memorial and turn right on Cedar Falls Road (SR 2226) heading east. Bear right as SR 2226 merges into Main Street (NC 22) in Franklinville, established in 1847. Writer William Least Heat-Moon came to Franklinville on his back-road journey across the United States, which he documented in his now-classic book, *Blue Highways*. The author was drawn here in search of an early ancestor's grave, supposedly located near Sandy Creek. Townsfolk sent him to an elder who would know how to find the graveyard in deep woods.

Thick muddy water in the ancient millrace of Randolph Mills at Franklinville curled in slow menace like a fat water moccasin waiting for something to come to it. The mill ran on electricity now, and the race was a dead end—what went in didn't come out. Inside, spoked flywheels tall as men spun, rumbling the wavy wooden floors and plankways, but no one was around. It seemed a ghost mill turned by Deep River. I knocked on the crooked pine doors; I tapped on a clouded window and pressed close to see in. On the other side, an old misshapen face looked back and made me jump.—From *Blue Highways: A Journey into America*, by William Least Heat-Moon (Boston: Back Bay Books, 1999), 44–45.

The writer finds his local guide and eventually, through deep and nearly impenetrable woods, comes upon a concrete marker that explains that his ancestor's grave is now under the waters of Sandy Creek.

The last Franklinville mill closed in 1979, and now local citizens are working to preserve the mill village architecture and to develop a four-mile rail/trail and greenway along the Deep River for hikers, bicyclists, and kayakers.

From Franklinville, take Andrew Hunter Road (SR 2235) south to US 64 and turn right. It's a pastoral drive, some thirty-three miles to Lexington, our next destination. Exit 64 onto US 70/29, which becomes North Main Street in downtown Lexington.

■ LEXINGTON

Lexington's town square, where Center and Main streets meet, is a good place to park and take in the town. If you have a sweet tooth, don't miss the Candy Factory under the red-and-white-striped awning at 15 North Main. Across the street and a few doors down, at 6 North Main, is Conrad and Hinkle Grocers, dating from 1925. At this classic old-time grocery, fresh liver mush is made daily, and all kinds of spreads—pimiento cheese, tuna fish, egg salad, chicken salad, and ham salad—are specialties of the house, along with banana pudding to go. This poem by North Carolina poet laureate Cathy Smith Bowers, a faculty member in creative writing at Queens University in Charlotte, evokes the history of such old establishments:

GROCERIES

I had a boyfriend once, after my mother
and brothers and sisters and I
fled my father's house, who worked
at the Piggly Wiggly where he stocked
shelves on Fridays until midnight
then drove to my house to sneak me out,

North Carolina poet laureate Cathy Smith Bowers is the author of The Love that Ended Yesterday in Texas *(Iris Press, 1992),* Traveling in Time of Danger *(Iris Press, 1999),* A Book of Minutes *(Iris Press, 2004), and* The Candle I Hold Up to See You *(Iris Press, 2009). Photo courtesy Chris Bartol.*

take me down to the tracks by the cotton mill
where he lifted me and the quilt I'd brought
into an empty boxcar. All night
the wild thunder of looms. The roar of trains
passing on adjacent tracks hauling
their difficult cargo, cotton bales
or rolls of muslin on their way
to the bleachery to be whitened, patterned
into stripes and checks, into still-life gardens
of wisteria and rose. And when the whistle
signaled third shift free, he would lift me
down again onto the gravel and take me home.
If my mother ever knew she didn't say, so glad
in her new freedom, so grateful for the bags
of damaged goods stolen from the stockroom
and left on our kitchen table. Slashed
bags of rice and beans he had bandaged
with masking tape, the labelless cans,
the cereals and detergents in varying

stages of destruction. Plenty
to get us through the week, and even some plums
and cherries, tender and delicious,
and floating in their own sweet juice.
—From *Traveling in Time of Danger*, by Cathy Smith Bowers
    (Oak Ridge, Tenn.: Iris Press, 1999), 9.

Lexington's mom-and-pop businesses speak to an earlier era, an environment that native son Jack Riggs explores in his coming-of-age novel, *When the Finch Rises*. Downtown Lexington and its adjoining neighborhoods are the haunts of Riggs's central characters. Raybert Williams and his friend Palmer Conroy ride bikes, sneak cigarettes from the grocery, play baseball, and generally make mischief during the era of Neil Armstrong's moon walk and the peak of Evel Knievel's fame. While Raybert and Palmer dream big dreams, reality constantly intrudes: Raybert's mother, Ellen, is mentally ill, and his father, Ray, handles his own stress with too much Jim Beam bourbon.

The novel is set in the fictional town of Ellenton. A number of Lexington sites—including Finch Park and Forest Hills Cemetery, close to the house where Riggs grew up—are important locations in the story.

Riggs studied with Fred Chappell at the University of North Carolina at Greensboro and now teaches writing in Atlanta. He urges visitors to sample a staple of the local diet that also figures in his novel—Lexington barbecue.

While more than twenty barbecue restaurants in the region are listed on a local visitor's map, Riggs recommends the recipe perfected by Honey Monk, the only actual Lexington name in his novel that the author did not change for purposes of fiction. The original Lexington barbecue was reportedly first produced using Monk's special recipe in the alley behind Conrad and Hinkle Grocers and was sold right off the cooker.

To reach the sit-down restaurant, turn onto West Center Street at the square. This route takes you by the neighborhood on Williams Street (called Robbins Street in the novel) where Jack Riggs's characters hung out. Because furniture is still manufactured here, you may notice along the way the scent of glue in the air. In 0.9 miles, turn right onto West Center Street Extension, then turn left in 0.2 miles onto the I-85 Business Loop Extension. Here the smell of glue gives way to the delicious scent of 'cue. Lexington Barbecue (336-249-9814) is immediately on the right, off I-85 Business.

The signature coleslaw on this restaurant's BBQ sandwiches is a sweet red concoction made with the unusual addition of ketchup and sugar. Of course, there are many other versions of pit-cooked pig, slaw, and pie to sample in

*Best known for its barbecue, the town of Lexington has assembled a
collection of pigs to celebrate its delicious reputation.*

town—Smokey Joe's, Smiley's, Speedy's, and Stamey's, to name a few. While
Henry James BBQ on Talbert Boulevard might seem to hold the promise of a
literary connection to the great writer, who once visited North Carolina's Bilt-
more House in Asheville, these Lexington (and Asheboro) restaurants simply
bear the first names of the owners, Henry and James. To dig deeper into the
finer points of such fanaticism found among barbecue buffs in Lexington, see
the highly literate treatment by John Shelton Reed and Dale Volberg Reed, with
William McKinney, in *Holy Smoke: The Big Book of North Carolina Barbecue*
(2008). For dessert, here's a tribute from Chapel Hill poet Margaret Rabb:

A SEASONING IN HELL
Carolina pit barbeque restaurant décor
invariably celebrates les cochons d'enfer.

Bandsawn plywood, cross stitched, sheet metal
porkers hang as worldly signs of a satiate cabal.

These aren't just happy pigs, either, apple
smugly stuffed, self-satisfied on the platter.

The secret is in the smoke.

Rather, these ecstatic swine lift meek forelegs
to praise Jesus who made divine mere shreds

And sauce. Amen, hogs. Dance on, shoulder
to shoulder, cheek by jowl, let hocks shudder,

Let hickory flames rise around you, consume
all flesh until it sputters into burnt communion.

Pass through living coals, brothers, leap after
each other, doused in vinegar and cayenne pepper.

Run two sheets before the wind, sanctify and seize
the flame azalea, its incense wasted bateau epiphanies.

Your bête noir serves the side dishes with a devilish
grin and spins the tray: red hot hell bent damn dervish.
—From *Granite Dives*, by Margaret Rabb (Kalamazoo, Mich.:
  New Issues Press, 1999), 29.

This tour concludes by following US 29 Business for ten miles northeast to
another historic manufacturing town, Thomasville.

Journalist, screenwriter, novelist, and publisher Jerry Bledsoe sets the beginning of his wistful memoir of small-town living in Thomasville, where he flourished as a boy:

> I turn onto the street, and the years peel away. I am twelve again, whizzing down the hill on my J. C. Higgins Special, no hands, my newspaper delivery bag flapping in the basket.
>
> I was five when we moved to Fifth Avenue in Thomasville, a small town in central North Carolina famed for its furniture factories. How the street came to be Fifth Avenue, I don't know. There were no First, Second, Third or Fourth avenues. I used to think my street was named for a candy bar, and it may well have been.
>
> Although it was only a few blocks from downtown, across the mainline Southern Railroad tracks, Fifth Avenue was a dirt street then, dusty in summer, muddy in winter. It wasn't paved until several years after we moved there. Improvements also brought a sidewalk that became a downhill raceway for kids on skates, scooters, tricycles, and wagons.

The candy theme continues as Bledsoe recounts the offerings at Noah's neighborhood store in Thomasville:

> The counter to the right was heaven to us kids. It stretched almost the length of the store, and on it were two low glass cases. The candy counter. We would scramble onto the benches in front of it, clutching a few pennies, and agonize over our decisions. Would we get Kits, Mary Janes, licorice twists, sour balls, caramel blobs, or candy cigarettes, pink-tipped and three to a pack? Would it be Kisses, Twoffers, Fireballs, Saf-T-Pops, Tootsie Rolls or Double Bubble gum wrapped with funny papers inside? How about a set of buckteeth made of sweet chewy wax? Orange lips? A mustache shiny black? Penny Nips—red, green and yellow in crumbly wax bottles?—From *Country Cured: Reflections from the Heart*, by Jerry Bledsoe (Marietta, Ga.: Longstreet Press, 1989), 5, 11.

Bledsoe's neighborhood on Fifth Avenue is at the end of this tour, but before reaching that destination, have a look around the town's central business district. As poet Barbara Presnell explains, the big chair at the center of downtown Thomasville still welcomes visitors to town, even though the town no

Thomasville's giant chair was once occupied by political candidate Lyndon B.
Johnson as he addressed a crowd assembled in the center of town.

longer makes chairs. In 1960, vice presidential candidate Lyndon Johnson rode
in on the train and spoke from the seat of this giant replica of a Duncan Phyfe
original. Today's visitor can only imagine life here when so much furniture was
made and shipped worldwide. Be sure and stop by the oldest remaining railroad depot in the state, at 44 West Main Street, which also houses Thomasville's
visitors' center.

Another significant literary contribution comes from Gerald White Johnson,
who grew up in eastern North Carolina but began his long career as a journalist in Thomasville, publishing the *Davidsonian* newspaper in the early twentieth century. Johnson would go on to publish more than three dozen books and
write for a number of newspapers, including the *American Mercury* and the
Baltimore Sun, where his columns often clashed with those of the paper's most

famous voice, H. L. Mencken. (Johnson, a Wake Forest alumnus, would be followed by W. J. Cash as the chief southern voice in the *Mercury*.)

Johnson's 1933 novel, *Number Thirty-six*, is set in Thomasville (called Rogersville in the book) early in the twentieth century, when the Civil War was yet a fresh memory to locals and the textile industry was just gaining momentum. The young protagonist, Donald Whyte Watson, is headed for a career in journalism. As the story opens, the daily trains that pass through the center of town hold much more attraction for the boy than the idea of a writing career:

> Into the square Don came slowly one June morning—slowly, because he didn't want to come. Papa had issued a ukase to the effect that he must begin to learn the printer's trade this vacation, and he didn't want to do it. Practical knowledge of printing, said Papa, was invaluable to a newspaper man. Sitting in an office all day long, writing, or reading newspapers and dull-looking books, or talking to duller people was no tempting prospect. He wanted to be outside where things happened. He wanted to be an engineer and drive Thirty-six every day up through Greensboro, and Danville and on to Monroe, Virginia, or bring Thirty-five down at night, through Rogersville and on to Spencer.—From *Number Thirty-six*, by Gerald W. Johnson (New York: Minton, Balch, 1933), 22.

Don Watson grows up, attends Wake Forest, fights in France, and returns to assume the reins of his father's newspaper (much like Johnson's own career). He soon confronts the challenge of his editorial career, when a cotton mill strike results in the death of several local workers. Watson's sympathies are torn between local mill owners and the workers. Both parties represent the town that his newspaper must serve to survive.

Though out of print, Johnson's novel is an important window on the prevailing attitudes of the era and the complex economic, political, and social legacy of North Carolina's once-booming textile industry.

■ LITERARY LANDSCAPE

Randolph Writers

randolphwriters@aol.com

Describing themselves as a loose association of area writers who want to share their work and learn more about the craft and business of writing, members meet monthly at the Moring Arts Center at 123 Sunset Avenue. They sponsor annual writing contests and host a recognition ceremony for the winners at the Asheboro Library downtown.

Lexington Branch Library

602 South Main Street, Lexington

<http://www.co.davidson.nc.us/community/LexingtonLibrary.aspx>

This downtown branch of the Davidson County library system is notable for its comprehensive collection of works by Lexington native Richard Walser. Until his death in 1988, Walser worked tirelessly to lift up North Carolina writers. He wrote or edited more than thirty books—especially anthologies—during his energetic career as a folklorist and teacher. He was called "North Carolina's literary evangelist" by Tom Wicker.

trail two

The Eastern Piedmont: Writers' Beginnings

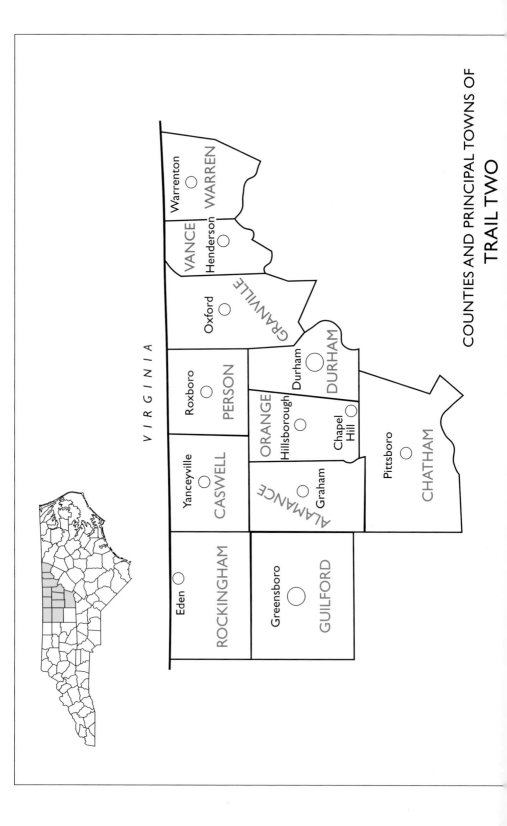

COUNTIES AND PRINCIPAL TOWNS OF
TRAIL TWO

So many literary careers launched in North Carolina in the last century have at their source at least one of the institutions of higher learning in the area that this trail encompasses. Phillips Russell, poet, novelist, biographer, and teacher of creative writing at the University of North Carolina at Chapel Hill from 1931 to 1955, gave credit to UNC president Frank Porter Graham for encouraging creative endeavors of many sorts at the university, including the work begun by Frederick Koch in the drama department and carried on by his protégé, Paul Green.

Woman's College in Greensboro (now UNC-Greensboro) has a similar tradition, and the faculty brought in before the school became coeducational reads like a roster of who's who in twentieth-century southern literature—Allen Tate, Caroline Gordon, Randall Jarrell, Robie McCauley, Frances Gray Patton, John Crowe Ransom, Hiram Haydn, Peter Taylor, and Fred Chappell. Similar literary traditions at North Carolina Central University and Duke University make this trail a rich undertaking—so many books, so many fine writers, and so many connections among them.

Connections are the story in North Carolina. In general, writers can be competitive. The writer/teachers in this region seem to have mastered the craft of kind but firm critique, making it possible for their students to take risks without fear of embarrassment.

Even beyond the classroom is the kind of support and nurture among a small band of Piedmont writers that gave birth in 1984 to the North Carolina Writers' Network. The Network rose to national prominence on the shoulders of a long succession of writers. One of them is Doris Betts, as an example, whose teaching skills are legendary. Betts was the beneficiary in the early 1950s of extraordinary support from one of her own teachers—a story Betts has told at a number of conferences and recorded in an interview by High Point University English professor Jane Stephens. The story is a fitting introduction to this trail.

Though Doris Waugh had already won several prizes for her student writing, she dropped out of Woman's College to marry her longtime sweetheart, Lowry Betts. The couple moved to South Carolina for Lowry to finish college and then moved back to North Carolina so he could attend law school. Before long, Doris was caring for two babies in the couple's tiny Chapel Hill apartment and trying to earn a little from newspaper writing while continuing to write fiction with what little time remained.

One day the doorbell rang. The short-story writer Frances Gray Patton, elegantly dressed, had come from Durham to call. Betts was mortified. She had been up all night with the children, who had the stomach flu. The bathroom pail was full of soiled diapers. The unmistakable smell of vomit was everywhere. The two women sat down to visit, but the babies kept crying. It was hard to talk. Finally, Mrs. Patton said she'd probably better get going, but asked if she could first use the restroom. Horrified, Doris showed her the way.

When Patton returned, she said her goodbyes, giving Doris her hand and a little wad of paper. Patton told her not to neglect the fiction writing and to get some help with the children. According to Jane Stephens's account, Patton said, "I have just sold *Good Morning, Miss Dove*, and it's a Book of the Month Club [selection], and I may never be able to do this again. All you have to do is, when the time comes, and you have a book in the Book of the Month Club, pass it on." When Patton departed, Betts opened her hand. In it was a check for five hundred dollars—a huge sum in the 1950s.

As Betts told Jane Stephens in the interview: "I did not cash the check, but I have kept the gift all my life." Doris Betts began passing the gift along at UNC in 1966. Her students have included Russell Banks, Tim McLaurin, Randall Kenan, and Robert Morgan. Fannie Patton's prediction came true: Betts's 1981 novel *Heading West* was a Book of the Month Club selection.

High Point : Centre : Greensboro

Visit Polecat Creek, a Quaker stronghold that gave rise to a surprising group of talented wordsmiths. Journey to High Point's furniture market with mystery writer Margaret Maron. Learn more about the extraordinary constellation of writers who came to teach at Woman's College, in Greensboro, and their influence on generations of writers who have followed.

Writers with a connection to this tour: Anjail Rashida Ahmad, Ethel Stephens Arnett, Nancy Bartholomew, Linda Beatrice Brown, Orson Scott Card, Fred Chappell, Quinn Dalton, Jonathan Worth Daniels, Burke Davis, Burke Davis III, Angela Davis-Gardner, Ann Deagon, Stuart Dischell, Candace Flynt, Marianne Gingher, Jennifer Grotz, O. Henry, Judith Hill, Randall Jarrell, Susan S. Kelly, Tom Kirby-Smith, Charles Kuralt, Burgess Leonard, Sarah Lindsay, Margaret Maron, Michael McFee, James McGirt, Kimberly Morton-Cuthrell, Edward R. Murrow, Valerie Nieman, Craig Nova, Michael Parker, David Roderick, Brenda Schleunes, Allison Seay, Elizabeth Sewell, Mark Smith-Soto, William Swaim, Alan Tate, Peter Taylor, Albion Tourgée, Robert Watson, Carole Boston Weatherford, Carolyn Beard Whitlow, Amy Jo Wood, Kathryn Worth, Lynn York, Lee Zacharias

■ HIGH POINT

Our foray into North Carolina's furniture manufacturing legacy and the literature about it begins on Main Street in High Point, site of the largest furniture industry trade show in the world. Though most of North Carolina's largest furniture companies have moved their manufacturing out of this country, High Point is still the destination for tens of thousands of furniture buyers and designers for ten days every April and October. The visitors fill the city with festivity, commerce, and sometimes intrigue, as novelist Margaret Maron would have us believe.

tour 12

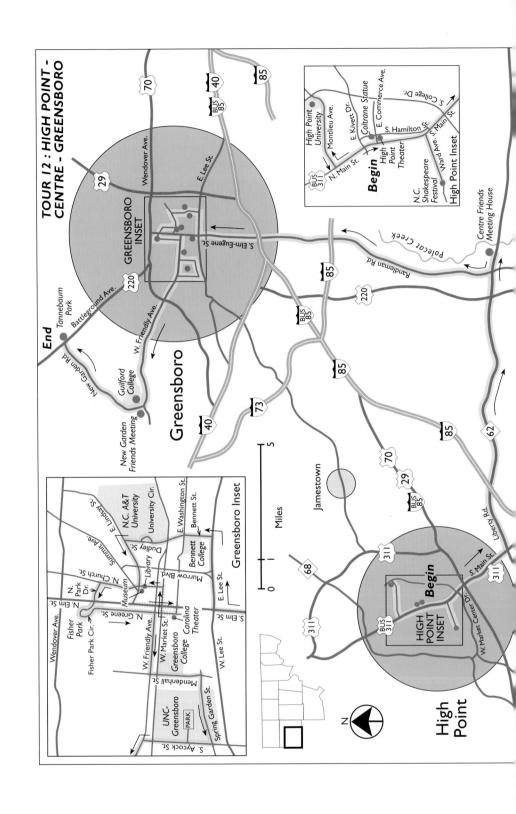

TOUR 12 : HIGH POINT - CENTRE - GREENSBORO

High Point Inset

High Point University
Montlieu Ave.
N. Main St.
E. Kivett Dr.
Coltrane Statue
E. Commerce Ave.
S. Hamilton St.
S. College Dr.
BUS 311
Begin
High Point Theater
Ward Ave.
S. Main St.
N.C. Shakespeare Festival
Centre Friends Meeting House

Greensboro Inset

Wendover Ave.
Fisher Park
Fisher Park Cir.
N. Elm St.
N. Church St.
N. Greene St.
N. Park Dr.
Summit Ave.
N. Lindsay St.
Dudley St.
University Cir.
N.C. A&T University
E. Washington St.
Bennett St.
Bennett College
Library
Museum
Murrow Blvd.
Fisher Park Cir.
W. Friendly Ave.
W. Market St.
Greensboro College
Carolina Theater
Mendenhall St.
UNC-Greensboro
PARK
S. Aycock St.
Spring Garden St.
W. Lee St.
S. Elm St.
E. Lee St.

Greensboro Inset

70
40
85
BUS 85
29
Wendover Ave.
GREENSBORO INSET
S. Elm-Eugene St.
E. Lee St.
220
Battleground Ave.
W. Friendly Ave.
End
Tannebaum Park
New Garden Rd.
Guilford College
New Garden Friends Meeting
Greensboro
40
73
Randleman Rd.
Polecat Creek
85
BUS 85
220
85
85
62
68
70
29
BUS 85
311
BUS 311
Jamestown
311
Begin
HIGH POINT INSET
S. Main St.
W. Market Center Dr.
Liberty Rd.
311

High Point

Miles
0 1 5

N

In the novel *Killer Market*, Maron's protagonist, Judge Deborah Knott, has come to town during market week and quickly finds herself trying to solve a murder for which there are more than enough interesting suspects. Knott's accidental tour guide in this adventure—a mysterious older woman named Matilda McNeill Jernigan—knows the ropes and maneuvers Knott through the throngs to see the market up close:

> With a sweep of chiffon, she gestured toward the big windowless buildings that could be seen from our table overlooking Main Street. "Seven million square feet of showrooms in a hundred and fifty places around the area and all the buildings are dark and silent for three hundred days of the year. Then we have a month of hustle—tearing out walls, putting in new ones, laying carpets, painting, hanging wallpaper, installing the furniture—just to get ready for nine days of buyers. Retailers come from all over the world to order the chairs and couches and case goods that will wind up in Mediterranean villas and Manhattan penthouses. Japanese decorators will buy outrageously expensive bibelots to grace a chain of hotels from Nagasaki to Sapporo. And those polyvinyl chaises that a newly famous Hollywood star will buy for her first swimming pool next fall? Someone will sell the line to a California distributor this week."—From *Killer Market*, by Margaret Maron (New York: Mysterious Press, 1997), 22.

Because the furniture market is limited to authorized professionals and their guests, Maron's novel is a great way to get an inside glimpse of the activity that takes place in High Point's maze of modern and historic buildings.

To see the heart of the market, going north on South Main, turn right onto East Commerce Avenue. At this corner one can see the maze of old and new buildings that is the market. The International Home Furnishings Center, at 210 East Commerce, houses High Point Theater, the Southern Circuit Film Festival, and the High Point Community Theater.

Don't miss the eight-foot-tall bronze statue of jazz saxophonist John Coltrane that stands at the intersection of Commerce Avenue and Hamilton Street. High Point's resident children's writer and poet, Carole Boston Weatherford, provides the story of Coltrane's youth in *Before John Was a Jazz Giant* (New York: Henry Holt, 2008).

Coltrane was born in Hamlet and then spent his first seventeen years in High Point. He joined a community music group and soon became a charter member of the school band at William Penn High School. An exhibition about his life and career is part of the High Point Museum.

Another children's writer from High Point, Burgess Leonard, had ten novels published from 1953 to 1960 that feature stories of athletes in baseball, basketball, and football. The books are set around the Piedmont, at the University of North Carolina at Chapel Hill, at North Carolina State University in Raleigh, and at Burgess's alma mater, Wake Forest University.

Book lovers may also be curious to visit the Bernice Bienenstock Furniture Library, at 1009 North Main Street, home to the world's largest collection of books on the history of furniture. It is open weekdays from 9 to 5 except for the noon lunch hour.

Continuing north on Main, turn right on Montlieu Avenue (US 29) to see High Point University. This institution has made a priority of creative writing. Among the writers who have taught here are Lynn York (whose work is considered in Tour 2), Quinn Dalton, a Greensboro-based novelist and short-story writer, and Carole Boston Weatherford, who now teaches at Fayetteville State University.

Backtrack to North Main Street. Turn left and return through downtown, heading south. Another main attraction for the literary traveler in High Point is Spirit Center, a 51,000-square-foot performing-arts campus located at 807 West Ward Avenue. It is headquarters for the North Carolina Shakespeare Festival (<http://www.ncshakes.org/>), a professional troupe of actors who regularly present works by the Bard and other more contemporary playwrights.

By now you may have noticed more than one eating establishment called Biscuitville. (There are five in High Point.) This Piedmont chain turns out to be popular with at least two Triad area (Winston-Salem, High Point, Greensboro) writers—novelist Susan S. Kelly and essayist Amy Jo Wood. Kelly, whose work comes a bit later on this tour, explains: "I wrote my first two novels in booths or at tables in Biscuitville and Bojangles. My children were small, and I'd hire babysitters and go there for the white noise and the anonymity."

For Amy Jo Wood, the attraction is a bit more complicated:

No matter how many veggie burgers I consumed, my Southern soul still craved ham biscuits. Some mornings I snuck into Biscuitville like a back-sliding Baptist, reveling in the rebellion of one going against the grain; the whole wheat grain of an era obsessed with health. A fat free friend in New York wonders why I won't give up foods from the past.

Wood, a prodigal who returned from Manhattan to her home turf after a turn at urban life, goes on to explain that it was more than just the seduction of comfort food from her childhood that drew her into Biscuitville for the first time. The customers seemed so familiar.

Their conversations reminded me of the chatter I'd endured on Sunday afternoons long ago, but I remained immune to the necessity of small talk. The Buddhas of Biscuitville plucked away at the petals of my cynicism.

The retired bank tellers, salesmen, and accountants who gathered in the back booths every morning didn't discuss the merits of forming communities, they saved seats for the latecomers and worried when a Biscuitville buddy didn't show.... A sliver of fat in the ham tried to con my taste buds into believing the food was just like grandma used to make. The dueling notions of nostalgia and revolution finally pushed me over the edge.

During free fall, I realized it was not the food which caused me to join my elders at Biscuitville. I was hungry for the details of the stories I missed the first time around, the momentary concerns of weather and neighbors. The important stuff.

An advertising banner flapping in the breeze beneath the air-conditioning duct read, "Biscuitville, 30 years and still rolling."

Me, too. As long as there are ham biscuits, I can always find my way home.

—From "The Buddhas of Biscuitville," in *White Bred, A Prodigal Jaunt to the Suburban South,* by Amy Jo Wood, <http://www.wampus.com>.

Beyond the Biscuitville at 2709 South Main Street, continue to the junction with NC 62 (Liberty Road) and turn left. It's approximately ten miles to the Centre Friends Meeting House, our next stop. Cross I-73 and Randleman Road and then watch on the left for a historical marker, the meeting house, several outbuildings, and a graveyard on the hill next to the church.

■ CENTRE

Though we are not taking the most direct route to Greensboro from High Point, this pilgrimage into rural Guilford County takes us to a significant literary site—Polecat Creek, a humble tributary that flows south from Greensboro, east of the Centre Meeting House, and eventually into the Deep River east of Randleman. A group of Quakers from Pennsylvania settled here around 1740 and were joined in the 1770s by Nantucket Islanders, who had made their living as whalers. Polecat Creek was the primary landmark in Centre, sometimes prone to flooding but generally helpful in the community's agricultural pursuits.

Though he was not a Quaker, writer William Swaim, born into the fourth generation of Swaims here in 1802, would leave Polecat Creek to become the owner and abolitionist editor of the *Greensboro Patriot* newspaper from 1829 to 1835. Of the newspaper business, Swaim wrote: "These are perilous times; and a responsibility awful as the tomb and extensive as eternity, hangs over every man who shall take upon himself the management of a newspaper."

Swaim's most famous publication was a pamphlet, "An Address to the People of North Carolina on the Evils of Slavery." As Swaim carried his abolitionist beliefs from Polecat Creek into Greensboro, he was harshly rebuked. At one point the North Carolina General Assembly debated whether to introduce a resolution charging him with sedition for his views.

Swaim died at age thirty-three, long before the birth of his grandson, William Sydney Porter, who would also take up a pen and write his way into history. As Charles Alphonso Smith, one of Porter's biographers, suggests, both men apparently had ink running in their veins. Porter, better known as O. Henry, would spend his youth in Greensboro and go on to become the most popular short-story writer of his time. He lived the last years of his life near Asheville.

Porter was born in 1862 in the spacious William Worth House—the "Mansion House" as the Centre locals called it. His great-uncle, also from Polecat Creek, was North Carolina governor Jonathan Worth (1865–68). For more on Swaim and Porter, see the companion biographies *William Swaim, Fighting Editor* (1963) and *O. Henry of Polecat Creek* (1962), written by Greensboro historian and poet Ethel Stephens Arnett.

O. Henry's successors on the Worth side of the family spawned yet more writers. The late Kathryn Worth, a great-granddaughter of the governor, wrote and dedicated a historical novel to her Centre ancestors in 1942. *They Loved to Laugh* is still in print and is a perennial favorite with pre-teen girls. It is a coming-of-age story that chronicles everyday Quaker life in Centre in the 1830s and also provides a dainty dose of adolescent romance.

Kathryn Worth published one other novel during her lifetime. She married Walter Clyde Curry, who was professor of English at Vanderbilt University for forty years and an early member of the Fugitive literary movement, which also figures in Greensboro's literary history.

Journalist and editor Jonathan Worth Daniels, who is featured throughout these trails, was also from the Worth side of O. Henry's family. He was the grandson of Governor Worth's younger brother, John M. Worth. Perhaps, then, ink in the bloodline is not such a far-fetched theory, or perhaps it was some-

Greensboro's memorial to the dean of American journalism, Edward R. Murrow, born south of the city on Polecat Creek near the Quaker settlement of Centre. The sculpture is the work of Ogden Deal.

thing in the water here, because the literary history of Polecat Creek includes one more eminent writer, unrelated to the Swaim and Worth families.

Edward R. Murrow, whose given name was actually Egbert, was born here in 1908 in a log cabin without running water, indoor plumbing, or electricity. His mother was overprotective, and his father was a relatively unsuccessful farmer, who grew corn and hay and a little tobacco on a tract of land right along Davis Mill Road (within sight of the Centre Meeting House). As Murrow's biographer explains, the boy's gift with words was obvious early on:

> The voice of Egbert Murrow was first heard publicly at the Centre Friends meeting. The meeting followed the Quaker custom of encouraging members to pray aloud, to exhort, to confess—whenever "moved by the spirit." And the spirit moved Egbert at age four. The boy had a booming voice, almost freakish coming from so small a body. Unprompted, he jumped to his feet and confessed that that morning he had trapped a rabbit and sold it for a dime, violating the Quaker commandment to rest on the Sabbath.
> —From *Edward R. Murrow: An American Original*, by Joseph E. Persido (New York: Dell, 1988), 22.

Murrow began his career by captivating listeners as he narrated the unfolding drama of World War II on CBS radio. His prose style was direct and clean. Later, Murrow moved into the new medium of television with a pathbreaking news and public affairs program called *See It Now*. The program allowed him to tackle the most challenging issues of his time, including the political witch hunts of the 1950s, which led him to a personal encounter with Senator Joseph McCarthy, documented in the 2005 film *Good Night and Good Luck*.

Murrow's other innovative interview program, *Person to Person*, featured guests who appeared in their own homes while Murrow interviewed them from his New York studio. Among Murrow's many subjects were Charlotte writer Harry Golden and evangelist Billy Graham. Murrow's crisp writing style, his distinctive voice, and the high ethical standards that were forged in his Quaker childhood on Polecat Creek have kept him at the top of most lists of the most influential journalists of the twentieth century.

Charles Kuralt was Murrow's colleague at CBS and had idolized the broadcaster as a child. Kuralt first met Murrow as a teenager and again as a student at the University of North Carolina at Chapel Hill. In an address in 1971 to the North Carolina Literary and Historical Association, Kuralt—with his own characteristic eloquence—said of Murrow:

> We remember him, finally, for his deep and abiding belief that we could take it; that there was never any excuse for insulating the people from reality; that escapism was the eighth, and deadliest sin; that the American people were wise beyond the comprehension of those who would trick us or delude us or tell us lies; that we were decent and responsible and mature and could be counted on every time if only we could be supplied our fair measure of the straight facts.
>
> We don't remember him for his honors. We remember him for how he honored us.
>
> —From "Ed Murrow's Inquiring Mind," by Charles Kuralt, in *North Carolina Historical Review* 48 (April 1971): 170.

Backtrack on NC 62 to Randleman Road and turn right. In a few miles, as Randleman forks to the left, bear right on South Elm/Eugene Street, which crosses I-40 and I-85 and leads into the heart of downtown Greensboro.

■ BENNETT COLLEGE FOR WOMEN

Greensboro's literary history is deep and rich, particularly because of the institutions of higher learning located here. Bennett College is one of the city's oldest, founded in 1873 as a normal school to serve African Americans recently emancipated from slavery. To reach Bennett, turn right on Lee Street from Elm/Eugene. The campus comes up on the left several blocks beyond Edward R. Murrow Boulevard. North Carolina Literary Hall of Fame poet, short-story writer, and magazine editor James Ephraim McGirt was born a year after Bennett College's founding in Robeson County. He moved to Greensboro as a child and attended public schools before earning a degree at Bennett in 1895. McGirt published his first collection of poems in 1899 and another in 1901.

THE SPIRIT OF THE OAK (EXCERPT)
The spirit of the oak am I,
With head uplifted to the sky,
Though hail and storm beat in my face,
Through weal or woe I hold my place,
With head uplifted to the sky,
The spirit of the oak am I.
—From *For Your Sweet Sake: Poems*, by James McGirt
    (Philadelphia: John C. Winston, 1906), 3.

McGirt most often wrote in dialect, though the poem above, from his last collection, takes a more formal tone. Ultimately frustrated by his poetry's poor reception, McGirt left Greensboro in 1903 and moved to Philadelphia to launch a general-interest monthly, *McGirt's Magazine*, which was a successful enterprise for several years. McGirt published one more book of poetry and a collection of short stories before returning to Greensboro in 1910 to start a thriving business in hair-care products. He died here in 1930 and is buried in Maplewood Cemetery in an unmarked grave. A branch of the Greensboro public library is named for McGirt and fellow poet George Moses Horton, of Chatham County.

Bennett became a women's college in 1926 and continues a proud tradition of literary engagement today. Among its alumnae is Greensboro native Kimberly Morton-Cuthrell, whose first novel, *Splinters of My Soul* (2006), found a large audience in Europe. She now lives and writes in Spain. Another Bennett alumna is poet, novelist, and professor Linda Beatrice Brown, who lives in Greensboro and has taught at the University of North Carolina at Greensboro, at Guilford College, and at her alma mater. Her work, which has been compared to Zora Neale Hurston's, depicts strong African American women. Her novels are *Rainbow Roun' Mah Shoulder* (1984; reissued in 1989) and *Crossing Over Jordan* (1994).

YOU PLAY IT ON THE EDGE (EXCERPT)
She walked out of the ocean
a black woman carrying her whole thing
in a bundle on her head/
she had a fist full of jewels
and three pomegranates in the other hand/
her cousin Venus came in on a shell
but "Miss Thang," she was,
and she came in on a gold shrimp boat
with satin sails
she walked out of the ocean/ a black woman
carrying her whole thing
in a bundle on her head.
—From "You Play It on the Edge," by Linda B. Brown, in *A Living Culture in Durham*, ed. Judy Hogan (Durham: Carolina Wren Press, 1987), 424.

Turn left from Lee Street onto Bennett Street in front of Bennett College to reach the next destination. Continue straight on Dudley Street.

■ NORTH CAROLINA A&T STATE UNIVERSITY

The Dudley Building on University Circle Drive is a good spot to stop on this historic campus. On the lawn, artist James Barnhill has installed his powerful statues of Franklin McCain, Joseph McNeil, Jibreel Khazan (formerly Ezell Blair Jr.), and David Richmond. These four A&T freshmen made history on the first day of February 1960, when they took seats normally reserved for white people at the lunch counter in Woolworth's dime store in downtown Greensboro. They encouraged others to employ a similar tactic as part of the civil rights movement in the South.

For three decades, A&T was the academic home of professor and writer Sandra Carlton Alexander, who has set several stories in a town called Innerville, which bears a resemblance to Greensboro. Alexander's first novel, *Impressions: Six Months in the Life of a Southern City* (2000), is a fictionalized account of the Greensboro sit-ins, primarily focusing on the efforts of a single white

A tribute to the four students who launched the sit-in at a Greensboro lunch counter—
a watershed moment in the civil rights movement and the subject of several books of
fiction and nonfiction. North Carolina A&T State University art professor James Barnhill
created the sculpture.

man who sought to mediate the conflict between white and black residents. The novel draws on the life of the late Edward R. Zane, a Burlington Industries executive who worked on behalf of the mayor to help ameliorate racial tension. (The planetarium in Greensboro's Natural Science Center bears his name.)

Today, poet Anjail Rashida Ahmad heads the creative writing program here. Ahmad began losing her sight in the late 1990s and has written powerfully about the experience. She has also been a strong advocate for public poetry programs in the city, working closely with the Greensboro Public Library. This poem describes her writing process:

the poet
    each morning I pull myself
    out of despair . . .
        —lucille clifton, book of light
each night, she climbs

with the bulb of her body
to the room at the top of the house
where she lies down in the dark
trellis of her bed.

her dreams gather,
   in the mouths of ancestors,
           whispering the bitter code
of what is possible.

when she awakens,
she remembers
the shape of her own breath,
pressing it
   into the heart of her words.
—From *necessary kindling*, by Anjail Rashida Ahmad
(Baton Rouge: Louisiana State University Press, 2001), 1.

Another poet and novelist on the faculty, Valerie Nieman, earned an MFA from Queens University, in Charlotte. Her 2006 poetry collection is *Wake, Wake, Wake* (Winston-Salem: Press 53).

■ DOWNTOWN GREENSBORO WALKING TOUR

Continue north on Dudley past the A&T campus to the intersection with Lindsay Street. Turn left, cross Murrow Boulevard, and at the next major intersection with Church Street turn left again. The Greensboro Children's Museum will be on your left with the Central Branch of the Greensboro Public Library on the right. Park in the public deck beyond the library to take a walking tour of downtown.

Greensboro's public library system is one of the busiest and most successful community-wide purveyors of literary activity in the state. The library (along with many others in North Carolina) regularly participates in "The Big Read," a program of the National Endowment for the Arts in which citizens read a single book and then attend discussions, lectures, and other celebrations of the book over the course of a month. Poetry GSO is the library's annual poetry festival, filling the entire month of April, which is also National Poetry Month. (GSO is the acronym of the Triad International Airport.) The celebration draws enthusiastic crowds to readings by top national poets and encourages poetry writing

In the rotunda of the Greensboro Public Library downtown, the late Mary Jarrell stands before a mural by artist Michael Brown featuring a likeness of her husband, UNC-Greensboro poet Randall Jarrell. Photo courtesy of Jan Hensley, photographer.

and reading by children and adults citywide. Information on these programs is available at the library and at <http://www.greensboro-nc.gov/departments/Library/One+Book/>.

Step inside the library to see *City Mural*, by artist Michael Brown, in the rotunda. Among the many prominent Greensboro figures in the work is Randall Jarrell, one of the most influential teachers, poets, and critics in twentieth-century literature. Jarrell taught at Woman's College, now UNC-Greensboro, from 1947 until his untimely death in 1965 at the age of fifty-one. Jarrell's work is complex. The following poem, first published in 1963 in *The Bat-Poet*—a charming children's book illustrated by Maurice Sendak—is addressed to young readers but carries an adult level of meaning, too. Literary scholar Stephen Burt suggests that the description of the mockingbird can be interpreted as Jarrell's paean to the country's best-known poet at the time, Robert Frost, "who owned the yard." (Frost read a poem at John F. Kennedy's inauguration, in 1961.)

Look one way and the sun is going down,
Look the other and the moon is rising.

The sparrow's shadow's longer than the lawn.
The bats squeak: "Night is here"; the birds cheep:
   "Day is gone."
On the willow's highest branch, monopolizing
Day and night, cheeping, squeaking, soaring,
The mockingbird is imitating life.

All day the mockingbird has owned the yard.
As first light woke the world, the sparrows trooped
Onto the seedy lawn: the mockingbird
Chased them off shrieking. Hour by hour, fighting hard
To make the world his own, he swooped
On thrushes, thrashers, jays, and chickadees—
At noon he drove away a big black cat.

Now, in the moonlight, he sits here and sings.
A thrush is singing, then a thrasher, then a jay—
Then, all at once, a cat begins meowing.
A mockingbird can sound like anything.
He imitates the world he drove away
So well that for a minute, in the moonlight,
Which one's the mockingbird? which one's the world?
—From *The Bat-Poet*, by Randall Jarrell
   (New York: HarperCollins, 1996), 28.

The Booklover's Shop, on the right as you exit the library, can outfit you with a free audio tour of the city along with a printed version featuring architectural and historical sites in the vicinity. Ahead are a few stops on that tour that have a literary slant.

From the library, the Greensboro Historical Museum (<http://www.greensboro history.org>) is around the next street corner to the left, at 130 Summit. Before you go into the building, look for the life-sized statue of O. Henry as a boy and a larger-than-life head of Edward R. Murrow on the lawn. Ogden Deal sculpted both. Inside, the museum has an exhibition of O. Henry memorabilia, including his top hat, wedding rings, a pair of sterling whiskey cups, and various photos and letters. This free museum is open every day except Monday.

Continue one block west on Lindsay Street to North Elm Street and turn left to reach 301 North Elm. Here a small park beside the United States Trust Center celebrates O. Henry's teenage connection to Greensboro in three sculptures by local artist Maria J. Kirby-Smith. (She is the first cousin of poet Tom Kirby-

Smith, a longtime English professor at UNC-Greensboro and founding editor of the literary journal *Greensboro Review*.)

Continue south on Elm across Friendly Avenue and Market Street. In the next block, at 121 South Elm, is a plaque commemorating the site of Porter Drug Store, where young William Sidney Porter worked for his uncle for five years. In the same building, Lunsford Richardson developed Vicks VapoRub after buying the drugstore from O. Henry's uncle in the 1890s.

Across the street, at 134 South Elm, is the F. W. Woolworth storefront (now Greensboro's International Civil Rights Center and Museum) where the sit-in movement of the 1960s is remembered. Carole Boston Weatherford has written a chronicle of the events for children in *Freedom on the Menu: The Greensboro Sit-Ins* (2005). Weatherford tells the story from the point of view of a young girl named Connie, who experiences firsthand the constraints of segregation and witnesses from afar the bravery of the four North Carolina A&T freshmen who began their protest here. Finally, Connie is able to sit at the Woolworth's lunch counter and order a banana split to celebrate the social change that has come to pass in her town.

A cartoon drawn by the young O. Henry satirizes the controversial jurist, writer, and editor Albion Tourgée, who left Greensboro in 1879 to return to the North where he wrote his best-known novel, A Fool's Errand, *based on his efforts on behalf of former slaves and his opposition to the Ku Klux Klan in Greensboro. Courtesy of Greensboro Public Library/ Greensboro Historical Museum Collection.*

At 232 South Elm, Triad Stage, a local theater company, has been presenting classic plays and new works by North Carolina playwrights following the renovation of its headquarters in what was once Greensboro's Montgomery Ward department store (box office: 336-272-0160).

Reaching the 300 block of Elm, you are close to a setting familiar to readers of *Stand by Your Man* (HarperTorch, 2001), a mystery by Nancy Bartholomew. The novel roams widely in and around Greensboro, along with protagonist Maggie Reid, a country singer and former hairdresser.

At the end of South Elm Street, another historical marker commemorates writer, educator, and judge Albion Winegar Tourgée, who helped to establish Bennett College. Tourgée, a white Civil War veteran from Ohio who moved South during Reconstruction, was repeatedly scorned and threatened in North Carolina for his radical Republican beliefs about the equality of black persons and for his efforts to document the activities of the nascent Ku Klux Klan. Ironically, he gave generous advice to a young Thomas Dixon at the beginning of Dixon's writing career, only to be mocked at the opening of *Birth of a Nation*, a film based on Dixon's inflammatory novels.

Tourgée left the region in 1879 to write two highly popular and profitable novels—*A Fool's Errand*, about Greensboro during Reconstruction, and *Bricks without Straw*, reissued in 2009 by Duke University Press. Tourgée started a magazine in 1882, the *Continent*, which published serialized fiction, the work of leading poets of the day, and a variety of opinion pieces. In 1896 he was tapped to argue the famous *Plessy v. Ferguson* case before the Supreme Court, unsuccessfully challenging the practice of racial segregation of interstate passengers traveling by rail. Tourgée died in 1905, while serving as U.S. consul to France.

One block west of Elm, at 310 Greene Street, is the final literary landmark on this walking tour. The Greek revival Carolina Theater opened as a vaudeville venue in 1927 and was reportedly the first commercial building in the state to be air-conditioned. Saved from demolition in 1977 and restored following a fire in 1981, this gilded and glittering arts facility now hosts the largest gatherings of the Poetry GSO festival each April. It was also the site of the world premiere of the movie *Full House*, on August 7, 1952. Narrated by novelist John Steinbeck, who makes a rare appearance on camera, the film was based on five short stories by O. Henry, including "The Gift of the Magi," with Jean Crain and Farley Granger. Each segment was created by a different Hollywood director. The film is now available on DVD.

Greensboro's visitors' center is at 317 South Greene Street (near the Carolina Theater), should you want more information during your visit. Otherwise, return to the municipal parking deck on Church Street and exit left onto Church. Follow Church north across Murrow Boulevard and watch for South Park Drive on the left. Go on past it and turn left at the next block onto North Park Drive to circle through a Greensboro neighborhood with several literary connections.

■ FISHER PARK

Fisher Park roughly circled a sloping wooded valley of city park threaded with footpaths and a sometimes creek. Its swing set, climbing fort, and basketball court had been attractive pluses to our house purchase. The blunt square roofs of high-rise buildings downtown were visible through the interlaced, winter-naked branches of trees. Two blocks to the left and behind us, raised railroad tracks ran between high kudzu-covered banks.

"We're just a close-to-downtown has-been neighborhood touted as newly stylish. A mixture of two-career childless types, fringe Strangeos, *artistes*, dying oldsters, and brave newcomers like yourself."

—From *How Close We Come: A Novel of Women's Friendships*, by Susan S. Kelly (New York: Grand Central Publishing, 1998), 31.

Novelist Susan S. Kelly is from Rutherfordton, in the North Carolina foothills, and lives in Greensboro. The settings of her novels cover the state, but much of the action in her first book takes place in Fisher Park, where two young mothers (the principal characters) bring their children to play. This quirky neighborhood, as Kelly describes it, has been popular with writers for generations. Kelly wrote part of her novel sitting in the park, she says.

Greensboro novelist Candace Flynt has a contemplative stop in Fisher Park in her third novel, *Sins of Omission*. Novelist John Hart, originally from Salisbury, makes his home in this neighborhood, and up ahead, at 114 Fisher Park Circle, is yet another of the houses once owned by short-story writer Peter Taylor and his wife, poet Eleanor Ross Taylor.

Before buying this house, the Taylors lived for a time in a duplex (now gone) at 1924 Spring Garden Street, near what was then the Woman's College campus. They co-owned the place with poet Randall Jarrell and his first wife, Mackie. A decade later, in 1963, after the Taylors had been away from North Carolina while Peter taught in Ohio, they returned and bought the Fisher Park residence, which Peter called "our biggest and ugliest house yet."

Going even farther back, to 1953, Fisher Park figures in Greensboro-native Edythe Latham's novel *The Sounding Brass*, which earned high praise from playwright Paul Green of Chapel Hill. The story begins after the Civil War and follows three generations of the fictional Chandley family, who lived in a grand house called Dunmeade, in a neighborhood that Greensboro residents recognized as a thinly veiled Fisher Park.

Continue around Park Drive and take Greene Street south. Cross Fisher Avenue and proceed all the way to Friendly Avenue and turn right. After three long blocks, turn left on Mendenhall Street. Greensboro College is on the left beyond Market Street. Continue on Mendenhall to the intersection with Spring Garden Street and turn right to visit the campus of UNC-Greensboro. (Spring Garden runs through campus on its south side. College Avenue is a pedestrian thoroughfare that leads into the heart of campus.)

Summer 1981, and I am riding around leafy, drowsy Greensboro, North Carolina, miles and miles and miles from sexy, circusy Chapel Hill where I used to teach, where I used to have a writing life. Now I'm too fat to teach or write. Too fat, too Great With Child, and drunk with the power of another kind of Creation. Today I am riding shotgun in my writer friend Candy's car. It's a vintage Lincoln Continental convertible, a turquoise parade float, loaded with flashing chrome. The radio's turned up full volume, some moldy oldie from the grooveyard playing something like "Stoned Soul Picnic," helping to revivify the late 1960s, when we were *really* young. We plan to cruise around in this thing with the top down, our long hair blowing like capes behind us, until our youth runs totally out.—From *Adventures in Pen Land: One Writer's Journey from Inklings to Ink*, by Marianne Gingher (Columbia: University of Missouri Press, 2008), 181–82.

This picture of two of Greensboro's most successful baby boom writers—Marianne Gingher and Candace Flynt—is from Gingher's 2008 memoir. In addition to an examination of her evolution as a writer, the book is also a spirited tour of Greensboro, beginning with scenes from her elementary school (Sternberger) to junior high (Kiser) to Greensboro's Grimsley High. Gingher then went to nearby Salem College and came back to the graduate program in creative writing at UNC-Greensboro. (The literary memoir also features sprightly illustrations by novelist Daniel Wallace, Gingher's colleague in the creative writing program at UNC–Chapel Hill, where she now teaches.)

Gingher, who still has a house in Greensboro, is the author of a novel, *Bobby Rex's Greatest Hit*; a collection of stories, *Teen Angel & Other Stories of Wayward Love*; and two other personal narratives—*How to Have a Happy Childhood* and *A Girl's Life: Horses, Boys, Weddings, & Luck*.

Candace Flynt, a graduate of Greensboro College, enrolled in the graduate program in creative writing at UNC-Greensboro during the same era as Gingher. She has three novels, which take place mostly in Greensboro: *Chasing Dad*, also partly set in Durham; *Sins of Omission*, a tale of a woman's reckless effort to undo the marriage of a local newspaper columnist; and *Mother Love*, a story told from multiple viewpoints about the challenging relationships among three sisters and their mother.

The list of successful writers who came through the creative writing program at UNC-Greensboro is staggering, and several besides Gingher and Flynt have made their homes here. Quinn Dalton is from a more recent generation of writers. She is the author of two story collections—*Bulletproof Girl* and *Stories from the Afterlife*—and a novel, *High Strung*. Poet and National Book Award finalist Sarah Lindsay is author of *Primate Behavior*, *Mount Clutter*, and *Twigs and Knucklebones*. She was a Randall Jarrell scholar at UNC-Greensboro and edited the *Greensboro Review*.

Orson Scott Card, a science-fiction and fantasy writer, moved to Greensboro to work for a computer magazine and ended up studying with novelist Lee Zacharias at UNC-Greensboro. Among Card's dozens of novels, *Lost Boys* is set in Greensboro and, he says, is his most closely autobiographical. Card's short story "Dogwalker," about a Greensboro computer hacker, is in the collection *Maps in a Mirror*, which also features long essays about his writing and family life.

So how did this particular state university evolve into a literary power-house? In the foreword to an anthology composed solely of writing by now-well-known students and faculty of UNC-Greensboro, Robert Watson—a poet, novelist, and emeritus professor of English—offered this theory:

> When I arrived in North Carolina fifteen years ago to teach at what was then called the Woman's College of the University of North Carolina, a my-thology had already grown up about the writers on campus. . . . I once asked Randall Jarrell why he thought writers found Greensboro congenial. He gestured toward the campus and said, "See, it's Sleeping Beauty." . . . If some-one asked me what Greensboro offered a writer, I would answer, "Bore-dom." What I mean is this: Greensboro puts the writer to his own resources, and he can compose without becoming entangled in the fads of the market place.—From *The Greensboro Reader*, ed. Robert Watson and Gibbons Ruark (Chapel Hill: University of North Carolina Press, 1968), xv, xvi.

Greensboro in the 1930s and 1940s was indeed a sleeping beauty—a town that felt much more rural and remote than it does today. In particular, it suited the sensibilities of Allen Tate, a member of the Fugitive poets—a group of writers at Vanderbilt University who launched a highly influential literary magazine by the same name in 1922. The Vanderbilt group later came to be known as the Agrarians for their controversial manifesto, issued in 1930, de-crying the demise of the preindustrial South. As North Carolina journalist Ed Yoder described Allen Tate in a *Washington Post* column in 1979: "He usually went against the grain—a classicist among romantics, a sectionalist among nationalists, an esthete (in no pejorative sense) in a political age, and a man

who sighed among the smokestacks for the South's agrarian past." Tate taught at Woman's College in the late 1930s and again in 1966.

Tate and his wife, novelist Caroline Gordon, were ringleaders in luring others to teach here: among them, Tate's Vanderbilt mentor, poet John Crowe Ransom; future *Playboy* fiction editor Robie MacCauley; and Hiram Haydn, who would later become editor in chief at Random House. They, in turn, brought their friends to lecture and read on campus—literary luminaries such as Flannery O'Connor, Eudora Welty, Saul Bellow, Robert Lowell, and Robert Penn Warren. It was into this heady milieu, sustained over a period of years, that future teacher/writers such as Eleanor Ross Taylor, Jean Ross Justice, Doris Betts, Sally Buckner, Emily Herring Wilson, and Heather Ross Miller arrived as undergraduates. A statewide literary tradition was in the making.

When Jarrell, after teaching in Greensboro over an eighteen-year period, was struck by a car and killed in Chapel Hill, in 1965, the literary flame dimmed for a time. But Jarrell's mantle as master poetry teacher at Woman's College was soon taken up by Duke alumnus Fred Chappell, who would serve as a generous and gentle mentor to upcoming writers for forty years, meanwhile managing his own prodigious output of poems, reviews, novels, stories, and critical essays. Poet Michael McFee once described Chappell's scholastic style: "Overshadowed by his more boisterous and attention-grabbing half—is Professor Chappell, a

Neo-classical polymath of the first order, deeply and widely read, profoundly learned: a genuine scholar. Professor Chappell speaks quietly but precisely; he alludes frequently but never shows off; his perspective is historical, across centuries and cultures" (*The Napkin Manuscripts*, by Michael McFee [Knoxville: University of Tennessee Press, 2006], 112).

Few writers in North Carolina have been so versatile or prolific as Fred Chappell. In this poem he describes the work of a poet with his usual irreverence:

CONSIDER THE LILIES OF THE FIELD
        "I'd like to do what you do
        but some of us have to work for a living."

maybe you'd like it   maybe you wouldn't

it takes longer than you probably think
to set down not only the pitch
of a birdsong but its rhythm
not *cheerily cheerily cheerily*
but *cheerily   teasinglycheerily*

and numbering the streaks of the tulip
is a long day's work because
of course you keep losing count
and sometimes it is hard to tell
if a line is a streak or the shadow of a stamen
you must wait for the sun to move

as for clouds, does that one there resemble
a whale   a hawk   a handsaw
a horsetail   a hamburger patty   a huckleberry bush?
decisions decisions decisions
Hamlet had the same problem

and then there is the play of light upon water
always a difficult subject
as is the play of water upon light

And is it the *drone* of traffic
or the *moan* or the *groan*?

well, *groan* if it is a semi
struggling up a grade in the early morning
drone if it is 5 o'clock

on the freeway a mile distant
if it is a single car
on two-lane asphalt at 3 A.M., *moan*

the tedium of it, you have no idea

as for the lilies of the field,
consider them considered
—From *Backsass*, by Fred Chappell (Baton Rouge:
Louisiana State University Press, 2004), 12–13.

Following the retirement of Fred Chappell and Robert Watson, a new crop of stellar writers filled the creative writing program at UNC-Greensboro, including eastern North Carolina novelist and short-story writer Michael Parker (whose work is considered in volume 3), novelist Craig Nova, and poets Stuart Dischell, Jennifer Grotz, David Roderick, Allison Seay, and Mark Smith-Soto.

To the campus visitor aiming to get a sense of this storied literary tradition, Michael Parker recommends, if nothing else, a visit to the campus library. "I like to walk the stacks," he says, "and imagine Randall Jarrell or Peter Taylor or Allen Tate or Bob Watson or recently retired but not at all forgotten Ole Fred and Lee Zacharias combing the same shelves. We have such a history of being a refuge for writers here, and the presence of those writers lingers nowhere more palpably than Jackson Library."

In its special collections, Jackson Library has Randall Jarrell's books and papers. An extensive section of women's history materials and women's detective fiction and a number of girls'-book series have also been collected since the early days of Woman's College.

Look for the library's distinctive white tower rising above the other campus buildings. It is accessible from the pedestrian walkway (College Avenue) or from the Walker Avenue parking deck. To reach the deck, take Spring Garden to South Aycock Street. Turn right and then right again onto Walker Avenue, which takes you into the center of campus. From the deck, look for the Elliot University Center–Library connector, which will lead you on foot to the library.

Among the roster of writers who have lived, worked, and visited here, one more bears mention. Poet Elizabeth Sewell was born in India and educated at Cambridge. She taught at Vassar, Fordham, Princeton, and Bennett, among other universities, but her final home was Greensboro, where, beginning in 1974, she taught in the department of religious studies at UNC-Greensboro. She wrote novels and poetry but was particularly interested in the intersection of literature and medicine.

To reach our next destination, return to South Aycock Street (US 29/70) and head north (right). Watch closely for the exit and follow the signs to West Friendly Avenue. Travel approximately 4.5 miles on Friendly to New Garden Road and turn right.

■ NEW GARDEN CEMETERY AND GUILFORD COLLEGE

Immediately on the left, at 801 New Garden Road, is the New Garden Friends Meeting House. A state historical marker in the yard notes the location of poet Randall Jarrell's grave in the cemetery behind the meeting house.

NEW GARDEN CEMETERY
Where gravel lies between the stones to keep the weeds away
the weeds come up, tall and immaculate:
the yellow dandelions whose grey age banners
the secret of perenniality.
When I have tired of rooting and uprooting greenery
I climb the path, ancient and budding still
between the subdivision and the graveyard
that beds Cornwallis' troops alongside Greene's.
   Now, their revolution done,
   year by year above them pass
   the revolution of the grass,
   the revolution of the sun.

The quiet folk who laid them there
themselves lay down beside them one by one
where now the crumbling markers range across the field.
This fertile mingling of their bones—
the men of conscience and the men of war—
brought forth these peaceful conflicts that divide our land,
   where pacifist and rebel share
   a revolution of new scope
   a new revolt of rising hope
   a new revolt against despair.

For even here where revolution ends
weeds still crack the roadbed, and I stoop
to pull a stubbornly rooted thornbush up.
We tend our gardens and our consciences

Longtime Guilford College faculty member and poet Ann Deagon sings at a gathering in the New Garden Cemetery. Photo courtesy of Ann Deagon.

<blockquote>

uncertain of the season. Have we reached

the turning point or the point of no return?

    Can new revolutions bring

    a peace all nature may enjoy—

    or will their clash instead destroy

    the sweet forever of the spring?

—From *Quaker Life*, May 1971, used by permission of Ann Deagon.

</blockquote>

Alabama-born Ann Deagon, a classics professor at Guilford College for many years, began writing poetry at age forty, about the time of this poem's composition. She came to Guilford in 1956 and was active in the peace movement during the Vietnam War. Her poem obliquely refers to the "revolutionary oak" that once stood in this cemetery from the time of the Revolutionary War. It was dynamited by vandals in 1955 when Eleanor Roosevelt came to the Guilford campus to speak to a racially mixed group about the recent *Brown v. Board of Education* ruling, which required integration of public schools. A stone monument to the oak still stands among the graves today.

    Deagon's literary contributions to North Carolina have been considerable. She directed Poetry Center Southeast, edited the *Guilford Review*, and was a founder of the North Carolina Writers' Network. She has written ten books of poetry and fiction and now, in her seventies, performs one-woman shows of her poems, stories, and songs. Her husband, Donald, is buried in this historic cemetery not far from Randall Jarrell.

Cross New Garden Road to walk the lush campus of Guilford College, founded in 1837 as a Quaker boarding school, which in 1888 became a four-year liberal arts college. It is the only college in the southeast founded by Quakers. For many years, poet Rebecca Gould Gibson taught here. (Her poetry is featured in volume 3.) Today, Carolyn Beard Whitlow is the Charles A. Dana Professor of English and the primary teacher of creative writing on campus. Whitlow is also an avid quilter, as suggested in this musical poem about the writing life:

SPACE
This, a must write night,
thoughts sieve through my mind,
grit, sand, head split off
its hinges, swinging
like a broken door.
I pour one cup of words,
slosh vowels in my saucer,
slurp, frittered remembrances
timid with spice.
Depth sounding failed,
letters jostle, spill,
mumbled pick-up stix,
pretty little prints.
A silent taste in my mouth,
sentences beaux-tired,
merry gentleman choruses
lip-synch Southern comfort,
joy, warble bassoons' bass
joviality, music unconscious,
inaudible, tinsel tinkling
ice. No screw driver handy,
pregnant with expectation,
like a Christmas package rum-
bled, dropped, oops, burps,
regurge, bursts, these lines break

open: red-eyed across tablecloth
rectangles, time squared,
I empty into space.
—From *Vanished*, by Carolyn Beard Whitlow
   (Detroit, Mich.: Lotus Press, 2006), 75.

To reach our final site on this tour, drive north four miles on New Garden Road, bearing right at the fork with Fleming Road. Continue on New Garden across Bryan Boulevard to Battleground Avenue (US 220) and turn right. Watch for Park Place on the left and turn left into Tannenbaum Park.

■ TANNENBAUM HISTORIC PARK

This park, near the much larger Guilford Courthouse National Military Park, commemorates Joseph Hoskins's 150-acre homestead, dating from 1778, which played host to General Cornwallis's troops during the Battle of Guilford Courthouse, in 1781. Hoskins's cabin and several restored outbuildings are the main attractions here.

In 1951, the Hoskins house, still standing though disguised as a residence with no interesting historical provenance, caught the attention of Durham-born novelist Burke Davis, his wife, Evangeline, and their two children, Angela and Burke III, as they were passing by on a Sunday drive to the site of the Battle of Guilford Courthouse. Davis's just-completed novel, *The Ragged Ones*, was about this very landscape and its dramatic role in the Revolutionary War. (Davis's day job at the time was as reporter for the *Greensboro Daily News*, and Evangeline served as the paper's book-page editor.)

The whole family fell instantly in love with the house they saw, which also happened to be for sale. As it turned out, clapboard and brick covered the original cabin that the Hoskins family had occupied so long ago. The Davises bought, remodeled, and lived in the house, and it was here that nine-year-old Angela began writing stories and a sometime-newspaper she called the *Cornwallis Weekly*.

Angela Davis-Gardner went on to study writing at Duke University with William Blackburn and to earn a graduate degree in creative writing at UNC-Greensboro, studying with Fred Chappell. She then taught at UNC-Greensboro, Guilford College, UNC–Chapel Hill, and North Carolina State University. Her second novel, *Forms of Shelter*, has at its center a towering emblem from the years the Davis family lived here: the magnificent Osage orange tree that still

Outside their historic home in the early 1950s in what is now Greensboro's Tannenbaum Park are novelist Burke Davis Jr. and his wife, Evangeline. Both were writers for the Greensboro Daily News. Their children, Angela Davis-Gardner and Burke Davis III, would go on to write their own novels. Photo courtesy of Angela Davis-Gardner.

stands on the grounds near the Hoskins cabin, now stripped back to its earliest form. Beryl, the novel's adolescent narrator, takes refuge in the tree house her stepfather, Jack, has built for her:

The Osage oranges were chartreuse, pimpled and irregularly shaped. Though the size of lopsided softballs, they more resembled brains because of the encircling lines that cleft the lumpy surface of each one. The unevenly pebbled skin of the Osage orange reminded me of a geographical relief map, like the one at school; that first autumn, as I sat in my tree house, stroking an Osage orange with my eyes shut, I like to imagine the hand of Mr. Snow, the handsome young science teacher, guiding mine over mountain ranges, continents. But when I inspected the fruit closely with my eyes open, I thought this was like looking at an organ in my own body,

Angela Davis-Gardner's second novel, Forms of Shelter, *was inspired in part by the extraordinary Osage orange tree in the yard where she lived as an adolescent in Greensboro.*

the poisonous color, the infected-looking swellings, all deliciously confirming my worst suspicions about my insides.—From *Forms of Shelter,* by Angela Davis-Gardner (New York: Dial, 2007), 68.

Burke Davis III would also write a novel based in Greensboro. *Dwelling Places,* published in 1980, received high praise from novelist Anne Tyler. Davis now lives in Virginia and is married to poet Kelly Cherry, a graduate of the creative writing program at UNC-Greensboro.

■ LITERARY LANDSCAPE

High Point Public Library
901 North Main Street, High Point
336-883-3660
<http://highpointpubliclibrary.com>
This facility's dramatic expansion project, completed in 2009, provides a much larger media center, room for new collections, a 125-seat auditorium, a new children's story room, and an expansive lobby area with lounge seating.

Tate Street Coffee House

334 Tate Street, Greensboro

336-275-2754

<http://tatestreetcoffee.com/>

Writer Ann Fitzmaurice Russ and her husband, Matt Russ, own this establishment, which sits alongside the UNC-Greensboro campus and brings an array of students, writers, and other locals in for music, food, and community updates.

Glenwood Community Bookstore

1206 Grove Street, Greensboro

New in 2008, this venture is the brainchild of Alan Brilliant, a veteran bookseller and a principal of Unicorn Press.

Writers Group of the Triad

336-854-0034

<http://www.triadwriters.org>

Founded in the 1950s as the Greensboro Writers Club by Judith Hill, this vibrant organization hosts workshop sessions at the Sternberger Artists Center, 712 Summit Avenue.

Barnes & Noble Friendly Center

3102 Northline Avenue, Greensboro

336-854-4200

Centrally located in one of Greensboro's older shopping centers, this busy store hosts many of the larger book signings arranged by the Writers Group of the Triad.

Touring Theatre Ensemble of North Carolina

113 North Church Street, #305, Greensboro

336-272-1279

<http://www.ttnc.org>

Under the artistic leadership of playwright and director Brenda Schleunes, this Greensboro-based group has adapted for the stage work by Nancy Bartholomew, Randall Jarrell, Randall Kenan, Jill McCorkle, Barbara Presnell, and Lee Smith, among others.

Madison : Eden : Reidsville : Yanceyville : Milton : Roxboro

This expedition can take two days, depending on how fully you master the pace of life in this pastoral landscape. Enjoy the long view of history and the small-town life that flourishes here on the banks of the Mayo, Dan, and Smith rivers.

Writers with a connection to this area: Sherwood Anderson, William Andrews, Daniel W. Barefoot, Jerry Bledsoe, Lisa Cantrell, P. T. Deutermann, R. S. Gwynn, Alex Haley, Larry Leon Hamlin, T. R. Pearson, Reynolds Price, Moses Roper, Dawn Shamp, David Spear, G. C. Waldrep, Manley Wade Wellman

This tour follows—from west to east—a swath of rural landscape that runs just below the Virginia state line and above the more densely populated corridor of I-40 connecting the Piedmont Triad (Winston-Salem, High Point, Greensboro) to the Triangle (Chapel Hill, Durham, Raleigh). Here in the Dan River basin, vestiges of the nineteenth- and twentieth-century dependence on bright leaf tobacco and homestead farming are everywhere: countless tobacco barns built of hand-hewn logs with roofs of rusted tin; broad, undulating fields; crossroads stores where hoop cheese and soda crackers are still staples; ancient oaks with limbs astride white clapboard houses; and churchyards with tumbledown tombstones. Again we encounter North Carolina's once-thriving textile-mill culture, which sprang up on the banks of the Dan River flowing east into Rockingham County, where we begin.

■ MADISON AND MAYODAN

Growing up in Madison, North Carolina, during World War II, I can remember the town being filled each Fall with such people bringing in their tobacco to sell. The

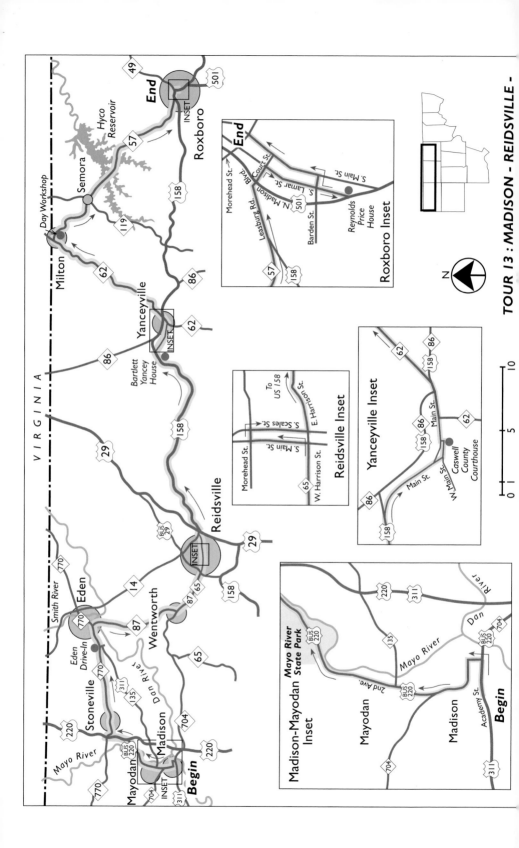

TOUR 13 : MADISON - REIDSVILLE -

Roxboro Inset
End
Morehead St.
Court St.
S. Madison Blvd.
Leasburg Rd.
N. Madison Blvd.
501
S. Lamar St.
S. Main St.
Barden St.
Reynolds Price House
57
158

Reidsville Inset
To US 158
Morehead St.
S. Scales St.
E. Harrison St.
S. Main St.
65
W. Harrison St.

Yanceyville Inset
62
158
86
86
Main St.
158
86
Main St.
62
86
W. Main St.
158
Caswell County Courthouse
Main St.

Madison-Mayodan Mayo River State Park Inset
220
311
135
River
Dan
Mayo River
BUS 220
2nd Ave.
BUS 220
Mayodan
704
BUS 220
Madison
Academy St.
704
311
Begin

VIRGINIA
Day Workshop
Milton
Semora
Hyco Reservoir
End
Roxboro
49
501
57
158
119
62
86
Yanceyville
62
INSET
Bartlett Yancey House
86
29
158
Reidsville
29
INSET
BUS 29
158
65
87
Wentworth
87
14
Eden
770
Eden Drive-In
770
770
Stoneville
311
135
Dan River
Smith River
770
220
Mayo River
BUS 220
Madison
Mayodan
704
INSET
311
Begin
704
220
65

N

0 1 5 10

town came alive with medicine shows, mule-drawn wagons, and families milling about town. These people survived on what they made from sharecropping tobacco and on what they were able to grow to eat. They were strong-willed and kept to themselves. There were thousands of families that had lived this difficult lifestyle after the Civil War and on into the mid-twentieth century. When the Industrial Revolution moved South after World War II, however, the landscape and people changed forever.—From *The Neugents: Close to Home*, by David M. Spear (Winston-Salem: Jargon Society, 1993), n.p.

Published by the late Black Mountain College poet Jonathan Williams, David Spear's photo-documentary book about the hardscrabble Neugent family offers an unusual window into the all-but-extinct practice of tenant farming in this region. Spear, the former publisher of Madison's weekly newspaper, turned to photography at age fifty and found as his first major subject the Neugents, his neighbors only a quarter-mile down Tobacco Road. Spear spent nearly six years visiting the family, whom he characterized in a radio interview as rugged, defiant, and unpretentious—members of "a lost tribe." His black-and-white portraits of the Neugents are captivating, and Spear also brings his uncluttered prose to the page to deepen the reader's appreciation of his subjects.

In more than one way throughout his career, Spear has followed in the footsteps of his legendary grandfather, short story master Sherwood Anderson, whose fictional but documentary-like portrait of a small town—*Winesburg, Ohio*—was published in 1919 and is considered a classic. In 1924, the year before Anderson's autobiography, *A Story-Teller's Story*, was published, the writer left the Midwest, where he had lived for most of his life, and bought a publishing company in Marion, Virginia. He began editing two local newspapers.

The itinerant Anderson had never spent much time with his children, all of whom came from the first of his four marriages. Later in life he did pass the newspaper business along to his son Bob and then built Ripshin, a personal writing retreat a few miles from Marion, in Troutdale, Virginia. When the newspaper in Madison, North Carolina, some hundred miles to the southeast, became available during the Depression, Bob Anderson encouraged his sister, Marion, and her husband to buy the paper. The couple had been living in New England. David Spear's father was a scholar of French literature who had aimed for a life in the academy. He had no experience in journalism. Nevertheless, the Spears took the challenge. They ran the Madison paper from 1934 to 1963 and then turned the business over to David.

David Spear and his siblings visited Sherwood Anderson at least once at

Ripshin. In turn, Anderson came down to Madison not long before his death. David's brother, Michael, recalls his grandfather's hearty appetite for pork chops and his nonstop storytelling that long winter evening in 1940. When the children rose the next morning, their grandfather had already departed. They would not see him again. While touring Panama in March 1941, Sherwood Anderson died of peritonitis, apparently after ingesting part of a toothpick that was embedded in a martini olive.

Like many other writers along this literary trail, Sherwood Anderson is remembered as an advocate for his literary friends. He was instrumental in the publication of William Faulkner's first novel. Ernest Hemingway carried a letter of introduction from Anderson to his first meeting in Paris with Gertrude Stein. Thomas Wolfe told Southern Pines novelist James Boyd that Sherwood Anderson was "the only man in America who ever taught me anything. Anything I know of writing, I have from him. He is our only sophisticate" (*Sherwood Anderson: A Writer in America*, by Walter Bates Rideout and Charles E. Modlin [Madison: University of Wisconsin Press, 2005], 291).

To honor their grandfather's generous spirit, in 1988 members of the Spear family established the Sherwood Anderson Foundation, which has been giving grants and scholarships to developing writers ever since.

DIRECTIONS

Madison and Mayodan are adjacent villages that sprang up near the confluence of the Mayo and Dan rivers. They are best reached by heading north on US 220 (Battleground Avenue) from Greensboro. Exit 220 at NC 704 and proceed left (west) and cross the Dan River to enter Madison.

Madison has two registered historic districts—Academy Street and Decatur-Hunter Street. The well-kept nineteenth-century houses here likely inspired local writer Lisa W. Cantrell's popular horror novel, *The Manse*. Cantrell, who has lived in Madison for more than three decades, has been called the female Stephen King. Her other titles include *Boneman*, *Ridge*, and *Torment*.

Madison, with a population of under 3,000, is home to the corporate headquarters of Remington Arms (the ammunition manufacturer) and to Gem-Dandy, a company dating back to 1914 that invented and patented the world's first fully adjustable garter and produced it for men, women, and children.

From Madison, continue north on NC 704 as it forks to the left to pass through the little village of Mayodan. Bear right on South Second Avenue (Business 220). Mayo River State Park, a few miles north on 220, is under development as of 2010, and both Madison and Mayodan have become popular destinations for

Poet R. S. Gwynn's father ran the Eden Drive-In during the writer's youth.

kayakers and canoeists who have easy river access near both towns. For more information, contact Three Rivers Outfitters, <http://www.3-R-O.com>, or call 336-627-6215.

Continue north on Business 220 as it merges with the 220 bypass. At the next exit, take NC 770 to the right (east). On the way to our next destination, you'll pass through Stoneville, a quaint town with a campground nearby on the Dan River.

■ EDEN

It's approximately nine miles on NC 770 to Eden. Where NC 135 comes in on the right, notice the entrance to the Eden Drive-In on your left, at 106 Fireman's Club Road. This nostalgic site (opened in 1949) is among the last outdoor movie theaters of its kind still operating in North Carolina, and it has a powerful literary connection.

R. S. (Sam) Gwynn—a formalist poet, poetry scholar, translator, and critic—was born in Eden in 1948. His father ran the drive-in when Gwynn was growing up. After high school, Gwynn left Eden to study at Davidson College and then ply his trade as a poet while also writing several important literary textbooks as a professor at Lamar University, in Beaumont, Texas. Gwynn is admired nationally among poets for his mastery of formal verse forms and his biting wit. The title poem from his first collection commemorates his origins:

THE DRIVE-IN

Under the neon sign he stands,
My father, tickets in his hands.
Now it is my turn; all the while,
Knee-deep in stubs he tries to smile,
Crying, You'll love it. Slapstick. Fights.
One dollar, please. Please dim your lights.
I pay and enter. Mother waits
In a black truck with dangling plates
And snag-toothed grillwork idling there
On the front row. She combs her hair
And calls for me to take my place.
The moon-lights dying on her face,
She lights another cigarette
And starts to sing the alphabet.
Quickly, I turn the speaker on:
The soundtrack is a steady drone
Of snoring. With his pockets full
My father gathers up his wool,
His pink tongue rolling up and down.
A wolf, dainty in hat and gown,
Appears, sneaking across the screen
Above my father. Then the scene
Expands to show a flock of sheep.
The wolf is drooling. In his sleep
My father smiles, my mother sighs,
And dabbing gently at her eyes
She goes across to sniff his breath.
A shepherd clubs the wolf to death,
The sheep dance lightly in the sun,
And now the feature has begun:
Union Pacific is its name.
I know it, know it frame by frame,
The tyranny of separation,
The lack of all communication
From shore to shore, the struggle through

Smashed chairs and bottles toward the true
Connection of a spike of gold.
I fall asleep. The night is cold.
And waking to the seat's chill touch
I hear the last car's slipping clutch,
And on the glass a veil of frost
Obscures this childhood I have lost.
The show is over. Time descends.
And no one tells me how it ends.
—From *No Word of Farewell: Selected Poems, 1970–2000*, by
R. S. Gwynn (Ashland, Ore.: Story Line Press, 2001), 160–61.

Continue east on NC 770, which becomes Washington Street in the historic district of "Olde Leaksville," the oldest of the three towns that now make up the single municipality of Eden.

"The Land of Eden" was the name that explorer and author William Byrd II gave to the 20,000-acre estate he claimed for himself while surveying the Virginia/North Carolina border in 1728. In 1967, when the historic textile and tobacco towns of Leaksville, Spray, and Draper voted with some reluctance to merge, they adopted Byrd's name for their new city. Despite the dissolution of old boundaries, these three communities still hold fast to their historic identities. Each town had a different story, but all were driven forward by a small band of industrial tycoons who lost and found their fortunes here, some several times over, by harnessing the prodigious water power of the Dan and Smith rivers to run their mills.

Leaksville was chartered in 1796. Its first cotton and woolen mills were built in the early 1800s and supplied uniforms to the Confederate Army. The historic district on Washington Street now features, among many shops, a popular outlet for the Karastan brand of rugs, still made in Eden today. Across the street from the rug dealer is a historic mural honoring the bateaux and boatmen who once ferried goods and people up and down the Dan. (A boat landing on the Dan is two blocks south.)

Managed by playwright Melissa Whitten, the Eden Historical Museum, at 656 Washington, is a new venture. The museum, the annual Charlie Poole Music Festival, in June, and the Eden RiverFest, in September, have increased awareness of the area's rich past. (Charlie Poole was a 1920s banjo master who was part of the famous Carolina Ramblers. He is buried in Eden.)

Spray, established just up the road in 1813, developed its own cotton and woolen mills and was the site selected in 1891 by the Moreheads, a leading

North Carolina family, to install the largest electric dynamo in the world, designed to smelt aluminum. The patented process for producing aluminum did not work as hoped, however. The family soon began experimenting with other chemicals and discovered that by mixing coal tar and lime in the smelter they could create calcium carbide. This inexpensive compound, when tossed into water, produced acetylene gas—a useful flammable material. The Moreheads seized this new discovery and went on to launch what would become the worldwide Union Carbide Corporation.

John Motley Morehead III would take his part of the family fortune from this venture to establish a foundation and prestigious undergraduate scholarship in 1951 at his alma mater, the University of North Carolina at Chapel Hill. Over the years, recipients of the scholarship have had a significant impact on American letters. They include novelist and historical nonfiction writer James Reston Jr., *New Yorker* columnist James Surowiecki, poet and translator Coleman Barks, environmental writer William deBuys, and Pulitzer Prize–winning historian Taylor Branch.

The third of Eden's former townships, Draper, was established as a planned community in 1906 on the far side of the Smith River from Spray and Leaksville. It became an expansion site for Fieldcrest Mills, an enterprise begun here in 1910 when the Marshall Field department stores of Chicago bought all the mills in the area, which had been founded by Eden's most prominent textile tycoon, Benjamin Franklin Mebane. Among its many innovations, Marshall Field created the first mass-produced Karastan rugs here, in 1928.

A second poem by R. S. Gwynn recalls the richness of the local vernacular once prevalent in these three mill towns. Gwynn has crafted verse from a collection of nicknames that were in use from the 1930s to the 1960s, listed by Richard "Spunk" Carter on a website dedicated to Leaksville history—<http://www.leaksville.com>:

LAMENT FOR THE NAMES LANG SYNE
Leaksville, N.C. (1797–1967)
Bootie, Cootie, Hootie, and Red,
Rooster, Jeepy, Sny, and June,
Hambone, Corky, and SwimmyHead,
Greenie, Weenie, Puss, and Moon,
Stinky, Winkie, Goat, and Spud,
Pinkie, Toodie, and Greasy J.,
Buddyro, Buddy, and just plain Bud
Timor mortis conturbat me.

Strangler, Babbie, Sis, and Twat,
Ikey, Eekie, Lum, and Buck,
Squabby, Knobby, Monk, and Squat,
Preacher, Rabbit, Sack, and Duck,
Bimbo, Fire Chief, Goof, and Jake,
Doodie, Rubber, Deuce, and Trey,
Whitey, Blackie, Bull, and Snake
Timor mortis conturbat me.

Puddin', Oggie, Bugg, and Tick,
Hoovie, Groovie, Ape, and Gam,
Buster, Punkin', Goat, and Slick,
Meatball, Big Train, Nub, and Ham,
Eudie, Stumpy, Chunks, and Shag,
Eeenie, Meenie, and Whatchasay,
Mustard, Turbo, Crab and Rag
Timor mortis conturbat me.

Prince Pedro, Skillet, Buffalo Bob,
Peewee, Little Bone, A.O.K.,
Slobber, Booger, Spit, and Blob
Timor mortis conturbat me.

To leave Eden, take South Hamilton Street (NC 87 south). Cross the Dan River and travel fourteen miles to reach the next destination.

■ REIDSVILLE

NC 87 intersects with Reidsville's Main Street. Turn left, and in a few blocks stop at Morehead Avenue. On your left is what locals call "the monkey house," a key site in T. R. Pearson's novel *A Short History of a Small Place*. The small place in this case is Reidsville, called Neely in the novel. Pearson's inimitable young narrator, Louis Benfield, tells the rambling and ultimately tragic story of Miss Myra Angelique Pettigrew, who lived right in town with her pet chimpanzee, Mr. Britches. Miss Pettigrew eventually comes unhinged and throws herself from the top of the water tower south of town.

The strongest part of the novel is the narrator's voice. In this passage, he describes a phenomenon well known to Piedmont residents—the delicious snow day, when all bets are off and a wholesale truce on normal activity is declared under the blanket of white.

Winter in Neely is a monotonous time of year and nothing much can really break the spell of the season except for a healthy snowfall, which tends to drive the good sense out of most people since very few of the natives have seen enough snow to have become indifferent to it. We are accustomed to sleet and to the sort of rain that freezes in treetops and downs powerlines, so even the rumor of flurries makes people's eyes bright....

There is a tendency among Neelyites to panic in the face of poor weather, and the reaction to snow is no less frantic, just a little more light-headed. Before the first few flakes have had time to settle in and melt, every school in the county closes down and any merchant who does not specifically deal in provisions, what are usually called groceries, has locked up his shop and gone home. When we children arrive from school, the mothers and housewives of Neely begin to expect the worst and busy themselves making shopping lists for such indispensable items as dish-powder and confectioner's sugar and institutional-sized cans of ravioli, just the sorts of things no family can be snowbound without. Since it is us children who will make the trip to the store, we set ourselves to rooting around in the bottoms of the closets looking for boots, which most of us usually find only one of and that one made to go on last year's foot. About the only citizens of Neely with boots that fit are the garbage men who have to stomp trash all day and who, of course, don't work when it snows. So we settle for Baggies over our sneakers, and while our mothers finish up their grocery lists, we go into the cellar after our sleds, which have usually had a full year to rust and deteriorate but which require only a little candle wax on the runners to be operational again.

—From *A Short History of a Small Place*, by T. R. Pearson (New York: Penguin, 2003), 68–69.

Thomas Reid Pearson grew up in Winston-Salem and studied at North Carolina State University. He started writing *A Short History* while living in Fuquay-Varina and painting houses. It was the first of three comic novels about Neely that Pearson loosely based on Reidsville, where his grandparents lived. The other two novels are *Off for the Sweet Hereafter* (1986) and *The Last of How It Was* (1987). For the literary traveler, reading the books and then visiting this old tobacco town will strike a resonant chord.

Pearson's tale of one town eccentric is fiction, but another writer, Jerry Bledsoe, takes up the bleak reality of two actual Reidsville citizens who also came unhinged and wrought disaster on their families in 1984 and 1985. *Bitter Blood: A True Story of Southern Family Pride, Madness, and Multiple Murder* documents

At the traffic circle in the heart of downtown Reidsville, visitors can catch a glimpse of significant icons from the town's history—a memorial to the Confederacy and the tobacco factory where R. J. Reynolds's signature brand, Lucky Strike, was first conceived.

the bizarre killing spree that stretched from Louisville, Kentucky, to Winston-Salem, Greensboro, and Reidsville, involving the paranoid son of a Reidsville physician. Fritz Klenner Jr. practiced medicine alongside his father with a fake Duke University medical degree and simultaneously lived the secret life of a Nazi sympathizer and survivalist, stockpiling guns and bombs that he and his cousin, Susie Sharp Newsom Lynch, eventually used to murder five members of Lynch's family. Then, after poisoning and shooting Lynch's two young sons, the cousins took their own lives.

This sordid saga captured worldwide headlines and raised questions at the highest levels of government about North Carolina's investigative and policing

A sign outside the Lucky City Book and Wine Bar on South Scales Street in Reidsville.

practices. Bledsoe's meticulous account sold some 800 copies in a single day when he came to Reidsville for a book signing in 1988 at Lucky City Books and Wine Bar. According to owner Richard Moore, the store has subsequently sold thousands of hardbound and paperback copies of Bledsoe's national bestseller over the years, which has, at times, literally kept the store in business.

From the corner of Main and Morehead, turn right on Morehead. A statue in the center of the traffic circle ahead commemorates Confederate soldiers from the Civil War. From this vantage point you can easily see the old tobacco factory buildings on the north side of town. Take South Scales Street in the opposite direction to visit Lucky City Book and Wine Bar, on the left in the first block.

The late playwright, actor, and director Larry Leon Hamlin, whose father worked for American Tobacco, was born in Reidsville, in 1948. Hamlin, who founded the National Black Theatre Festival, discovered acting in first grade. Hamlin's mother encouraged his passion for the theater throughout his high school years in Reidsville. He went on to study business in the Northeast and then enrolled in theater classes at Brown University. When Hamlin returned to North Carolina, the lack of African American theater in the state discouraged him. In response, he established the North Carolina Black Repertory Company in Winston-Salem in 1979 and launched the National Black Theatre Festival a decade later. Hamlin, who died in 2007, had a profound influence on the vitality of African American theater across the United States.

Reidsville's newest writer-in-residence is P. T. Deutermann, who has set three of his first dozen suspense novels in North Carolina. A U.S. Navy veteran who has lived around the world, Deutermann began writing in retirement and settled here in 2005 on a horse farm. His North Carolina protagonist, retired police officer Cam Richter, of Manceford County, pursues cases across the state, in *Spider Mountain*, *Cat Dancer*, and *Moonpool*. Deutermann says his next novel takes his characters to Caswell County, where this tour is now headed.

Continue on South Scales to the intersection with West Harrison Street (US 158) and turn left (east). Yanceyville is approximately twenty-four miles ahead, on 158.

■ YANCEYVILLE

As we head east toward Yanceyville, the seat of Caswell County, it is easy to see why agriculture, and specifically tobacco, figures conspicuously in the stories from this region.

Founded during the American Revolution, Caswell had become one of the wealthiest counties in the state and one of North Carolina's top five leading tobacco producers by the beginning of the Civil War. The lingering presence of so many antebellum houses is a testament to that material success, a boom initiated in part by the accidental discovery around 1839 of a new tobacco-curing technique that produced North Carolina's famous bright leaf.

The story goes that one night Stephen, a slave owned by Captain Abisha Slade, hastily threw a heap of charcoal into a curing fire that had gone out. The intense heat from the charcoal caused the tobacco leaves to turn bright yellow. This quick process also happened to intensify the sugar content of the leaf and made smoke from it easier to inhale. Slade shared this efficient "flue-curing" technique all across the Dan River basin where the poor, sandy soil was perfect for growing the kind of tobacco that responded well to flue-curing. By 1855, the region had taken over the market. The Civil War would soon spread the appetite for golden leaf far and wide.

Caswell's affluence was not just created by a product but was also made possible by the endless toil of the enslaved people, who outnumbered landowners in the county. According to the 1976 bestseller, *Roots*, among these workers were Kizzy, the daughter of author Alex Haley's African forebear Kunta Kinte, and Kizzy's son, Chicken George, who lived on a Caswell plantation belonging to Tom Lea, a notorious breeder of gamecocks used for fighting. Today, Alex Haley's son, William Alexander Haley, lives in North Carolina. Of his father's monumentally successful book and television miniseries, he once said: "It changed the impression of people about how the African-American people came through that period. They had values, they had a culture, and both black and white people identified with that culture."

One of the most stinging firsthand accounts of slavery in the United States also comes from Caswell. According to University of North Carolina at Chapel Hill literary scholar William Andrews, Moses Roper's 1848 "Narrative" was more widely read in England and the United States than other accounts because of its brutal candor.

I was born in North Carolina, in Caswell County. I am not able to tell in what month or year. What I shall now relate, is what was told me by my mother and grandmother. A few months before I was born, my father married my mother's young mistress. As soon as my father's wife heard of my birth, she sent one of my mother's sisters to see whether I was white or black, and when my aunt had seen me, she returned back as soon as she could, and told her mistress that I was white, and resembled Mr. Roper very much. Mr. Roper's wife not being pleased with this report, she got a large club-stick and knife, and hastened to the place in which my mother was confined. She went into my mother's room with a full intention to murder me with her knife and club, but as she was going to stick the knife into me, my grandmother happened to come in, caught the knife and saved my life. — From "Narrative of the Adventures and Escape of Moses Roper from American Slavery," in *The North Carolina Roots of African American Literature: An Anthology*, ed. William Andrews (Chapel Hill: University of North Carolina Press, 2006), 96.

Roper's light skin made his youth especially difficult. He was sold away from his mother and passed among some fifteen owners across the southern states. Eventually his skin color worked to his advantage as he made his escape to the North and finally to England, often passing for white.

Coming from Reidsville, as you are nearing Yanceyville on US 158, watch for Hatchett Road on the right, and then shortly thereafter you will see the Bartlett Yancey House (pink roof, purple/gray siding) on the right.

Beyond this landmark, Yanceyville's Main Street is 0.3 miles ahead. Turn right and follow East Main Street one mile and bear right onto Hooper Road. In 0.2 miles, turn left on West Main.

The meticulously restored Caswell County Courthouse in Yanceyville,
site of a politically motivated murder and an oft-told ghost story.

The Yanceyville Courthouse is the site of the infamous murder of state senator John Walter "Chicken" Stephens, so named as a young man for his first ar-
rest in the matter of two stolen chickens. Stephens, originally from Rockingham
County, was by turns a harness maker, tobacco buyer, and Bible salesman. By
the time he moved to Yanceyville, his reputation was also secured as a scoun-
drel and a thief and as one who had avoided serving in the Confederate Army.
As prolific storyteller Manley Wade Wellman describes it in *Dead and Gone:*
Classic Crimes of North Carolina (Chapel Hill: University of North Carolina Press,
1954), Stephens went so far as to kill his widowed mother: "On June 30, 1869, she
was found with her throat cut to the very neck bone, and her son announced
that she had fallen against the jagged edge of a broken chamber pot" (140).

Though Stephens was acquitted of the murder and soon elected to the state
senate, he mysteriously met his fate in a wood storage room on the second
floor of the Yanceyville courthouse, even as public business was in full swing.
Stephens was strangled and stabbed by a band of men that included Tom Lea, a
former sheriff, and the head of the local Ku Klux Klan. Though the perpetrators
were tried, none was convicted. The head of the Klan confessed his part in the
action in a memoir unsealed at his death, in 1935.

Detail from one of the many antebellum mansions now deteriorating in Caswell County. Here Roots *author Alex Haley traced his enslaved ancestors, who worked in the tobacco fields that fueled the county's economic prosperity before the Civil War.*

Writer Daniel Barefoot also tells the tale and contextualizes the event in terms of statewide politics at the time: "Should you visit the historic courthouse at Yanceyville, you can see the room where Chicken Stephens worked and died. But take care if the door closes behind you, for the ghost of the senator—which is said to visit the room on occasion—may very well be the responsible party" (from *Piedmont Phantoms*, by Daniel W. Barefoot [Winston-Salem: John F. Blair, 2002], 18).

Follow Yanceyville's Main Street east from the square to the intersection with NC 62 north, which goes all the way to Milton, a tiny village some twelve miles ahead on the Virginia state line. This official scenic byway rides a dramatic ridge that affords long views across farms dotted with decaying tobacco barns and stunning two-story houses with multiple chimneys.

As you ponder Caswell County's past, here's a poem from G. C. Waldrep, an Amish writer who studied at Duke and lived for five years in the county before taking a teaching position at Bucknell University, in Pennsylvania. Waldrep wrote this pastoral poem as his valedictory to Yanceyville:

GEODESY II

Monochrome prospect at moonset. I always liked
the view from the mow: dark square lightened
by the deeper barn dark, felt presence of hay
drowsing in staggered rows—Flemish bond, two-
to-one—accomplishment I could touch, could breathe,
inhale the tang, dried sweat and lespedeza.
Through that arch: bright glow of house-roof, silver
instead of tin in this burnish, dull prickle
of gravel lane and garden-stipple. Wire fence
just visible like spiderweb after heavy rain.
Fritter of moonglow in these last moments: it's not
the place I'll miss so much, but the idea of place.
In the morning this ladder will be first to go.
—By G. C. Waldrep, from *West Branch* 53 (Fall 2003): 33.

NC 62 comes to a stoplight in Milton. The Dan River and the Virginia state line are to the left. Milton's business district is to the right, on Broad Street (NC 57).

■ MILTON

Thomas Day is still Milton's best-known citizen. Born in 1801 to a free black woman, he came from Halifax County, Virginia, to North Carolina around 1823. For the next thirty-six years, he made furniture in the village of Milton.

Tom probably had white friends, but if he ever felt relaxed about his free status, the icy hand of North Carolina law woke him up. Though he was legally free, he was treated like a slave.

Every month he watched a local militia, the Milton Blues, drill on New Bridge Street. Tom wasn't allowed to join because North Carolina law stated that free Negroes couldn't serve in the military except as musicians. He couldn't bear witness against a white person in court. Worst of all, he couldn't collect money owed to him by whites unless he owned property. . . .

Worry scratched him like sandpaper. As he got closer to the dream of striking out on his own, North Carolina lawmakers tightened the screws that held free blacks in place. In 1826 they ruled that *no* free blacks could

The village of Milton still claims furniture maker Thomas Day as its best-known resident.

enter the state. Free blacks were "unfortunate and troublesome," the legis-
lators fumed, and "a public nuisance."

—From *Master of Mahogany: Tom Day, Free Black Cabinetmaker*, by Mary E.
    Lyons (New York: Scribner, 1994), 11–12.

Writer Mary E. Lyons spent her adolescence in Charlotte, took two degrees at
Appalachian State University, and taught school in Graham before becoming
a librarian and then a writer. She has published a number of juvenile nonfiction titles. Her book on Milton's most famous resident pieces together the scant
known historical facts of Thomas Day's life. Today he is celebrated in Milton,
which calls itself a museum without walls.

In 1850, Day's workshop (on the right as you come into town on Broad Street)
once housed the Union Tavern. Day turned it into the largest furniture-making
enterprise in North Carolina and employed free blacks, whites, and enslaved
people. Day was a pioneer in the mass production of furniture and used steam-
powered tools. By the time of his death, on the eve of the Civil War, however, his
business was failing, as was the local economy.

Though much of Thomas Day's handiwork is in private collections, you can see pews he made in the Milton Presbyterian Church and his crown molding and stair railing in the Woodside House. A general store, several antique stores, and an art gallery make a nice walking tour of town. Maps outlining a longer historic tour of Milton and directions for six county bike routes are available at <http://www.miltonnc.com>.

From Milton, proceed southeast on NC 57 for eighteen miles through the crossroads of Semora and Concord and across Hyco Lake to Roxboro.

■ ROXBORO

Roxboro is the seat of Person County. Novelist Reynolds Price (born sixty miles east, in Macon, in 1933) lived here in the mid-1930s. His father, Will, sold electric appliances for Carolina Power and Light. Price swears he remembers lifting a pair of scissors off a dresser top while still in his crib and cutting himself a hula skirt out of a window shade in their Roxboro house. He also writes in his memoir that his "first sustained memory" is of an evening in Person County in the late spring of 1936:

We'd finished supper and, to give the house a chance to cool, we left all the windows open and awarded ourselves that peaceful pleasure of roomy prewar America, "going to ride."

. . . We drove out aimlessly to the open country that lay no more than a quarter mile south of our house—flat fields and wild grass that I see as almost gray, no later than early May then. Planted like dummies in the grass, real cows gazed at us as if we were some entirely new creature. We stopped at the creamery for Dixie cups of vanilla ice cream. Then we sat in the creaking car, in the graveled parking lot, and ate slowly from the quarter-pint cups of waxed cardboard with wood paddle-spoons that tasted as good as the cream (you could also rub them pleasantly on gums swollen with the buds of new teeth).

. . . Sometime in the ten-minute last leg of that ride—before we stopped in the drive by the white rock steps of our house on the hill on South Lamar Street, there on the rough cloth of a back seat—I knew for the first and final time that we were all married: Elizabeth, Will and Reynolds. We were now in this car, in all the world and in all our lives from here out, three people who'd trust each other for good; and that trust would last on every side.

—From *Clear Pictures: First Loves, First Guides*, by Reynolds Price (New York: Atheneum, 1989), 41–42.

The mimosa-festooned Roxboro residence that novelist Dawn Shamp had in mind for the entrepreneurial Wheeler family in her first book, On Account of Conspicuous Women.

Follow NC 57, and as it joins NC 49 and US 158, stay on 158 (Leasburg Road) to the intersection with US 501 (Madison Boulevard) and cross Madison to Court Street. Take Court one block to Lamar Street. Turn right to drive down South Lamar and see the neighborhood where Reynolds Price lived. The house he writes about is 508 South Lamar, the last one on the left before Lamar runs back into 501.

Backtrack on South Lamar a couple blocks and turn right on Barden and then left on South Main. Ahead are several landmarks featured in Roxboro-native Dawn Shamp's novel, *On Account of Conspicuous Women.*

The year is 1919 and debutante Ina Fitzhugh arrives from Richmond to help teach at Roxboro's one-room school. She's been hired by Mrs. Wheeler, prominent wife of the owner of the local telephone company. The elegant Victorian house on the left just past the post office on your right on South Main Street was Shamp's inspiration for the Wheeler house, but Miss Fitzhugh will not be staying here. She is boarding in a more modest residence with the Daye family.

A train pulled into the depot of a small village in North Carolina around four o'clock in the afternoon. It was August, as hot a day as one could possibly imagine. No hat brim wide enough, no paper fan large enough. The air itself smelled like a fiery flatiron scorching damp cotton.

Ina stepped down from the platform with her train case and waited for the remainder of her luggage. She was wearing a simple ivory blouse of silk georgette crepe, a dark skirt with a sweep just above the ankle, and a becoming hat fashioned from imported forget-me-nots. Everything appeared lit to burnt orange, electrified by the sun. She gave her eyes a moment to adjust, then took in the view of what was to be her new, albeit temporary home. . . .

"Well, this would be Roxboro," Miss Daye said, turning onto the paved crossroad. "Best not to blink if you wanna catch it all in."

It looked like a picture postcard to Ina, the epitome of an up-and-doing small town. Dark red brick on both sides of the street, cream-colored awnings over the windows of storefronts. People on the go, in one door and out another.

—From *On Account of Conspicuous Women*, by Dawn Shamp (New York: Thomas Dunne, 2008), 31, 34.

In this novel, written in a style appropriate to its era, Shamp's conspicuous women, Ina Fitzhugh and Bertie Daye joining forces with Doodle Shuford and Guerine Loftis, promote women's suffrage and the civil rights of Roxboro's African American population. They tangle with Mr. Wheeler, whose phone company is based on the real Morris Telephone Company, which was headquartered, says Shamp, in the two-story building still standing at the corner of Main and Depot streets. The operators, or "Hello Girls," who worked there (including Shamp's own grandmother) sometimes hung out the windows and summoned passersby who were receiving a call.

Sergeant & Clayton's Grocers, another actual site in Shamp's novel, is across the street from the former phone company headquarters, now home to Cole's Pharmacy, at 117 North Main Street. Locals gather in Cole's these days for gossip, excellent fresh-squeezed orangeade, and pimiento cheese or chicken salad sandwiches at lunchtime.

Rockingham Public Library

<http://www.rcpl.org>

With branches in Madison, Mayodan, Eden, and Reidsville, this library system has its own monthly radio show and offers regular story times for children and computer classes for adults.

Person County Public Library

319 South Main Street, Roxboro

336-597-7881

<http://library.personcounty.net>

Part of the Hyconeechee Regional Library system along with Orange County's libraries to the south, this library has a rich collection of materials about the colonial history of Person and Orange counties.

Rock of Ages Winery & Vineyard

1890 Charlie Long Road, Hurdle Mills

336-364-7625

<http://www.rockofageswinery.com>

An elegant rock building houses the winery and gift shop, which sells books. The owners occasionally host readings and signings by North Carolina writers. From NC 49 on your way south to the next tour in Hillsborough, turn left on Charlie Long Road at Brushy Fork.

Hillsborough : Efland : Mebane

Explore the historic community that has drawn writers for decades as a place to settle down and get the work done. Hike along the Eno River on the Poet's Walk. Visit the cemetery where relatives of Alex Haley, the author of *Roots*, are buried.

Writers with a connection to this area: Darnell Arnoult, Hal Crowther, Cathy Davidson, Annie Dillard, Elon G. Eidenier, Inglis Fletcher, Jaki Shelton Green, Allan Gurganus, Alex Haley, Debra Kaufman, Wallace Kaufman, Elizabeth Hobbes Keckley, Randall Kenan, John Lawson, Zelda Lockhart, Amanda Mackay, Michael Malone, Doug Marlette, Frances Mayes, Jill McCorkle, Pauli Murray, Craig Nova, David Payne, Robert Richardson, Eleanor Ross Taylor, Peter Taylor, Clarissa Thomasson, Lee Smith, Martha Witt, Edwin Yoder

From Roxboro, on the last tour, take NC 49 southwest and pick up NC 86 south in Prospect Hill, and you'll be on the stretch of highway that writer Darnell Arnoult had in mind in this early scene of her first novel, *Sufficient Grace.*

Gracie maintains her light touch on the wheel and drives on into the dreary day. She feels light. Her fingers play the wheel as if it is a keyboard. She makes various rest stops along the way, and, after leaving I-85, visits three roadside hamburger stands in search of safe food.

I wouldn't eat that if I were you, the voices say at Top's Barbecue Shack on Highway 86, and then again farther up the road at Bill's Dairy Bar. As Gracie backs out of her parking spot at the second drive-in, a soft voice says, *I'd get rid of that purse, too. They can keep track of you with it.* Gracie pulls alongside the Dumpster. *It gives off a homing signal,* another voice says. *Toss it,* says another. Gracie extends one leg out of the open car door and, with her right hand still on the steering wheel, she raises up enough to fling

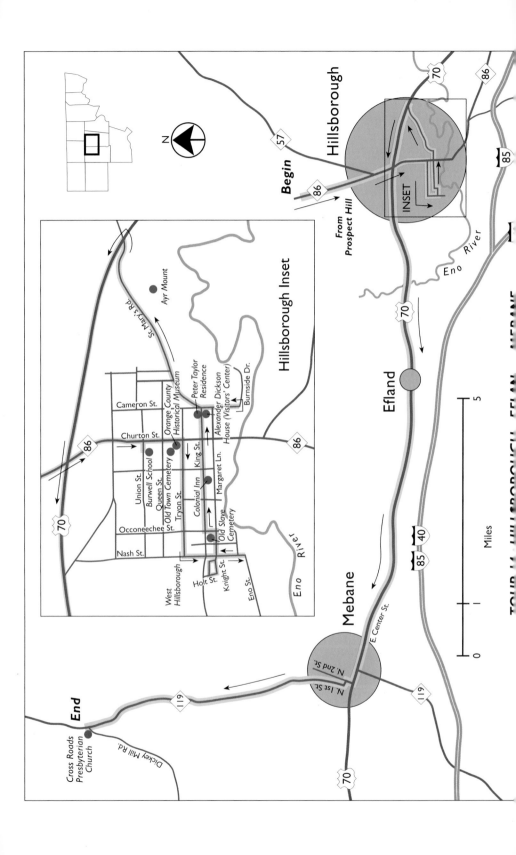

Begin Hillsborough

From Prospect Hill

Hillsborough

INSET

Eno River

Efland

Mebane

E. Center St.

N. 2nd St.

N. 1st St.

End

Cross Roads Presbyterian Church

Dickey Mill Rd.

Miles

0 1 5

N

Hillsborough Inset

St. Mary's Rd.

Ayr Mount

Cameron St.

Churton St.

Union St.

Burwell School

Queen St.

Old Town Cemetery

Occoneechee St.

Nash St.

West Hillsborough

Holt St.

Knight St.

Eno St.

Tryon St.

Colonial Inn

King St.

Margaret Ln.

Old Slave Cemetery

Orange County Historical Museum

Peter Taylor Residence

Alexander Dickson House (Visitors' Center)

Burnside Dr.

Eno River

her Coach shoulder bag up and over the roof of the car and into the Dumpster. *Two points*, says another voice. *Two! Two!* The voices cheer in unison. —From *Sufficient Grace*, by Darnell Arnoult (New York: Free Press, 2006), 14.

And so begins the quixotic journey of Arnoult's character Gracie, whose schizophrenic break takes her to a nurturing family of strangers in Virginia, while her husband, Ed, and daughter, Ginger, back home in a town much like Burlington, try to understand what they must have missed in Gracie's behavior that would account for her sudden disappearance. Arnoult is a graduate of the creative writing program at North Carolina State University and is also the author of a collection of poems, *What Travels with Us*.

NC 86 soon meets US 70 at the Hillsborough city limits. Downtown Hillsborough is straight ahead as 86 becomes Churton Street, the central thoroughfare.

"You're going to love it," she said. "Linda says Eno is the best-kept secret in the region. 'This quaint little old mill town is becoming the hottest, hippest place in the area to live.' It's still just enough off the radar to attract writers and artists and university professors." —From *The Bridge*, by Doug Marlette (HarperCollins, 2002), 41.

Hillsborough (called Eno in Marlette's novel) gives a new meaning to the term "writer's block." Here, nationally known writers live on nearly every block, where, as Marlette's narrator puts it, "historic markers were as prevalent on the downtown streets as parking meters" (92).

Perhaps it is the sheer scope and drama of Hillsborough's past that appeals to the writers in residence here. It's a history rife with stories of rebellion—from the scrappy Orange County Regulators of the 1770s to the mill workers of 1934 who staged an uprising against their bosses that turned violent. (Marlette's grandmother, a mill worker, sustained stab wounds from the National Guard in the melee—a story that piqued Marlette's curiosity and led to the novel.)

But beyond the sheer volume of stories that haunt Hillsborough, there's also the word-of-mouth factor. For the most part, the writers who live here have known each other for years, and one by one they have become neighbors. For example, Virginia-born novelist Lee Smith had something to do with Annie Dillard's decision to renovate the Cameron-Nash Law Office (built about 1881) as an occasional office space and writing retreat for herself and her husband, eminent biographer Robert Richardson. Smith and Dillard, a Pulitzer Prize–winning nonfiction writer and poet, were Hollins College classmates in the 1960s.

The 1881 Hillsborough residence that biographer Robert Richardson and poet/essayist Annie Dillard bought for their visits here. Across the street is the Cedar Walk, which figures in Lee Smith's twelfth novel, On Agate Hill.

Just across the street from Dillard's house is a residence belonging to novelist and Henderson native David Payne. The Cedar Walk—a narrow path now marked by a sign—runs beside the ancient cedars that flank Payne's house. This little wooded corridor also figures in Lee Smith's novel *On Agate Hill*.

Novelist Jill McCorkle, who is from Lumberton, returned to North Carolina after a number of years in Massachusetts, where she taught creative writing at Harvard and at Bennington College, in Vermont. She and her husband, Tom Rankin—a photographer, filmmaker, and folklorist—live outside of town on the banks of the Eno River, not too far from the farmhouse that Georgia-born poet and memoirist Frances Mayes (*Under the Tuscan Sun*) has been helping her daughter to remodel.

Zelda Lockhart, whose novels include *Fifth Born* and the historically based *Cold Running Creek*, settled in Hillsborough after earning advanced degrees in English literature and filmmaking. She was selected in 2010 as the second Piedmont Laureate, a yearlong position that involves the presentation of public readings and workshops promoting the value and impact of literature. Craig Nova, author of the novels *The Good Son* and *The Congressman's Daughter*, among many others, has built a house outside Hillsborough and is said to be working on his first book with a North Carolina setting. Eastern North Carolina writer Randall Kenan has also found the allure of Hillsborough irresistible, and he settled here when he began teaching at the University of North Carolina at Chapel Hill.

Hal Crowther, the curmudgeonly columnist on all things southern for *Oxford American* and former editor and critic on the staffs of *Time* and *Newsweek*, confirms the power of the ghosts that live around the house he shares with his wife, Lee Smith:

> Not long ago, my wife and I moved into a house in Hillsborough, North Carolina, that was built before the Civil War. It's of no special interest to historians, as far as we know. But it has an aura. It belonged to a family of undertakers, for one thing. . . . We own a decrepit carriage house from a previous century and an ancient freestone wall half-buried under honeysuckle, and out back a brick summer kitchen, older than the house, where someone's slaves cooked supper when Andrew Jackson was president. . . .
>
> History lives in the bricks and stones. For a price, established by a realtor, you can listen to those stones day and night. In the South, as so many writers have noted, they never shut up.
>
> —From "The Twelve Apostles," in *Cathedrals of Kudzu*, by Hal Crowther (Baton Rouge: Louisiana State University Press, 2000), 79.

For Allan Gurganus, author of *The Oldest Living Confederate Widow Tells All*, Hillsborough was a natural choice for literary inspiration. The Victorian house that he bought and restored is in sight of the eighteenth-century cemetery where William Hooper, the Hillsborough resident who signed the Declaration of Independence, is buried.

As Dannye Romine Powell explains in her book *Parting the Curtains, Interviews with Southern Writers*, it was back in the early 1990s when Doug Marlette's wife, Melinda, had a real estate broker call Gurganus the instant the Hillsborough house went on the market, knowing he'd been hunting for just such a place. The 1860 Gothic windows Gurganus installed in the former kitchen—now his writing office—came from St. Matthews Episcopal Church in town, known to be the oldest Gothic revival church building still standing in North Carolina.

With this high concentration of imaginations at work in the midst of such historic fascinations, it's not surprising that Hillsborough itself has become fodder for fiction. On occasion, the village scribes have found themselves writing about one another. Doug Marlette's first novel, in fact, stirred up an unwelcome controversy among his literary neighbors. The painful dispute, however, now seems inconsequential in light of Marlette's tragic death in 2007 on a rain-slick highway in Mississippi, where he'd gone to witness a high school production of the musical *Kudzu*, based on the cartoon strip he had created before his foray into fiction. Marlette was fifty-seven. His second novel, *Magic Time*, a thriller set in Mississippi, had come out just months before the accident.

■ BURWELL SCHOOL

As you come into town on Churton Street, note the Burwell School (ca. 1821), set back from the road on the right at the corner of Union Street. This institution, established in 1837, served as a boarding and day school for young women until 1857. In Lee Smith's twelfth novel, *On Agate Hill*, Burwell served as the inspiration for Gatewood Academy, where the novel's intrepid and winsome narrator, Molly Petree, a Civil War orphan, must endure the difficult headmistress, Mariah Snow. The rules and purpose of Gatewood Academy are described by its headmaster, Cincinnatus Snow:

The primary object of our course of instruction is to qualify young ladies for the discharge of the duties of subsequent life. We seek to cultivate in every pupil a sense of her responsibility for time and for eternity. Our instruction in every branch is thorough and rigorous. "Not how much, but how well," is our motto. — From *On Agate Hill*, by Lee Smith (Chapel Hill: Algonquin Books of Chapel Hill, 2006), 141.

Turn right on Union Street and drive uphill to visit Burwell School, which offers docent-led tours Wednesday through Sunday. The small cottage behind the main house also has a literary connection. Elizabeth Hobbes Keckley, an enslaved teenager who worked for the Burwells, lived here and was raped by a white man, whose identity she kept secret. Keckley left Hillsborough in 1839 and became a dressmaker. She was eventually prosperous enough to buy freedom for herself and her son, George. Later she became First Lady Mary Todd Lincoln's dressmaker and confidante. Keckley's 1868 memoir, which followed her service in the White House, did not shine a favorable light on her early years with Richard Burwell and his wife:

One morning he went to the wood-pile, took an oak broom, cut the handle off, and with this heavy handle attempted to conquer me. I fought him, but he proved the strongest. At the sight of my bleeding form, his wife fell

Small quarters behind the Burwell School in Hillsborough where memoirist Elizabeth Hobbes Keckley worked and lived as a teenager. She later became Mary Todd Lincoln's dressmaker at the White House.

upon her knees and begged him to desist. My distress even touched her cold, jealous heart. I was so badly bruised that I was unable to leave my bed for five days. I will not dwell upon the bitter anguish of these hours, for even the thought of them now makes me shudder. The Rev. Mr. Burwell was not yet satisfied. He resolved to make another attempt to subdue my proud, rebellious spirit—made the attempt and again failed, when he told me, with an air of penitence, that he should never strike me another blow; and faithfully he kept his word. These revolting scenes created a great sensation at the time, were the talk of the town and neighborhood.—From *Behind the Scenes: Thirty Years as a Slave and Four Years in the White House*, by Elizabeth Hobbes Keckley (New York: G. W. Carleton, 1868), 37–38.

Though Keckley's memoir cast Mary Todd Lincoln in a sympathetic light, the first lady ended their friendship upon its publication, saying that she felt her confidence had been betrayed.

Return to Churton Street and continue south. In the next block on the left, at the intersection with Queen Street, is Dickerson Chapel AME Church, the oldest AME church in town, which began as a Quaker school for black children. After the terrible hardships of the Civil War, some African Americans in the Hillsborough area finally began to prosper. As writer Pauli Murray describes in her memoir, *Proud Shoes*, her great-grandparents arrived in Hillsborough from Pennsylvania on the evening train in 1869. Met by their son, Pauli Murray's grandfather, Robert Fitzgerald, the family took only ten days to buy a 158-acre plantation called Woodside, on the banks of the Eno River southeast of Hillsborough. The farm was successful, and Murray's grandfather soon started a school for African Americans. Their primary challenge came from a local chapter of the Ku Klux Klan, who made constant threats against the family and other successful African Americans in the area. (For more on Pauli Murray, see Tour 17.)

■ ORANGE COUNTY HISTORICAL MUSEUM

Lee Smith conducted extensive research among the holdings of this museum for her novel *On Agate Hill*. For more than fifty years, there has always been a dedicated band of Orange County citizens who have collected artifacts and papers on the history of Hillsborough. The building, at the corner of Tryon and Churton, once served as the town library. In addition to the exhibits that lift up the many layers of town history, the museum gift shop offers several books, including fine-art photographer Elizabeth Matheson's *A Sense of Place: A Hillsborough Memoir*. Matheson is a Hillsborough native whose photographs of the town's architecture and landscape are accompanied by the voices of various Hillsborough residents throughout history, selected by poet Elon G. "Jerry" Eidenier.

Around the corner from the museum, on Tryon Street, past the Presbyterian Church, is the Old Town Cemetery on the right, a fascinating place to wander and wonder at the many lives lived here.

■ WEST HILLSBOROUGH

At the beginning of the twentieth century, Hillsborough became a textile mill town. In addition to the grand Colonial, Federal, and Victorian houses that are preserved here, a great many of the old mill houses are still intact.

In East Hillsborough, there were gardens and tended lawns; driveways were paved or neatly filled with small gravel. The sun rose promptly there, spent the day shining, preparing to roll toward the other side, where it

A bottle tree decorates the yard of the Bateman Mill House, built in 1922 by the Belle-Vue Cotton Manufacturing Company. This Hillsborough neighborhood figures in the novel Broken as Things Are, *by Martha Witt.*

could set in a wild abandon of oranges and reds. Ginx and I walked west together that evening, watching as the sun sank, breaking over the trailers and the small houses, their weather-beaten porches scattered with children's clothing and parts of dolls and trucks. There was a yard with plastic statues of Snow White and the Seven Dwarfs; a small Bambi grazed at the feet of one of the dwarfs. We passed by Cone Mill, where I thought we would see what Uncle Pete had spoken of. But all we saw was a group of men there, some desperately still and others who laughed loudly enough for everyone. No one, though, was missing limbs as far as I could tell.—From *Broken as Things Are*, by Martha Witt (New York: Henry Holt, 2004), 56.

Martha Witt uses her hometown of Hillsborough as the setting for a touching and somewhat dark novel about a girl and her autistic brother whose imaginations are fired by tales of the dangers of mill work, as told by their older relatives. To visit the neighborhood she writes about, follow Tryon four blocks west to Nash Street and turn left. Follow Nash across West King Street and turn right onto Webb Street, which leads straight ahead to Knight Street. On Knight, note the Bateman Mill House on the right, built by the Belle-Vue Cotton Manufacturing Company around 1922. This residence was one of twenty-nine mill houses that the company constructed on Knight, Holt, and Webb streets, according to a neighborhood historian, Candice Cobb. At the south end of Nash Street, near the river, the company also built a commercial area with a drugstore, café, barbershop, and movie theater.

At the end of Knight, look to your left to see the old mill. Turn right on Holt and right again on Webb, where a collection of yard art much like Martha Witt describes in her novel is proudly displayed. Follow Webb back to Nash and turn right to see the little commercial village and mill at the bottom of the hill. Nash ends at Eno Street, which runs alongside and then crosses the river. This was the site of Hillsborough's train depot. Doug Marlette's character Mama Lucy describes the old days:

> "Mill village life was like a family," she continued. "They took care of you. You knew everybody in that town and everybody knew you. Two hundred, two hundred fifty families. Neighbors always borrowin' from each other. An egg or a piece of fatback. Maybe a couple of Irish potatoes. We looked after one another. Not like today." Lucy's eyes sparkled as she warmed to the subject and her memories filled her up. "I remember lyin' in bed late at night when I was a girl, in the summertimes when the windows was up, smellin' the yard mixed in with the wisteria and the honeysuckle, and starin' through the window screens up the hill to the factory lit up like a Christmas tree and listenin' to the roar of the looms. It was real soothin', would put you to sleep like the poundin' of waves on a beach. Like a lullaby." — From *The Bridge*, by Doug Marlette (HarperCollins, 2002), 87–88.

Backtrack on Nash to Margaret Lane and turn right. Hillsborough's Old Slave Cemetery is on your far left. The names of the known dead are commemorated on a single plaque mounted on a large boulder in the center of the lawn. Continue back toward the business district on Margaret and turn left on Occoneechee and then right on West King Street.

Beyond the beautifully maintained residences along this block and just before the commercial district begins, the badly aging Colonial Inn is on the right.

COLONIAL INN
Cornwallis, circa 1781
It's finger lick'n chicken,
okra, oysters, fried nuggets

A century ago, Hillsborough's Colonial Inn welcomed guests to King Street, a simple, tree-lined dirt road. Photo courtesy of the Hillsborough Historical Society.

on the plate,
and cobbler close behind,
that make the trip worth while.

Amidst all this food, is the raised
standard, but you won't care who slept
where or with whom, in this venerable
Inn, in continuous operation since Aaron Burr.

To get there, go west on the King's
Highway just off Churton, cobbled
by Cornwallis, so red coats could
march out of mud. Even if Cornwallis

didn't sleep here, you might make
a night of it. He surely did eat here, or
somewhere near—marching all
his ten thousand men.
—Used by permission of Elon G. Eidenier.

Poet "Jerry" Eidenier, retired manager of Duke University's Gothic Bookshop, takes a comic turn on the much-embroidered history of the Colonial Inn. Neither George Washington nor Charles Cornwallis slept here, nor does the inn even date from the colonial era. However, those who remember the fried chicken and vegetables of this establishment's last incarnation in the 1990s are still mourning its closing.

First named Spencer's Tavern and built in 1838, the inn is the primary subject of a novel, *Defending Hillsborough*, by Clarissa Thomasson, a Nags Head writer, who researched her great-great-grandmother's career as proprietor here. At the end of the Civil War and following her husband Henry's death from influenza, Sarah Holeman Stroud was running the inn, then called the Orange Hotel. (Henry is buried in Old Town Cemetery.) At the book's dramatic conclusion, as Sherman's soldiers invade Hillsborough and begin hauling off the inn's furnishings and all her family's possessions, the widow Stroud hangs her husband's Masonic apron out a window. Seeing the apron, a Union officer recognizes it as the Masonic distress signal and identifies himself to Sarah as a Mason. He calls off the looting, and Stroud's livelihood is saved.

Continue to Churton Street and note the historical marker commemorating the Regulators, who gave themselves the name because they aimed, in 1770, to regulate their own affairs rather than be ruled by British officials. After a battle near Alamance Creek, in 1771, six Regulators were hanged, only five years shy of the Declaration of Independence, which would make their cause a national movement. In 1957, novelist Inglis Fletcher wrote *The Wind in the Forest*, a novel that dramatizes this era in local history.

■ HILLSBOROUGH VISITORS' CENTER

Follow King Street across Churton to the intersection with Cameron Street. On the right, the Alexander Dickson House, now the Orange County Visitors' Center, offers additional information on other Hillsborough sites that may be of interest.

Directly across King is a house designated as William Reed's Ordinary and Still House Lott. Short-story writer Peter Taylor and his wife, poet Eleanor Ross Taylor, bought this residence in 1949—yet another fancy of Peter's, which he soon declared would be their last in a long string of real estate deals. According to Peter Taylor's biographer, Hubert H. McAlexander, the Taylors were happy here. They commuted to Greensboro three days a week, where Peter taught creative writing at the University of North Carolina at Greensboro and Eleanor

The King Street residence that was once home to poet Eleanor Ross Taylor and short-story master Peter Taylor. Robert Penn Warren, Frances Gray Patton, Randall Jarrell, and other notable writers visited the Taylors here.

took poetry classes with Randall Jarrell. Eleanor, who was raised in a family of writers, confessed to houseguests that, for her, taking up poetry was a way to avoid being overshadowed by her husband's literary success. Her work so impressed Jarrell that he once drove the forty miles from Greensboro to Hillsborough just to tell his new student how much he liked her latest batch of poems.

At the beginning of their tenure in Hillsborough, Peter was selling stories to the *New Yorker* at a regular clip and was in frequent, giddy correspondence with Katharine White, his editor there. He was so enthralled by the house that he began to feel he couldn't write anywhere else.

The Taylors also started attending St. Matthews Episcopal Church, just across Cameron Street, and they frequently entertained literary luminaries from out of town. Poet Robert Lowell and his second wife, novelist Elizabeth Hardwick, were houseguests, and fellow *New Yorker* writer Frances Gray Patton often came to call from Durham.

In the spring of 1950, Robert Penn Warren (*All the King's Men*) came to visit, which thrilled the Taylors. But trouble arrived not long after: Randall Jarrell came over to announce that he was divorcing his wife, Mackie. He said they would need to sell a Greensboro duplex that the Taylors and the Jarrells owned jointly. About the same time, Peter's fortunes with the *New Yorker* reversed, when founding editor Harold Ross turned the magazine over to his successor, William Shawn. Peter grew frustrated and restless. He arranged for Fannie Patton to take his classes at Greensboro while he took guest-teaching assignments elsewhere. Ultimately, the Taylors sold the Hillsborough house, and long-suffering Eleanor endured, continuing her own writing. Years later, she published this poem in the *New Yorker*:

KITCHEN FABLE
The fork lived with the knife
    and found it hard—for years
took nicks and scratches,
    not to mention cuts.

She took tedium by the ears:
    nonforthcoming pickles,
defiant stretched-out lettuce,
    sauce-gooed particles.

He who came down whack.
His conversation, even, edged.

Lying beside him in the drawer
   she formed a crazed patina.
The seasons stacked—
   melons, succeeded by cured pork.

He dulled; he was a dull knife,
while she was, after all, a fork.
—From *Late Leisure*, by Eleanor Ross Taylor (Baton Rouge:
   Louisiana State University Press, 1999), 67.

From the corner of King and Cameron streets, walk or ride down Cameron to the right (south). As Margaret Lane comes in from the right, note the driveway across Cameron that leads to a private house called Burnside. You can only get a glance from the street of the pristine white house, built in 1883 by industrialist Paul Cameron. It was here that the six Regulators were hanged from one of the Burnside trees.

This house was the first that Doug and Melinda Marlette restored in Hillsborough. Marlette called it Oaklawn in *The Bridge*. The estate now belongs to Durham-born novelist Michael Malone and his wife, Maureen Quilligan, a Renaissance scholar at Duke. You can tour the house if you are lucky enough to be in town during Hillsborough's annual candlelight Christmas tour in December.

Continue down Cameron toward the river to see a replica of the original village of the Occaneechi-Saponi, the first settlers in the region and the smallest and last Indian tribe to be recognized by the State of North Carolina. Occaneechi Town was located on the banks of the Eno along the Great Indian Trading Path. Explorer and prolific journal writer John Lawson met here with the Indians on the banks of the Eno in 1701.

Backtrack on Cameron Street to the intersection with St. Mary's Road and go right on St. Mary's Road, past Saint Matthew's Episcopal Church. In a half mile, watch for the entrance to your right for Ayr Mount, our next stop.

■ AYR MOUNT

Once a plantation twice its present size (265 acres), this property has been lovingly restored and put into a land trust. Tours of the house are conducted for a fee, but the grounds are open to the public free of charge. The Poet's Walk, which begins beside the parking area, is a one-mile excursion first among huge magnolias beside the lawn and then down to the banks of the Eno. Dogwoods and maples in profusion make this walk especially colorful in spring and fall. Picnickers are welcome. (Plans call for this path along the Eno to be paved and

Along the Poet's Walk in Ayr Mount.

extended from the mill village in West Hillsborough all the way to Occaneechi Mountain, a state natural area and the highest point in Orange County, farther downstream.)

A thriller by Durham writer Amanda Mackay explains a bit about the Eno River, which was once threatened by development from here and into Durham County. Mackay's protagonist, Hannah Land, is a professor of political science at Duke:

> The Eno River meanders through tobacco country and woodland, coming close to Durham, North Carolina. It's a private wild river, for all the bustle around it. Practical city fathers in Durham think it would make a reservoir. Passionate ecologists want it for a park. But those who love the river best are those who live along it. For them it is a place to fish, or water the mule, and also, in seasons when the water is high, to get out in a boat. Though in some places scarcely more than a creek, the Eno has good stretches for canoeing, and such frivolous craft are sometimes seen there. Indeed, when the water's high, a canoe can go from Hillsborough to Durham, a good five hours, and not see ten houses. —From *Death on the Eno*, by Amanda Mackay (Boston: Little, Brown, 1981), 4.

Gaines Chapel AME Church was an early influence in the life and work of the first Piedmont Laureate, Jaki Shelton Green.

From Ayr Mount, continue on St. Mary's Road to the intersection with US 70 and turn left (west).

■ EFLAND

Heading west on 70 Business, be sure to avoid the upcoming ramp onto I-85. Instead, stay on 70 and watch for Gaines Chapel AME Church on the left, a little less than two miles beyond the I-85 ramp and five miles beyond NC 86 in Hillsborough.

You are now in Efland, the hometown of the first Piedmont Laureate, Jaki Shelton Green, who was appointed to the post in 2008 by a consortium of the arts councils for Raleigh and Wake, Durham, and Orange counties. Green, who works in a variety of settings as teacher, poet, and literary activist, won the North Carolina Award for Literature in 2003 and is the author of four poetry collections. Her extended family has lived in this area for generations. Gaines Chapel was the church of Green's beloved grandmother, Eva White Tate, an elder among the church ladies who once prepared for Martin Luther King Jr. when he came to call in the 1960s.

THAT BOY FROM GEORGIA IS COMING THROUGH HERE (EXCERPT)

they changed curtains
waxed floors
aired out the front company room
sent for camphor to lay throughout the house
they cooked all night
boiled bath water all day
cornbread, okra, turnip salad, stewed chicken,
fried chicken, dressing,
killed the prized hen
gravy, corn, potatoes, rice, sweet potato custard,
lemon pie, rice pudding, coconut cake,
chocolate cake, lemonade, and your chittlins,
martin,
all for you martin,
word was given sunday
that you was coming
to their corner
so they swept dirt yards
put the chickens up
hung out the special quilt
laid out the catalog sheets
put fresh oil in all the lamps
cause you could never tell
just how long you'd want to stay
a war on evil takes a lot of planning
takes a lot to get troops
stirred up.
so stewed corn with fatback, fried chicken
sliced tomatoes and cucumbers in vinegar
were passed around several times
soldiers need meat on their bones
martin
walking through dustbowls
hailstorms
riding on the blade
of a lightning rod
those old sisters

opened

their front rooms for you

—From *Breath of the Song: New and Selected Poems*, by
    Jaki Shelton Green (Durham: Carolina Wren Press, 2005), 42.

About ten miles south of this spot is the site of another literary inspiration—
a housing development created by poet and environmentalist Wallace Kaufman. Novelist Joyce Allen lived there for many years. Behind her house, Allen
discovered a big stone hearth and the footprint of a small cabin. "I used to go
out there a lot and wonder about who had lived there," Allen explains. "I found
their well (filled in), and in the winter, when the growth was down, you could
still see the furrows from their field."

Allen knew the inhabitants could have been black, white, or Indian, given
the area's history. "So I began to think of someone who might be of any race,
and who remained a cultural outsider whoever she was." The result is *Hannah's
House*, Allen's sometimes spooky 2008 novel that moves between past and
present in the lives of two women living more than a century apart but who
inhabited the same ground.

■ MEBANE

You enter Mebane the way you enter many small North Carolina towns—
from the expressway, turning off, slowing down. Just beyond the I-85 exit
is the main residential thoroughfare, tree-lined with elegant turn-of-the-
century homes, neatly painted, freshly restored. There is a small business
section and, clustered nearby, the tidy homes of working people. Mebane
would seem like a quietly prosperous place were it not for the hulk of the
old White Furniture company, looming at the center of town. . . . The history of Mebane is a microcosm of the American furniture industry. The
glory of that history is White's.—From *Closing: The Life and Death of an
American Factory*, by Cathy N. Davidson, photographs by Bill Bamberger
(New York: W. W. Norton, 1998), 23.

And so begins Duke English professor Cathy Davidson's narrative that accompanies Bill Bamberger's sensitive photographs documenting the final days
of White Furniture Company. The old factory, some five miles west of Efland, is
on the right as you come into the village of Mebane on US 70. This documentary volume introduces the people and history of an old-fashioned town that is

also the birthplace of Edwin M. Yoder, Pulitzer Prize–winning columnist for the *Washington Post*. In this excerpt from a New Year's Day column in 1976, Yoder looks back at the Mebane of his youth in the 1940s from the perspective of a homecoming visit at Christmas:

> There were four distinct classes of people in my town, if you counted the farm folk who lived at country places called Hebron and Woodlawn and the millworkers of "Mexico" whose cottages perched in rows near the abandoned clay mine. All the town's known Republicans were tagged, like exotic migratory birds, and it was unkindly whispered that they all descended from carpetbaggers. On a fine Sunday morning you could set your watch, the furniture factory whistle being silent, by the ferocious roar of Miss Emma H's old auto, as with elaborate stuttering and popping she readied her noon departure from the First Presbyterian Church. Traffic parted to make way, like the Red Sea before the Children of Israel. . . .
>
> These towns endure, even with new faces and houses and habits. Perhaps it is fancy to believe they were more interesting then, in their cloistered and time-set ways—more interesting than, to tell the truth, they seemed at the time. Were they more interesting when familiar people sat on the front porches on hot summer evenings, counting the fireflies and listening to the crickets, than now when unfamiliar people sit unseen in back rooms watching fantasies on their television screens? *O lost, and by the wind grieved, ghost, come back again!* cried Thomas Wolfe.
>
> But these musings do not last long on a Christmas day walk. The air chills, the light fades, the eggnog waits amid the littered wrappings at home, and there are long distances to go tomorrow.
>
> —From *The Night of the Old South Ball, and Other Essays and Fables*, by Edwin M. Yoder (Oxford, Miss.: Yoknapatawpha Press, 1984), 59–61.

Among Yoder's many books, this one may be of most interest, because the writer provides his eloquent perspective on other North Carolina writers also considered in these trails: among them Harry Golden, Phillips Russell, Thomas Wolfe, W. J. Cash, and the Fugitive poets from out of state who taught at the University of North Carolina at Greensboro—John Crowe Ransom and Allen Tate.

Holding up the banner for poetry in Mebane today is Debra Kaufman, a poet, playwright, and former staff member at Duke University Press, who has made her home in town for more than two decades. In this poem she celebrates the advantages of the contemplative life in the country:

ALMOST FIFTY IN AUGUST

What calls you out—
the cicadas' shimmer-song,

the jasmine-scented air,
that extra glass of wine you drank?

Or something wilder in your blood
driving you to pass

the porch lights you know
and keep on going,

past the abandoned
textile mill, past the county's

last family farm, down a dark
gravel road that dead-ends in deep pine woods?

What are you waiting for
here in the muggy night

where insects won't stop screaming,
where spiders spin out their ordinary lives?

This may be as good as it gets—
counting on the cycles (summer turns

to fall, predator finds prey),
walking alone into an unknown plot,

terrified but longing
to meet your shadow

under the ancient, dusty moon
soon to be new again.
—Used by permission of Debra Kaufman.

This tour concludes with a trip a few miles north of Mebane on NC 119 north
(Second Street), which comes up on the right as you continue through town.
Follow 119 for about nine miles and watch for the Cross Roads Presbyterian
Church on the left at the intersection with Dickey Mill Road (SR 1912).

■ CROSS ROADS PRESBYTERIAN CHURCH

This congregation was organized perhaps as early as 1783. It was to this church that writer Alex Haley came in the early 1970s to find a key link between his relatives in Caswell County and the generation that was sold to the Murray family, in Alamance County. According to a story by reporter James Thorner in the *Greensboro News & Record*, Haley was finishing the manuscript of what would be his enormously successful book, *Roots*, published in 1976. He needed to know more about the story of his great-grandfather, Tom Murray, a master blacksmith who left Alamance County and settled in Henning, Tennessee—Haley's birthplace—at the end of the Civil War. The author tracked down a female descendant of Andrew Murray, a white tobacco planter in this area who might have been Haley's great-grandfather's master before emancipation. The landowner's heir, Ila Murray Bryan, in turn managed to find Effie Murray White, the daughter of slaves, still living in the Cross Roads community at the age of ninety-six. Mrs. White's husband had been the cemetery custodian here. Haley came immediately to Cross Roads to meet Mrs. White, who told him what she knew. (Mrs. White was also first cousin to Eva White Tate, grandmother to poet Jaki Shelton Green, whose work is presented earlier in this tour.)

Haley found the grave of Andrew Murray, his great-grandfather's former master, in the Cross Roads cemetery. Alongside his large tombstone are the unmarked graves of some of the African Americans who worked for him, including Alex Haley's great-great-uncle, Enoch Wright Murray, brother to Tom. Upon finding these relatives, Haley could finish his story:

> Nearly every Sunday afternoon, unless the Murrays had gone somewhere themselves, various of the local plantation families would pay them welcoming visits, along with their old friends from Burlington, Graham, Haw River, Mebane and other towns around. In showing their guests about the big house and yards, the Murrays always proudly pointed out different examples of Tom's craftsmanship. Few of their farm or township guests left without urging that the massa permit Tom to make or repair something for them, and Massa Murray would agree. Gradually more of Tom's custom-made articles appeared about Alamance County, as word of mouth further advertised him.—From *Roots: The Saga of an American Family*, by Alex Haley (New York: Vanguard, 2004), 753–54.

After the book's extraordinary success, Haley came back to Cross Roads in 1977 for a family reunion, which was documented in a CBS television program,

Roots: One Year Later. The church has an autographed copy of Haley's book in its library.

■ LITERARY LANDSCAPE

Purple Crow Books
109 West King Street, Hillsborough
919-732-1711
This independent bookseller is a likely place to find autographed books by Hillsborough writers, if not the writers themselves.

Hillsborough Cup-a-Joe
120 West King Street, Hillsborough
919-732-8056
This hole-in-the-wall purveyor of caffeine, pastries, and artisan-roasted coffees by the cup and the bag is a likely place to spot one or more of Hillsborough's writers. Hillsborough's poet of the streets, Mike Troy, might also burst in with a poem he's just written to share with the patrons.

Haw River : Graham : Burlington : Snow Camp : Liberty : Silk Hope : Siler City : Pittsboro : Fearrington

Welcome to a land of contrasts. Here urban sprawl and rural isolation are neighbors and writers wrestle with the stories that have come from the ups and downs of North Carolina's product-based economy. The ghosts of a colorful past occupy this landscape, while the contemporary residents have taken up new occupations.

Writers with a connection to this tour: Dorothy Robinson Barnwell, Doris Betts, Ellen Bland, Virginia Boyd, Paul Cuadros, Robin Greene, John W. Harden, William Hardy, Leon Hinton, Lynne Hinton, Judy Hogan, George Moses Horton, Marjorie Hudson, Drew Lasater, Duncan Murrell, Lawrence Naumoff, Michael Parker, Nancy Peacock, Dale Ray Phillips, Diane Silcox-Jarrett, Mark Sumner

This tour travels into Alamance and Chatham counties, places that still move at a slower pace than the booming urban centers to the west and east. Nevertheless, the area's new agricultural pursuits—including organic dairy farming, wineries, strawberry fields, poultry, goats, vegetables, and even Christmas trees—are a testament to the resilience of the residents, despite the decline of textiles. These two counties have also attracted newcomers in recent years, residents drawn by the relative quiet and natural beauty. Among them are filmmakers, purveyors of outdoor adventures, artists, craftspeople, and musicians who participate in events such as the twice-yearly Shakori Hills Music Festival, held on a farmstead near Pittsboro.

tour 15

SILK HOPE - SILER CITY - PITTSBORO - FEARRINGTON

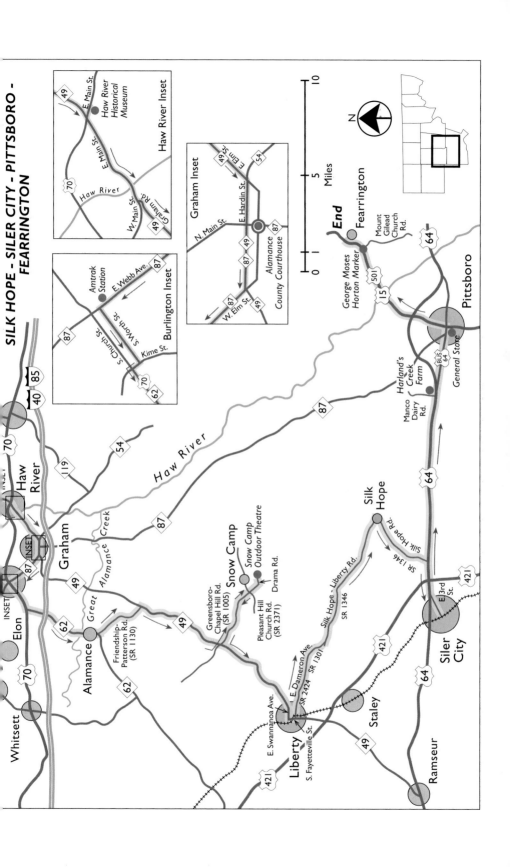

Haw River Inset

E. Main St.

Haw River Historical Museum

E. Main St.

70

Haw River

Graham Rd.

W. Main St.

49

Burlington Inset

Amtrak Station

E. Webb Ave.

87

S. Church St.

S. Worth St.

Kime St.

70

62

Graham Inset

F. Elm St.

49

54

N. Main St.

E. Hardin St.

87 49

Alamance County Courthouse

87

W. Elm St.

87

49

Miles

0 1 5 10

N

End
Fearrington

George Moses Horton Marker

Mount Gilead Church Rd.

501

15

64

Pittsboro

Harland's Creek Farm

Manco Dairy Rd.

BUS 64

General Store

64

87

Haw River

70

Whitsett

Elon

70

Haw River

INSET

87

INSET

Graham

62

49

Great

Alamance

Creek

119

54

87

Silk Hope

Silk Hope Rd.

SR 1346

Alamance

Friendship-Patterson Rd. (SR 1130)

Snow Camp

Greensboro-Chapel Hill Rd. (SR 1005)

Snow Camp Outdoor Theatre

Pleasant Hill Church Rd. (SR 2371)

Drama Rd.

62

49

Silk Hope - Liberty Rd.

SR 1346

421

E. 3rd St.

Siler City

421

421

E. Dameron Ave.

SR 2424 SR 1301

Liberty

E. Swannanoa Ave.

S. Fayetteville St.

64

Staley

49

Ramseur

421

40

85

70

From the last tour, follow Dickey Mill Road west to NC 49 and turn south. NC 49 runs directly into the village of Haw River.

On the east the woods were cut short by the Haw River, where some of the backwaters had been dammed to make Jake's All Nite Carp Pond. Here men waiting to hop a freight train to distant places loitered alongside the out-of-work. A few old men fished eternally for a carp with a tag on its tail which would win a grand prize. Women were rumored to have disappeared around the pond, and once, after we had carved hearts and our names in the tops of the tallest trees, I watched with the other boys as the men with grappling hooks unsuccessfully dragged the muddy water for a missing person. All this and the fact that Jake sold cigarettes and bootleg whiskey to minors made the place irresistible.—From "The Woods at the Back of Our Houses," by Dale Ray Phillips, in *This Is Where We Live: Short Stories by 25 Contemporary North Carolina Writers*, ed. Michael McFee (Chapel Hill: University of North Carolina Press, 2000), 82.

Dale Ray Phillips was born in Alamance County in 1955 and was raised in Burlington. He portrays life along the Haw River during his desultory youth. Today, what was once a mill town is being reclaimed as part of a recreational corridor for nature enthusiasts.

Before crossing the Haw River on NC 49, watch for the intersection with US 70. If it's the weekend, turn right on 70, and in a very short distance you'll find the Haw River Historical Museum, at 201 East Main Street, open only on Saturdays and Sundays. The museum offers a window on the town's critical contributions to the state's textile industry, specifically in the development of water-powered cotton mills. Across the street from the museum is Granite Mill, built in 1844 on a granite outcropping.

Return to NC 49 (West Main Street) to cross the Haw River, which has become the focus of a regional conservation effort to create a dedicated multi-use trail stretching some sixty miles from Haw River State Park, in southern Rockingham County, all the way to Jordan Lake State Recreation Area, near Pittsboro, in Chatham County. The trail follows alongside the Haw, which has several long stretches suitable for canoeing and kayaking. Paddling the Haw is a different way to experience the history of the mills that once hummed along its banks (see <http://www.thehaw.org>).

■ GRAHAM

Because of the pervasiveness of textile factories and the housing develop-ments built for their workers, the boundaries between the towns of Haw River, Graham, and Burlington are practically indistinguishable to the first-time visi-tor. NC 49 becomes East Elm Street and then East Harden Street in Graham, the county seat. As 49 crosses Main Street, look south to see the county courthouse and town center.

Graham was the birthplace of John W. Harden, a journalist who began his career at the *Burlington Times-News* and went on to write for papers in Raleigh, Charlotte, Salisbury, and Greensboro. Harden is best remembered for his *Tales of Tarheelia*, broadcast in the 1940s on WPTF radio, in Raleigh. The series later became the basis of *The Devil's Tramping Ground and Other North Carolina Mystery Stories* (1949) and *Tar Heel Ghosts* (1954), both published by the Univer-sity of North Carolina Press.

■ BURLINGTON

As West Harden Street comes to a fork on the other side of Graham, bear right on NC 87, which leads into Burlington. The town lent its name to a brand that became synonymous with plaid fabrics and all manner of socks, linens, hosiery, and apparel. J. Spencer Love founded Burlington Mills in 1923. Because he took a chance on a new fiber called rayon, by the early 1960s he had built the company into the largest textile manufacturer in the country.

Burlington poet and short-story writer Leon Hinton remembers when Burlington was known as the hosiery center of the South. "Huge companies were here, like Standard Hosiery Mills, which later became Kayser-Roth," says Hinton, who also says that mom-and-pop hosiery mills even sprang up in garages and in small buildings behind private homes. From the 1920s to the 1950s nearly everyone in Burlington worked in textiles or in hosiery.

To passersby on the interstate, Burlington is recognized as the town that turned from mills to malls—specifically outlet malls featuring seconds, over-runs, and bargain merchandise from a slew of manufacturers. Though this dis-count shopping strategy has spread across the nation, with strategically placed outlet malls along interstates in every direction, Burlington was an early leader in the concept. Hillsborough writer Lee Smith could hardly resist this retail milieu for a story:

Melanie stands dreaming against the open door, the entrance to Linens N' Things in the outlet mall in Burlington, North Carolina. It's raining. Melanie loves how the rain sounds drumming down on the big skylight at the center of the mall right over The Potted Plant and Orange Julius, it sounds like a million horses running fast, like a stampede in a western movie. She loves movies, she loves Clint Eastwood, now what if *he* came in the outlet mall right now and walked over to her and said, Excuse me, ma'am, I need a king-size bedspread in a western décor? She'd say, Why yes, come this way sir, I've got exactly what you need. Only the trouble is that he won't come in probably, or any other real man either, men don't come to outlets unless of course they happen to work there, especially not to Linens N' Things, which is where Melanie works.—From "The Interpretation of Dreams," in *Me and My Baby View the Eclipse*, by Lee Smith (New York: Ballantine, 1990), 129.

Likewise, Darnell Arnoult's character Ed Hollaman in her novel *Sufficient Grace* is another Burlington retailer who profits by proximity to the interstate:

Ed had wanted to name his business Tire King, but that name was taken. In the end he came to like the sound of Tire Man. *Sounds like a superhero*, Gracie said. *And who will people want when they have troubles but a superhero?* She used to look on the bright side of everything.

Not long after he opened Tire Man, he had nailed a good contract with Jessie Burgess's towing service. They bring in the motorists stranded on the interstate, the ones always glad to find a real garage open on the weekends. From the beginning, everyone in town has known that Tire Man goes far beyond tires. Practically everything related to auto mechanics is possible in the bays of Tire Man except transmission and body work. Ed's fingers fly over the adding machine.

—From *Sufficient Grace*, by Darnell Arnoult (New York: Free Press, 2006), 73.

It's notable that Arnoult's contemporary character still uses an adding machine instead of a computer. So it goes in this region of transition from old-fashioned to newfangled, from solo entrepreneurs to big-box stores.

NC 87 (East Webb Avenue) leads into Burlington's central business district. With the train depot on the right, turn left on South Worth Street and explore downtown. Zack's, famous for its hot dogs since 1928, is located on the corner of Worth, at 201 West Davis Street. This historic eatery is proud to claim that it is now supplying used cooking oil to a local biodiesel producer—another example of how old is meeting new.

Among the literary legends here, Burlington was home to a hardy writer and high school English teacher, Robinson Barnwell, who published two novels for young people, *Head into the Wind* (1965) and *Shadow on the Water* (1967), about the hardships and rewards of growing up in the country. Like North Carolina writers Olive Tilford Dargan (aka Fielding Burke) and Frances Fisher Tiernan (aka Christian Reid), who found it necessary to write under names that might disguise their then-lesser status as females, Robinson Barnwell left off her first name for the first two books. Then, in 2005, at the age of ninety, Barnwell published her third novel, *Years from Home*, under her first name, Dot.

Diane Silcox-Jarrett, who also lived in Burlington and who graduated from Elon University, wrote a valuable and imaginative biography of the life of Charlotte Hawkins Brown. Brown established the Palmer Memorial Institute, a school for African Americans, in 1902. Silcox-Jarrett was inspired to write the book, *Charlotte Hawkins Brown: One Woman's Dream*, after her first visit to the state historic site and museum that commemorate Brown's life and legacy, some fourteen miles west on US 70.

To reach our next destination, follow Worth Street to a right on West Kime, then turn left onto South Church Street (US 70/62). At the intersection with NC 54, follow the sign for NC 62 (Alamance Road) south. After crossing the interstate, it's approximately four miles to the village of Alamance on Alamance Creek, once the site of E. H. Holt's enormous cotton mill.

NC 62 curves sharply to the right just as Bellemont-Alamance Road comes in on the left. Take the second left on Friendship–Patterson Mill Road (SR 1130), which, in several miles, will connect with NC 49. Turn right on 49, heading south.

In this landscape, where soybeans and corn are more likely crops than yesteryear's tobacco and cotton and where brightly clad bicyclists now ride for miles on roads with sometimes challenging elevations, the old ways of country living are nevertheless still in practice.

Novelist Lynne Hinton was born in Durham and raised in Fayetteville. She attended the North Carolina School of the Arts and the University of North Carolina at Greensboro before going to seminary to become an ordained minister. She served for a time as a hospice chaplain in Rockingham County and then became pastor of Mount Hope United Church of Christ, in Whitsett, about ten miles west of Liberty. Hinton drove these rural roads that carry the name "Friendship" as she began to imagine what would become her first best-selling novel.

In *Friendship Cake*, Hinton tells the story of five women at the fictional Hope Springs Community Church who decide to publish a cookbook, which, in turn, leads to a deepening of their friendships, even as they weather the hardships of aging, loss, and family crises. This passage, written in the voice of tough-minded Margaret Peele, explains the importance of cooking to these church ladies and, like many other passages on this tour, explores North Carolina's rural/urban divide, this time from a culinary angle:

> As far as cooking goes, I'm considered only fair by the women in this com-munity. Out here, everybody grows their own vegetables, has their own livestock, kills, milks, and cans. So every recipe begins with something like "Strip all the feathers from the bird" or "Make sure the roots and stems are cut." The standards are a little higher than say, Greensboro, where I took my sweet potato casserole to a women's meeting; and having set it down next to all the KFC boxes and the Winn-Dixie potato salad, was treated like I was Cordelia Kelly from Channel 2's cooking show.
>
> Here, in the country, women grew up learning to cook before they were tall enough to reach the stove. It was the mother's and the grandmother's responsibility to make sure all the girls in the family could make a meal out of one strip of meat and a cup of beans. So we learned to cook. And we learned to be creative. We learned how to stretch dough across two weeks at three squares a day. We learned how to make soup from old bones and old potatoes. And we learned to knead our sorrows and our dreams into loaves of bread and our worthiness into cherry pies and fatty pork chops.
> —From *Friendship Cake*, by Lynne Hinton (New York: HarperCollins, 2002), 6.

This unusual novel, which includes recipes, refers to several local landmarks, including Fran's Front Porch, an establishment that for some twenty-eight years was the top choice in these parts for a Sunday dinner out. Fran Holt, who closed the restaurant in 2004, had been cafeteria manager at Nathanael Greene Elementary School, in Liberty. She was also a lifelong member of the church Hinton served in Whitsett. Fran's famous chicken pie compelled Sunday diners to travel great distances to enjoy the specialty of the house, not to mention the dozen or more desserts she prepared. Some guests even came in private planes, which landed at the small airstrip across the road from the family home place with the wraparound porches that Fran and her daughters enclosed to make more dining space. Though Fran died in 2008 at the age of ninety-one, her recipe for chicken pie lives on in the cookbook she published and sold through six printings.

Since the publication of *Friendship Cake*, Lynne Hinton has written two other novels about the Hope Springs community. She is also the author of a series of mysteries published under the pseudonym Jackie Lynn. Though she now serves a church in Albuquerque, New Mexico, Hinton writes a regular column for the *Charlotte Observer*'s Faith and Values section.

From NC 49, it's hardly a mile to the flashing light at the intersection with SR 1005 (Greensboro–Chapel Hill Road). Turn left and go 3.4 miles to another flashing light. Follow the signs straight ahead to the site of the Snow Camp outdoor dramas, *Sword of Peace* and *Pathway to Freedom*. From the flashing light, it's 0.2 miles to Drama Road. Turn left.

■ SNOW CAMP OUTDOOR THEATRE

On this historic site, the legacy of outdoor drama that was germinated at the University of North Carolina at Chapel Hill continues as it does in many such amphitheaters around the county. The Snow Camp Historical Drama Society produces two plays during the summer months in these woods where Quakers settled before the Revolutionary War. The play *Sword of Peace* details the events surrounding General Cornwallis's encampment at Simon Dixon's home here, a few days after the Battle of Guilford Courthouse, in 1781.

The late Chapel Hill writer and stage director William Hardy wrote *Sword of Peace* on commission in 1972. By that time, he had worked for many years on the management team of Paul Green's best-known outdoor drama, *The Lost Colony*, in Manteo, and then served for thirty years as manager of Kermit Hunter's play *Horn in the West*. He had also directed *Unto These Hills*, in Cherokee.

Hardy was a pioneer in the organization that led to the creation of the Institute for Outdoor Drama and was the author of a novel about World War II and three other historical dramas set elsewhere in the United States.

A second outdoor drama regularly presented here is *Pathway to Freedom*. It focuses on the North Carolina participants in the Underground Railroad—a clandestine means of passage to the North and Midwest for slaves seeking freedom before the Civil War. Some 50,000 Africans and African Americans fled North Carolina in the thirty years before the Civil War, and the Quakers on Cane Creek helped many of them escape. Several historic buildings on the grounds of Snow Camp also help tell this story.

Among his many plays, Asheville native Mark Sumner wrote *Pathway to*

Freedom in 1994. Sumner, who lives in Chapel Hill, was director of the Institute for Outdoor Drama for twenty-five years, served as president of the American Theater Association, and was instrumental in the founding of some thirty outdoor theater companies around the country.

Get in touch with the theater for a schedule of its annual productions, summer youth camps, and off-season special events (336-376-6948 or <http://www.snowcampdrama.com>).

Backtrack to NC 49 to continue the tour.

◼ LIBERTY

NC 49 rolls into Liberty, a classic town divided by railroad tracks. Though once an agricultural center, Liberty is best known these days for its antique festivals held every April and September, which bring in more than four hundred dealers. The Liberty Showcase, held in the town's remodeled theater, brings musical acts to town. Robin Greene's poem remembering her time in Liberty speaks to a present-day transience that contrasts with earlier generations, which were more likely to settle in one place. Greene is professor of English and writing at Methodist University in Fayetteville, where she also presides over Longleaf Press.

LIBERTY, NC
Half a decade I lived here, but now passing through,
it all seems as distant as the smallest

dot on my gas station map. Crossed
by the red and black arteries of Routes 49 and 421,

the landscape remains obscure, foreign as I drive
slowly down Main Street, past the Liberty Theater,

First Union Bank, the veterinary clinic
where I used to work—closed now, I hear,

in this town where for several years I trespassed,
owner of farmhouse and land, as if it were possible

to claim the red fox and cornsnakes, wild poke
and blackberries. My first child was born

in Liberty, in this place where I never belonged—
woods, kudzu, unkept pasture, clay soil and weeds,

neighborhood dogs howling all night for a bitch
in heat. Ten years. And still I can't recognize

why loss haunts like a half-remembered song,
or a dream forgotten after waking.
—From *Memories of Light*, by Robin Greene (Carrboro, N.C.:
North Carolina Writers' Network, 1991), 5.

NC 49 comes through downtown Liberty and makes a sharp left instead of crossing the railroad tracks. (Note the handsome restored depot on the far side of the tracks.) Follow 49 as it makes this turn. In a few more blocks, 49 crosses the tracks. Take the next left on East Dameron Avenue (SR 2424), which soon becomes Silk Hope–Liberty Road (numbered first as SR 1301 and then as SR 1346). This glorious thirteen-mile ride through the countryside passes through Crutchfield Crossroads and continues as SR 1346 into Chatham County and the crossroads known as Silk Hope.

■ SILK HOPE

Silk Hope is a farming community twenty-five miles west of Chapel Hill, North Carolina.

In the mid-1800s, an American sailor who had spent time in China planted mulberry trees in the same area, hoping to establish a silk industry. When the trees matured enough to harvest their leaves, he discovered that the silkworms he'd hatched would not eat the leaves. He'd planted the wrong variety of mulberry tree.
—From *Silk Hope*, by Lawrence Naumoff (New York: Harcourt Trade
Publishers, 1995), n.p.

This epigraph launches Lawrence Naumoff's fourth novel, set in the Silk Hope community where he lived off and on from 1971 to 2005. The story centers around two sisters who must decide, following their mother's death, whether they will honor her wishes and maintain the old home place or sell it. One sister, Frannie, decides to settle down and gets a job packing men's briefs in boxes at the mill where her sister also works. She keeps a hog she names Alice. She tries her riding skills at the local rodeo and wins. Frannie grows fond of her new life in Silk Hope. By contrast, Frannie's sister, Natalie, and her boyfriend, Jake, have other ideas about the dispensation of the family property, which creates the novel's tension.

On the road to Silk Hope, the subject of a novel by Lawrence Naumoff.

Throughout the novel, Naumoff, who has worked by turns as a carpenter, farmer, bulldozer driver, and creative writing professor, shares his sharp eye for the finer points of farmhouse architecture:

The interior walls of this house were beaded pine boards. It was thought this was a premium way to finish a house, and a couple today finding such a house rejoiced. Actually in times past, the boards were considered second to plaster, but plaster houses in the country were rare and expensive, and wood could be cut and milled off your own property (12).

Naumoff also offers a hefty dose of authentic local color, as when the sisters travel to Hillsborough for the annual Hog Day Celebration—an actual event held each June.

When the novel appeared, Silk Hope residents didn't know what to make of it. Naumoff says the idea of using a landscape and its history for entirely made-up characters and their story "was too new" for some readers, who complained that they could not find anyone they recognized in the book. The 1999 movie version of the novel, starring Farrah Fawcett, did stir some community pride, but then it was Naumoff's turn to be disappointed.

Today, Silk Hope offers the Old Fashioned Farmer Days Festival on Labor Day and the Shakori Hills Music Festival each spring and fall. The Silk Hope Winery, Chatham County's first vintner, is located at one of the highest points in the area, straight ahead a few miles from the crossroads store, just off Silk Hope–Gum Springs Road.

To continue the tour, turn right at the crossroads onto Silk Hope Road (SR 1003), pass the Silk Hope Grill, and come to US 64. Turn right on 64 for a short ride to Siler City.

■ SILER CITY

Perhaps best known in popular culture as the town where the actress Francis Bavier, who played Aunt Bee on the *Andy Griffith Show*, spent the last twenty years of her life, Siler City also has several literary distinctions. It is the birthplace of novelist and short-story writer Michael Parker and hometown of writer Virginia Boyd. Her small-town upbringing inspired her 2007 novel-in-stories, *One Fell Swoop*. Shock waves race through Boyd's fictional town of Riley, in Matthews County, when the marriage of a prominent couple explodes in a murder-suicide. Boyd offers multiple viewpoints on the tragedy and gradually unpacks the force of the event on the whole community over a period of three decades. She also cleverly manages to illuminate the way in which small-town life inevitably and inescapably connects people despite differences in age, income, racial identity, and religious faith.

Riley's residents generally prefer the slow pace of rural life, are suspicious of outsiders, and would rather avoid the world beyond their bubble. Not the character Delma Matthews, however. She's a hairdresser whose husband, Troy, works in a local dog food plant. (Siler City did have such an enterprise—Chatham Dog Food—which burned to the ground in 1981.) Troy explains his wife's penchant for news of the world beyond Riley:

When Delma first told me she wanted to subscribe to the daily newspaper, sent every day all the way from Raleigh, I was right proud. Most folks are happy catching what kind of news they can in the little old Matthews County paper. But not my Delma. She said, "There's more going on out there than we know, and I aim to find out what it is." And I thought, *Well, I'll be, I married me a smart little cookie, now didn't I.*

Delma has always been curious and likes to study up on things, so I was not taken totally by surprise. She's told me all about how important it is to support your spouse in their efforts to grow and improve, and I thought

Siler City's best-known hamburger purveyor is a favorite spot of writer Virginia Boyd.

that was the case here. So, I said, "Sweet cakes, you read all the papers you want." I had no idea where all this would lead.

—From *One Fell Swoop*, by Virginia Boyd (Nashville: Thomas Nelson, 2007), 61.

To experience Siler City's flavor firsthand, Boyd recommends a stop first at Johnson's, on US 64 a quarter-mile beyond the intersection with US 421. Established in 1946, Johnson's, housed in a brick stand-alone storefront, is famous for cheeseburgers. "But you have to get there early," says Boyd, "because once they run out of fresh hamburger, they close up shop and that happens earlier in the day than you would think." Claxton Johnson makes each burger to order and serves it on a toasted bun with a serious slice of sharp cheddar cheese. The restaurant is cozy (twelve seats at the counter and six booths), and the walls are covered with family photos. For dessert there's chocolate or lemon icebox pie. Johnson's is closed on Sundays and Mondays.

From Johnson's, continue a block west on 64 and turn left on East Third Street to reach downtown, which is laid out in a grid with numbered streets running roughly east and west and numbered avenues running north and south. Follow Third Street as the avenue numbers decline and turn left on what should be First Avenue but is instead North Chatham Avenue—the main street in the historic district. Along these blocks are several art galleries, a business incubator for artists, and Courtyard Coffee and Soda Café, a popular spot for visitors. Park and enjoy.

In 2000, Siler City made national headlines as the site of an anti-immigration rally led by David Duke, a former member of the Ku Klux Klan who had come up from Louisiana. Chatham County is home to a large number of immigrant workers who have found employment in the fields and in the chicken-processing plants here. The assimilation of this new population is the subtext of *A Home on the Field*, a memoir by Peruvian-born journalist Paul Cuadros, who moved to the area to study immigration and ended up coaching soccer for Jordan-Matthews High School during the era of David Duke's visit. (Cuadros now teaches journalism at the University of North Carolina at Chapel Hill.)

So much of their lives had already been spent getting around rules, being informal, bending the law. Many of them owed their presence in North Carolina to deceit. Their parents worked with *chuecos*, fake documents they paid handsomely for, sometimes just to get a job at the chicken plant. . . .

I needed them to learn that there was a right way to do things and a wrong way. I wanted the team to live in an environment that was honest and up-front. The team was here to help its members in more ways than just winning games. The boys needed to know there was one place where things were absolute. They knew instantly where they stood on the team. They were either eligible or not. No in between. They had to make the grades and stay in school or they couldn't play. There would be no compromises, no deals, no informality about these rules. They needed to learn that the things they wanted in life came at a price. There would be no *chuecos* on this team.

—From *A Home on the Field: How One Championship Team Inspires Hope for the Revival of Small Town America*, by Paul Cuadros (New York: HarperCollins, 2006), 84.

One more Siler City fascination is worth mentioning. Though our tour does not go to the famous Devil's Tramping Ground a few miles south of town, the literary visitor will remember the mention of a book so-titled earlier in the tour. Driving directions to this circle of land where nothing ever grows are easily available on the Internet, and John W. Harden's book, still in libraries, provides the background for this spooky curiosity. Like the Brown Mountain Lights near

Morganton, the Devil's Tramping Ground has brought many curious travelers to speculate on its origins.

From here, our tour heads east on US 64 toward Pittsboro, the Chatham County seat. Backtrack from downtown Siler City on Third Street to US 64. Turn right and watch the mileage as you travel east. At eleven miles, begin watching for Manco Dairy Road (SR 1514) on the left and turn left. Then take an immediate right on Plantation Drive.

■ HARLAND'S CREEK FARM

This certified organic farm grows produce, herbs, and heirloom flowers that were probably grown here in the 1800s, when the property was a plantation. The Alston-Degraffenried House, on the National Register of Historic Places and built in 1810, is the magnificent plantation house now occupied by the owners of the farm, who began their organic operation in 2001 after uncovering several old flower beds amid the ancient trees. The farm welcomes visitors who are interested in horticulture and the literary connection here. See <http://www.harlands-creek-farm.com> for more information.

Novelist Nancy Peacock, who grew up in Chapel Hill, rented the tenant house beside the plantation house as she began her novel *Home Across the Road*, a story of two families with the same last name. The intertwined story of the white and black Redd families that began on a Chatham County plantation took shape for Peacock as she made daily walks through the surrounding woods and fields. Peacock also learned from her neighbors how in 1977, when the television miniseries based on Alex Haley's book *Roots* was first broadcast, the occupants of the Alston-Degraffenried House found themselves answering queries from their African American neighbors with the surname Alston. They wanted to know if their relatives might have lived and worked on the old plantation. Haley's story set off a new interest in genealogy nationwide.

China crossed the field. She walked past the piles of rocks laid there by the field hands clearing the land, rocks now partially hidden by the high, weedy grasses of Chatham County. China kicked at one as she went by.

She walked past the tumble of logs that had once been cabins. She walked up the rutted carriage trail that led into the woods. She walked across the bridge that spanned the Haw River, up the hill and past the white Redds' cemetery.

—From *Home Across the Road*, by Nancy Peacock (Atlanta: Longstreet, 1999), 107.

The Alston-Degraffenried house near Pittsboro inspired the novel
Home Across the Road *by Nancy Peacock.*

Piles of field stones are scattered along the carriage trail, which is discernible not far from the big house even now. A walk in these woods makes Peacock's novel even more vivid.

Return to US 64 East and take exit 378 to reach the Pittsboro business district.

■ PITTSBORO

US 64 Business leads directly into town. Park beside the Pittsboro General Store, just before the traffic circle that surrounds the old county courthouse, and have a look around. You'll see a popular soda shop, several antique shops, a toy store, and the local arts council gallery.

Like Hillsborough to the north of Chapel Hill, Pittsboro to the south has become a popular refuge for writers and retirees who want to be close to the Triangle cities but who appreciate the quiet, the historic homes, and the possibility to spread out and even raise animals in this vicinity. At last count, novelist Doris Betts had fifteen horses, two dogs, and one goat on her farm just outside town. Writer Marjorie Hudson, who worked tirelessly to see that Chatham County's resident poet from the 1800s, George Moses Horton, was duly commemorated with a state historical marker, lives near Betts. (Hudson's book, *Searching for Virginia Dare*, is discussed in volume 3.)

Pittsboro is a relatively new address for writer Duncan Murrell, a former Algonquin Books editor and frequent contributor to *Harper's* magazine. Murrell's essay "Pittsboro Haunts" describes some of the sources of his inspiration in town:

> Our house in Pittsboro is ninety years old. I am almost forty. My wife and I are the fourth owners of the place, a tin-roofed country bungalow with a wide porch and a perfect view of the poultry trucks that gear up for the hill just as they pass.
>
> On the wall of our house are three photographs of a woman named Sankie Reed, whom we have never met. She was the daughter of the man who built the house, Mr. Glenn, and after a brief marriage to a man nearly fifty years older, Sankie settled back in the old home place and lived there until 1989.
>
> The photos show the house in its youth, when Hillsboro Street through Pittsboro was a raised road, and people like Miss Sankie grew peavines in their front yards instead of lawns. In each of the photos she stands buttoned up in proper church clothes, her mouth drawn straight across her small, china-white face.
>
> It was not long after we began attending services at the old Pittsboro Presbyterian Church, after we had been sitting in the same spot in the same pew for months, that one of the older members took us aside. "Have you heard of Miss Sankie?" he asked. Why, yes, in fact we have her photos on our wall. "She used to sit in that very spot."
>
> Pittsboro is small and old, so small and so old that very little separates us from each other or our ghosts. The longer I live here, the more often I have the vertiginous moment, the instant certainty that I've just walked into someone else's story still being written by, for instance, Miss Sankie.
>
> Then there's Doris Betts, who sits in the pew across from and behind us most Sundays. She is, of course, one of America's greatest writers, the

author of eight works of fiction that, if there is any justice, will be remembered at least two hundred years, which is how long the old former saloon and boy's academy with the secret dance floor, now called the St. Lawrence House, has been standing in Pittsboro. Sometimes I have the great pleasure of sitting over beers with Doris to talk about writing and publishing. We meet at The City Tap, which is in the building that once housed the department store that served the black townfolk who gathered one day in front of the lens of the great photographer Dorothea Lange. Are we all living in one another's stories?

The images, the strange coincidences, the hilarity, the pain, and the joy of living close by others, the old rivalries, the surprising gifts of grace, the mysteries of the dead laid neatly in our many old cemeteries—these are the strata of a history that, here in Pittsboro, seem sliced open and exposed all at once like rings on the world's oldest holly tree, which once stood behind the old Blair Hotel. This is my place. Here I can write, and though it is not always clean or well lighted, it is crowded with ghosts, charged with memory, and I have no lack of inspiration. I have written half a dozen stories set in the fireplace room of the Pittsboro Bait Shop. I look out my window and I see willow oaks and pin oaks and black walnuts and pecan trees and I can see the huge circle of a flight of vultures, and there is nearly too much to write about.

—Used by permission of Duncan Murrell.

One of North Carolina's most vigilant poets and literary organizers, Judy Hogan, has lived in Chapel Hill, Saxapahaw, and now Moncure, near Pittsboro. Hogan has coached scores of would-be writers to publication. She was the mastermind behind the North Carolina Writers' Network and later developed a lively exchange between groups of poets in Russia and North Carolina. Most important, Hogan founded Carolina Wren Press, still a vital publishing house in Durham. Before leaving Pittsboro, read one of Hogan's poems, a complement to Duncan Murrell's piece.

CENTURY OF LIGHT IV

January 10, 1999
I carry a century on my shoulders.
A walking stick carved from twisted wood
helps me find my footing. The Carolina wren
celebrates sun. The stream is not frozen;
it runs across the pebbles. Some oak leaves

at the edge of the water look red. I found
lightwood, knocking the rotten wood
off a long-dead pine until the knots showed
themselves. More holly trees and more berries
in them than I had noticed before. The last
year of the century begins, and I have work
enough for another century. But the rill over
the pebbles reminds me: do what you can.
  I look at my land: broken and uprooted
trees, but some grow tall and flourish. If John Muir
could fight for national parks and win, I can guard
and tend my acres of woods and field. Sun on
brown leaves; white limbs against a grey blue sky.
To reach my house I walk uphill. I want to know
every tree and shrub by heart. I will. A large
bird flies over: hawk, eagle? I saw his shadow
first and then his wings.
    One tree root crosses
the water at its widest point and goes into the bank
opposite. Probably from that old holly tree.
This wood grows holly well. Holly, winter's crown.
—Used by permission of Judy Hogan.

Travel around the traffic circle in the middle of Pittsboro and take US 15/501 north toward Chapel Hill. On the way out of town, you'll pass the old Chatham Mill on the right, now transformed into retail and office spaces. In 2004, Central Carolina Community College instructor and playwright Ellen Bland and her former student Drew Lasater created *The Millworker,* a musical drama based on the book *Like a Family: The Making of a Southern Cotton Mill World.* Jacqueline Hall and her colleagues gathered hundreds of oral histories from former mill workers—stories that, at their best, read like Dickens. Bland's play, which adapted some of these stories for the stage, was performed in empty mills all around the Piedmont, including Chatham Mill. Many former mill workers, some of whom had never before attended live theater, declared the production accurate and powerful.

Continue north on 15/501. Just before the bridge that crosses the Haw River, on the left side of the highway, is the site of an old hippie commune called the Banana Farm, long gone but the basis of another Nancy Peacock novel, *Life*

The original cast of The Millworker—*a stage play written by Central Carolina Community College drama and humanities instructor Ellen Bland, along with her former student Drew Lasater.*

without Water. This area also inspired the opening scene in Doris Betts's novel *Souls Raised from the Dead.* The author explains:

> On my daily commute to the University of North Carolina–Chapel Hill, I came upon a chicken-truck wreck beside the highway. Seventy-five hundred capons, raised in houses heated and lit by electric current—chickens that had never set foot to ground before—were loose from the overturned poultry truck. They flew; they hobbled with bloody wings, banged into passing windshields. Neighbors were catching some in tow sacks for lunch and dinner. Imbedded in this scene, with wounded chickens flapping past his head, a state trooper was trying to bring order out of chaos in a tableau both horrible and funny. And the look on his face? Pure existentialist despair. If Jean-Paul Sartre had lived in Chatham County, North Carolina, he would have recognized this as Page One, though perhaps we would have written different paragraphs at the end. In my case, that chicken-truck wreck opens a novel in which a highway patrolman longs to protect his daughter from all harm at all times, to rear her as perfectly as if she could

be kept in unnatural isolation like those chickens. But of course, there is no way to give children a perfect or a perfectly safe life. There will be wrecks in their lives, too. There will be escapes, freedom. And in time there will be injury.—From "Whispering Hope," by Doris Betts, *Image* 7 (Fall 1994) (<http://imagejournal.org/page/journal/articles/issue-7/betts-essays>).

It's approximately three miles from the Haw River bridge to Mount Gilead Church Road and the end of this tour, where a state historical marker on the right commemorates the remarkable poet George Moses Horton, an enslaved man whose master, William Horton, had a 400-acre farm nearby. Horton, who was born in Northampton County and moved to Chatham with his master, taught himself to read by firelight. While tending cattle, Horton began composing poems and committing them to memory, because, though he could read, he could not write. On Sunday trips to Chapel Hill, he began reciting his poems to university students and soon discovered they would pay for his compositions. Horton walked the long road to Chapel Hill as often as he was allowed, hoping to earn enough money to buy his freedom.

Beyond his commissioned love poems, Horton's subject matter was broad. According to scholar Joan R. Sherman, he was the first American slave to protest his bondage in verse. On the next tour, we'll visit the site of his recitations on the Chapel Hill campus.

Here in the countryside, near the present-day community of Fearrington, imagine the night sky that Horton witnessed well more than a century ago:

REFLECTIONS FROM THE FLASH OF A METEOR

Psalm xc. 12

So teach me to regard my day,
How small a point my life appears;
One gleam to death the whole betrays,
A momentary flash of years.
One moment smiles, the scene is past,
Life's gaudy bloom at once we shed,
And thinly beneath affliction's blast,
Or drop as soon among the dead.
Short is the chain wound up at morn,
Which oft runs down and stops at noon;
Thus in a moment man is born,
And, lo! the creature dies as soon.
Life's little torch how soon forgot,

Dim burning on its dreary shore;
Just like that star which downwards shot,
It glimmers and is seen no more.
Teach me to draw this transient breath,
With conscious awe my end to prove,
Early to make my peace with death,
As thus in haste from time we move.
O heaven, through this murky vale,
Direct me with a burning pen;
Thus shall I on a tuneful gale
Fleet out my threescore years and ten.
—From *The Black Bard of North Carolina: George Moses*
Horton and His Poetry, ed. Joan R. Sherman (Chapel Hill:
University of North Carolina Press, 1997), 105.

■ LITERARY LANDSCAPE

May Memorial Library

342 South Spring Street, Burlington
336-229-3588
<http://www.alamancelibraries.org>
One Sunday a month, the May Library brings in regional writers to read and answer questions about their work.

Burlington Writers Club

<http://www.burlingtonwritersclub.org>
Founded in 1958, this group works across genres offering critique services, contests, workshops, member readings, and general camaraderie for beginning and established writers.

Elon University

101 East Haggard Avenue, Elon College
336-278-2000
<http://www.elon.edu>
The college was given the name Elon (Hebrew, meaning oak) upon the school's founding, in 1889, because of the old grove of trees on these grounds. Today's up-and-coming university offers a concentration in creative writing for English majors.

The barn at Fearrington Village is the site of many literary events associated with McIntyre's Books across the lane.

McIntyre's Books

2000 Fearrington Village Center, Pittsboro
919-542-3030
<http://www.fearrington.com/village/mcintyres.asp>

A broad collection of North Carolina books distinguishes this bookstore, launched in 1989. Nationally recognized writers command the barn at Fearrington, where the store often sponsors special literary events and celebrations.

Chapel Hill : Carrboro

Writer/musician Bland Simpson offers a special excursion through the Old Chapel Hill Cemetery, where dozens of esteemed writers from North Carolina's past are at rest, though their works live on. More recent generations of dedicated wordsmiths have also launched their careers in these two towns that surround the first state-supported university in the United States.

Writers with a connection to this area: Milton Abernathy, Alice Adams, Daphne Athas, Ellyn Bache, Doris Betts, Will Blythe, Anthony Buttitta, Michael Chitwood, Jane Toy Coolidge, Libba Cotten, Pam Durban, Charles Edward Eaton, John Ehle, William Faulkner, Lawrence Ferlinghetti, Candace Flynt, Shelby Foote, Roland Giduz, Marianne Gingher, Edward Kidder Graham, Frank Porter Graham, Elizabeth Lay Green, Paul Green, Edwin Greenlaw, Caroline Lee Hentz, Fred Hobson, Linda Whitney Hobson, George Moses Horton, Robert B. House, Noel Houston, Langston Hughes, Wallace Kaufman, Randall Kenan, Robert Kirkpatrick, Frederick Koch, Charles Kuralt, Phillip Manning, Michael McFee, Ruth Moose, Josefina Niggli, Frances Gray Patton, Peggy Payne, Walker Percy, Reynolds Price, Lillian Hughes Prince, William Meade Prince, Jessie Rehder, Louis D. Rubin Jr., John Russell, Phillips Russell, David Sedaris, Phillip Shabazz, Alan Shapiro, Bland Simpson, Betty Smith, Cornelia Phillips Spencer, Elizabeth Spencer, Max Steele, Gertrude Stein, James Street, James Taylor, Daniel Wallace, Thomas Wolfe, Richard Wright, Jonathan Yardley, Valerie Raleigh Yow

From the low plateau on which the town of Pinehill is built many roads wind down and down and out in various directions: toward the coast, or the western mountains, or north, up to New York, Boston, Canada, all that. Going east, the coastal direction, is a fairly new two-lane highway. (This state is famed for its highway system; much more

tour 16

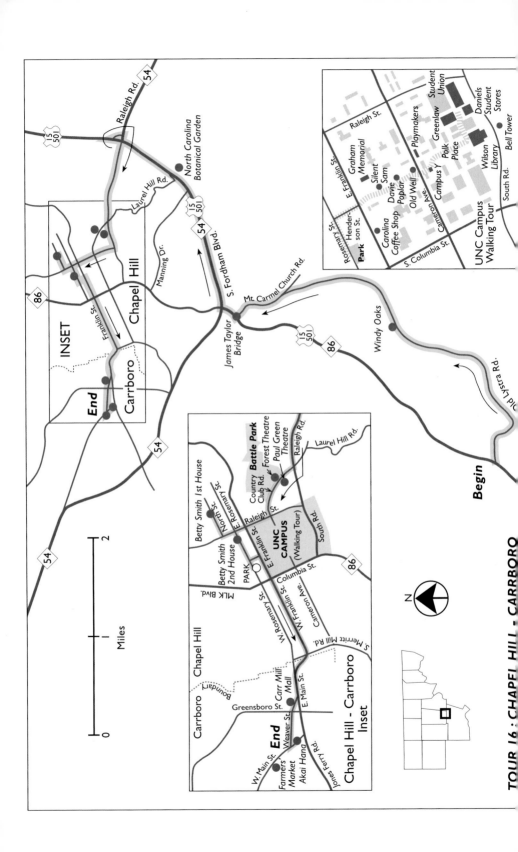

TOUR 16 : CHAPEL HILL - CARRBORO

money is spent on highways than on schools, as local professors are fond of pointing out, shaking heads and muttering of the future.) On both sides of this eastern drive are deep and seemingly infinite woods, pines and oaks and maples and poplars, and a rich, indistinguishable undergrowth of bushes and thick vines. Recently a dirt road has been built that goes back into these woods. Not very far out of town. At the end of this road, in an old refurbished farmhouse, Russ Byrd and Brett and all those children live. A marvelous spread, which a great many people in town have never seen.

—From *A Southern Exposure*, by Alice Adams (New York: Alfred A. Knopf, 1995), 44–45.

The two-lane roads Alice Adams remembers from her youth in Chapel Hill (which she called Pineville in this novel) are now four-lane or wider. Adams was born in 1926, the daughter of an aspiring writer, Agatha Boyd Erskine, and her husband, Nicholson Adams, who was soon to take an appointment as professor of Spanish at the University of North Carolina at Chapel Hill.

Adams wrote nine novels and is probably best known for her short stories, which appeared year after year in the *New Yorker*. Her parents moved to Chapel Hill in the heyday of playwright Paul Green's literary eminence. It was a heady time on the UNC campus, with nationally prominent writers coming to visit and sometimes stay to collaborate with Green, who had won the Pulitzer Prize in 1927 for *In Abraham's Bosom*, the first of his six Broadway plays. Green might have been part of the inspiration for Adams's character Russ Byrd in the novel, though Byrd is more egotistical and less appealing than was the genuinely humble Paul Green.

Speaking in 1984 of her childhood in Chapel Hill, Adams told CBS interviewer Don Swain on his show, *Book Beat*: "Thomas Wolfe had been there when I was growing up in the 1930s. Betty Smith [*A Tree Grows in Brooklyn*] was there, too. She was a local heroine. The message I got from the air there is that writing books is a superior calling."

Adams would spend most of her life in San Francisco, though Chapel Hill was never far from her thoughts. She told CBS that on one occasion when she sent her son to Chapel Hill on a family errand, he returned saying that he understood why his mother had become a writer. Adams asked how he knew. "Because everyone in that town is writing a book," he said.

Not much has changed in the ensuing years. The literary output of Chapel Hill and Carrboro has not diminished since Paul Green's day, making this tour one of the most densely packed in the state. As Louis D. Rubin Jr., founder of Algonquin Books of Chapel Hill, once put it, "Good writers—like grapes and overdrafts at the bank—usually come in bunches. Where there is one, there are likely to be others turning up about the place."

■ WINDY OAKS

Appropriately then, we approach Chapel Hill and Carrboro from the south on US 15/501 to see the last home of Paul Green, the man who, perhaps more than any other single playwright, first put Chapel Hill on the literary map. At the intersection with Old Lystra Road, a state historical marker commemorates Paul Green, also the creator of the first successful outdoor drama, *The Lost Colony*. The show has been produced on the North Carolina coast every summer since 1937, except for a hiatus during the blackouts of World War II.

In 1965, Green moved from his longtime residence on Greenwood Road, closer to the UNC campus, to this rural area. He would spend the rest of his life on the small farm that he and his wife, Elizabeth Lay Green, also a writer, named Windy Oaks. These later years were the period when Green organized North Carolinians against the Death Penalty—a passionate crusade that has continued since his death in 1981.

In addition to *The Lost Colony*, Green created fifteen more outdoor dramas. A number of these shows are still in production across the country in theaters that are constituent members of the nationwide Institute for Outdoor Drama, an organization headquartered at UNC–Chapel Hill. Our next stop is the present site of the log cabin where Green did much of his writing.

Continue beyond Windy Oaks on Old Lystra Road. At the end of Old Lystra, turn left onto Mount Carmel Church Road, which intersects US 15/501 in a half mile. To the right on 15/501 is the James Taylor Bridge. Singer/songwriter James Taylor wrote some of his earliest hit songs as a teenager growing up outside Carrboro near University Lake. Taylor's mother and four siblings were also musicians. His father became dean of the UNC–Chapel Hill Medical School in 1963.

It is fitting that Taylor's lyrical contributions are commemorated by a bridge, because that is also a term for the transitional portion of a song that prepares the listener to return to the verse and chorus.

Taylor's "Carolina in my Mind" has become a regional anthem. Among his more recent works are two songs—"New Hymn" and "Copperline"—that he wrote with lyrics supplied by Duke professor and novelist Reynolds Price. The latter song whimsically touches on a key component in the making of moonshine (a copper line) and gives the name of the creek that runs under the James Taylor Bridge: "Half a mile down to Morgan Creek / Leaning heavy on the end of the week / Hercules and a hog-nosed snake / Down on copperline."

Windy Oaks was the last home of playwright and social justice advocate Paul Green.

From Mount Carmel Church Road, turn right, cross the James Taylor Bridge, and take the on-ramp on the right to US 15/501 North. Follow the brown signs to the North Carolina Botanical Garden, which comes up on the right in a little over a mile.

■ NORTH CAROLINA BOTANICAL GARDEN

These pleasant grounds offer profuse plantings of native flora, educational materials about them, and many winding paths for hiking. The literary traveler can also get a peek inside the log cabin that playwright Paul Green used for many years as a writing studio, relocated from his former home on nearby Greenwood Road.

Green, who began his career at Carolina as a professor of philosophy, was a prolific writer in nearly every genre and continued writing long after he retired from teaching in 1944. A dozen of his film scripts were produced in Hollywood from 1932 to 1964, including an adaptation of *State Fair*, starring Will Rogers and Janet Gaynor. Green wrote or adapted scores of plays, several collections of short stories, essays, a collection of poems, two novels, and a hefty two-volume encyclopedia of words and colloquialisms inspired by the colorful language he heard growing up in Lillington, North Carolina.

Green's wife, Elizabeth Lay Green, daughter of a clergyman and a member of the Carolina Playmakers in her youth, collaborated with her husband on several writing projects and published literary study guides. Today the Paul Green Foundation carries on the Greens' work against the death penalty and in support of human rights and playwriting that shines a light on issues of social justice. The Green children and grandchildren continue the work of their forebears as writers and activists.

■ UNC CENTER FOR DRAMATIC ARTS

To reach the UNC campus from the Botanical Garden, turn right on 15/501 (South Fordham Boulevard) and continue to the second exit ramp for NC 54 (Raleigh Road) toward Chapel Hill. Ascend the hill one mile to the intersection with Country Club Road. UNC's Center for Dramatic Arts is to the right a few hundred yards down Country Club on the left. This facility houses both the 500-seat Paul Green Theatre (home to Playmakers Repertory Company, now a resident professional company) and the Kenan Theatre (where additional Playmakers shows and student productions are mounted).

■ FOREST THEATRE

A bit farther down on the right is the historic Forest Theatre, an amphitheater dedicated to Frederick Koch, who came to Carolina from North Dakota in 1919 to start the drama department. Koch created Carolina Playmakers—a group that performed plays as fast as his students could write them. His focus was on the stories of real people—"folk plays," as he called them. Among Koch's students were Thomas Wolfe, Paul Green, and Charles Edward Eaton, the Winston-Salem poet. Eaton described Koch as "a brilliant and colorful teacher with his Norfolk jackets, lavender shirts, the inevitable pipe, exuding the glamorous world of the many famous playwrights and actors he knew" (*The Man from Buena Vista: Selected Nonfiction, 1944–2000*, by Charles Edward Eaton [Cranbury, N.J.: Associated University Presses, 2001], 23).

Backtrack on Country Club Road to the intersection with NC 54, which becomes South Road to the right. Park in a metered spot along South to visit the Old Chapel Hill Cemetery, our next destination, described by Chapel Hill writer and UNC–Chapel Hill creative writing professor Bland Simpson:

THE OLD CHAPEL HILL CEMETERY (1798)

Within the rock walls of the Old Chapel Hill Cemetery, which dates to 1798, repose a number of significant figures in the state's and university's literary heritage. Though Thomas Clayton Wolfe is buried two hundred miles west in Asheville, two of Wolfe's favorite professors at Carolina in the late 1910s lie less than a hundred yards apart here. Wolfe characterized Edwin Greenlaw (author of *Literature and Life*) as Professor Randolph Ware in his novel *The Web and the Rock* ("I am a Research Man! . . . I get the Facts"). Horace Williams (author of *The Education of Horace Williams*), who came here from Gates County in isolated Dismal Swamp country and spent a lifetime in Chapel Hill becoming one of the college's most popular professors, appeared as Professor Virgil Weldon in *Look Homeward, Angel*, where Wolfe celebrated him: "Oh, my old Sophist, he thought. What were all the old philosophies that you borrowed and pranked up to your fancy to you, who were greater than all? What was the Science of Thinking, to you who were Thought?"

Along or near the cemetery's easternmost lane lie Wolfe's playwriting classmate Paul Green, who won the 1927 Pulitzer Prize for Drama with *In Abraham's Bosom*, two years before *Look Homeward, Angel* was published, and who virtually invented outdoor (Green's term was "symphonic") drama with the 1937 opening of Roanoke Island's *The Lost Colony*; Frederick "Proff" Koch, who taught that playwriting class and founded the Carolina Playmakers, and to whom the nearby Forest Theatre is dedicated; Frank Porter Graham, the great southern progressive, first president of the consolidated university system, U.S. senator, and author of *The Faith and Hope of an American*; harmonica-playing Robert B. House, Carolina's first chancellor and author of the memoir *The Light That Shines*; poet-professor Robert Kirkpatrick; and, beside him, Max Steele, longtime director of the creative writing program at Carolina (*Where She Brushed Her Hair*), and fiction writer Alice Adams (*After You've Gone*; *The Last Lovely City*).

Other literary figures and artists buried here include William Meade Prince, illustrator and memoirist, whose book title gave the town its most abiding nickname, the Southern Part of Heaven; beside him, his sister, Lillian Hughes Prince, who for many seasons portrayed Queen Elizabeth in Green's *Lost Colony*; near them, journalist and broadcaster Charles Kuralt, *CBS Sunday Morning* host and author of *North Carolina Is My Home*; bandleader Kay Kyser, the "Old Professor" whose Kollege of Musical Knowledge was a national radio success; playwright and novelist Noel Houston (*The Great Promise*); journalist and fiction writer James Street (*Oh, Promised Land*; *The Biscuit Eater*); and memoirist Jane Toy Coolidge (*Growing Up with Chapel Hill*).

■ CARMICHAEL AND WOOLLEN GYMS

Continuing on South Road, deeper into campus, are the pre–Dean Dome haunts of the UNC men's basketball team. First on the left is Carmichael Gym (where the women's team now plays). Next to it is Woollen Gym, which preceded Carmichael as Tar Heel basketball nirvana.

The history of hoops in this town has long been a topic irresistible to writers. The thousands of foul shots, layups, and dunks made in these gyms are documented in UNC humanities professor Fred Hobson's *Off the Rim: Basketball and Other Religions in a Carolina Childhood*. Hobson, who is coeditor of the *Southern Literary Journal*, begins his tale four days after President John F. Kennedy came to speak on campus, in 1961. Even that monumental event was trumped in Hobson's undergraduate mind by the opportunity to try out in Woollen Gym for a walk-on spot on the varsity squad. Hobson made the team.

Chapel Hill writer William McCranor Henderson, author of *Stark Raving*

Elvis and *I Killed Hemingway*, confesses his method of never missing a Carolina basketball game at Woollen Gym as an adolescent:

> On game days, we would play pickup ball in Woollen until late afternoon, when they cleared the gym to prepare for the evening event. But instead of leaving, we would file surreptitiously into the spacious corner men's locker room, lock ourselves into the stalls, and sit patiently, waiting for six o'clock.... At a given signal (a single flush by whoever had a watch), we filed out and merged into the entering crowd stream, picking our spots along choice bleacher rows and squeezing politely left or right if challenged by a real ticket holder.—From "The Return of the Native," by William McCranor Henderson, in *Close to Home: Revelations and Reminiscences by North Carolina Authors*, ed. Lee Harrison Child (Winston-Salem: John F. Blair, 1996), 39.

Former *Esquire* editor Will Blythe (grandson of Charlotte writer LeGette Blythe) provides his take on the eternal conflict between light blue and dark blue teams in the not-so-simply titled *To Hate Like This Is to Be Happy Forever: A Thoroughly Obsessive, Intermittently Uplifting, and Occasionally Unbiased Account of the Duke–North Carolina Basketball Rivalry* (2006).

As you reach the far end of Woollen Gym, turn right on Raleigh Street, cross Cameron, Franklin, and Rosemary streets, and then turn right onto North Street. At 506 North Street is the house where in 1936 writer Betty Smith first settled in Chapel Hill with her two daughters.

■ THE RESIDENCES OF BETTY SMITH

At age thirty-nine, Betty Smith was divorced and had never finished high school, but she had managed with great determination to win a playwriting award and study the craft at Yale. She then secured employment (not easy during the Depression), first as an administrator and then as an actor in the Works Project Administration's Federal Theater Project. Chapel Hill writer and biographer Valerie Yow picks up the story:

> She was coming home from acting in a Federal Theater play one day when she saw in a bookstore window a copy of Thomas Wolfe's *Of Time and the River*. She hesitated for a second, then used three dollars of grocery money to buy it. She read without stopping until she finished it sometime early the next morning. The book set her on fire. She underlined heavily and

wrote in the margins and jotted down on a blank page at the back, "Notes for a Novel I'll Write Someday." It was a novel about growing up in Brooklyn. —From *Betty Smith, Life of the Author of* A Tree Grows in Brooklyn, by Valerie Raleigh Yow (Chapel Hill: Wolf's Pond Press, 2008), 84.

Not long after, when a touring play took Smith to Raleigh, she caught a bus to Chapel Hill between shows, hoping to meet Frederick Koch, Thomas Wolfe's teacher. As luck would have it, the first person that Brooklyn-born Betty spotted on the UNC campus was Walter Spearman, now remembered as a legendary professor of journalism, who also acted and wrote plays and short stories. Smith couldn't understand Spearman's southern accent when he tried to tell her how to find Koch, so he simply escorted her to Murphey Hall. She met Koch and his apostle, Paul Green, and convinced them to hire her for a federally funded WPA position on the drama staff.

Betty Smith wrote *A Tree Grows in Brooklyn* in a one-room apartment on the second floor of the North Street house. In the same way that many southern-born writers have found their muse in the North or elsewhere, Betty Smith was apparently better able to fictionalize her difficult Brooklyn upbringing from a distance.

Mexican American author Josefina Niggli arrived in 1935 to study with the Carolina Playmakers and remained in Chapel Hill for some twenty years. Photo courtesy of the North Carolina Collection Photographic Archives, Wilson Library, UNC–Chapel Hill.

Early on, Paul Green invited her to join his writing group, which included Betty's boyfriend and writing partner, Robert Finch, short-story writer Max Steele, Josefina Niggli, one of the first Latina writers to have her work published in the United States, and Jessie Rehder, a Wilmington native whom Smith's biographer, Valerie Yow, characterizes as "a woman with ideas about writing that people disputed at their peril" (96).

Meanwhile Smith's daughters thrived in the Chapel Hill schools and soon befriended a classmate, future novelist Daphne Athas.

The house Smith occupied in her later years, until senile dementia made it impossible for her to live alone, is at 315 East Rosemary Street, now the home of illustrator Dianne Manning and environmental writer Phillip Manning (*Afoot in the South: Walks in the Natural Areas of North Carolina*). From North Street, return to Raleigh Road and turn right on Rosemary. It was in this house (on the right) that Betty Smith took in a bright young boarder named William Ivey Long Jr., who was studying art history at Carolina. Long, whose theatrical family had been involved in productions of Paul Green's *The Lost Colony* on the coast

A mural by artist Michael Brown on Chapel Hill's Henderson Street.

for many summers, planned to earn a Ph.D. in art history at Yale. Smith encouraged him instead to study design in the drama department. Taking her advice, Long applied, was accepted, and roomed at Yale with Sigourney Weaver. Long's other classmates included Meryl Streep, Christopher Durang, and Wendy Wasserstein. Long's trajectory as a Tony Award–winning costume designer on Broadway has been meteoric.

After Betty Smith's death, in early 1972, another writer, Bland Simpson, moved into the house at 315 Rosemary for his senior year as a political science major at UNC. Simpson, whose literary gifts range from fiction to historical nonfiction to songwriting, was invited to join the UNC creative writing faculty in 1982. He left teaching to join the legendary Red Clay Ramblers string band, as a pianist, in 1986. His first novel, *Heart of the Country, A Novel of Southern Music*, was published the next year. Simpson and his musical colleagues have scored films, appeared on Broadway, and won a Tony Award. He returned to the creative writing program in 1989 and became its director in 2002.

Proceed on East Rosemary to the intersection with Henderson Street, noting the #2 pencil mural on the wall on the far left side of Henderson. From here it's easiest to park in the public deck on the left side of Rosemary just beyond the backside of the old post office building. This tour continues on foot across

Franklin Street and into the shady parklike quad on campus known as McCorkle Place.

■ MCCORKLE PLACE

The first monument on the lawn here is Silent Sam, a memorial to the university's alumni who died in the Civil War and to all the UNC students who joined the Confederate Army. *The Activist's Daughter*, a novel by Ellyn Bache, who studied English here, is set on the UNC campus as the civil rights movement is gaining momentum all across the South in 1963. In the novel, undergraduate Beryl Rosinsky has come from Washington, D.C., to college, delighted at last to get away from her liberal, crusading mother. But Beryl cannot escape. She finds the UNC campus awash in political debate. For the first time in her life, Beryl confronts Old South bigotry and witnesses the wounding power of "whites only" shops and restaurants in downtown Chapel Hill. She also confronts her own second-class status as a female student. Eventually Beryl is drawn into the struggle.

On the quad in front of Graham Memorial, I stopped to read the inscription on the statue of Silent Sam — silent because he was supposed to shoot his gun every time a virgin walked by. Ironically, the deeply Southern message at his feet was about the utmost importance of duty, a sentiment my mother would have cheered. A few hundred yards away, down on Franklin Street, a protest march was just ending in front of the post office. — From *The Activist's Daughter*, by Ellyn Bache (Duluth, Minn.: Spinster's Ink, 1997), 75.

Bache mentions Graham Memorial, the large building on the left as you are facing Silent Sam. On the second floor, during the 1950s and 1960s, hoards of scribbling students spent late nights producing the student newspaper, the *Daily Tar Heel*, here. Among the alumni of UNC's student newspaper who went on to literary prominence were Thomas Wolfe, who took the paper from weekly to twice weekly long before it became a daily, CBS raconteur Charles Kuralt, beat poet Lawrence Ferlinghetti, and *Washington Post* book columnist Jonathan Yardley.

John Ehle chronicled student activism in his first-person account of desegregation on the UNC campus, *The Free Men* (1965), reissued in 2007 by Press 53, in Winston-Salem. *Move Over, Mountain* (1957), Ehle's first and only novel set in Chapel Hill, began as a short story that Paul Green suggested he lengthen. It, too, dealt with segregation but in a more daring form. Ehle's viewpoint character, Jordan Cummings, is a black man with bold aspirations, living in Tin Top, a poor neighborhood on the fringes of town. The novel earned critical notice, particularly by reviewers in the North, who were impressed with Ehle's sensitivity in portraying Cummings, but it was rejected by many booksellers in the South. In 2007, it was reissued in a fiftieth-anniversary edition, also by Press 53 in Winston-Salem.

Well more than a century before the era of civil rights activism, enslaved poet George Moses Horton, introduced on the last tour, recited his work and solicited business from UNC students on the lawn here. The students paid Horton to write sentimental acrostics based on their girlfriends' names. During these entrepreneurial literary ventures, Horton was befriended by novelist Caroline Lee Hentz, a white woman who stridently opposed abolition through her writing yet saw fit to help Horton by transcribing his work and sending it out on his behalf for publication. (Horton hoped for royalties sufficient to buy his freedom from his Chatham County master.)

In 1829, Horton's collection *The Hope of Liberty* became the first book of poems published by a black person in more than half a century and the first ever by an African American in the South. Horton eventually persuaded his master to allow him to live in Chapel Hill, paying him twenty-five cents per week for the privilege. After Horton's *Poetical Works* came out in 1845, the campus literary magazine began publishing some of his work. His largest collection, *Naked Genius*, was issued in 1865. After decades of trying to earn his freedom to no avail, Horton was emancipated at the end of the Civil War. He moved to Philadelphia but never again published. He died in 1883.

As you proceed deeper into campus, note the massive tree known as the Davie Poplar. (A couple of its heirs are nearby.) This legendary tree, more than two centuries old, is reputed to have been named by writer Cornelia Phillips Spencer a hundred years after Revolutionary War general William R. Davie selected these grounds for the university. UNC opened in 1795 and is, by most accounts, the first state university in the nation.

■ **THE OLD WELL, OLD SOUTH, CAMPUS Y, PLAYMAKERS THEATRE**

The town of Ephesus was called the oasis of the South. This was because of the University. The university vied with the University of Georgia in claiming to be the oldest state university in the nation. It had a liberal tradition. There were only three thousand students. Everybody knew everybody else. Tuition was cheap. Many students were poor. Learning was respected. Phi-

losophy was on everybody's lips. . . . The campus was centered around an old well, over which had been built a fresh white canopy with columns. Old North and Old South were dormitories that had been designated state landmarks and planted with plaques. Dogwoods perforated spring like snow. Oftentimes classes were held outdoors. Teachers came from the North and West and spread the school's fame. It took on a cosmopolitan air. —From *Entering Ephesus* (Twentieth Anniversary: Classic Edition), by Daphne Athas (Sag Harbor, N.Y.: Permanent Press/Second Chance Press), 43.

Daphne Athas, daughter of a Greek immigrant, came to Carrboro as a teen in the late 1930s. Her father ran a local business. She went to high school in Chapel Hill and earned her undergraduate degree at UNC–Chapel Hill before beginning a teaching and writing career that took her around the world. Though Athas published novels before and after *Entering Ephesus*, this coming-of-age story offers the most vivid picture of life in Chapel Hill during the same era as Alice Adams's novel, though Athas more gleefully satirizes the pretensions of Chapel Hill with her brisk, no-punches-pulled prose.

Athas mentions the Old Well—now and forever UNC's symbol. Directly across Cameron Avenue is Old South, headquarters to the university administration, another site of occasional student protests. To the right of Old South and set back a ways from the street is the Campus Y building, where Thomas Wolfe wrote in a room on the second floor during his student years at Carolina.

On the other side of Old South is the original Playmakers Theatre, built in 1851 as the university's first library. As the building outgrew the university's library holdings, it was used as the law school. Finally the building was renovated for the Carolina Playmakers in 1925, long after Thomas Wolfe played the title role in his own play, *The Return of Buck Gavin*, his first as a student in Frederick Koch's class, in 1918.

■ WILSON LIBRARY

Immediately behind South Building is a long stretch of lawn called Polk Place, and at the far end is Wilson Library, home of the North Carolina Collection. This vast repository of books, manuscripts, and artifacts relating to North Carolina writers and the state's 400-year history is unparalleled. Although most of the books in the North Carolina Collection are not available in open stacks and must be requested by visitors, Wilson also presents rotating exhibits in the North Carolina Collection Gallery in addition to a permanent display of Thomas Wolfe memorabilia. Most any book referenced in the *Literary Trails* series can be found in this library if nowhere else. Don't miss the inspiring rare book room and galleries upstairs.

Among the many materials available for further research are novelist Walker Percy's enormous cache of manuscripts and papers and his personal library of books annotated in his hand. All are housed in the Rare Book Collection and the Manuscript Department.

Walker Percy came to Chapel Hill as a freshman in 1933 from his home in Mississippi. His Uncle Will, a Harvard graduate, sent his nephew to Chapel Hill, believing it to be the best state university in the South. As Percy told Charlotte poet Dannye Romine Powell in a 1980 interview, it helped that tuition was one hundred dollars.

Though he had no particular interest in writing at the time, Percy told another interviewer, Ashley Brown, that he was required to prove his writing skills upon his arrival: "I took the qualifying English test in Faulknerian style (I had been reading *The Sound and the Fury*). I wrote one long paragraph without out punctuation. The result was that I was put in a retarded English class."

Percy was apparently the star of his remedial writing group but nevertheless opted for a major in chemistry, with minors in math and German. One of

On Franklin Street, moviegoer Walker Percy (center, in khaki pants with foot outstretched) during his undergraduate years in Chapel Hill. Photo courtesy of the North Carolina Collection Photographic Archives, Wilson Library, UNC–Chapel Hill.

his most vivid memories from his Carolina days, however, was literary. Percy told Dannye Powell that he recalled sitting on the porch of the Sigma Alpha Epsilon fraternity house, lost in a biography of Robert E. Lee.

The Second Coming, Percy's only novel set in North Carolina, is, in part, about the rise of wealth and evangelistic Christian fervor in the New South. In a 1981 interview with literary scholar and writer Linda Whitney Hobson, he explained his rationale. "I chose North Carolina because it's kind of a no man's land be-tween Virginia—which is a country all to itself, drenched in all sorts of blood and history—and the deep South, where one is apt to be overtaken by all the literary clichés which are hard to get rid of, and because it's away from New Orleans. North Carolina is a neutral sort of place; it has the best and maybe the worst of both North and South."

Shelby Foote, Walker Percy's childhood playmate and lifetime correspon-dent, was as obsessed as Percy with the South and its history. He joined his friend in Chapel Hill in 1935. Though Foote had not been admitted to the uni-versity, he talked his way into a battery of tests and gained admission. His academic performance, however, was checkered. Foote skipped about half his classes to dig into the treasures of Wilson Library, where he reportedly spent the night at least once.

Foote left UNC in 1937. He would go on to write six novels but was finally best known for his series of nonfiction books on the Civil War. Wilson Library is the repository of his correspondence with Percy.

■ GRAHAM STUDENT UNION

Out the front door of Wilson to the right is House Undergraduate Library and, beyond that, the Pit, a rallying place for students that flanks the Frank Porter Graham Student Union, so named for the president of the university from 1930 until 1949. Graham was appointed to the U.S. Senate in 1949 to fill an unexpired term. He later lost his primary bid to return to the Senate to Willis Smith, whose negative campaign was engineered in part by a young journalist named Jesse Helms.

Helms, who would later win the Senate seat himself, was the likely inspiration for a character named Joe Crain in a novel by UNC alumnus John Russell. The book fictionalizes the Graham era in the university's history:

Joe Crain for instance. Didn't even go to Chapel Hill. Nobody knew him. Yet there he was, from some down East swampwater town, leading a slick, Red-baiting, Bible-beater crusade against Dr. MacGiver. Crain was everywhere—on the radio, giving newspaper interviews, mobilizing the large youth religious organization he apparently controlled—and he was all of twenty-five years old.—From *Favorite Sons*, by John Russell (Chapel Hill: Algonquin Books of Chapel Hill, 1992), 104.

Another interesting literary anecdote turns on Frank Porter Graham's brother. Archibald Wright "Moonlight" Graham played baseball for Carolina and graduated to the minor leagues. He advanced to play only a single inning in the major leagues—a story depicted in the novel *Shoeless Joe*, by W. P. Kinsella, which in turn inspired the 1989 movie *Field of Dreams*.

■ GREENLAW HALL

As you face the Student Union, on your left is Greenlaw Hall, home to the English department and UNC's creative writing program. Though it was not always so, Carolina undergraduates today can minor in creative writing or in writing for stage and screen. Poets Michael McFee, James Seay, Michael Chitwood, and Alan Shapiro teach here. Fiction writers Pam Durban (who has written extensively about South Carolina) and Daniel Wallace (whose works focus

on his native Alabama) are on the faculty, along with Marianne Gingher, Bland Simpson, Lawrence Naumoff, Daphne Athas, and Ruth Moose—all of whom appear elsewhere in this volume. Randall Kenan, whose fiction is largely centered in his native eastern North Carolina, joined the faculty in 2003.

The list of graduates nurtured in their writing here is far too long to inventory, but several faculty members from the past, who each in turn helped bring the program to its present stature, must be considered.

Rockingham native Phillips Russell taught creative writing to English and journalism students at Carolina from the 1930s to the 1950s, launching a somewhat unusual tradition for the times. Creative writing was not always deemed a credit-worthy academic discipline in many English departments across the country. Russell's good work, however, set the stage for Jessie Rehder's energetic appearance on the scene in 1947. Rehder helped students get published and coached them most kindly, says her former student, Robert Morgan.

Rehder died unexpectedly, in 1966, and is remembered in a short story, "The Tin Can," written by her successor, Max Steele. In Steele's fictional treatment, Sally Gupton, a colleague with whom the story's nameless central character has shared a campus office for years, dies suddenly and his world is upended. He cannot sleep; he imagines that the buildings on campus are disappearing one by one:

> When he shut his eyes he saw the light on the Bell Tower disappear and then the whole building, leaving the boxwood maze surrounding nothing.
>
> He felt foolish, dressing and driving up to the campus and parking across from the Bell Tower in the middle of the night but it was better than lying alone sleepless. Gupton had told him about Gertrude Stein coming to the campus in the thirties and saying later that it was interesting that everyone took her to see the Bell Tower and all of them had said the same thing. "Those boxwoods are little now. But someday they will be big." It was then he realized how much she loved Gertrude Stein.
>
> —From *The Hat of My Mother*, by Max Steele (Chapel Hill: Algonquin Books of Chapel Hill, 1994), 239–40.

Poet, Duke alumnus, and environmental writer Wallace Kaufman co-authored a textbook, *The Act of Writing*, with Jessie Rehder. Kaufman remembers that Rehder's beloved student Lawrence Naumoff once described his teacher as someone who "came into the classroom like a school bus on fire." Kaufman wrote a poem at Rehder's death, a portrait of her last visit to the pond opposite his house in Chatham County.

OLD WOMAN FISHING
   For Jessie Rehder
In sneakers, khaki pants
and brother's flannel shirt
you slosh the mud, weeds
and willow shoots that rim
the green glass pond.
Frogs describe long arcs
in forewarned flight and wrens
from woven nests inscribe
the air with rapid script.
Cricket shrill is cut
absolutely still.

Gallumphing woman clown,
with sportsman's rod and reel,
you should not leave the car,

you have no right to stumble,
plod great holes and splash
where no one laughs.
Anyhow, you stop
to fasten lure to line.

Your broad arm whips the fiber
pole, the silver minnow leaps
against the sky,
slows to a perfect curve,
descends far off, small
plip that rings the glass.
In cool depths the fish
are wakened by the glint
that sways toward you beneath
the ripples spreading green
all ways in perfect
O's.
—Used by permission of Wallace Kaufman.

When Max Steele took charge of the creative writing program, he hired Doris Betts and then Daphne Athas to help. Together they built a curriculum and a following, adding courses over the years and enlisting guest faculty at every turn. Two literary legends—Mississippi novelist Elizabeth Spencer and writer/teacher/publisher Louis D. Rubin Jr.—moved to Chapel Hill and taught in the program. Betts even coaxed her mentor, Frances Gray Patton, into the classroom. As more and more of Carolina's creative writing graduates have published books, they, too, have done stints on the faculty, and the volumes by UNC writers keep piling up on library shelves.

Today, outside Greenlaw, retrace your route back to Franklin Street. You're likely to hear the Bell Tower across the street behind Wilson Library as it chimes the hour, a local landmark that Gertrude Stein did indeed see on her visit in the spring of 1935. And yes, the boxwoods are much larger now.

■ FRANKLIN STREET

Most locals would admit that it has lost some of its luster in recent years, but Franklin Street is saturated with literary history. The haunts of writers and would-be writers, professors, and hangers-on have changed with time. A few of the older establishments remain, but the strongest literary connection still belongs to the Carolina Coffee Shop at 138 East Franklin. Founded in 1922, this restaurant is where novelist Doris Betts, before her retirement from the university, could often be seen reading student stories and meticulously making indelible comments in the margins with an instrument from her exotic collection of fountain pens. Here, too, humor writer David Sedaris once washed dishes:

> I longed for a home where history was respected—and, four years later, I finally found one. This was in Chapel Hill, North Carolina. I'd gone there to visit an old friend from high school—and because I was between jobs, and had no real obligations, I decided to stay for a while and maybe look for some dishwashing work. The restaurant that hired me was a local institution, all dark wood and windowpanes the size of playing cards. The food was O.K., but what the place was really known for was the classical music that the man in charge, someone named Byron, pumped into the dining room. Anyone else might have thrown in a compilation tape, but he took his responsibilities very seriously, and planned each meal as if it were an evening at Tanglewood. I hoped that dishwashing might lead to

a job in the dining room, bussing tables, and, eventually, waiting on them, but I kept these aspirations to myself. Dressed as I was, in jodhpurs and a smoking jacket, I should have been grateful that I was hired at all. — From "This Old House," by David Sedaris, *New Yorker*, July 9, 2007.

Across the way and up the street at 119 East Franklin is the old home of the Intimate Bookshop, now marked by a lone plaque on the brick storefront. The last owners, Wallace and Brenda Kuralt (brother and sister-in-law of Charles Kuralt), bought the Intimate in 1965 from Bunny and Paul Smith, rare book dealers who'd owned it since 1950. Before that, according to the late Chapel Hill columnist Roland Giduz, the bookshop belonged for a time to Kemp Battle Nye, a colorful character who also ran a popular record shop on Franklin that was eventually lost to fire.

The Intimate originated, however, in the dorm room of Milton "Ab" Abernathy, an undergraduate who also sold books from a wheelbarrow he pushed around campus, according to Giduz. The first volumes in the "store" were donated by Paul and Elizabeth Green.

Ab's business partner and roommate was Anthony "Tony" Buttitta, who later ran an Intimate satellite in Asheville and befriended a troubled F. Scott Fitzgerald.

Ab and Tony were the bold founders of a campus literary magazine, *Contempo*. Many of the books they received for review ended up as stock in their bookstore. The *Contempo* editors corresponded with the writers of the day and solicited their work. They even managed to entice a few celebrated authors to the UNC campus. Buttitta writes:

William Faulkner came to Chapel Hill, N.C. on a two-week visit one late fall day in 1931, carrying a small valise and a little canvas bag. The bag contained the manuscript of *Light in August*, written in his tiny cryptic handwriting which only his publisher's secretary could decipher. He was running away from New York and all the hullaballoo that was being made over him, following the success of his gothic thriller *Sanctuary*. . . .

Bill stayed with us on the second floor of a Chapel Hill office building which housed the office of the magazine and our Intimate Bookshop. He had a room to himself, where he rested and slept, guzzled bootleg corn whiskey and talked of himself and his work. After a week of this, he jumped up one day and said, "I want out." We had a barber come in and shave him. We pressed his suit for him, and in no time Bill was the im-

maculate little dandy that earned him the title of "The Count" in his native Oxford, Mississippi.
—From "A Memoir of William Faulkner in His Early Days of Fame," by Anthony Buttitta, in *San Francisco Chronicle*, July 15, 1962, "This World" Section, 20.

Once cleaned up, Faulkner had the students take him to a movie in Durham, which he soon found boring. He later made an appearance in Phillips Russell's writing classes and took questions on his writing technique.

Poet Langston Hughes also came to Chapel Hill at the invitation of Paul Green and faculty colleagues, but before his arrival Abernathy and Buttitta wrote to request a poem and an essay for *Contempo*. They also extended an invitation to the poet to stay with them.

The day of Hughes's arrival, *Contempo* came out with his essay and poem on the front page. The poem immediately scandalized some readers. Entitled "Christ in Alabama," it was considered blasphemous and inflammatory according to existing Jim Crow standards. Hughes had written a commentary to go with the poem on the Scottsboro rape trials taking place at the time in Alabama. As a consequence of the brouhaha, Hughes later explained in his autobiography, the young *Contempo* editors were instantly evicted from their apartment, so they couldn't provide the writer with a place to stay. Still, Abernathy and Buttitta insisted on taking Hughes to dinner that day. He writes:

I had by afternoon been housed with the leading Negro family of the town. But that evening I dined with my two intrepid white hosts at a *white café* on the main street in the company of several other white students. If they were willing to go through with dinner in a public restaurant in the tense atmosphere of that small town, I was willing, too. . . . The next morning all the newspapers in the state carried dispatches concerning the excitement attendant on my appearance at Chapel Hill.—From *The Collected Works of Langston Hughes, Volume 14, Autobiography: I Wonder as I Wander*, by Langston Hughes, Dolan Hubbard, and Arnold Rampersad (Columbia: University of Missouri Press, 2001), 77.

In its last years, the Intimate Bookstore was best known for its remaindered book bargains, creaky wooden floors, and the unmistakable boom of Wally Kuralt's baritone, similar to his famous brother's. After a fire that destroyed the inventory and nearly gutted the building, in 1992, the Kuralts went bravely

forward at a location at the Eastgate Shopping Center, while they rebuilt the Franklin Street building. The Intimate's last incarnation closed in 1998.

One more literary landmark comes at the end of this cherished block: the former Carolina Theater at 108 East Franklin. The theater—which moved around the corner for a time and was run by children's author Bruce Stone, who now runs the Chelsea Theater—was closed for good in 2005. In its heyday, however, the theater hosted the 1965 world premiere of *Joy in the Morning*, a movie based on Betty Smith's novel starring Richard Chamberlain. The actor came to a reception at the Carolina Inn and then saw the premiere. Several thousand Chapel Hillians came to see Chamberlain.

Life in Chapel Hill does exist beyond the bounds of the university, as Apex novelist Peggy Payne tells it in *Revelation*. This comic novel revolves around a Presbyterian clergyman who one day hears the voice of God right in his own backyard in Chapel Hill. When Swain Hammond speaks of the incident from the pulpit, his congregation of dispassionate intellectuals begins to worry about their pastor. They struggle between their political belief in free speech and their concern that Hammond may require psychological counseling.

Greensboro writer Candace Flynt's 1987 novel, *Mother Love*, provides yet another perspective on life beyond the university. Judith, one of the three sisters central to the book, is adapting to a new sense of freedom as a divorced woman in Chapel Hill, which she finds so unlike the more conservative Greensboro she has left behind.

> Ahead of her on the sidewalk is a guy walking a bicycle. He has short hair, but she can tell by his age and his clothes—a fatigue jacket and blue jeans—that he's one of the sixties hippies who never left here. Some of the hippies have become entrepreneurs, as chefs or real estate men or even lawyers. Some like this man, have made a fad into real life....
>
> She doesn't completely know Chapel Hill yet. But people she has met have told her that, unlike other places, you can be yourself here.
> —From *Mother Love*, by Candace Flynt (New York: Farrar, Straus & Giroux, 1987), 308, 309.

We continue west on Franklin Street toward Carrboro with this poem from Carrboro resident and veteran creative writing teacher Phillip Shabazz:

FRANKLIN STREET
The nights I love glisten with rain
sliding down windows, like notes on air.

Old-fashioned streetlamps light the sidewalk,
soft glow, and pale as suds in beer.

Hills swell beneath the gray
unprotected coat of asphalt causing cracks.

Someone in the sky is dying for my sins;
and I can't blame the rain.

A black moon rolls north side of the coffeehouse.
Someone ends the hour.

It is jazz night at the club: foot traffic,
rain tracks on the hardwood floor.

Cars shine like June bugs taking their time
where rain comes and goes on this night.

Someone stole the stars or the rain hides them
like bones piled in a closet.

To walk this street in the rain means
someone will say things; I won't lose sleep;

I won't undermine the spearmint gum
in my mouth to spar with someone,

some face more bruised than the leaf
lying in a puddle, face wet like mine.

Even the falling rain has a face
visible in the same puddle,

a sweet face directed toward everyone;
the rain moves in that way;

the rain moves this street, the beauty
on all four sides, beauty that draws me

deeper into its turn and touch
and live jazz swinging at this table,

this window, this night life inside the club,
as if the music leads to

a new here and now, with affection,
and cared for by the same rainfall.

Then, from its miracle, a streak
of lightning slices the sky apart

over this street, as if the ever falling rain
could bring back the dead.
—Used by permission of Phillip Shabazz.

■ CARRBORO

West Franklin Street goes into a sharp curve at the restaurant, Crook's Corner, and then Carrboro begins. Daphne Athas describes the transition between her fictional towns of Ephesus and Haw:

A one-track railroad brought coal in once a week for the university power plant. The railroad track separated Ephesus from its adjunct, a settlement called Haw, originally Saxapahaw, Indian for "Dirty Feet in Muddy River." Although Haw was the original settlement, a weaving mill had been put there in 1910. The mill had gone out of business during the Depression, and the low brick building sat like a ghost. . . .

Haw was a scattering of mill houses clumped along dirt roads. Each mill house teetered on four stones at the corners. There were no foundations. The dirty white clapboards were stained red on the bottom from clay. Yards were grown up with weeds, choking bushes, or kudzu vines that had multiplied dangerously. Paths had been worn through the yards by bare feet. These paths were more traveled than the roads. The tin roofs gave off a feverish luster on hot afternoons in summer when the sun began to go down. People sat on their broken porches. Through the groan of swings they stared out of sharp faces, the color of turnips, and chewed tobacco. Underneath the houses dogs howled in their dreams.

—From *Entering Ephesus* (Twentieth Anniversary: Classic Edition), by Daphne Athas (Sag Harbor, N.Y.: Permanent Press/Second Chance Press), 44–45.

Athas offers a not-so-exaggerated look at the enormous cultural divide that was once marked by the railroad tracks between Chapel Hill and Carrboro. Traffic is heavier now in the middle of Carrboro than it was forty years ago. The same mill shacks Athas describes are now custom renovated, and some are worth upwards of a half million dollars. Their owners drive, bike, or hike to any number of fancy eateries or stop by the renovated mill to shop for health food, local artwork, high fashion clothing, and outdoor gear.

The down-and-out Carrboro of the 1950s and 1960s was the setting Betty Smith had in mind when she wrote *Joy in the Morning*. A later, up-and-coming Carrboro is where Doris Betts put the home of her character, Sergeant Frank Thompson, the officer on hand for the chicken-truck wreck at the Haw River bridge described in the last tour. Sergeant Thompson's daughter, Mary, rides her bike back and forth from Chapel Hill to their Carrboro apartment even though her father has told Mary not to exert herself. Her kidney disease, which requires her to undergo frequent dialysis, provides the novel's dramatic focus:

It was an easy ride downhill on West Cameron, past the university laundry plant with its smokestack, and on into Carrboro. Its boundary reminded her of melting Jell-O, as there was no way now to tell where Chapel Hill left off and Carrboro began. Once the railroad tracks had marked the line, but when the trains stopped coming, all the book lovers had poured across from Chapel Hill and turned Carrboro into its imitation. On the whole she preferred the faded mill town that used to be, Carrboro before cosmetics. . . . In repainted Carrboro, where former mill houses were now considered "historically restored," still lived the orderlies and clerks and cooks and repairmen and highway patrolmen; and their physical work propped up the mental work of doctors and lawyers and professors who lived over the line in Chapel Hill. —From *Souls Raised from the Dead*, by Doris Betts (New York: Alfred Knopf, 1994), 192–93.

Carrboro was once the side of segregated Chapel Hill that was reserved for blacks and purportedly the only place where novelist Richard Wright could safely spend the night when he came in 1941 to collaborate with Paul Green on the stage adaptation of *Native Son*. Carrboro is also where Elizabeth "Libba" Cotten, a nationally recognized singer/songwriter, was born (1895) and learned to play guitar upside down and backwards, because she was left-handed. Along these same railroad tracks, Cotten was inspired to write her best-known song, "Freight Train," at the age of twelve. The bike path that runs alongside the railroad tracks and behind the storefronts on Carrboro's Main Street bears her name.

Today's hip and upwardly mobile Carrboro bills itself on the town website as "the Paris of the Piedmont—a little to the left of Chapel Hill and always one degree cooler." Carrboro boasts two weekly newspapers and its own poet laureate, selected annually. It is also a town made for walking.

Bear right at the fork onto Weaver Street alongside Carr Mill Mall and take a right at the traffic light onto Greensboro Street. The parking lot beside Carr Mill Mall, on the right, is a good place to leave your car for a stroll around the neighborhood.

Weaver Street Grocery, or the Weave, as locals refer to it, is at one end of the mill/mall. The lawn that fronts Weaver Street is Carrboro's outdoor living room. Here you can get a good sense of the diverse residents living in this village. On Thursday evenings and Sundays at noon folks come out for live music and dancing.

Carrboro's famous Farmers' Market (Saturday mornings and Wednesday afternoons) is on the far western end of Weaver Street next to Town Hall. Nearby, at 206 West Main, is Akai Hana, the hugely successful sushi restaurant founded by novelist Lee Smith and essayist Hal Crowther. Only the exquisitely sweet iced tea and the fresh flowers every Tuesday give a hint of Smith's southern appetites. (It's also the only restaurant in North Carolina that hosts an annual haiku competition.)

This tour concludes with a poem about everyday life in Carrboro by local writer and poet Maura High:

CYCLING THROUGH CARRBORO
I lurch out of the driveway
into the predawn dark, lights
flashing white, red. And lay
a track up the road, scooping
past two early walkers, more
early risers in their lit kitchens
and bedrooms, traces
of dog trot and sniff
along the curbs and bushes,
spoor and specimen, memoranda:
of the roadmakers and patchers,
and before them, tillers
of this poor dirt, woodlot
scavengers, shot squirrels,
a squawk and scatter of crows,
deer viscera, arrowheads.
The moon is full and setting.
I bring all of my weight
to bear down on the pedals.
—Used by permission of Maura High.

■ LITERARY LANDSCAPE

Chapel Hill Public Library
100 Library Drive, Chapel Hill
919-968-2777
<http://www.chapelhillpubliclibrary.org>
This dazzling collection—the largest circulation library per capita in the state—emphasizes popular fiction and has many books on North Carolina history. Friends of the Library regularly host author teas.

Carolina Quarterly

<http://www.unc.edu/depts/cqonline>

Now published three times a year, this campus literary journal has been presenting emerging and nationally known writers of fiction, poetry, reviews, interviews, and criticism since 1948.

Bull's Head Bookshop

Daniels Building, UNC campus

919-962-5060

First housed in a faculty office and now on the second floor of student stores, this bookshop carries most every Chapel Hill author named in this tour along with many beautiful commemorative books about the university.

The Bookshop

400 West Franklin Street, Chapel Hill

919-942-5178

<http://www.bookshopinc.com>

Since 1985 this used and rare book dealer has been an important resource for out-of-print titles.

Flyleaf Books

752 Martin Luther King Jr. Boulevard, Chapel Hill

919-942-7373

<http://flyleafbooks.com>

Owned by three longtime Chapel Hill residents, this community bookstore is an energetic newcomer to the literary scene with a host of events for children and adults weekly.

Carrboro ArtsCenter

300 East Main Street #G, Carrboro

919-929-2787

<http://www.artscenterlive.org>

This community organization has provided creative writing classes, playwrights workshops, staged readings, and theater productions by local writers. It is home to the Carrboro PlaySlam! and The Roundtable, a play development lab.

Durham

Durham is a hotbed of literary pursuits, with as many writers past and present as Chapel Hill or Hillsborough. With its historic African American corporate interests and the presence of North Carolina Central University, Duke University, the legendary Durham Bulls baseball team, and the Duke family's once prominent American Tobacco Company, there's an unparalleled mix of ingredients in Durham that have fired the imaginations of many a writer.

Writers with a connection to this area: Julie Tetel Andresen, James Applewhite, Christina Askounis, Helen Bevington, William Blackburn, Michele Andrea Bowen, Kevin Boyle, Guy Davenport, Osha Gray Davidson, Angela Davis-Gardner, Ariel Dorfman, Clyde Edgerton, Peter Filene, John Hope Franklin, Laurel Goldman, David Guy, Pete Hendricks, Oscar Hijuelos, Judy Hogan, Zora Neale Hurston, Mac Hyman, Doris Iarovici, Frank Lentricchia, Michael Malone, Melissa Malouf, Katy Munger, Pauli Murray, Lawrence Naumoff, Gwendolyn M. Parker, Frances Gray Patton, Peggy Payne, Catherine Petroski, Henry Petroski, Deborah Pope, Joe Ashby Porter, Susie Ruth Powell, Reynolds Price, Wendy Rountree, Lewis Shiner, Darrell Stover, William Styron, Eleanora Tate, Anne Tyler, Samm-Art Williams, Tom Wolfe

The transformation of Durham's old tobacco warehouses into condos, retail and office space, and research facilities has put a new burnish on the red brick history of the city's first incarnation as a factory town. The sweet molasses smell of tobacco is gone. Now Durham is best known for its excellent medical facilities and high tech enterprises. For the literary traveler, there are many riches here lurking beneath the surface.

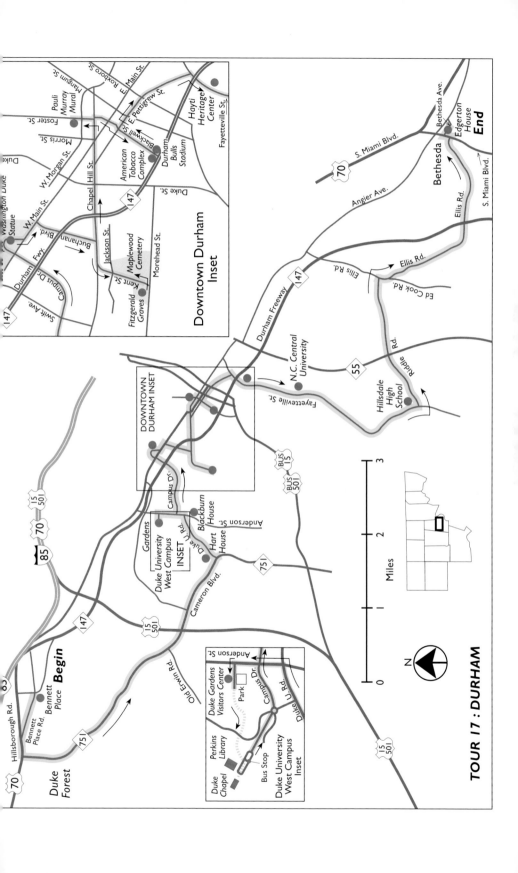

TOUR 17 : DURHAM

Downtown Durham Inset

Duke University West Campus Inset

N

Miles
0 1 2 3

■ BENNETT PLACE

4409 Bennett Memorial Road (off US 70)

We begin at a momentous site from the past: the farmstead where Generals Sherman and Johnston signed the first official surrender of the Civil War. Elon University poet Kevin Boyle offers a powerful lyric poem on this destination:

A LULLABY OF HISTORY

I put the bookmark in the page after Lincoln's
silence during the 1860 campaign, after no one
in the Gulf States cast a single vote for him,
then march off to the car, car seat in tow, drive on
cruise mainly to the site in Durham where Sherman
coaxed the Southern general—Johnston—
to submit twice, sign twice. The six-hundred-thousand
dead were like the shucks inside the reconstructed
bed, the smoke the chimney slewed, the clayish mud.
In the museum, name-tagged women watch our daughter,
four months here, while we investigate the flags
with gunshot holes, the uniforms with gunshot holes,
the shells of the Union Army with three rings, the shells
of the Confederate's with two. We take our daughter
to the film strip where she sleeps through
the stills of uniformed corpses in ditches, and cries
at war's end, one flag for all these states. We ride,
strapped, to the Greek restaurant known for its sauces
and lamb, stroll inside the tobacco warehouse transformed
into a mall, each glass pane so large a truck
could drive through and pick up brightleaf to ship.
They say this section profited when South met North
and troops took in the smoke of this leaf, spreading
by word of mouth the flavor, until the profits
were so large owners began to donate. In the antique store
we happen onto a map my father might love
of Ireland before division, just as it appeared
when he was born, the north a section, not another country,
Ulster's six counties awash in the orange mapmakers
stained it. But we can't commit to buy for this price,

or prevent our daughter from falling asleep as we discuss
facts the map makes clear: battles marked in bold,
our side losing again and again, the Flight of the Earls,
Vinegar Hill, the Battle of the Boyne, and we donate
our time during the drive home to feel for a moment
the weight of the centuries' dead, almost cry for all
those men who gave their skin to the ground so young,
so young brought their lips to earth and let their mouths
cave in, accept the soil as their voice. We did not wake
our girl through this. Let her sleep, we said.
—From *A Home for Wayward Girls*, by Kevin Boyle
    (Kalamazoo, Mich.: New Issues Press, 2005), 9.

■ DUKE FOREST

Not far from Bennett Place, NC 751 leads into Durham passing through one section of the more than 7,000 acres of woodlands that make up Duke Forest—a living laboratory for the university. Novelist Reynolds Price, James B. Duke Professor of English, lives and writes in this vicinity. His ranch house and a second rental house built by novelist and carpenter Lawrence Naumoff are set back in the woods by a pond. This is where Price has managed his prodigious output of novels, plays, poetry, stories, and essays—more than fifty books over fifty some years.

■ DUKE UNIVERSITY

In approximately three miles on NC 751, the road comes to a traffic circle. Take the second exit and continue ahead on 751. At the fourth traffic light, the Washington Duke Inn and Golf Club is on the right, and Duke University's sports complex begins on the left. At the next traffic signal, turn left onto Duke University Road and note the Hart House on the corner. Here the grandparents of Salisbury novelist John Hart made their home when Dr. Deryl Hart was university president. Richard H. Brodhead, whose scholarship has focused in part on the works of North Carolina writer Charles Chesnutt, is the first Duke president since Hart to occupy the residence.

By way of introduction to the literary traditions of Duke University, we turn first to the late Helen Bevington—poet, essayist, travel writer, and much-beloved teacher of writing. Bevington came to Duke in 1942 when her husband,

Merle, joined the English department. From her perspective as a dyed-in-the-wool Yankee from upstate New York, Bevington pokes wicked fun at the decidedly southern university she found upon her arrival:

The poor South. Already guilty of slavery, it became guilty of cigarettes....

From this glittering fortune rose Duke University, paved not with gold but with golden tobacco leaves. In 1924, a year before Buck Duke died one of the world's richest men, he bought himself a monument. He offered Trinity College, a little Methodist school off Main Street, a gift of forty-odd millions provided it assume the stature of a university like Yale or Harvard and change its name to Duke.

Buck Duke never went to college and was glad of it, a ruthless self-made man. "If I amount to anything in this world," he said, "I owe it to my daddy and the Methodist Church." He had no need to read books—witness his prodigious wealth—but apparently some people had. If they wanted an education, they might avail themselves in his name of whatever good came of book learning.

—From *The House Was Quiet and the World Was Calm*, by Helen Bevington
(New York: Harcourt Brace Jovanovich, 1971), 13–14.

▓ WEST CAMPUS

Driving along this stretch of Duke University Road, the main entrance to Duke's West Campus is off to the left. Continue 0.8 miles to Anderson Street and turn right to see the former home of Duke's legendary creative writing teacher William Blackburn, immediately on the left at 713 Anderson. Novelists Reynolds Price, Anne Tyler, Angela Davis-Gardner, and William Styron were among Blackburn's writing students, as were North Carolina's distinguished poets Fred Chappell and James Applewhite. South Carolina–born Guy Davenport—visual artist, lifelong book critic, and writer of experimental narratives—also studied with Blackburn, as did Georgia-born Mac Hyman, the author of *No Time for Sergeants*.

Though not as well known today, Mac Hyman's novel was an immediate hit in 1954 and was soon adapted for television, the Broadway stage, and, finally, a 1958 film, which combined to fortify the nascent acting career of North Carolina's favorite son, Andy Griffith, who played the central character, Will Stockdale, in all three productions. Later, the Stockdale persona became the inspiration for Jim Nabors's role in the television series *Gomer Pyle, U.S.M.C.*

Hyman died of a heart attack before his fortieth birthday. William Black-

Dark blue meets light blue: creative writing students from Carolina and Duke meet to share manuscripts. Duke's William Blackburn (top row, far left) and UNC's Phillips Russell (hands on hips near Blackburn) were the instructors. Future novelist William Styron stands behind Russell on the right. Photo courtesy of Duke University Archives.

burn edited the posthumous *Love, Boy: The Letters of Mac Hyman* (Baton Rouge: Louisiana State University Press, 1969).

Blackburn remained fiercely loyal to all of his favorite students and encouraged them in their careers. He nominated both Styron and Price for the Rhodes Scholarship, which Blackburn himself had won. (Price was a successful Rhodes candidate, but Styron's miserable grades in physics kept him from the honor.)

Blackburn frequently brought his published protégés back to campus to speak and read at an annual literary festival he began at Duke in 1959, which now bears his name. Recently, his son, Alexander, detailed the Blackburn family's life at Duke in a wistful 2004 memoir. In the book's introduction, Fred Chappell describes his professor's approach to the classroom:

> His reluctance to criticize a new work or one in progress in detail was another characteristic of his modesty. He intuited the nearly preternatural esteem in which his favorites held him and feared to utter a mistaken judgment that might imperil the project underway. I speak now of the

stories and novels undertaken by his friends in their early professional stages. Toward their undergraduate themes and essays he was pitiless. Of the old fashioned school, he held to the view that undergraduate composition courses comprised a sort of intellectual boot camp where the necessary first step was to knock the nonsense out of the tenderfoot.—From *Meeting the Professor: Growing Up in the William Blackburn Family*, by Alexander Blackburn (Winston-Salem: John F. Blair, 2004), xi.

Chappell says that though Blackburn never published a single short story or poem, students often speculated that he kept reams of his own writing hidden away. Another of his students, James Applewhite (now a longtime professor at Duke), expressed his gratitude to his mentor in the following poem:

WILLIAM BLACKBURN, RIDING WESTWARD (EXCERPT)
Here in this mild, Septembral December, you have died.
Leaves from the black oaks litter our campus walks,
Where students move, or stand and talk, not knowing
Your wisdom's stature, illiterate of the book of your face.

So often we walked along the old stone wall at night,
Looked up at your window, where lamplight cleft your brow,
And knew you were suffering for us the thornier passages,
Transfixed by *Lear*, or staring ahead to the heart
Of Conrad's Africa. Sometimes we ventured inside,
To be welcomed by an excellent whiskey, Mozart's *Requiem*.
—From *Selected Poems*, by James Applewhite
    (Durham: Duke University Press, 2005), 9.

To continue the tour, backtrack on Anderson to the intersection with Duke University Road. (Duke's Nasher Museum of Art will be on the right.) Continue on Anderson straight through the traffic light at Campus Drive. Ahead on the left is the entrance to the Sarah P. Duke Gardens—generally an easy parking spot (for a fee) from which to take a short literary walking tour of Duke's West Campus.

Duke psychiatrist and writer Doris Iarovici takes advantage of the romantic setting of Duke Gardens in a piece from her debut collection, *American Dreaming and Other Stories*, published by Novello Festival Press in 2005. In the story, a Romanian man and his imported bride finally reconnect after she has left him and their young daughter to complete her medical studies. The estranged couple come to the garden to talk, and it is soon clear who has the upper hand:

"She smiles, takes his arm, then paces them at a stroll, steering toward the small gazebo at the top of the formal gardens. Its cap of fragrant wisteria rains lavender petals on them" (56). They take in the roses, the wisteria, and then talk for a time on the stone steps of the Gardens—a conversation that will forever change their relationship.

Proceed through the Gardens to the opposite side from the parking lot. Climb the hill in the general direction of Duke Chapel and take one of the walkways between buildings to reach the main quad of West Campus. Perkins Library, on the right as you are facing the unmistakable Duke Chapel, is the first stop.

This world-class library houses many rare editions. The manuscript collections are so extensive that it's only possible to mention a few. Novelist Anne Tyler's papers are here, including a draft of an early novel that Tyler curiously printed by hand on unlined paper with painstakingly straight right and left margins, as if the document were an actual typeset version of her novel-to-be. Perhaps the effort helped her believe in the prospect of publication.

Tyler studied with William Blackburn and was also one of Reynolds Price's first students when he joined Duke's English department. Price found Tyler already to be a remarkable writer who set a high bar for his subsequent students. "She's as close to a fulfilled prophecy as we'll ever have," said English professor Carl Anderson, when introducing Tyler years later when she came back to Durham for a campus reading.

Tyler, who'd been admitted to the university straight out of the same Raleigh high school that Reynolds Price had attended (Broughton), was only nineteen when she graduated from Duke in 1961. She then did a year of graduate study at Columbia University before returning to work in Perkins Library as a Russian bibliographer. Her first novel was published in 1964. She has since published some eighteen novels; six have been adapted for film.

Perkins Library also houses one of the most extensive collections of Walt Whitman material in the world, along with the papers of contemporary writers Fred Chappell, Reynolds Price, and William Styron. The papers of South Carolina novelists Padgett Powell and Josephine Humphries (a Duke graduate and former student of Reynolds Price), Georgia novelist Carson McCullers, feminist writer Robin Morgan, Virginia poet laureate George Garrett, Carolina Wren Press founder and poet Judy Hogan, Kentucky novelist and literary philanthropist Sallie Bingham, and the Georgia-born twin brothers and novelists Robert and Richard Bausch are also housed here.

The John Hope Franklin Collection of African and African American Documentation is another exceptional resource in Perkins. It includes first-person accounts from African Americans from the era of slavery to the present and a special collection of materials about African Americans in Durham, including the papers of novelist Gwendolyn M. Parker. The late John Hope Franklin, a prolific author, recipient of the Congressional Medal of Freedom, and James B. Duke Professor Emeritus of History, donated his personal and professional papers to the collection.

As you are facing the chapel, Perkins Library is on the right side of the main quadrangle. The entrance is a couple of steps below sidewalk level, with stone benches flanking the patio entryway. Upon entering the library, turn left at the first hallway. Rare Books and Manuscripts are on this floor. Take the stairway on the right to the second floor to visit the Gothic Reading Room (210), an impressive setting for study that now features an exhibition on the history of the university. William Styron frequented this spot in his years at Duke and remembered it this way:

> I read everything I could lay my hands on. Even today I can recall the slightly blind and bloodshot perception I had of the vaulted Gothic reading room, overheated, the smell of glue and sweat and stale documents, winter coughs, whispers, the clock ticking toward midnight as I raised my eyes over the edge of *Crime and Punishment*. The library became my hangout, my private club, my sanctuary, the place of my salvation; during the many months I was at Duke, I felt that when I was reading in the library I was sheltered from the world and from the evil winds of the future; no harm could come to me there. It was doubtless escape of sorts but it also brought me immeasurable enrichment. God bless libraries. —From *Havanas in Camelot: Personal Essays*, by William Styron (New York: Random House, 2008), 79–80.

Styron began his first novel while at Duke and published it to critical acclaim at the age of twenty-six, following a brief stint in 1947 at McGraw-Hill, where he was fired for sailing paper airplanes out a window. He continued his studies for a time at the New School, in Manhattan. In the early 1950s, he lived in Paris and helped his friends George Plimpton and Peter Matthiessen launch the *Paris Review*, a literary journal best known for its author interviews. *The Confessions of Nat Turner*, Styron's sweeping and most controversial novel, in which the author assumed the persona of a rebellious slave, was published in 1967, in the midst of the civil rights struggle. He weathered the controversy sparked by his use of the voice of an African American man as his narrator. Styron went on to confront another charged period of history—the Holocaust—with his 1979 novel, *Sophie's Choice*. He did not publish another novel during his life, though his essay collections and the memoir *Darkness Visible* about his struggles with mental illness revealed much of the man.

Duke has never offered a degree program in creative writing, yet a significant number of fiction writers, playwrights, and poets serve as faculty across many departments. Among them are short-story writers Melissa Malouf and Joe Ashby Porter, poet Deborah Pope, young adult science fiction novelist Christina Askounis, internationally acclaimed playwright and novelist Ariel Dorfman, Cuban-born novelist Oscar Hijuelos, Mario Puzo expert and novelist Frank Lentricchia, and romance writer and publisher Julie Tetel Andresen.

Novelist David Guy, who studied with Reynolds Price, teaches writing to public policy students. Civil engineering professor Henry Petroski has penned a dozen popular and eminently readable books that might also interest the literary visitor, including *The Pencil: A History of Design and Circumstance* (1990) and *The Book on the Bookshelf* (1999). Petroski's wife, Catherine Petroski, is a children's writer and young adult novelist.

Duke Medical Center has also been declared a leader among health care providers for its literary endeavors. Through the Health Arts Network at Duke, visual and performing artists share their work with patients on a regular basis, and the hospital employs a literary arts coordinator and a writer-in-residence, who work with patients and caregivers who wish to write about their experiences with illness and recovery. In addition, the Osler Literary Roundtable is a weekly meeting in the hospital of published and aspiring writers; among them are many Duke physicians and medical professionals.

Leaving the Gothic Reading Room, turn left and walk to the end of the building. A portrait of Reynolds Price by artist Will Wilson is on the right. A stairway to a ground floor exit is on the left. Return to the quad and take in a fuller view of the Gothic campus that was at least part of Tom Wolfe's inspiration for his fictional Dupont University in *I Am Charlotte Simmons*. Wolfe's daughter graduated from Duke in 2002, also the year in which her father gave the commencement address. Wolfe spent several months researching his controversial novel here and at Harvard and Stanford universities.

To visit Duke's other campus to the east, which was the sole province of female students until 1972, you can take a five-minute bus ride from the traffic circle in front of the chapel or return to your car in the Gardens parking lot. From the Gardens entrance on Anderson, turn right and then left onto Campus Drive. East Campus is less than a mile ahead.

On the way from West to East Campus is another literary landmark. Where Swift Avenue crosses Campus Drive at the flashing light, there is a quiet neighborhood off to the right where many Duke faculty members built homes in the

1940s and 1950s, including English professor Lewis Patton and his wife, writer Frances Gray Patton.

Fannie Patton was born in Raleigh, the daughter of the editor of the *Raleigh Times*. She studied at Duke and later attended the University of North Carolina at Chapel Hill, where she wrote plays and earned a Playmakers Fellowship for her acting.

As a Duke faculty wife and the dedicated mother of three children, Patton crafted comedic short stories that have a tongue-in-cheek flavor. Some critics accused her of sentimentality, apparently missing the ironic edge in her work.

Fannie Patton wrote what she knew—narratives of well-off 1950s housewives and their preoccupations with gardening, bird-watching, child-rearing, and husband-pleasing. She also faithfully portrayed the relationships between these white women of privilege and their African American hired help in the still-segregated South.

In "A Piece of Luck"—a story with actual place-names from Durham, including Five Points, Duke Hospital, "Haiteye," and Lincoln Heights—Patton assumes a voice that is unabashedly autobiographical. She offers up what she calls in the story "a little street scene, a comedy of manners," where she, the only white person in a throng of African Americans at "the transfer junction for most bus riders in town," observes the clash of class differences being played out among her fellow passengers. Patton is the most privileged among them—which she is aware of—and she is not the hero of the drama. The story was one of many that Patton published over the course of four decades in the *New Yorker*.

Frances Gray Patton was best known, however, for her best-selling 1954 novel *Good Morning, Miss Dove*, made into a movie the following year. As Alexander Blackburn tells it, the novel was actually based on his fifth-grade geography teacher, Mrs. Lorraine Pridgen, who also taught Patton's daughters at the George Watts Elementary School downtown and was principal there from 1945 to 1962.

■ EAST CAMPUS

If it's a weekend, you may park along either side of Campus Drive beyond Washington Duke's statue. Here at the Main Street entrance to East Campus is the East Duke Building, which dates back to 1912. As his son explains, William Blackburn had his office here:

> When Father arrived in Durham in 1926 to begin his long career at Duke, he sought for his exclusive use a classroom that could also serve as his

Washington Duke's statue is at the entrance to Duke University's East Campus, where young writers come to summer camp to hone their skills through Duke Youth Programs.

office.... He found a small rectangular storeroom on the second floor of East Duke Building, an old Trinity structure. Located beneath the balcony of a Victorian auditorium, approached over floorboards that creaked and flapped like a plank road in wilderness, the storeroom had large, old-fashioned sash windows, pigeons a-flutter on their ledges, and a bucolic vista of elephant-trunk magnolias with waxen green leaves and bridal flower-cones, also of a lily pond with goldfish.... He would later add mementos of brilliant students: a painting by Guy Davenport, a framed dust jacket of William Styron's first novel, *Lie Down in Darkness* (187).

Little has changed on the outside of East Duke Building, and it is almost possible to imagine the campus as it was at Blackburn's arrival only a year after the cornerstone of Duke Chapel was laid. The floors still moan and creak on the second floor of East Duke, and the Victorian auditorium—now the Nelson Music Room—is still used for concerts and readings. Blackburn's old office, however, has unceremoniously been given over to storage. In a letter, Alexander Blackburn suggests that visitors "will have to use imagination to conjure up images of the literary souls who once discovered themselves in it . . . and the literary giants who visited it, such as Tennessee Williams and Elizabeth Bowen."

For her part, writer Helen Bevington had come to Durham expecting to raise her children and assume the role of faculty wife, but she was soon enlisted to take over a class in Woman's College and was ultimately given a permanent teaching position. By 1946 she had published her first collection of poems, and not long after her work began appearing in the *New Yorker*. Despite this early success, Bevington approached her role as teacher with characteristic modesty and humor:

> I told them to set down whatever they liked, but preferably to draw it from their own backyard and make it visible. In general they did. Writing is a personal thing, I said (as if I knew what it is). Be an authority on yourself; write to please yourself. Tell what is true, it being more entertaining and a lot more plausible than the untrue. Keep a notebook (oh, I told them). A writer is first and last a notetaker or he isn't a writer. Collect places and people instead of inventing them. Why imagine an incident if you have a reliable memory of one? The knack is to find a way of looking, a talent for experience (62).

Bevington's light touch in the creative writing classroom has been echoed in more recent years by a number of instructors who offer noncredit courses for community members at Duke Continuing Studies, headquartered in the old Bishop's House at the far northeastern corner of East Campus. (The Bishop's House was named for Methodist bishop John Kilgo, a bachelor who served as Trinity president from 1894 to 1910 and who was often seen walking the perimeter of campus with his gangly hound dog.)

Remarkably, a writing class begun here by novelist Laurel Goldman (*Sounding the Territory*, *The Part of Fortune*) in the 1980s is still meeting off campus after nearly thirty years. In most Continuing Studies writing classes, participants learn how to serve as peer teachers, reading their manuscripts to each other for encouragement and critique. From Goldman's first writing group have come at least a half-dozen published novels, including Angela Davis-Gardner's *Forms of Shelter*, Peggy Payne's *Revelation*, Pete Hendricks's *The Second War*, and Peter Filene's *Home and Away*.

The *Bishop's House Review* is a literary magazine that is produced by Duke Continuing Studies students from time to time. Duke Youth Programs, also headquartered in the Bishop's House, offer middle school and high school students a chance at intensive creative writing courses each summer. At the other end of the age spectrum, the Osher Lifelong Learning Institute, for community members over fifty, offers poetry, memoir, and fiction writing classes, usually taught by retired authors and scholars.

■ MAPLEWOOD CEMETERY

Our tour proceeds from East Campus toward East Durham by means of another important writer who found her earliest inspiration in this town. Pauli Murray was raised in a neighborhood behind Durham's Maplewood Cemetery by her maternal grandparents and an aunt. She attended Durham's segregated Hillside High School, graduating at the top of her class, and went on to finish a degree with honors at Hunter College in New York.

In 1938, Murray sought to do graduate study in sociology at the University of North Carolina but was turned away because of her skin color. She went instead to law school at Howard University, graduating at the top of her class, a distinction that usually resulted in a fellowship to Harvard University, but Murray was once again denied admission, this time because she was female. Murray took a fellowship instead at Boalt Law School at the University of California and then began a long career as an activist—first in the field of civil rights for African Americans and later as one of the founders of the National Organization for Women. In 1956, after four years away from her law practice for the purposes of research, Murray published a memoir, *Proud Shoes: The Story of an American Family*. The book documents her heritage in North Carolina and the earliest pains of rejection in Durham. A volume of Murray's poetry followed in 1970.

Pauli Murray eventually entered seminary at the age of sixty-two, and, despite the threat of more rejection, she sought to become the first African American female priest to be ordained by the Episcopal Church. Her bid for the priesthood was successful, and she went on to preside over worship at the Chapel of the Cross, a Chapel Hill sanctuary where her ancestors had once worshipped in the slave balcony. Pauli Murray's final memoir was published two years after her death, in 1987.

Grandfather was buried in the Fitzgerald family graveyard where Great-Grandfather Thomas, Great-Grandmother Sarah Ann, Uncle Richard and other relatives already rested. It was on the west side of Chapel Hill Road next to the old section of Maplewood Cemetery. Only an iron picket fence separated the Fitzgeralds from their white contemporaries who had been early settlers in Durham, but a far wider gulf separated the living descendants. And it was in Grandfather's death that I found a symbol which would somehow sustain me until I grew older and found other ways of balancing loyalty with revolt.

Grandfather died in 1919 and it would be a number of years before the graves of World War I veterans appeared. Meanwhile the white cemetery from our back door to Chapel Hill Road and beyond was filled with Confederate dead. Every Memorial Day or Decoration Day, the cemetery hillside was dotted with crossbarred Confederate flags. As a Union veteran, Grandfather was entitled to a United States flag for his grave, so every May I walked proudly through a field of Confederate flags hugging my gold-pointed replica of Old Glory. I crossed Chapel Hill Road to the Fitzgerald family burial ground and planted it at the head of Grandfather's grave....

I spent many hours digging up weeds, cutting grass and tending the family plot. It was only a few feet from the main highway between Durham and Chapel Hill. I wanted the white people who drove by to be sure to see this banner and me standing by it. Whatever else they denied me, they could not take from me this right and the undiminished stature it gave me. For there at least at Grandfather's grave with the American flag in my hands, I could stand very tall and in proud shoes.

—From *Proud Shoes: The Story of an American Family*, by Pauli Murray (New York: Harper, 1956), 274–76.

DIRECTIONS

From the entrance to Duke's East Campus, turn left onto Main Street and right at the next intersection onto Buchannan Boulevard. At the next traffic light turn right onto West Chapel Hill Street. In another 200 yards or so, at another traffic light, bear left onto Kent Street. Pass Jackson Street on the right. At the beginning of the fence surrounding Maplewood Cemetery on the right are the Fitzgerald family graves. For closer inspection, turn right into the cemetery gate and park. Walk back down the fence line alongside Kent Street where you've just come.

Though the iron fence Pauli Murray describes is no longer there to separate black families from white, the gravestones of African Americans are set along the cemetery margins, far below the ground level of the white graves, almost in a ditch. Note Washington Duke's massive mausoleum, on the highest ground in the center of this section of Maplewood. Pauli Murray's grandparents' tombstones are close to the road and beside a holly bush.

Here as perhaps nowhere else in twenty-first-century Durham is such a visceral expression of the two Durhams, east and west, black and white. Pauli

Murray's legacy of hope and determination is fortunately celebrated by a more fitting tribute downtown, our next destination.

■ DOWNTOWN DURHAM

Return to West Chapel Hill Street and turn right toward downtown. In 0.5 miles, the road crosses over the Durham Freeway and runs along beside the towering North Carolina Mutual Insurance Company, founded in the Hayti district of Durham in 1898 by Charles C. Spaulding. For years, it was the largest African American business on the planet.

Next door, Durham's police headquarters is notable for its literary connection to the crime novels of Michael Malone and Katy Munger. The prolific Michael Malone worked for years writing Emmy-winning scripts, including a long run as head writer for the soap opera *One Life to Live*. After two comic novels, he then turned to crime writing in a popular series of books that are set in fictional Hillston, a university town that bears a strong resemblance to Durham. His central characters are an unlikely pair—the rather elegant Lieutenant Justin Bartholomew Savile V, the aristocratic head of the homicide division, and Vietnam vet and police chief Cudberth "Cuddy" Mangum, whose tastes run to fast food. In the 2002 novel *Time's Witness*, Cuddy describes himself as a "Carolina Will Rogers without the rope tricks." In these smart, funny, and fast-paced books, Malone also manages to tackle serious topics such as white supremacy, the death penalty, and election fraud. Dubbed the "American Dickens," Malone claims that his astute ear for dialogue came from serving as his deaf mother's "ears." Faylene Jones Malone was a fourth-grade teacher in Durham.

Writer Katy Munger's intrepid detective Casey Jones is an up-by-her-own-bootstraps Triangle private investigator who is smart-alecky, sometimes vulgar, and hard drinking. In *Better Off Dead*, Jones investigates a series of rapes on the Duke campus. In *Out of Time*, she is hired by a woman on death row in Raleigh who is accused of killing her husband, a local police officer. In *Money to Burn*, Casey rubs shoulders with Durham's upper class whose fortunes were made in tobacco.

Beyond the police station and North Carolina Mutual, the road soon ducks under a railroad overpass. Continue to Five Points and proceed straight ahead on West Chapel Hill Street. Turn left on Foster Street and cross Morgan Street. Look on the left for the TROSA Furniture and Frame Shop at 313 Foster and turn into the parking lot just beyond the brick facade. A mural portrait of Pauli Murray has been painted on the side of this building as part of a larger public art project around town that is designed to salute Murray.

Entitled Pauli Murray and
True Community, *this mural
is one of five in Durham
created by artist Brett Cook
to celebrate the life of poet,
memoirist, and clergywoman
Pauli Murray.*

Backtrack to the intersection of Foster and West Chapel Hill Street and continue straight ahead onto Corcoran Street. Note the large bronze bull standing on the edge of the open plaza on the right. The sixteen-story Washington Duke Hotel (later called the Jack Tar) once stood here. From its construction in 1925 up until its demolition fifty years later, the hotel was the place where most visiting dignitaries, including many important writers, stayed when they came to Durham.

Continue on Corcoran through the center of downtown. Cross Main Street, Ramseur, the railroad tracks, and Pettigrew Street. Corcoran becomes Blackwell Street along this stretch, so named for the first tobacco company established in Durham. The renovated factory building on the right is part of what is now known as the American Tobacco Campus, billed as downtown Durham's entertainment district. On the left is the Durham Bulls Athletic Park, opened in 1995 to replace the original Durham Athletic Park (still in existence) where the movie *Bull Durham* was filmed.

In Durham's manufacturing heyday, workers poured into this area around the clock for three shifts. Durham native Mary E. Mebane describes the American Tobacco workplace in 1949 in an autobiography that she began as a series for the *New York Times*. As a teenager, Mebane stood in a crowd in the summer sun for hours hoping to be hired on in "the green season" to process new tobacco for cigarettes. On the second day of her vigil, she was finally called in and put to work:

It was a cavernous room, long and tall. The man who led me there called to the boss, who came over to tell me what to do, but the machinery was so loud that I couldn't hear him and I was so startled by my new surroundings that I didn't really concentrate on what he said. I was afraid to take a deep breath, for the room was so cloudy with tobacco dust that brown particles hung in the air. I held my breath as long as I could and then took a deep breath. I started to cough and my eyes watered, I saw lots of women and some men, each doing a task seemingly unrelated to the others', but I knew that there must be a plan.

My job had something to do with a conveyor belt. It was shaped like a child's sliding board, only it had a deep trough and it moved. Shredded tobacco was on this belt—I think that it came from upstairs—and my job was to sit by the belt and pick out the pieces whose stems were too large, for the belt was constantly moving, and obviously I couldn't pick out every single stem on the belt. I looked at the others, but I couldn't see what method they were using. I was in misery, for this was my first "public" job and I didn't want to do badly on it. I did the best that I could but soon the boss came and told me he was going to put me on the belt upstairs. I was glad, for my back was hurt from bending over, trying to pick out stems. Maybe I could do better upstairs.

—From *Mary: An Autobiography*, by Mary E. Mebane (New York: Viking, 1981), 161–62.

The late Mary Mebane, raised just outside Durham in a close-knit rural community of African Americans, would go on to study at North Carolina Central University and earn a Ph.D. in English from UNC–Chapel Hill. She pursued an academic career at universities in South Carolina and Wisconsin. The second volume of her autobiography is titled *Mary: Wayfarer* (1999).

Backtrack to Pettigrew Street and turn right. In three blocks, turn right onto Fayetteville Street, which crosses over the Durham Freeway to Durham's historic Hayti community.

The history of the racial divide in Durham has been told from many angles. Notably, Osha Gray Davidson, a frequent contributor to *Rolling Stone* and *Mother Jones* magazines, captured the story of Ann Atwater, an African American single mother who became a civil rights activist in the 1960s here, and C. P. Ellis, a white man of limited means who joined the Ku Klux Klan as a Durham youth. *The Best of Enemies* documents the evolution of Atwater and Ellis in their separate camps and their eventual reconciliation and remarkable friendship. The book also contrasts Durham's much-touted African American monied class with the harsh economic realities for common laborers, both black and white, who once worked here in textile and tobacco manufacturing. At the beginning of the twentieth century, both W. E. B. Du Bois and Booker T. Washington visited Hayti and wrote about Durham in the national press, promoting the city's economic and racial progress.

By the mid-twentieth century, Durham's situation was changing. Lewis Shiner's 2008 novel *Black & White* fictionalizes the checkered history of urban renewal in Hayti, which began in 1958 with the demolition of parts of the community, based on politicians' promises of new and better storefronts and residential sections in the district. Instead, the community was forever divided by the concrete canyon that was dug to install Durham's East–West Expressway in the 1970s. Scores of African American homes and businesses were permanently displaced by the freeway, and only the former St. Joseph's AME Church and the adjoining Hayti Heritage Center at 804 Old Fayetteville Street bear witness to the more illustrious past of Hayti.

In the novel, Lewis Shiner's protagonist, Michael Cooper, comes to Durham in 2004 to take care of his father, who is dying from lung cancer at Duke Medical Center. The elder Cooper, a white man, finally gives up two long-held secrets—his participation in the cover-up of the murder of a Hayti activist in the 1970s and the fact that his son's mother is an African American woman from Hayti. With a tip from Cooper, authorities soon uncover the murdered activist's body in a concrete form at the Fayetteville Street overpass. The rest of the book unpacks the history and evolution of Hayti, including the contemporary Hayti Heritage Center. Shiner's details and sharp descriptions of contemporary Durham, east and west, are so familiar that the historic conflict he fictionalizes takes on a credibility that's both disturbing and satisfying.

"Stop here for a second," Michael said. Along the south retaining wall someone had painted names and primitive likenesses of famous Hayti

Haitian vévé — a voodoo symbol — tops the spire of Durham's historic St. Joseph's AME Church, now the Hayti Heritage Center. This landmark figures in Lewis Shiner's 2008 novel, Black & White.

residents: Moore, Merrick, and Shepard, who'd founded North Carolina Mutual Life, along with other names that Michael didn't know. Steps led up to the brick and steel of the Heritage Center, and above it all towered the steeple.

Michael reached for the car door.

"You getting out here?" the driver asked nervously.

"Just for a second."

From where he stood, resting his hands on the open door, he could see the thing at the top of the steeple clearly. It was made of black wrought iron, an intricate design of intersecting curves, heart shaped, on an axis like a weather vane.

Michael reached into the cab and dug a sketchbook out of one of the plastic bags. "Keep the meter running," he told the driver. He got the thing down in a couple of minutes. Roger could tell him exactly what it was, but Michael didn't need him to know it had no business on top of a church.

He got in the cab. "You know what that is?" he asked the driver.

"It's a church, sir."

"The thing on top of the steeple. Where the cross should be."

"I never saw that before."

"It's called a *vévé*," Michael said. "It's the symbol of a voodoo god."

—From *Black & White*, by Lewis Shiner (Burton, Mich.: Subterranean Press, 2008), 4.

The voodoo symbol Shiner describes indeed sits atop the St. Joseph's steeple. The 450-seat sanctuary, now a performance hall, dates from 1891 and features a colorful pressed tin ceiling, elegant chandeliers, and twenty-four stained glass windows. Duke professor Tim Tyson, author of *Blood Done Sign My Name* (considered in the next tour), has taught an unprecedented academic class in this spirit-filled room. "The South in Black and White" is open to Duke, North Carolina Central, and UNC–Chapel Hill students and community members. Tyson has filled the sanctuary with students eager to learn more about the history of Hayti in the broader context of racial conflict in the twentieth-century South. He uses readings from African American writers Richard Wright, Zora Neale Hurston, and Ernest Gaines, along with their white counterparts: William Faulkner, Eudora Welty, and Lillian Smith.

Hayti Heritage Center also sponsors an array of spoken word events every year, in addition to the Bull Durham Blues Festival. This poem, by Darrell Stover, sings the music of this section of Durham:

STEPPED IT UP AND GONE ON
City Marker Commemoration June 16, 2001 for Blind Boy Fuller
Hayti Hayti Handed down
    Handed down
        Hayti Hayti Handed down
    Rev. Gary Davis
    Told this man
    To tell Brownie McGee
    To hook up with Sonny Terry
    'cause there's some dancin' to be done
    some 'baca to be sold
    some stories to be told
    by a string singin'
    git pickin'
    Blind, Bad
    Durham dude
    Wadesboro

BOY

WHIPPIN' WICKEDLY

WONDERFUL LICKS

LIKE BLACK LEAGUES

OF SOUTHERN STRUGGLIN'

LOOKIN' FOR LOVE

IN ALL THE WRONG PLACES

RECORDIN' BOOCOO

HISTORY

TELL TELLIN'

SPIDER MAN

ON THE STRINGS

LOOKIN' LIKE MY GRANDADDY

UP FROM THE CAROLINAS

FULTON HIM MACK DADDY

SLICK DAPPER

DAN GENIUS

CLEAR SEEIN' THIRD EYE

PREACHIN' PARTY PARTY

MAN CHILD

PLAYIN' NATIONAL STEEL

IN A COTTON RAG LAND (HAYTI HAYTI HANDED DOWN . . .)

—Used by permission of Darrell Stover.

Continue ahead on Fayetteville Street. In 0.3 miles on the left is another historic community meeting place, the Stanford L. Warren Library, opened in 1940 as the second home of Durham's "colored" library, which dates back to 1913, when it began in the basement of White Rock Baptist Church.

Just beyond the Warren Library are the larger homes that Durham's elite African American families occupied in the 1940s and that Gwendolyn Parker describes in her elegantly written novel *These Same Long Bones*. Parker's story begins with the sudden death of the daughter of one of Hayti's most prominent entrepreneurs:

Sirus stood now, some thirty-five years past his birth, in the late summer of 1947, in this town of Durham, North Carolina, which bustled with progress, in a house on Fayetteville Street that was one of dozens he'd built, wishing he were the one who was dead. From his bathroom, the sun streaming in the window, Sirus could still hear the cars as they slowed to pass his house. He stood his shaving brush on its base, bristles up, to dry, and carefully shook the last drops of water from his razor. He looked at his face, now clean shaven, in the mirror....

Long before this day, before his successes, his marriage, before Durham and buildings and struggle, there was just Sirus, a young boy, and his parents, Eubie and Mattie, living together in the small town of Carr. It wasn't this future that beckoned then, but just the moment, captured in a land defined by tobacco, cotton, sun, and trees, where what was coming was all motion and movement. Sirus's childhood was like all children, even for colored boys, and no matter how brief, it was a place out of time, set into itself, a vivid dream.... In this dream there was no other place than Carr; there were no other people than his own. The facts, of course, were different, as facts always are, but it wasn't the facts that mattered.... To Sirus, in that very rural and very small town, places like Durham and Raleigh were little more than names, without faces or smells or memories attached. His family was the world, and all of the world was his family.

—From *These Same Long Bones*, by Gwendolyn McDougald Parker
(New York: Plume Books, 1995), 7, 36.

Few novels depict so vividly an African American family in the context of a patchwork community of poverty and prosperity in the mid-twentieth-century South. Coincidentally, McDougald Terrace, Durham's oldest and largest public housing project, on nearby Lawson Street, bears Parker's mother's family name. In the novel, Parker's protagonist, Sirus McDougald, unhappily partners with a group of white businessmen to develop such a housing project as the story progresses.

Parker, born in 1950, lived in Durham until her ninth birthday. Her great-grandfather, Aaron McDuffie Moore, was cofounder of the North Carolina Mutual Life Insurance Company and founder of the Mechanics and Farmers Bank. He was also involved in the establishment of North Carolina Central University. Parker went on to attend Radcliffe College and New York University Law School and to work as a Wall Street attorney, before beginning her writing career from her home in Connecticut. Her second book, a memoir, *Trespassing: My Sojourn in the Halls of Privilege* (1997), also details her Durham childhood and the discrimination she later experienced in the boardrooms of corporate America.

Another half-mile ahead, this distinguished university, with its law school, new biotechnology laboratories, and strong communications and library sciences programs, dates back to 1910 when it opened as the National Religious Training School and Chautauqua. It later was known as the North Carolina College for Negroes and became the first state-supported liberal arts college for African Americans. NCCU adopted its present name in 1969 and joined the University of North Carolina system in 1972.

Dr. James E. Shepard, whose statue stands before the central administration building just beyond the campus's main entrance on the left, was the college president until 1947. He was a traditional man of great convictions, with a firm hand at the helm. Shepard was not quite prepared for the charming but feisty independence of the writer he hired in the fall of 1939 to create a drama program for the college.

Zora Neale Hurston arrived on campus driving a sporty convertible and wearing her signature beret. According to Hurston biographer Valerie Boyd, the flamboyant author filled out her faculty information card in red ink, describing her marital status as "Married (getting divorced)." Given this fact, Dr. Shepard apparently expected Hurston to live in unmarried female faculty housing on campus. Hurston insisted that she needed solitude to write and rented a cabin several miles away. In a letter to a friend in New York, Hurston describes the place:

> I have no telephone out at the shack, which is out on Highway #15,
> Hope Valley Road about two mile[s] on the town side of the Country Club.
> But if you will send me a wire to my mail box, (which I am watching these
> days like a cat watches a mouse hole,) I will know what is what. Also in
> case you decide to come tell me where to meet you. The Washington Duke
> is considered the best hotel in Durham. My log house is in a yard with two
> little log cabins in back. It used to be a tourist camp, complete with a filling
> station. None of it is in use now. I just live in the house which is on the left
> side of the road as you drive out towards the golf club.—From *Zora Neale
> Hurston: A Life in Letters*, ed. Carla Kaplan (New York: Doubleday, 2002), 454.

The tourist cabins are long gone on Hope Valley Road, but Hurston spent her brief tenure in Durham there, driving back and forth to campus and on Sundays to Chapel Hill to study with playwright Paul Green.

Just after her arrival, Hurston gave a presentation at the invitation of the

At a football game at what is now known as North Carolina Central University in Durham. In the fall of 1939, folklorist and writer Zora Neale Hurston (standing, center) had recently arrived to help launch a drama program on campus. Photo by Alex Rivera, courtesy of Robert Lawson.

Carolina Playmakers at UNC–Chapel Hill, which was, of course, an all-white institution. Hurston regaled the group with her plan to create "a Negro folk theater" at North Carolina College for Negroes. "She opened her talk with a story," writes biographer Valerie Boyd (*Wrapped in Rainbows*, New York: Scribner, 2003). "As she was driving onto the campus in her convertible, she said, a Tarheel student tried to insult her, but she ended up getting the last word. 'Hi nigger!' he called out. 'Hi, freshman!' she replied" (328).

Hurston met UNC drama professor Paul Green that night. He invited her to join his playwriting seminar on the segregated campus. One member of his seminar group objected to Hurston's joining, and Green promptly told the disgruntled student that she'd be missed in class.

Hurston's 1937 novel, *Their Eyes Were Watching God*, had just been issued in England and Italy, and she enthralled her fellow students at Carolina with segments from a folk opera she was writing about backwoods Florida. Hurston hoped that she and Green might strike up a writing partnership for the theater, and she stayed in touch with him even after she left North Carolina in March 1940. Frustrated by the lack of artistic freedom under Shepard's watch and by resources that were inadequate to build a quality theater program, Hurston had been unable to produce a single play on campus in her first semester. Given her flamboyant reputation, there were also unhelpful rumors that she might have dated one of her students. In any case, President Shepard was reportedly relieved to see her go, and Hurston was happy to be on her way.

She immediately began an oral history project in Beaufort, South Carolina, collecting details on the Gullah culture of the region. She wrote Green one last time hoping for an alliance, but by that time Green had invited Richard Wright to come to Chapel Hill for a playwriting collaboration, following the enormous success of his novel *Native Son*, published the same month that Hurston left Durham.

Other prominent writers have served on the NCCU faculty over the years. In fact, it was on this campus that thirty-two-year-old John Hope Franklin received a contract from Alfred A. Knopf to begin his research on what would become the landmark volume *From Slavery to Freedom*, published in 1947, which forever changed the way history was written about the African American experience.

Children's author and folklorist Eleanora Tate served on the faculty in the School of Library Science. Among her many honors, Tate, along with John Hope Franklin, received the 1999 Zora Neale Hurston Award from the National Association of Black Storytellers. Though she was raised in Missouri, Tate has written a number of books for children in which North Carolina folklore and African American traditions are celebrated.

Wendy Rountree, whose specialty is African American literature, teaches in the English department and is the author of *Lost Soul*, a young adult novel.

Burgaw-native Samm-Art Williams, an actor, director, and playwright whose work has been produced on Broadway, has taught in the theater/drama department.

Take a walk beyond the administration building and around this handsomely landscaped campus. If you have time, step into NCCU's Shepard Memorial Library where the Treasure Room on the second floor features first editions of novels by Paul Lawrence Dunbar, Phillis Wheatley, Charles W. Chesnutt, W. E. B. Du Bois, and Countee Cullen, among others.

■ FAYETTEVILLE STREET

Beyond NCCU, another half mile down Fayetteville Street, is a bustling area of commerce and historic side street neighborhoods. This section of Fayetteville Street might well be the location for Durham writer Michele Andrea Bowen's fictional shop, Miss Thang's Holy Ghost Corner and Church Woman's Boutique, "the most perfect today's-black-woman-friendly store in the Triangle cities of Raleigh, Durham, and Chapel Hill, North Carolina" (1). *Holy Ghost Corner* is Bowen's first novel set in Durham. Her second, *Up at the College* (2008), is also set in the neighborhood.

Continue south on Fayetteville Street down and up a steep hill. The historic White Rock Baptist Church is at the top of the hill on the right. Durham playwright, poet, and librarian L. Teresa Church wrote this poem that might well speak to joyful celebrations that take place regularly at White Rock.

PEPPER AND PRAYER
Runs streak our caramel calves like keloids,
when briars snag cinnamon-brown nylons
while we wind paths in Sunday-dress.

Us girls bounce petroleum-jelly-fried curls,
let our shoulder blades jab pastel sleeves,
elbow-hunch air like bantam roosters.

We vow for front-row seats,
giggle when the Starlight Quartet travels through.
Guitars strung with foot-pattin' songs

raise money for church building funds,
help wise saints steady-up God's house
where mothers clutch prayer shields,

hide their single gals behind the cross,
dust our tracks with pepper and prayer
every time the lead singer wails,

nearly knots us into his necktie,
red silk noose that somehow seems
loosened on purpose.
—"Pepper and Prayer," by L. Teresa Church, from
    Pembroke Magazine, no. 39 (2007): 6.

In another 0.4 miles on the left is Pauli Murray's alma mater, Hillside High School, relocated to this site in 1995. Dating back to the 1880s, the institution is now the oldest historically black high school still operating in North Carolina after desegregation.

■ BETHESDA

Our last stop, Bethesda, is like a great many old farming communities that were once small crossroads on the outskirts of Durham. Bethesda had its own special identity and a tight-knit population, as depicted in the novels of Clyde Edgerton, who was born here in 1944. Edgerton was raised by his extended family, including grandparents and a raft of aunts and uncles.

On the front and back flyleaves of Edgerton's seventh novel, *Where Trouble Sleeps*, the author provides a map of fictional Listre (based on Bethesda) as it was in the 1950s and then as it appeared fifty years later. Like so many other crossroads nearby—Lowe's Grove, Few, and Nelson (where novelist Sylvia Wilkinson was raised)—Bethesda's identity has been swallowed up in the development of Research Triangle Park, which now links Raleigh, Durham, and Chapel Hill into a major metropolitan matrix.

DIRECTIONS

From Fayetteville Street immediately past Hillside High, turn left onto Riddle Road, which then crosses NC 55, goes under the freeway (NC 147), and ends at Ellis Road. Turn right on Ellis and follow it several miles to its end at South Miami Boulevard and turn left. Immediately on the right at the intersection with Bethesda Avenue is the house where Edgerton's grandfather, aunt, and uncle lived, at 1901 South Miami Boulevard. Turn right onto Bethesda Avenue. The brick house where Edgerton was raised is the second on the left, the same house depicted in this excerpt from Edgerton's second novel:

The dog was a tan fice—cowlicked, thin pointed sticks for legs, a pointed little face with powerful whiskers, one ear flopped and one straight.
    He was lying on the back steps of Mattie Riggsbee's brick ranch one

The fictional town of Listre was based on novelist Clyde Edgerton's home community of Bethesda on the outskirts of Durham. This is the street where he was raised.

summer Saturday morning when she opened the door to throw out a pan of table scraps for the birds. She placed her foot on the step beside him. She was wearing the leather shoes she'd cut slits in for her corns. The dog didn't move. Holding the bowl, Mattie stepped on out into the yard and tried to see if it was a him or a her so she could decide whether or not it *would* have been possible to keep it if she were younger and more able.

—From *Walking across Egypt*, by Clyde Edgerton (Chapel Hill: Algonquin Books of Chapel Hill, 1997), 1.

Though the older generation is nearly gone, the Edgerton family is still given to frequent reunions, often held in nearby John Umstead Park at the site of the family's old graveyard. *Killer Diller* and *Lunch at the Piccadilly*—Edgerton's fourth and eighth novels, respectively—deal with taking care of aging relatives, something Edgerton has done for his mother and aunts in Durham. He also spoofs Duke's famous diet programs in his work.

At least Bethesda Avenue hasn't changed much, Edgerton says. But one block up Miami Boulevard at the intersection with Angier Avenue everything is different. This crossroads was "a one-blinker-light corner," Edgerton explained in correspondence, "with a grocery store, general store, service station, auto shop, and grill. The church (much changed today) was on down Miami Boulevard and the school was across from it. The ball field is at the same place, and the woods beyond it. That whole area—that half square mile in there or so—is where I see very much of my fiction in my mind."

Fiction also preserves the past in another Durham writer's work. This tour of the Bull City concludes with a passage depicting the rural edge of Durham from several decades back. Susie Powell, a former law professor at NCCU, echoes Edgerton's memories of a more idyllic community life in this vicinity, before the emergence of Research Triangle Park:

> It was a place in which people gave each other rides, asked after each other, watched to see what cars visited one's driveway or guessed by the direction in which one went, where one was going; and if unsure, might call up and ask, "Where was you going when I seen you go pass the store?" It was a place in which people took dinner to church to feed each other at revival time even if they had clashed over something said about their children or their husbands and at least two of the men sold illegal whiskey and gave the money to their wives to buy the chickens to fry and eggs and flour to make pound cakes. Some of the men were church deacons and trustees. Some families had no men at all; only children and women, some of the women quite old, all shipwrecks or widows. Only five old men lived in the neighborhood. The wino, Rabbit, was at least fifteen years younger than he looked. Hiding behind madness, he touched everything.—From "Chapter One," by Susie Ruth Powell, in *A Living Culture in Durham*, ed. Judy Hogan (Durham: Carolina Wren Press, 1987), 38.

■ LITERARY LANDSCAPE

Regulator Bookshop
720 Ninth Street, Durham
919-286-2700
<http://www.regbook.com>

For more than thirty years, this Durham institution has been a steady literary anchor on Durham's vibrant Ninth Street. The roster of writers who have read here over the years rivals that of any bookshop in the nation.

Durham County Library
300 North Roxboro Street, Durham
919-560-0100
<http://www.durhamcountylibrary.org>
Housed here is a remarkable collection of materials on the history of North Carolina and the city in particular, now digitized and accessible online.

Stagville : Oxford : Henderson : Warrenton : Macon

This tour begins on the site of an antebellum plantation, a source of inspired material from writers who give voice to the enslaved and the slaveholder. We end these Piedmont tours at the birthplace of Duke University's most revered novelist, playwright, essayist, and poet, Reynolds Price.

Writers with a connection to this area: Hilda Gurley-Highgate, David Payne, William T. Polk, Connie Rose Porter, Reynolds Price, Sam Ragan, Annella Rockson, Andrea Selch, Frank G. Slaughter, Thad Stem, Eleanor Ross Taylor, Peter Taylor, Timothy Tyson

On the way out of Durham to reach our first destination in this final tour, we begin with a literary fantasy by poet Andrea Selch, who lives in the countryside north of Durham and east of Hillsborough. Selch studied creative writing at the University of North Carolina at Greensboro and earned a Ph.D. at Duke, where she taught creative writing for several years. She is president and executive director of Carolina Wren Press, a nonprofit press begun in 1976 by poet Judy Hogan. In Selch's quest for the perfect country breakfast in Durham and Orange counties, she has had many favorites over the years, but few of these eateries seem to stay in business. For the moment, she recommends Honey's, in Durham where Guess Road intersects I-85.

THE PLEASURE DOME
What journey was it, or did I
only dream the poetry jukebox?
Fifty cents a poem or three for a dollar—
while I waited for my grits and bacon
I scanned the plastic rotary

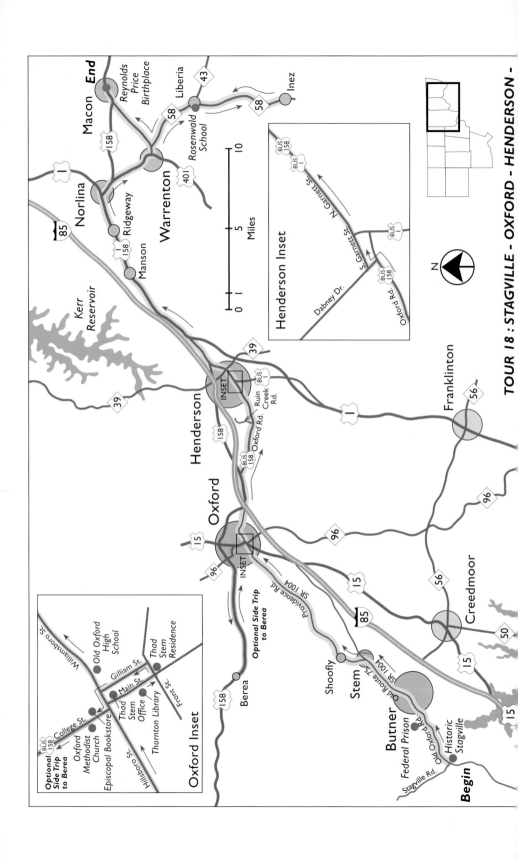

TOUR 18 : STAGVILLE - OXFORD - HENDERSON -

N

Kerr
Reservoir

Henderson

Oxford

Macon **End**

Reynolds
Price
Birthplace

Liberia

43

58

Inez

58

158

Norlina

1

Ridgeway

158

Manson

Warrenton

401

Rosenwald
School

85

Henderson Inset

BUS
158
BUS
1

N. Garnett St.

S. Garnett St.

Dabney Dr.

BUS
1

BUS
158

Oxford Rd.

10

5

Miles

5

0

1

39

39

INSET

BUS
1

Ruin
Creek
Rd.

158

BUS
158

Oxford Rd.

1

Franklinton

56

96

96

15

INSET

96

15

85

56

Creemoor

50

15

15

Providence Rd.

SR 1004

**Optional Side Trip
to Berea**

15

Shoofly

Stem

SR 1004

Old Route 75

Butner

Federal Prison

Old Oxford Rd.

Stagville Rd.

*Historic
Stagville*

Begin

158

Berea

Oxford Inset

Williamsboro St.

Old Oxford
High School

Thad
Stem
Residence

Gilliam St.

Front St.

Main St.

Thad Stem
Office

Thornton Library

BUS
158

College St.

Oxford
Methodist
Church

Episcopal Bookstore

Hillsboro St.

**Optional
Side Trip
to Berea**

for some whose words I thought I'd know.
Like 45s they ranged in pairs —
all the "A"s rang too familiar,
while the "B"s were full of passionate intensity.

Moving from Frost to Pound,
from Pound to Rich,
I chose a poem
and had it with my breakfast, like USA Today
or 91.5fm.
Now as I was young and easy under the apple boughs
the waitress wondered if I'd like more coffee,
yes, and if there were cream,
a little cream somewhere to lighten things
unruly sun. . .shine here to us
ah, what pleasure there in one booth lay!

For three years, out of step with my time
I've tried to relocate that dark café:
I have stopped in diners, roadhouses, greasy spoons,
I have eaten eggs — eggs over easy and over done —
and grits with cheese and more grits
and livermush (I too dislike it;
eating it, however, with a perfect contempt for it,
one gleans an appreciation for pastiche, the poetry
of butchers working in their frozen stalls at market).
Sundays too, I got up early
and loaded my Honda Odyssey™
with backroads maps and crisp one dollar bills
to prowl the two-lanes and "Old Route" something-somethings,
my stomach growling and the radio turned off.

You might ask how long I'll travel thus, impetuously.
There is no hunger like the taste for poetry —
even in these bountiful times I feel
it calling me to slip behind the wheel:
each Scenic Route glistens with dew
and heads off — toward Xanadu.
—Used by permission of Andrea Selch.

North of Durham, at 5828 Old Oxford Road, is one of the finest examples of an antebellum plantation for public touring in North Carolina, thanks to the dedication of historians and archaeologists who have probed this site and its existing buildings and artifacts. The seventy-one acres, given to the State of North Carolina by Liggett and Myers Tobacco Company, represent only a fraction of what were once the landholdings of the Cameron and Bennehan families who lived here. They owned some 30,000 acres by 1860.

Stagville figured prominently in the research of Hillsborough novelist Lee Smith as she wrote *On Agate Hill*. Smith was inspired by a cowrie shell that researchers had found in 1977 in the hearth of one of the slave cabins here. "It gives me chills just to think about it," Smith says.

Coincidentally, Smith's novel begins in the attic of a plantation house with the contemporary discovery of a diary and a dusty box with many curious items, including "marbles, rocks, dolls, and a large collection of bones, some human and some not" (3). These artifacts set in motion the story of Smith's protagonist, Molly Petree—a young white girl who kept the diary and box of treasures. Molly was orphaned by the Civil War and lived for a time in the ruins of a plantation house.

Later in the novel, Smith's character Liddy, a former slave who is preparing to run away, digs out the cowrie shells that she had hidden in her cabin on the Agate Hill plantation. Molly Petree narrates:

> Liddy opened the top and emptied the box out onto her palm while Washington held the candle right there. It was a pile of shiny little shells—six or seven of them. Liddy sucked in her breath and said something I could not understand. The shells glowed like pearls in her hand. Their tops were rounded like snail shells or like the dinner rolls that Liddy used to make for company so long ago. The bottom of each shell had two rows of teeth, almost like a little open mouth.
>
> From Africa, Liddy said.
>
> I grabbed one. It felt solid and warm and good in my hand, like a little rock. Can I have it? I asked, for suddenly I wanted it most in the world.
>
> No. Liddy did not look at me. She took the shell from me, then one by one she put them all back in the box and closed the top.
>
> —From *On Agate Hill*, by Lee Smith (Chapel Hill: Algonquin Books of Chapel Hill, 2007), 114.

Stagville Plantation plays a role in the Addy series of American Girl books by children's author Connie Rose Porter.

The discovery of a cowrie shell at Stagville also inspired writer Connie Rose Porter in the creation of her character Addy Walker in the American Girls Addy series. Porter researched the first book in the series, *Meet Addy*, at Stagville and based the tobacco plantation where Addy lived on this site. The actual Walker family, owned by the Camerons at Stagville, fled the plantation and ended up in Philadelphia—a fact Porter dramatizes in the book. A doll that was found in the trunk room of the Bennehan house at Stagville also figures in Addy's story. Stagville eloquently testifies to the experiences of the enslaved people who worked and lived here. Both Lee Smith's novel and Connie Porter's children's books are available in the Stagville gift shop. For hours, call 919-620-0120.

■ BUTNER

From Stagville, continue up Old Oxford Road toward Butner. In 2.4 miles, notice the concrete and metal edifice that is a maximum security federal penitentiary. Beyond it are the grounds of old Camp Butner, where in January 1944 short-story writer Peter Taylor and his army unit were stationed for training before their overseas deployment in World War II. At the time, Taylor had only recently married Norwood native and future poet Eleanor Ross. He had also written perhaps his most personal story, "Rain in the Heart," which reveals the writer's lifelong obsession with finding the perfect house to settle into, a wish made more urgent by his status as a newlywed about to go to war. Eleanor stayed in Durham to be near her husband until March, when he was sent to New York and thence to Europe.

Sadly, the state mental hospital, also along this route in Butner, was a brief way station for Chapel Hill writer Betty Smith, author of *A Tree Grows in Brooklyn* and *Joy in the Morning*. She was institutionalized here in 1971, when senile dementia made it impossible for her to live alone. She died in January 1972 in a hospital in Connecticut. (For more on Betty Smith, see Tour 16.)

DIRECTIONS

Old Oxford Highway continues northwest, skirting the west side of the town of Butner. From there it is referred to as Old Route 75. From Stagville it's about 8.5 miles to the town of Stem. At 14 miles, the road crosses the Tar River and begins switching back and forth across the railroad tracks that run alongside it. This two-lane changes names again, becoming Providence Road as it passes through the crossroads of Providence and draws closer to Oxford, the Granville County seat. Providence Road ends at Oxford's Hillsboro Street. Turn right and watch for the entrance to the Elmwood Cemetery on the left.

■ **OXFORD**

Old Man Rufe built the first mausoleum in Oxford insofar as I can determine. It was, is, a handsome marble structure, designed in the manner of a miniature Grecian temple. He called it his "mossy-lee," and he used it, from spring to fall, as a combination office and playhouse for several years. I think the "mossy-lee" was built at least fifteen years before Old Man Rufe died.

He said it was the coolest place in town, next to the ice plant, and each morning, in pretty weather, he took his newspaper and stumbled and jerked over to the cemetery to his "mossy-lee."

He would sit in the doorway in a rocking chair, read his paper, sing and whistle his songs, and smoke his roll-your-own cigarettes.

. . . A few times I took oddments to Old Man Rufe, in the "mossy-lee." There was a small table inside which he and his cronies used for checkers and for set-back and for poker.

Old Man Rufe kept jugs of buttermilk, which he used for a chaser, and mason-jars of Just Plain Snake Imboden's homemade whiskey. On the shelves, where the coffins went, ultimately, were apples and pears, in season, and there was a huge glass filled with horehound candy.
—From *Entries from Oxford*, by Thad Stem (Durham: Moore Publishing Company, 1971), 39–40.

Local historian, poet, and raconteur Thaddeus Garland Stem Jr. grew up in Oxford, went away to college at Duke, and then came back home to the house where he was born. Over his lifetime, Stem sold some 8,000 of his homespun pieces to North Carolina newspapers, predominantly the *Raleigh News and Observer* and the *Southern Pines Pilot*. Stem kept an office in downtown Oxford, a few blocks from his house. There he also wrote a weekly column, short fiction, and scores of poems and essays. In all, Stem published sixteen books, none with a nationally known publishing house, but even as his body began failing him in his mid-seventies, he kept writing. Stem's grave is ahead off the center driveway in the Elmwood Cemetery, on the left near the Moon family graves. Who knows if the mausoleum tale, excerpted here, is true or which of the aboveground tombs in this cemetery was the one Old Man Rufe occupied for card-playing and the cool temperatures?

Backtrack to the cemetery entrance on Hillsboro Street and turn left toward town. At Main Street, turn right and note the building on the left at 125 Main. Stem's office was on the second floor above the former Hall's Drug Store, now a gift shop that also sells used books.

In the next block on the right is Oxford's Thornton Library, at 210 Main. This library's North Carolina Room preserves a complete collection of the works of Thad Stem, many titles by the physician and writer Frank G. Slaughter, who went to high school in town, and several works by North Carolina's late poet laureate Samuel Talmadge Ragan, who was born a few miles west of Oxford in the little crossroads of Berea.

Thad Stem would have been pleased if not surprised to find himself a central character in a best-selling book about his home town, *Blood Done Sign My Name*, written by former Oxford resident and scholar of African American history Timothy Tyson. Tyson, a white man, was the son of a Methodist preacher who made no secret of his sympathies in the 1960s with the movement launched by Martin Luther King Jr. After weathering a controversy stirred up by having an African American clergyman preach to the all-white congregation he was serving in Sanford, Rev. Vernon Tyson decided to accept the pastorate that was offered him at Oxford Methodist Church. The church parsonage, at 415 Hancock Street, was right around the corner from Thad Stem's house, and, as Tim Tyson tells it in his book, the preacher's family arrived in Oxford as African Americans in this part of North Carolina were organizing to press harder for their civil rights. Thad Stem was a staunch supporter of the movement and would quickly befriend the new, progressive pastor in town. Tyson, still in elementary school when his family landed in Oxford, remembers Stem:

> The ever irascible Thad must have been around fifty when I met him. He had silver hair and wore black turtlenecks and blue jeans, tweed jackets and white Converse All-Stars, strange attire for a grown-up. (I had never heard of bohemians or intellectuals.) . . . Thad, who called himself "a militant, if not particularly sophisticated New Dealer," soon visited Daddy's office regularly to rail against the "tithing racists" and "mealy-mouthed miscreants" who beset them both and to remind his new friend to keep the faith.—From *Blood Done Sign My Name*, by Timothy B. Tyson (New York: Three Rivers Press, 2004), 82.

By 1970, however, everyone in Oxford had their faith challenged one way or another, when Henry "Dickie" Marrow, a military veteran, was accused of making a flirtatious remark to a white woman outside a crossroads store. Marrow, an African American in his twenties, was instantly confronted by Larry Teel, the son of the owner of the convenience store. Marrow pulled a knife. The store owner, Robert Teel, also rumored to be a member of the local Ku Klux Klan, went for his shotgun. Henry Marrow took flight, with Teel and his sons in pursuit. Teel shot Marrow on the street.

Tim Tyson was ten years old at the time of the murder, and Gerald Teel, the killer's son, was his playmate. The book details the fallout from this explosive act. Writing from the dual perspective of historian and child eyewitness, Tyson navigates the story as if it were a novel. The book has now been adapted for a film, which was largely shot in Statesville, on the western side of the Piedmont.

Ahead, Main Street ends at Front Street, and on the right is the house where Robert Teel lived. Turn left on Front. Note Hancock Street on the right, where the Tyson family lived. Thad Stem's birthplace and lifelong residence is at 104 East Front. With such close proximity, it's extraordinary to imagine the tension that must have existed in this neighborhood as Tyson's father tried to intervene in the chaos that followed the murder. Oxford's African American community protested, local tobacco warehouses went up in flames, and the Klan made constant threats.

Oxford United Methodist Church, where writer Tim Tyson's father was pastor during the incidents described in Tyson's memoir, Blood Done Sign My Name.

Continue up Front Street and turn left on Gilliam Street. Follow Gilliam back to Williamsboro Street and turn left. Then turn right on College. Oxford Methodist Church, where Tim Tyson's father was minister, is at the corner of College and West McClanahan.

Though it is not on the tour, if you're curious to see the village of Berea, where poet and journalist Sam Ragan was born, continue ahead on College. Pass the Oxford Orphanage and then follow NC 158 to the left toward Roxboro. It's a little over thirteen miles through beautiful countryside to Berea.

To reach Henderson, our next destination, return to Williamsboro Street and continue on US 158 east out of town. As you leave town, note City Hall on the right, past Belle Street. The building formerly served as Oxford High School, where novelist Frank G. Slaughter graduated at age fourteen. Slaughter was the son of a mail carrier and, like Sam Ragan, grew up on a farm near Berea. He graduated from Trinity College (now Duke) at seventeen and then took a medical degree at Johns Hopkins. Slaughter never gave up his career as a surgeon but somehow managed simultaneously to write more than seventy popular novels, mostly under his own name but some under a pen name, C. V. Terry. In his lifetime, Slaughter sold more than 60 million books.

Continue on Williamsboro and bear right at the fork, where Salem Road goes straight ahead. Stay on Williamsboro Street as it merges with 158 (Oxford Loop) and follow it past I-85. Bear right again on 158 Business (Oxford Road) as US 158 forks to the left.

■ HENDERSON

Henderson residents will tell you right off that this town is a place with many untold stories. Tobacco sales at auction here once rivaled Durham and Winston-Salem in dollars and pounds. Touted as the home of "the best cotton in the world," Henderson also had two important mills—Harriet and Henderson—and was headquarters for the Carolina Bagging Company, the largest manufacturer of jute bags used to cover cotton bales in its day. But Henderson's prosperity took a hit in 1956, when a strike at the Harriet and Henderson mills shook the community to its roots.

Boyd E. Payton, international vice president of the Textile Workers Union, went to prison for his part in the strike. He tells his story in *Scapegoat: Prejudice/Politics/Prison* (1970). Historian Daniel J. Clark's more recent examination of the strike is *Like Night & Day: Unionization in a Southern Mill Town*. Both books provide an interesting backdrop to *Ruin Creek*, a novel by Henderson native David Payne.

When I was off from school, I went to work with Pa sometimes. He'd stop by the house and pick me up at seven and take me out to breakfast at the Scuppernong Hotel, which was across the street from the railroad station in downtown Killdeer. Uncle John Landis would be there, who was the president of Carolina Fidelity Bank, and Uncle Herbert Kincannon, who owned the Dixie Bagging Mill—they were Pa's best friends. There'd be buyers down from Reynolds and American and Philip Morris up in Richmond for the sales at the Bonanza and Top Dollar, which was our competition, and you knew they were important, the buyers, because they all looked like the president or king of something. There were traveling salesmen, too, which you could tell by the different kind of suits they wore, which wouldn't hang just right and looked a little shiny. They might have a gold tooth or a gent's diamond or a tattoo peeking out from under a cuff, and they'd think they could pull a swift one on us, like that time they tried to sell Pa some timberland in the middle of the Dismal Swamp. Pa said they figured we were simple country boys who came from a hick burg, but if they messed with us, especially Pa or Uncle Johnny, boy, they'd wish the Seaboard Railroad never let them off in Killdeer, North Carolina.—From *Ruin Creek*, by David Payne (New York: Doubleday, 1993), 21–22.

Ruin Creek, from which Payne's novel derives its name, was once the site of a dairy farm. Ruin Creek Road comes up on the left on 158 as you enter Henderson, the seat of Vance County. The downtown district still has many of its early landmarks, though the Vance Hotel (called the Scuppernong in Payne's fictional town of Killdeer) closed in 1976. The Vance was indeed a gathering spot for hard-nosed local business executives and salesmen sharing breakfast in the late 1950s and early 1960s, when Payne's story takes place. Although much of the novel takes place on the Outer Banks (a landscape Payne often uses in his fiction), the family tobacco business and its entanglements with the mills in town provide the basis for the paternalistic traditions that Payne explores in his story.

This is also the downtown district where television talk-show host Charlie Rose grew up. Henderson native Annella Rockson writes about it in this poem.

HOME TO HENDERSON
The land called you back: faded gray barns,
ivy-trimmed, seemed to grow there, the collection
of deserted house and three barns you saw each time
on the way to the airport, the glow of autumn
mornings, rose-dappled twilight, cows in a field
of new-mown hay, and your little town halfway between
mountains and ocean: pointed steeple of graystone
church silhouetted against the red clock tower, drawing
you to the end of Main Street. Beneath the tower,
the fire station and rock-bordered pool where
your father took you to watch the goldfish
when you were five. The library was on that street
and the courthouse, Confederate soldier guarding
out front.

You turned right, drove under the concrete underpass
and came upon the high school, its interplay
of pale old brick and sandstone-trimmed

Gothic windows. Broad steps led to the front
doors. Inside, the floors gleamed like travertine.
Two blocks away stood the old Vance Hotel:
dark red brick, columned porch with rocking
chairs where your father sat when he was a young
man and lived at the hotel, where he'd watch your mother
skim under the stopped train when she was late for school.
She was a teacher. He was a tobacco man, an all right
thing in those days for Southern men, who knew the country,
country ways, could talk to farmers about their crops,
the state of rain and weather, while children
tumbled from the porch and swung from tires
hung from trees in the yard.
On Sundays your father would drive to the farm.
The car stopped at the wooden gate. You would jump
out when the car stopped, run, and swing on the gate
to open it. Your father drove in, past the barn, cows
meandering in and out, up to the big old white house,
one half built before the Revolutionary War,
the other half just before the next one. Your father
talked to the tenant farmer who lived there while you
ran to the garden where overgrown boxwood had formed
a green house. You'd sit in its branches, dreaming.

Everything was there in your town: the green train station,
the little house made of coal where coal was sold. The small
grocery store delivered. Your father could walk to the service
station on the corner to talk in the evenings or walk the other
way during daytime to talk to the banker, whose father he knew
when they were boys in the country. Two maple trees blazed
out front in autumn, and next door there were four pecan trees.
Crepe myrtle bloomed from August on, wisteria in spring,
and all the little flowers all year long.

In April you'd fly down from New York to take off your shoes
and walk barefoot in the grass beneath those maple trees,
watch the apple trees bud out back, and listen to soft voices,
the turn of seasons echoing in long vowels, drawn out diphthongs,
    old stories.
—Used by permission of Annella Rockson.

To see these landmarks in downtown Henderson, follow 158 (Oxford Road) to Dabney Drive and turn left. Then turn right on South Garnett Street, the main artery downtown. Note the house at the corner of Garnett and Young Avenue on the left. It was the home of one of Thomas Wolfe's Harvard roommates, Skinner Kittrell.

After you've spent some time poking around Henderson, continue out of town on Garnett, which is still US 158. It joins up with US 1 at Middleburg and continues through Manson and Ridgeway. If you happen to be traveling during the summer months, consider stopping at a fruit stand along the way. The farms in Ridgeway are known for the quality of their melons and berries. There are also a number of historic houses in various degrees of repair along this route.

At Norlina, before US 1 splits off and heads north toward Virginia, take US 401 south. Bear right as US 158 splits off to the left toward Macon. Follow 401 into Warrenton, the seat of Warren County. Close to town, 401 first is called Ridgeway Street and then takes a right turn to follow North Main Street to the center of town.

■ WARRENTON

What, you don't remember your Uncle Hall! Pshaw, boy, you're as bad as these people that never had delirium tremens—"you ain't been nowhere and you ain't seen nothing." Ah, Lord, they broke the mold when they made him. No, that's right, you wouldn't remember him, he died—yes, and went to hell—ten years before you were born, and if you ever get down there yourself—as you probably will if you're like most of these young folks nowadays—and see a big, bald-headed man following a pack of hounds after a fox over those brimstone bogs with sparks flying off his tail like a comet, that will be your Uncle Hal.—From "The Fallen Angel and the Hunter's Moon," by William Polk, in *North Carolina in the Short Story*, ed. Richard Walser (Chapel Hill: University of North Carolina Press, 1948), 110.

This lively bit of narrative launches a short story by William Tannahill Polk, the grandnephew of President James K. Polk and the mayor of Warrenton, elected several times before World War II. Polk went to the University of North Carolina at Chapel Hill, where he edited the student newspaper and graduated the same year as Thomas Wolfe. Both Wolfe and Polk then set off for Harvard, where Wolfe studied writing and Polk studied law. As a practicing lawyer back in his hometown of Warrenton, Polk began to write and publish a number of spirited short stories. He also helped create the Citizen's Library Movement, to establish county libraries across the state, and was president of the North Carolina Literary and Historical Association, in 1936. Polk finally gave up his legal practice here and moved to Greensboro to become associate editor of the *Greensboro Daily News.*

Macon-born novelist Reynolds Price describes Warrenton as a "one street town" in his novel *Kate Vaiden.* His no-nonsense narrator, Kate, though critical of the town's limitations, also declares her indebtedness to the local librarian, Miss Mabel Davis, for leading her to just the right book at just the right time as she was grieving her parents' death. Otherwise, by Vaiden's account, the town was a dull place, except on weekends, when folks from the countryside poured in to shop and to exchange gossip. Today, Warrenton bears the patina of all the colorful history that Price and Polk describe and has also had a few face-lifts in select spots.

The Hardware Café, on the corner of Main and Macon—directly across from the public library and the courthouse square—is a good stop to get your bearings. Like some other towns on this trail that sit in the rural corridor between the Virginia state line and the urban centers to the south (in this case, Raleigh), Warrenton is a town built on the shoulders of African Americans and the tobacco they worked.

Hilda Gurley-Highgate's parents were raised in Warren County. Her novel, *Sapphire's Grave,* follows several generations of African American women, beginning with the arrival of Sapphire's mother from Sierra Leone to enslavement in Charleston, South Carolina. The story soon jumps ahead to Warren County in 1863.

At first the people did not believe; not when they were gathered together, the music of their whispered prayers, their plaintive sighs, silenced; hoes in hand, their faces expectant; their feet caked with the red mud of the field, the lush, May grass beneath them, they listened but did not hear the message, the messenger, through lies and deceit, having lost the faith of the congregants many decades ago. They could go, or they could stay—it was up to them entirely. . . .

It was not until they were dismissed, by the nod of the messenger, his face crimson, his eyes afraid, that they turned en masse to return to the fields, the stables, the kitchens and parlors of their labor. In these, their places, they resumed their work—the mindless, often backbreaking toil that blunted their senses and made possible the breaking of their spirits,

An old homestead near Shocco Springs, once a tourist destination, now a remote corner of Warren County and part of the landscape in Hilda Gurley-Highgate's novel Sapphire's Grave.

that part of them which might have otherwise been free. They would not believe. They set their faces. They would not believe until God himself said it.

—From *Sapphire's Grave*, by Hilda Gurley-Highgate (New York: Doubleday, 2000), 9, 10.

Disbelief in the era of emancipation and the stories that follow this opening scene in Gurley-Highgate's novel inform the experience of traveling south on NC 58 (Macon Street) from Warrenton. The crossroads known as Liberia is four miles ahead. Watch for the forestry tower on the left. On the right is a restoration of an African American schoolhouse, one of dozens in North Carolina built by Chicago philanthropist Julius Rosenwald, the president of Sears, Roebuck and Company, who sought to improve education for black people in the early twentieth century. (For more on the Rosenwald story, see High Point writer Carole Boston Weatherford's 2006 children's book, *Dear Mr. Rosenwald*.)

Bear right on NC 58 at Liberia and travel another seven miles to reach Inez—now a very remote aggregation of historic plantation houses set among enormous oaks and cedars. It is 3.7 miles from Liberia to the first road sign for the village, but continue another 3 miles to reach the center of Inez. Drive at least as far as Cherry Hill, a grand house on the right, before turning back.

Gurley-Highgate's novel takes place among these old sites and also at Lick Skillet (a crossroads several miles west) and Shocco Springs, once the site of a popular health spa from the 1830s to the 1850s. In these two communities very little related to the novel remains for a visitor to see, however.

Backtrack on NC 58, and then take US 158 on the right toward Macon.

■ MACON

Reynolds Price has written extensively in his fiction and nonfiction and more obliquely in his poetry about his humble birthplace. As Price's unforgettable character Kate Vaiden says, "In Macon, N.C., if you were a girl, and unless your people farmed, you had as much chance of useful work as a Luna moth." So, too, for the genius of Reynolds Price, who, as this guidebook has explained, grew up in towns all across the Piedmont—Roxboro, Asheboro, Warrenton, and finally Raleigh, where his English teacher, Phyllis Peacock, encouraged the application of his considerable gifts. Price studied at Duke University, earned a Rhodes scholarship to Merton College at Oxford University in England, and then returned to Duke to teach. *A Long and Happy Life*—his first and some say his finest novel—has Warren County as its setting. Its central character, young

A fading sign on the side of a store in downtown Macon, the birthplace of novelist, poet, playwright, and essayist Reynolds Price.

Rosacoke Mustian, ponders the attractions of life in the big city of Norfolk to the east with skepticism, while her boyfriend, Wesley Beavers, buzzes back and forth to Tidewater, Virginia, on his macho motorcycle. Price would write more about the Mustian family—Rosacoke's brothers Milo and Rato and their kin— and almost three decades later he returned in the novel *Good Hearts* to Rosacoke and Wesley Beavers, by then middle-aged and settled in Raleigh, a couple who had weathered many years together and were in much better shape than their hometown of Macon.

Today Macon is much as Price describes it—a town of fewer than two hundred people, all variously housed along what had been the thrumming Seaboard rail line running from Raleigh to Norfolk. There have never been more than a few businesses on the side of the highway that faces the finer houses across the tracks, Price's family home among them. In a post-9/11 novel, Price's character Mabry Kincaid returns home to visit his father:

As he turned his rented van over the tracks, Mabry waited for the comforting lift and thump of iron rails beneath him. But he crossed as smoothly as a rowboat on a pond. *Damn, these new cars have got plush shock absorbers!*

When he slowed and looked back through the mirror, he reminded himself. Maybe five years ago the railroad had come through and torn up the tracks from here to Raleigh, more than 60 miles. They could ship the old iron to Japan for scrap and let these little railroad towns die.

As he moved on forward, the Methodist church was there in place, with the tacky steeple his cousin had donated thirty years ago. It sat on the honest squat brick building like a well-earned dunce cap, but any one of the three new houses in the grove of oaks that stretched past the church—the site of his play in a childhood happier than he tended to recall—would make a feasible vacation house for occasional visits to the scene of his youth. A hundred yards more, though; and Mabry braced himself for his goal.

He hadn't seen the homeplace in nearly three years; and he'd heard sad reports of neglect and rot and the depredations of migrant workers, here for a season of tobacco or pulpwood, renting the old place and mailing their savings back to families in Mexico or Guatemala. As he pulled into the drive, though, the first impression was better than he'd feared. The tin roof had rusted in broad streaks, some palings were gone from the long porch rail, and the porch floor seemed to be rotting in spots. Still, as he stopped, the low rambling house felt like the only home he'd known.... Mabry was born in a bright bedroom in the far west wing.

—From *The Good Priest's Son*, by Reynolds Price (New York: Scribner, 2005), 23–24.

Within view of the room where Reynolds Price was born, the Piedmont Literary Trails end. Price's observations about his birthplace easily echo many of the losses and gains, contrasts and contradictions, that have been lifted up along this expedition by the region's most observant writers. Facing east, the ocean and the stories of North Carolina's beginnings are yet ahead.

■ LITERARY LANDSCAPE

Episcopal Bookstore
134 College Street, Oxford
This bookshop carries many local titles of regional interest, including *Granville County: Looking Back*, by Lewis Bowling.

Perry Library
205 Breckenridge Street, Henderson
252-438-3316
<http://www.perrylibrary.org>
In 2006, this new, two-story facility opened with ample accommodations for computer users and genealogical researchers.

ACKNOWLEDGMENTS

This second volume in the Literary Trails series has been enthusiastically supported by North Carolina's Secretary of Cultural Resources Linda Carlisle, North Carolina Arts Council Director Mary Regan, and Deputy Director Nancy Trovillion.

Debbie McGill, former literature director at the N.C. Arts Council, first edited the manuscript with her usual clear-eyed remedies, even as she was preparing to begin a new chapter in her professional life as publications editor for a global nonprofit. She is sorely missed. However, the N.C. Arts Council's Rebecca Moore and Jeff Pettus soon stepped in to help with suggestions for streamlining a still unwieldy manuscript, while Jennifer Huggins managed the enormous task of gathering permissions for the excerpted poems and prose. To these professionals who work every day to support the arts in the State of North Carolina, I am deeply grateful.

Donna Campbell, the creator of all the contemporary photographs in this book and the previous volume, *Literary Trails of the North Carolina Mountains*, has been a firm source of encouragement, wit, and companionship as we have combed the back roads of the Piedmont and climbed the stairs of every major institution of higher learning in the region. Even more than her good eye for an image, Donna is a cheerful spirit and eager reader. Her knowledge of North Carolina is vast and her patience with this process has been critical to my own. Thank you, dear Donna.

Over the years I have made the acquaintance of a great many writers in North Carolina. It was to these experts and friends that I turned in compiling the stories behind the Piedmont's literature. In several cases, local wordsmiths provided me with personal tours to the sources of their inspiration. Singular appreciation goes to Heather Ross Miller, Dawn Shamp, Nancy Peacock, and Charleen Swansea for their willingness to reveal the backstories in their own backyards.

Historian and poet Mary Kratt long ago canvassed the city of Charlotte, hunting down its literary luminaries. Special thanks to Mary for her willingness to share her findings and, in turn, measure my work for accuracy.

A number of writers were also kind enough to provide work created or shaped specifically for this book. I am grateful to Jean Ross Justice, Duncan Murrell, Aimee Parkison, Barbara Presnell, and Bland Simpson.

Another group of writers endured my e-mails and phone calls to verify their personal stories or to mine their vast knowledge of North Carolina letters. Doris Betts, Virginia Boyd, Sally Buckner, Ann Deagon, Pam Duncan, Clyde Edgerton, Sue Farlow, Angela Davis-Gardner, Nancy Gates, Jaki Shelton Greene, Judy Goldman, John Hart, Betty Hodges, D. G. Martin, Susan Meyers, Ruth Moose, Lawrence Naumoff, Jacqueline Ogden, Reynolds Price, Jack Riggs, Lee Smith, David Spear, Gene Stowe, Tim Tyson, Amy Rogers, Ann Wicker, Edwin Graves Wilson, Emily Herring Wilson, and Lynn York have been invaluable resources in this process.

A number of dedicated librarians provided on-the-spot fact-checking: Jane Johnson at Hamlet Library, Mark Thomas at Duke's Perkins Library, Sam Brownlee at the Forsyth County Library, Steve Summerford at the Greensboro Public Library, Joy Gambill at Wake Forest University's Reynolds Library, and Marilyn Schuster in Special Collections at the Atkins Library at UNC-Charlotte. Particular appreciation goes to Bob Anthony and his staff at the North Carolina Collection at UNC–Chapel Hill, who welcomed my many requests for books sequestered deep in the closed stacks at Wilson Library.

Personal help and advice came from a number of scholars, including Durham ethnographer Barbara Lau, Zora Neale Hurston biographer Valerie Boyd, and Betty Smith biographer Valerie Raleigh Yow and from avocational historians Linda Carmichael, Allen Dew, Annie Gulley, Lynn and Mike Harper, Bridget Huckabee, Dianne Pledger, Jeff Michael, Les Young, and Elissa and Eddie Yount. I also gathered local lore from Mark Bishopric in Eden, Eddie McGee and his assistant Sharon Williams at the Stokes Arts Council in Danbury, Sarah Domenech at the Stanly County Arts Council in Albemarle, April Krause at the Person County Historical Museum, Greensboro photographer Jan Hensley, and the kind folks at the Greensboro Historical Museum. Thanks go to the North Carolina Writers' Conference for the invitation to preview parts of this book and their enthusiastic reception of it at their 2009 gathering.

And last (only because their process results in the final product), I thank the professionals at the University of North Carolina Press, who have provided steady guidance and good ideas: David Perry, Paul Betz, Heidi Perov, Kim Bryant, Vicky Wells, Zach Read, Dino Battista, Gina Mahalek, Laura Gribbin, Susan Garrett, and the diligent crew at Longleaf Services. Major appreciation goes to copyeditor Dorothea Anderson, who caught more inconsistencies than I care to admit, and to Michael Southern, who masterfully prepared the maps.

I have often suggested to my writing students that if someone asks how long it took you to write a certain book, the only proper answer is to give your age. Exploring the enormous volume of books inspired by this region is truly a lifetime's work, hardly something to be summarized between two covers. Therefore, this representation of the Piedmont's literary riches is by definition incomplete, but I have tried to apply myself with hope, delight, and a certain blindness to the enormity of the task. The joy, for me, has come in the surprising connections among Piedmont writers and in the lyricism and insights they have brought to us in their words. I wish the same for every reader.

A NOTE ON THE NORTH CAROLINA
LITERARY TRAILS PROGRAM

North Carolina Literary Trails is a program of the N.C. Arts Council, an agency of the N.C. Department of Cultural Resources. The first volume, *Literary Trails of the North Carolina Mountains*, is also available from UNC Press. With the completion of the final guidebook, on eastern/coastal North Carolina, you'll be able to see the entire state through our writers' eyes. When complete, the project will include sites related to literature across the state. Because new books and authors emerge constantly, it is impossible to be all-inclusive of North Carolina's literary treasures. The tours that make up the trails have been devised to represent the following priorities:

—historic sites where North Carolina authors have lived and worked;
—visitable sites that figure prominently in the published poetry, fiction, creative nonfiction, and plays of North Carolina writers and other writers who have spent significant time here;
—libraries with notable collections of manuscripts, books, and other literary artifacts related to North Carolina authors that are publicly accessible;
—bookstores and other venues where North Carolina authors take part in public programming or are represented in exhibits, events, performances, and other activities; and
—other local amenities related to each tour itinerary as recommended by contemporary authors familiar with the area who have, in some cases, been commissioned to write brief pieces for inclusion in these guidebooks.

The N.C. Arts Council would like feedback on your experience with this guidebook. Please e-mail us at Ncarts@ncdcr.gov and tell us if you used Literary Trails to plan a vacation or weekend getaway, or purchased the book as a gift. If you are inspired to tell us more, feel free to post a comment on our blog, http://ncartseveryday.org/.

A companion website, http://www.ncliterarytrails.org/, is an online travel guide and supplements the guidebooks with videos of poets, novelists, and other writers; listings of literary events; and news from North Carolina writers. The information is updated regularly, so please visit often.

PERMISSIONS

Unless otherwise indicated, the copyright holder is the author.

POEMS

Abbott, Anthony: "The Man Who Loved Mondays," from *The Man Who...* (Main Street Rag Publishing Company), copyright © 2005.

Ahmad, Anjail Rashida: "the poet," from *necessary kindling* (Louisiana State University Press), copyright © 2001.

Applewhite, James: "State Road 134" and "William Blackburn, Riding Westward" (excerpt), from *Selected Poems* (Duke University Press), copyright © 2005.

Beam, Jeffrey: "The Loom," from *What We Have Lost: New & Selected Poems, 1977–2001* (Green Finch Press), copyright © 1995.

Bowers, Cathy Smith: "Groceries," from *Traveling in Time of Danger* (Iris Press), copyright © 1999.

Boyle, Kevin: "The Lullaby of History," from *A Home for Wayward Girls* (New Issues Press), copyright © 2005, used by permission of New Issues Press.

Brown, Linda B.: "You Play It on the Edge" (excerpt), from *A Living Culture in Durham*, ed. Judy Hogan (Carolina Wren Press), copyright © 1987 Carolina Wren Press.

Buckner, Sally: "Cedar," from *Potato Eyes*, vol. 17/18, copyright © 1998.

Cannon, Marion: "Creation," from *Another Light* (Red Clay Books), copyright © 1974, used by permission of Charleen Swansea.

Chappell, Fred: "Consider the Lilies of the Field," from *Backsass* (Louisiana State University Press), copyright © 2004.

Church, L. Teresa: "Pepper and Prayer," from *Pembroke Magazine* 39, copyright © 2006.

Deagon, Ann: "New Garden Cemetery," from *Quaker Life*, May 1971, copyright © 1971.

Eaton, Charles Edward: "The Appraisal," from *The Man from Buena Vista: Selected Nonfiction, 1944–2000* (Associated University Presses), copyright © 2001, used by permission of Associated University Presses.

Eidenier, Elon G.: "Colonial Inn," copyright © 2008.

Editions, Ltd.), copyright © 2008, used by permission of BOA Editions, Ltd., www.boaeditions.com.

Powell, Dannye Romine: "At Morrow Mountain," from *At Every Wedding Someone Stays Home: Poems* (University of Arkansas Press), copyright © 1994, used by permission of University of Arkansas Press, www.uapress .com.

Presnell, Barbara: "Industrial League Bowling" and "The Unwearing: A Benediction," from *Piece Work* (Cleveland State University Poetry Center), copyright © 2007.

Rabb, Margaret: "A Seasoning in Hell," from *Granite Dives* (New Issues Press), copyright © 1999.

Rash, Ron: "Listening to WBT," from *Eureka Mill* (The Bench Press), copyright © 1998.

Redding, Sandra: "Naomi Wise," from *North Carolina's 400 Years: Signs along the Way—An Anthology of Poems by North Carolina Poets to Celebrate America's 400th Anniversary*, ed. Ronald H. Bayes with Marsha White Warren (Acorn Press), copyright © 1986, used by permission of Acorn Press.

Rockson, Annella: "Home to Henderson," copyright © 2008.

Selch, Andrea: "The Pleasure Dome," copyright © 2005.

Shabazz, Phillip: "Franklin Street," copyright © 2008.

Sullivan, Chuck: "The Chime of Love and Honor," excerpt from *Zen Matchbox* (Main Street Rag Publishing Company), copyright © 2008.

Taylor, Eleanor Ross: "Kitchen Fable," from *Late Leisure* (Louisiana State University Press), copyright © 1999, used by permission of the author; "These Gifts," from *Late Leisure* (Louisiana State University Press), copyright © 1999, used by permission of Louisiana State University Press.

Waldrep, G. C.: "Geodesy II," from *West Branch* 53 (Fall 2003), copyright © 2003.

Weatherford, Carole Boston: "Trane Travelin'" (excerpt), from *Stormy Blues* (Xavier Review Press), copyright © 2002, used by permission of Xavier Review Press and the author.

Whitlow, Carolyn Beard: "Space," from *Vanished* (Lotus Press), copyright © 2006.

Williams, Robert F.: "Go Awaken My People," copyright © 1953, used by permission of Mabel R. Williams and John C. Williams.

Wilson, Dede: "The Carnegie Library," copyright © 2008.

Wilson, Emily: "From a Far Place," from *Balancing on Stones* (Jackpine Press), copyright © 1979.

INDEX

Page numbers in italics refer to photographs and captions. Page numbers in boldface refer to maps.